THE NEW
THEMATIC
CONCORDANCE

THE NEW
THEMATIC
CONCORDANCE

For the use of
Ministers, Missionaries, Teachers
and Christian Workers

Edited with additional material by
DANIEL MORRISON MILLER

'SEARCH THE SCRIPTURES.' (JOHN 5:39)

FURTHER REVISED BY
GEOFFREY STONIER

CHRISTIAN FOCUS

Copyright © Geoffrey Stonier 2004

ISBN 1-85792-931-4

10 9 8 7 6 5 4 3 2 1

Published in 2004,
Reprinted 2005
by
Christian Focus Publications,
Geanies House, Fearn, Ross-shire,
IV20 1TW, Scotland

www.christianfocus.com

Cover Design by Alister MacInnes

Printed and bound by
Norhaven Paperback, Denmark

Editor's Preface

The plan of this book is to provide topical outlines of a variety of major themes for the guidance of students and workers engaged in Christian service at home and in all parts of the world. The study of the Bible topically is one of the most interesting and perhaps one of the most fruitful methods. The value of these outlines to the busy Christian worker and missionary overseas is incalculable.

The outlines provide the basic material for specific subjects, or for a series of studies under such subjects as The Gospel, The Holy Spirit, Christian Life and Service - and a host of other matters. The value of The Topical Bible Concordance to Christian workers cannot be overstressed, providing as it does a balanced framework, skilfully prepared by master builders of the Christian faith.

In many foreign countries, nationals are often without either a concordance or a Bible containing references, and here is a compilation of vital subjects that cannot but give direction and inspiration, and provide sure foundations, for a healthy and useful Christian upbuilding.

The original manuscript of this volume made its appearance over one hundred and fifty years ago, dispensing blessing and giving spiritual direction to multitudes. This up-to-date issue, slightly revised and edited to meet present-day requirements, is sent forth with the prayer that, under God, it may fulfil its mission of goodwill and sound teaching to the Christians of this generation.

Daniel Morrison Miller

A Word of Commendation

When I first started preaching in my youth and inexperience, I fell back constantly upon two books: Thompson's Chain Reference Bible and Miller's Topical Concordance. Indeed, there are thousands of sermons to be found in this Concordance on nearly all gospel themes imaginable.

There are also some very valuable sections at the end of many of the Topics by way of example. This helps the preacher to reach into all parts of the Bible to find practical examples and applications, even for today. This Concordance is just as it claims - a concordance and not a commentary. Yet, it is more than that, for it is a small book of theology. Under each topic, you will find many headings and Bible verses arranged in such a way that they lend themselves easily to become the 'points' of a sermon.

So valuable did Charles Haddon Spurgeon, the greatest of all Baptist preachers, find this Topical Concordance that he commended its use to his preachers and students by including it whole in his re-issue of Matthew's Henry's Commentary on the New Testament. Here it is again in a modern dress! It is an essential tool for busy preachers.

Rev. Dr. Geoffrey Stonier.
(International Director, Preachers' Help)

Note that in order to save space, reference is often made to a single verse, although the matter referred to may be contained in several connected verses. Therefore, make reference to the context, which is vitally important.

A

ACCESS TO GOD

Is of God. *Ps. 65:4.*

Is by Christ. *Jn. 10:7, 9; Jn. 14:6; Rom. 5:2; Eph. 2:13, 3:12; Heb. 7:19, 25, 10:19; 1 Pet. 3:18; 1 Tim. 2:5.*

Is by the Holy Spirit. *Eph. 2:18.*

Obtained through faith. *Acts 14:27; Rom. 5:2; Eph. 3:12; Heb. 11:6.*

Follows upon reconciliation with God. *Col. 1:21-22.*

In prayer. *Deut. 4:7; Mat. 6:6; 1 Pet. 1:17.* (See Prayer)

In his temple. *Ps. 15:1, 27:4, 43:3, 65:4.*

To obtain mercy and grace. *Heb. 4:16.*

A privilege of the saints. *Deut. 4:7; Ps. 15:2-5, 23:6, 24:3-4.*

The saints have, with confidence. *Eph. 3:12; Heb. 4:16, 10:19, 22.*

Vouchsafed to repenting sinners. *Hos. 14:2; Joel 2:12.* (See Repentance)

The saints earnestly seek. *Ps. 27:4, 42:1-2, 43:3, 84:1-2.*

The wicked commanded to seek. *Is. 55:6-7; Jas. 4:8.*

Urge others to seek. *Is. 2:3; Jer. 31:6.*

Promises connected with. *Ps. 145:18; Is. 55:3; Mat. 6:6; Jas. 4:8.*

Blessedness of. *Ps. 16:11, 65:4, 73:28.*

Typified. *Lev. 16:12-15 with Heb. 10:19-22.*

An example in **Moses**. *Ex. 24:2, 34:4-7; Deut. 5:5.*

ADOPTION

Explained. *2 Cor. 6:18.*

Is according to promise. *Rom. 9:8; Gal. 3:29.*

Is by faith. *Gal. 3:7, 26.*

Is of God's grace. *Ezek. 16:3-6; Rom. 4:16-17; Eph. 1:5- 6, 11.*

Is through Christ. *Jn. 1:12; Gal. 4:4-5; Eph. 1:5; Heb. 2:10, 13.*

The saints are predestined to. *Rom. 8:29; Eph. 1:5, 11.*

Of Gentiles, predicted. *Hos. 2:23; Rom. 9:24-26; Eph. 3:6.*

The Adopted are gathered together in one by Christ. *Jn. 11:52.*

The new birth is connected with. *Jn. 1:12-13.*

The Holy Spirit is a Witness of. *Rom. 8:16.*

Being led by the Spirit is an evidence of. *Rom. 8:14.*

The saints receive the Spirit of. *Rom. 8:15; Gal. 4:6.*

A privilege of the saints. *Jn. 1:12; 1 Jn. 3:1.*

The saints become brothers of Christ by. *Jn. 20:17; Heb. 2:11-12.*

The saints wait for the final consummation of. *Rom. 8:19, 23; 1 Jn. 3:2.*

Subjects the saints to the fatherly discipline of God. *Deut. 8:5; 2 Sam. 7:14; Prov. 3:11-12; Heb. 12:5-11.*

God is longsuffering and merciful towards the partakers of. *Jer. 31:1, 9, 20.*

Should lead to holiness. *2 Cor. 6:17-18, with 2 Cor. 7:1; Phil. 2:15; 1 Jn. 3:2-3.*

Should Produce

Likeness to God. *Mat. 5:44-45, 48; Eph. 5:1.*

Child-like confidence in God. *Mat. 6:25-34.*

A desire for God's glory. *Mat. 5:16.*

A spirit of prayer. *Mat. 7:7-11.*

A love of peace. *Mat. 5:9.*

A forgiving spirit. *Mat. 6:14.*

A merciful spirit. *Lk. 6:35-36.*

An avoidance of outward show. *Mat. 6:1-4, 6, 18.*

Safety of those who receive. *Prov. 14:26.*

Confers a new name. *Num. 6:27; Is. 62:2; Acts 15:17.*

(See Titles of the Saints)

Entitles to an inheritance. *Mat. 13:43; Rom. 8:17; Gal. 3:29; Gal. 4:7; Eph. 3:6.*

Is to be pleaded in prayer. *Is. 63:16; Mat. 6:9.*

Illustrated in **Joseph's sons**: *Gen. 48:5, 14, 16, 22.* **Moses**: *Ex. 2:10;* **Esther**: *Esther 2:7.* Typified in **Israel**: *Ex. 4:22; Hos. 11:1; Rom. 9:4.*

An example in **Solomon**:
1 Chron. 28:6.

AFFECTIONS, THE
Should be supremely fixed on God. *Deut. 6:5; Mk. 12:30.*
Should be fixed
  On the commandments of God. *Ps. 19:8-10, 119:20, 97, 103, 167.*
  On the house and worship of God. *1 Chron. 29:3; Ps. 26:8, 27:4, 84:1-2.*
  On the people of God. *Ps. 16:3; Rom. 12:10; 2 Cor. 7:13-15; 1 Thess. 2:8.*
  On heavenly things. *Col. 3:1-2.*
Should be zealously engaged for God. *Ps. 69:9, 119:139; Gal. 4:18.*
Christ claims the first place in. *Mat. 10:37; Lk. 14:26.*
Enkindled by communion with Christ. *Lk. 24:32.*
Blessedness of making God the object of. *Ps. 9:114.*
Should not grow cold. *Ps. 106:12-13; Mat. 24:12; Gal. 4:15; Rev. 2:4.*
Of the saints, supremely set on God. *Ps. 42:1, 73:25, 119:10.*
Of the wicked, not sincerely set on God. *Is. 58:1-2; Ezek. 33:31-32; Lk. 8:13.*
Worldly desires should be mortified. *Rom. 8:13, 13:14; 1 Cor. 9:27; Col. 3:5; 1 Thess. 4:5.*
Worldly desires are crucified in the saints. *Rom. 6:6; Gal. 5:24.*
False teachers seek to captivate. *Gal. 1:10, 4:17; 2 Tim. 3:6; 2 Pet. 2:3, 18; Rev. 2:14, 20.*
Of the wicked, are unnatural and perverted. *Rom. 1:31; 2 Tim. 3:3; 2 Pet 2:10.*

AFFLICTIONS
Are God-appointed. *1 Kings 22:19-23; 2 Kings 6:33; Job 1:6, 12; Ps. 66:11; Amos 3:6; Mic. 6:9.*
God dispenses as he will. *Job 11:10; Is. 10:15, 45:7.*
God regulates the measure of. *Ps. 80:5; Is. 9:1; Jer. 46:28.*
God determines the continuing of. *Gen. 15:13-14; Num. 14:33; Is. 10:25; Jer. 29:10.*
God does not willingly send. *Lam. 3:33.*
Man is born to. *Job 5:6-7, 14:1.*
The saints are appointed to. *1 Thess. 3:3.*
Consequent upon the Fall. *Gen. 3:16-19.*
Sin produces. *Job 4:8, 20:11; Prov. 1:31.*
Sin is visited with. *2 Sam. 12:14; Ps. 89:30-32; Is. 57:17; Acts 13:10-11.*
Often severe. *Job 16:7-16; Ps. 42:7, 66:12. Jonah 2:3; Rev. 7:14.*
Always less than we deserve. *Ezra 9:13; Ps. 103:10.*
Frequently end in good. *Gen. 50:20; Ex. 1:11-12; Deut. 8:15-16; Jer. 24:5-6; Ezek. 20:37.*
Are tempered with mercy. *Ps. 78:38-39, 106:43-46; Is. 30:18-21; Lam. 3:32; Mic. 7:6-9; Nahum 1:12.*
The saints are to expect. *Jn. 16:33; Acts 14:22.*
Of the saints, are comparatively light. *Acts 20:23-24; Rom. 8:18; 2 Cor. 4:17.*
Of the saints, are only temporary. *Ps. 30:5, 103:9; Is. 54:7-8; Jn. 16:20; 1 Pet. 1:6, 5:16.*
The saints experience joy under. *Job 5:17; Jas. 5:1.*
Of the saints end in joy and blessedness. *Ps. 128:5-6; Is. 61:2-3; Mat. 5:4; 1 Pet. 4:13-14.*
Often arise from a profession of the gospel. *Mat. 24:9; Jn. 15:21; 2 Tim. 3:11-12.*
Show the love and faithfulness of God. *Deut. 8:5; Ps. 119:75; Prov. 3:12; 1 Cor. 11:32; Heb. 12:6-7; Rev. 3:19.*

AFFLICTED SAINTS
God is with. *Ps. 46:5,7; Is. 43:2.*
God is a refuge and strength to. *Ps. 27:5-6; Is. 25:4; Jer. 16:19; Nahum 1:7.*

God comforts. Is. 49:13; Jer. 31:13;
Mat. 5:4; 2 Cor. 1:4-5,7:6.
God preserves. Ps. 34:20.
God delivers. Ps. 34:4, 19; Prov. 12:13;
Jer. 39:17-18.
Christ is with his. Jn. 14:18.
Christ supports his. 2 Tim. 4:17;
Heb. 2:18.
Christ comforts his. Is. 61:2;
Mat. 11:28-30; Lk. 7:13; Jn. 14:1; Jn. 16:33.
Christ preserves his. Is. 63:9; Lk. 21:18.
Christ delivers his. Rev. 3:10.
Should praise God. Ps. 13:5-6, 56:8-10,
57:6-7, 71:20-23.
Should imitate Christ. Heb. 12:1-3;
1 Pet. 2:21-23.
Should imitate the prophets. Jas. 5:10.
Should be patient. Lk. 21:19;
Rom. 12:12. 2 Thess. 1:4. Jas. 1:4. 1 Pet. 2:20.
Should be resigned. 1 Sam. 3:18;
2 Kings 20:19; Job 1:21; Ps. 39:9.
Should not despise chastening.
Job 5:17; Prov. 3:11; Heb. 12:5.
Should acknowledge the justice
of their chastisements. Neh. 9:33;
Job 2:10; Is. 64:5-7; Lam. 3:39; Mic. 7:9.
Should avoid sin. Job 34:31-32; Jn. 5:14.
Should trust in the goodness of
God. Job 13:15; Ps. 71:20; 2 Cor. 1:9.
Should turn and devote them-
selves to God. Ps. 116:7-9; Jer. 50:3-4;
Hos. 6:1.
Should keep the pious resolu-
tions made during affliction.
Ps. 66:13-15.
Should be frequent in prayer.
Ps. 50:15, 55:16-17.
(See Affliction, Prayer under)
Should take encouragement from
former mercies. Ps. 27:9; 2 Cor. 1:10.
Some examples of afflicted saints.
Joseph: Gen. 39:20-23; Ps. 105:17-19.
Moses: Heb. 11:25. **Eli**: 1 Sam. 3:18.
Nehemiah: Neh. 1:4. **Job**: Job 1:20-22.
David: 2 Sam. 12:15-23. **Paul**: Acts 20:22-
24, 21:13. **The Apostles**: 1 Cor. 4:13; 2
Cor. 6:4-10.

AFFLICTION, PRAYER DURING
Exhortation to. Jas. 5:13.
That God would consider our
trouble. 2 Kings 19:16; Neh. 9:32; Ps. 9:13;
Lam. 5:1.
For the presence and support of
God. Ps. 10:1, 102:2.
That the Holy Spirit may not be
withdrawn. Ps. 51:11.
For divine comfort. Ps. 4:6; 119:76.
For the mitigation of troubles.
Ps. 39:12-13.
For deliverance. Ps. 25:17, 22, 39:10;
Is. 64:9-12; Jer. 17:14.
For pardon and deliverance from
sin. Ps. 39:8, 51:1, 79:8.
That we may be turned to God.
Ps. 80:7, 85:4-8; Jer. 31:18.
For divine teaching and direction.
Job 34:32; Ps. 27:11, 143:10.
For the increase of faith. Mk. 9:24.
For mercy. Ps. 6:2; Hab. 3:2.
For restoration of joy. Ps. 51:8, 12,
69:29, 90:14-15.
For protection and preservation
from enemies. 2 Kings 19:19;
2 Chron. 20:12; Ps. 17:8- 9.
That we may know the causes of
our trouble. Job 6:24, l0:2, 13:23-24.
That we may be taught the
uncertainty of life. Ps. 39:4.
That we might be made alive.
Ps. 143:11.

AFFLICTION, CONSOLATION DURING
God is the Author and Giver of.
Ps. 23:4; Rom. 15:5; 2 Cor. 1:3, 7:6; Col. 1:11;
2 Thess. 2:16-17.
Christ is the Author and Giver of.
Is. 61:2; Jn. 14:18; 2 Cor. 1:5.
The Holy Spirit is the Author and
Giver of. Jn. 14:16-17, 15:26, 16:7; Acts 9:31.
Promised. Is. 51:3, 12, 66:13; Ezek. 14:22-23;
Hos. 2:14; Zech. 1:17.
Through the Holy Scriptures.
Ps. 119:50, 76; Rom. 15:4.
By ministers of the gospel.
Is. 40:1-2; 1 Cor. 14:3; 2 Cor. 1:4, 6.

Is abundant. *Ps. 71:21; Is. 66:11.*
Is strong. *Heb. 6:18.*
Is everlasting. *2 Thess. 2:16.*
Is a cause of praise. *Is. 12:1, 49:13.*
Pray for. *Ps. 119:82.*
The saints should administer to
each other. *1 Thess. 4:18. 1 Thess. 5:11, 14.*
Is sought in vain from the world.
Ps. 69:20; Eccl. 4:1; Lam. 1:2.
To those who mourn for sin.
*Ps. 51:17; Is. 1:18, 40:1-2, 61:1; Mic. 7:18-19;
Lk. 4:18.*
To the troubled in mind. *Ps. 42:5,
94:19; Jn. 14:1, 27, 16:20, 22.*
To those deserted by friends.
Ps. 27:10, 41:9-12; Jn. 14:18, 15:18-19.
To the persecuted. *Deut. 33:27.*
To the poor. *Ps. 10:14, 34:6, 9-10.*
To the sick. *Ps. 41:3.*
To the tempted. *Rom. 16:20;
1 Cor. 10:13; 2 Cor. 12:9; Jas. 1:12; Jas. 4:7;
2 Pet. 2:9; Rev. 2:10.*
In prospect of death. *Job 19:25-26;
Ps. 23:4; Jn. 14:2; 2 Cor. 5:1; 1 Thess. 4:14;
Heb. 4:9; Rev. 7:14-17; Rev. 14:13.*
Under the weaknesses of old
age. *Ps. 71:9, 18.*

AFFLICTIONS MADE BENEFICIAL
In promoting the glory of God.
Jn. 9:1-3, 11:3-4, 21:18-19.
In show the power and faithful-
ness of God. *Ps. 34:19-20; 2 Cor. 4:8-11.*
In teaching us the will of God.
Ps. 119:71. Is. 26:9; Mic. 6:9.
In turning us to God. *Deut. 4:30-31;
Neh. 1:8-9; Ps. 78:34; Is. 10:20-21; Hos. 2:6-7.*
In keeping us from departing
again from God. *Job 34:31-32; Is. 10:20;
Ezek. 14:10-11.*
In leading us to seek God in
prayer. *Judg. 4:3; Jer. 31:18; Lam. 2:17-19;
Hos. 5:14-15; Jonah 2:1.*
In convincing us of sin. *Job 36:8-9;
Ps. 119:67; Lk. 15:16-18.*
In leading us to confession of
sin. *Num. 21:7; Ps. 32:5, 51:3-5.*
In testing and showing our
sincerity. *Job 23:10; Ps. 66:10; Prov. 17:3.*

In trying our faith and obedience.
*Gen. 22:1-2 with Heb. 11:17; Ex. 15:23-25;
Deut. 8:2, 16; 1 Pet. 1:7; Rev. 2:10.*
In humbling us. *Deut. 8:3, 16;
2 Chron. 7:13-14; Lam. 3:19-20; 2 Cor. 12:7.*
In purifying us. *Eccl. 7:2-3; Is. 1:25-26,
48:10; Jer. 9:6-7; Zech. 13:9; Mal. 3:2-3.*
In exercising our patience. *Ps. 40:1;
Rom. 5:3; Jas. 1:3; 1 Pet. 2:20.*
In rendering us fruitful in good
works. *Jn. 15:2; Heb. 12:10-11.*
In furthering the gospel. *Acts 8:3-4;
Acts 11:19-21; Phil. 1:12; 2 Tim. 2:9-10;
2 Tim. 4:16-17.*

Some examples. **Joseph's
brothers**: *Gen. 42:21.* **Joseph**:
Gen. 45:5, 7-8. **Israel**: *Deut. 8:3, 5.* **Josiah**:
2 Kings 22:19. **Hezekiah**: *2 Chron. 32:25-
26.* **Manasseh**: *2 Chron. 33:12.* **Jonah**:
Jonah 2:7. **Prodigal Son**: *Lk. 15:21.*

AFFLICTED, DUTY TOWARD THE
To pray for them. *Acts 12:5; Phil. 1:16,
19; Jas. 5:14-16.*
To sympathise with them. *Rom. 12:15;
Gal. 6:2.*
To pity them. *Job 6:14.*
To bear them in mind. *Heb. 13:3.*
To visit them. *Jas. 1:27.*
To comfort them. *Job 16:5, 29:25;
2 Cor. 1:4. 1 Thess. 4:18.*
To relieve them. *Job 31:19-20; Is. 58:10;
Phil. 4:14; 1 Tim. 5:10.*
To protect them. *Ps. 82:3. Prov. 22:22,
31:6.*

AFFLICTIONS OF THE WICKED, THE
God is glorified in. *Ex. 14:4. Ezek. 38:22-23.*
God holds them in derision.
*Ps. 37:13;
Prov. 1:26-27.*
Are multiplied. *Deut. 31:17; Job 20:12-18;
Ps. 32:10.*
Are continual. *Job 15:20; Eccl. 2:23;
Is. 32:10.*
Are often sudden. *Ps. 73:19; Prov. 6:15;
Is. 30:13; Rev. 18:10.*
Are often judicially sent. *Job 21:17;*

Ps. 107:17; Jer. 30:15.

Are examples to others. Ps. 64:7-9; Zeph. 3:6-7; 1 Cor. 10:5-11; 2 Pet. 2:6.

Are ineffective in and of themselves for their conversion. Ex. 9:30; Is. 9:13; Jer. 2:30; Hag. 2:17.

Their persecution of the saints is a cause of. Deut. 30:7; Ps. 55:19; Zech. 2:9; 2 Thess. 1:6.

Impenitence is a cause of. Prov. 1:30-31; Ezek. 24:13; Amos 4:6-12; Zech. 7:11-12. Rev. 2:21-22.

Sometimes humble them. 1 Kings 21:27.

Frequently harden. Neh. 9:28-29; Jer. 5:3

Produce slavish fear. Job 15:24; Ps. 73:19; Jer. 49:3, 5.

The saints should not be alarmed at. Prov. 3:25-26.

Some examples. **Pharaoh and the Egyptians:** Ex. 9:14-15, 14:24-25. **Ahaziah:** 2 Kings 1:1-4. **Gehazi:** 2 Kings 5:27. **Jehoram:** 2 Chron. 21:12-19. **Uzziah:** 2 Chron. 26:19-21. **Ahaz** etc: 2 Chron. 28:5-8, 22.

ALLIANCE AND SOCIETY WITH THE ENEMIES OF GOD

Forbidden. Ex. 23:32, 34:12; Deut. 7:2-3, 13:6, 8; Josh. 23:6-7; Judg. 2:2; Ezra 9:12; Prov. 1:10, 15; 2 Cor. 6:14-17; Eph. 5:11. Leads to idolatry. Ex. 34:15-16; Num. 25:1-8; Deut. 7:4; Judg. 3:5-7; Rev. 2:20.

Have led to murder and human sacrifice. Ps. 106:37-38.

Provoke God's anger. Deut. 7:4, 31:16-17; 2 Chron. 19:2; Ezra 9:13-14; Ps. 106:29, 40; Is. 2:6.

Provoke God to leave men to reap the fruit of them. Josh. 23:12-13; Judg. 2:1-3.

Are ensnaring. Ex. 23:33; Num. 25:18; Deut. 12:30; Deut. 13:6; Ps. 100:36.

Are enslaving. 2 Pet. 2:18-19.

Are defiling. Ezra 9:1-2.

Are degrading. Is. 1:23.

Are ruinous to spiritual interests. Prov. 29:24; Heb. 12:14-15, 2 Pet. 3:17.

Are ruinous to moral character. 1 Cor. 15:33.

Are a proof of folly. Prov. 12:11.

Children who enter into, bring shame on their parents. Prov. 28:7.

Evil consequences of. Prov. 28:19; Jer. 51:7.

The wicked are prone to. Ps. 50:18. Jer. 2:25.

The wicked tempt the saints to. Neh. 6:2-4.

Sin of, to be confessed, deeply repented of, and forsaken. See Ezra chapter 10.

Involve the saints in their guilt. 2 Jn. verses 9-11; Rev. 18:4.

Involve the saints in their punishment. Num. 16:26; Jer. 51:6; Rev. 18:4.

Unbecoming in those called saints. 2 Chron. 19:2; 2 Cor. 6:14-16; Phil. 2:15.

Exhortations to shun all inducements to. Prov. 1:10-15; Prov. 4:14-15; 2 Pet. 3:17.

Exhortations to hate and avoid. Prov. 14:7; Rom. 16:17; 1 Cor. 5:9-11; Eph. 5:6-7; 1 Tim. 6:5; 2 Tim. 3:5.

A call to come out from. Num. 16:26; Ezra 10:11; Jer. 51:6, 45; 2 Cor. 6:17; 2 Thess. 3:6; Rev. 18:4.

Means of preservation from. Prov. 2:10-20, 19:27.

Blessedness of avoiding. Ps. 1:1.

Blessedness of forsaking. Ezra 9:12; Prov. 9:6; 2 Cor. 6:17-18.

The saints grieve to meet with it in their contact with the world. Ps. 57:4; 120:5-6; 2 Pet. 2:7-8.

The saints grieve to witness it in their brothers. Gen. 26:35; Ezra 9:3; Ezra 10:6.

The saints hate and avoid. Ps. 26:4-5, 31:6, 101:7; Rev. 2:2.

The saints deprecate. Gen. 49:6; Ps. 6:8, 15:4, 101:4, 7, 119:115, 139:19.

The saints are separate from. Ex. 33:16; Ezra 6:21.

The saints should be careful

when accidentally thrown into.
Mat. 10:16; Col. 4:5; 1 Pet. 2:12.
Pious parents prohibit to their
children. *Gen. 28:1.*
Persons in authority should
denounce. *Ezra 10:9-11; Neh. 13:23-27.*
Punishment of. *Num. 33:56; Deut. 7:4;
Josh. 23:13; Judg. 2:3; Judg. 3:58; Ezra 9:7, 14;
Ps. 106:41-42; Rev. 2:16, 22-23.*

Some examples. **Solomon**:
1 Kings 11:1-8. **Rehoboam**: *1 Kings 12:8-9.*
Jehoshaphat: *2 Chron. 18:3, 19:2, 20:35-
38.* **Jehoram**: *2 Chron. 21:6.* **Ahaziah**: *2
Chron. 22:3-5.* **Israelites**: *Ezra 9:1-2.*
Israel: *Ezra 44:7.* **Judas Iscariot**: *Mat.
26:14-16.*

Examples of avoiding. **A man of
God**: *1 Kings 13:7-10.* **Nehemiah**, etc:
Neh. 6:2-4, 10:29-31. **David**: *Ps. 101:4-7,
119:115.* **Jeremiah**: *Jer. 15:17.* **Joseph
of Arimathea**: *Lk. 23:51.* **Church in
Ephesus**: *Rev. 2:6.*

Examples of forsaking. **Israelites**:
Num. 16:27; Ezra 6:21-22, 10:3, 4, 16-17.
Sons of the priests: *Ezra 10:18-19.*

Examples of the judgements of
God against. **Korah**, etc: *Num. 16:32.*
Ahaziah: *2 Chron. 22:7-8.* **Judas
Iscariot**: *Acts 1:18.*

AMBITION, WORLDLY

God condemns. *Gen. 11:7; Is. 5:8.*
Christ condemns. *Mat. 18:1, 3-4, 20:25-26,
23:11-12.*
The saints avoid. *Ps. 131:1-2.*
Vanity of. *Job 20:5-9, 24:24; Ps. 49:11-20.*
Leads to strife and contention.
Jas. 4:1-2.
Punishment of. *Prov. 17:19; Is. 14:12-15;
Ezek. 31:10-11; Obad. verses 3-4.*
Connected with
  Pride. *Hab. 2:5.*
  Covetousness. *Hab. 2:8-9.*
  Cruelty. *Hab. 2:12.*

Some examples. **Adam and Eve**:
Gen. 3:5-6. **Builders of Babel**: *Gen. 11:4.*
Miriam and Aaron: *Num. 12:2.*
Korah, *etc:* *Num. 16:3.* **Absolom**:
2 Sam. 15:4, 18:18. **Adonijah**: *1 Kings 1:5.*
Sennacharib: *2 Kings 19:23.* **Shebna**:
Is. 22:16. **Sons of Zebedee**: *Mat. 20:21.*
Antichrist: *2 Thess. 2:4.* **Diotrephes**:
3 Jn. verse 9.

AMUSEMENTS AND WORLDLY PLEASURES

Belong to the works of the flesh.
Gal. 5:19, 21.
Are transitory. *Job 21:12-13; Heb. 11:25.*
Are all vanity. *Eccl. 2:11.*
Choke the word of God in the
heart. *Lk. 8:14.*
Formed a part of idolatrous
worship. *Ex. 32:4, 6, 19* with *1 Cor. 10:7;
Judg. 16:23-25.*
Lead to
  A rejection of God. *Job 21:14-15.*
  Poverty. *Prov. 21:17.*
  A disregard of the judgements
  and works of God. *Is. 5:12;
  Amos 6:1-6.*
  Sorrow. *Prov. 14:13.*
  Probably greater evil. *Job 1:5;
  Mat. 14:6-8.*
  The wicked seeking for happi-
  ness in. *Eccl. 2:1, 8.*
Indulgence in
  A proof of folly. *Eccl. 7:4.*
  A characteristic of the wicked.
  *Is. 47:8; Eph. 4:17, 19; 2 Tim. 3:4; Titus 3:3;
  1 Pet. 4:3.*
  A proof of spiritual death.
  1 Tim. 5:6.
  An abuse of riches. *Jas. 5:1, 5.*
Wisdom of abstaining from.
Eccl. 7:2-3.
Shunned by the early saints. *1 Pet. 4:3.*
Abstinence from, seems strange
to the wicked. *1 Pet. 4:4.*
Denounced by God. *Is. 5:11-12.*
ExcludeS from the kingdom of
God. *Gal. 5:21.*
Punishment of. *Eccl. 11:9; 2 Pet. 2:13.*

An example of renunciation in
Moses: *Heb. 11:25.*

ANGELS
Created by God and Christ.
Neh. 9:6; Col. 1:16.
Worship God and Christ. *Neh. 9:6;*
Phil. 2:9-11; Heb. 1:6.
Are ministering spirits. *1 Kings 19:5.*
Ps. 68:17, 104:4; Lk. 16:22; Acts 12:7-11;
Acts 27:23; Heb. 1:7, 14.
Communicate the will of God
and Christ. *Dan. 8:16-17, 9:21-23, 10:11,*
12:6-7; Mat. 2:13, 20; Lk. 1:19, 28; Acts 5:20,
8:26, 10:5, 27:23; Rev. 1:1.
Obey the will of God. *Ps. 103:20;*
Mat. 6:10.
Execute the purposes of God.
Num. 22:22; Ps. 103:21; Mat. 13:39-42, 28:2;
Jn. 5:4; Rev. 5:2.
Execute the judgements of God.
2 Sam. 24:16; 2 Kings 19:35; Ps. 35:5-6;
Acts 12:23; Rev. 16:1.
Celebrate the praises of God.
Job 38:7; Ps. 148:2; Is. 6:3; Lk. 2:12, 14.
Rev. 5:11-12; Rev. 7:11-12.
The Law given by the ministra-
tion of. *Ps. 68:17; Acts 7:53; Heb. 2:2.*
Announced
   The conception of Christ.
   Mat. 1:20-21; Lk. 1:31.
   The birth of Christ. *Lk. 2:10-12.*
   The resurrection of Christ.
   Mat. 28:5-7; Lk. 24:23.
   The ascension and second
   coming of Christ. *Acts 1:11.*
   The conception of John the
   Baptist. *Lk. 1:13, 36.*
Minister to Christ. *Mat. 4:11; Lk. 22:43;*
Jn. 1:51.
Are subject to Christ. *Eph. 1:21;*
Col. 1:16, 2:10; 1 Pet. 3:22.
Will execute the purposes of
Christ. *Mat. 13:41, 24:31.*
Will attend Christ at his second
coming. *Mat. 16:27, 25:31; Mk. 8:38;*
2 Thess. 1:7.
Know and delight in the gospel
of Christ. *Eph. 3:9-10; 1 Tim. 3:16;*
1 Pet. 1:12.

Ministration of, obtained by
prayer. *Mat. 26:53; Acts 12:5, 7.*
Rejoice over every repentant
sinner. *Lk. 15:7, 10.*
Have charge over the children of
God. *Ps. 34:7, 91:11-12; Dan. 6:22;*
Mat. 18:10.
Are of different orders. *Is. 6:2;*
1 Thess. 4:16; 1 Pet. 3:22; Jude verse 9;
Rev. 12:7.
Are not to be worshipped.
Col. 2:18; Rev. 19:10, 22:9.
Are examples of meekness.
2 Pet. 2:11; Jude verse 9.
Are wise. *2 Sam. 14:20.*
Are mighty. *Ps. 103:20.*
Are holy. *Mat. 25:31.*
Are elect. *1 Tim. 5:21.*
Are innumerable. *Job 25:3; Heb. 12:22.*

ANGER
Is forbidden. *Eccl. 7:9; Mat. 5:22;*
Rom. 12:19.
Is a work of the flesh. *Gal. 5:20.*
Is a characteristic of fools.
Prov. 12:16, 14:29, 27:3; Eccl. 7:9.
Connected with
   Pride. *Prov. 21:24.*
   Cruelty. *Gen. 49:7. Prov. 27:4.*
   Clamour and evil-speaking.
   Eph. 4:31.
   Malice and blasphemy. *Col. 3:8.*
   Strife and contention. *Prov. 21:19,*
   29:22, 30:33.
Brings its own punishment.
Job 5:2; Prov. 19:19, 25:28.
Grievous words stir up. *Judg. 12:4;*
2 Sam. 19:43; Prov. 15:1.
Should not betray us into sin.
Ps. 37:8; Eph. 4:26.
In prayer, be free from. *1 Tim. 2:8.*
May be averted by wisdom.
Prov. 29:8.
Meekness pacifies. *Prov. 15:1;*
Eccl. 10:4.
Children should not be provoked
to. *Eph. 6:4; Col. 3:21.*
Be slow to. *Prov. 15:18, 16:32, 19:11;*
Titus 1:7; Jas. 16:32.

Avoid those given to. *Gen. 49:6; Prov. 22:24.*

Examples of justified anger. **Our Lord**: *Mk. 3:5.* **Jacob**: *Gen. 31:36.* **Moses**: *Ex. 11:8, 32:19; Lev. 10:16; Num. 16:15;* **Nehemiah**: *Neh. 5:6, 13:17, 25.*

Examples of sinful anger. **Cain**: *Gen. 4:5-6.* **Esau**: *Gen. 27:45.* **Simeon and Levi**: *Gen. 49:5-7.* **Moses**: *Num. 20:10-11.* **Balaam**: *Num. 22:27.* **Saul**: *1 Sam. 20:30.* **Ahab**: *1 Kings 21:4.* **Naaman**: *2 Kings 5:11.* **Asa**: *2 Chron. 16:10.* **Uzziah**: *2 Chron. 26:19.* **Haman**: *Esther 3:5.* **Nebuchadnezzar**: *Dan. 3:13.* **Jonah**: *Jonah 4:4.* **Herod**: *Mat. 2:16.* **Jews**: *Lk. 4:28.* **High Priest**, etc: *Acts 5:17, 7:54.*

ANGER OF GOD, THE

Averted by Christ. *Lk. 2:11, 14; Rom. 5:9; 2 Cor. 5:18-19; Eph. 2:14, 17; Col. 1:20; 1 Thess. 1:10.*

Is averted from those who believe. *Jn. 3:14-18; Rom. 3:25, 5:1.*

Is averted upon confession of sin and repentance. *Job 33:27-28; Ps. 106:43-45; Jer. 3:12-13, 18:7-8, 31:18-20; Joel 2:12-14; Lk. 15:18-20.*

Is slow. *Ps. 103:8; Is. 48:9; Jonah 4:2; Nahum 1:3.*

Is righteous. *Ps. 58:10-11; Lam. 1:18; Rom. 2:6, 8, 3:5-6; Rev. 16:6-7.*

The justice of, not to be questioned. *Rom. 9:18, 20, 22.*

Manifested in terrors. *Ex. 14:24; Ps. 76:6-8; Jer. 10:10; Lam. 2:20-22.*

Manifested in judgements and afflictions. *Job 21:17; Ps. 78:49-51; Ps. 90:7; Is. 9:19; Jer. 7:20; Ezek. 7:19; Heb. 3:17.*

Cannot be resisted. *Job 9:13, 14:13; Ps. 76:7; Nahum 1:6.*

Aggravated by continual provocation. *Num. 32:14.*

Specially reserved for the day of wrath. *Zeph. 1:14-18; Mat. 25:41; Rom. 2:5, 8; 2 Thess. 1:8; Rev. 6:17, 11:18, 19:15.*

Against

The wicked. *Ps. 7:11, 21:8 9; Is. 3:8, 13:9; Nahum 1:2-3; Rom. 1:18, 2:6; Eph. 5:6; Col. 3:6.*

Those who forsake him. *Ezra 8:22; Is. 1:4.*

Unbelief. *Ps. 78:21-22; Heb. 3:18-19; Jn. 3:36.*

Impenitence. *Ps. 7:12; Prov. 1:30-31; Is. 5:13-14; Rom. 2:5.*

Apostasy. *Heb. 10:26-27.*

Idolatry. *Deut. 29:20, 27, 28, 32:19, 20, 22; Josh. 23:16; 2 Kings 22:17; Ps. 78:58-59; Jer. 44:3.*

Sin, in the saints. *Ps. 89:30-32, 90:7-9, 99:8, 102:9-10; Is. 47:6.*

Is extreme, against those who oppose the gospel. *Ps. 2:2, 3, 5; 1 Thess. 2:16.*

The folly of provoking. *Jer. 7:19; 1 Cor. 10:22.*

Is to be dreaded. *Ps. 2:12, 76:7, 90:11; Mat. 10:28.*

Is to be deprecated. *Ex. 32:11; Ps. 6:1, 38:1, 74:1-2; Is. 64:9.*

Removal of, should be prayed for. *Ps. 39:10, 79:5, 80:4, Dan. 9:16; Hab. 3:2.*

Tempered with mercy to the saints. *Ps. 30:5; Is. 26:20; Is. 54:8, 57:15-16; Jer. 30:11; Mic. 7:11.*

To be borne with submission. *2 Sam. 24:17; Lam. 3:39, 43; Mic. 7:9.*

Should lead to repentance. *Is. 42:24-25; Jer. 4:8.*

Examples of God's anger. **The old world**: *Gen. 7:21-23.* **The builders of Babel**: *Gen. 11:8.* **Cities of the Plain**: *Gen. 19:24-25.* **Egyptians**: *Ex. 7:20, 8:6, 16, 24, 9:3, 9, 23, 10:13, 22, 12:29, 14:27.* **Israelites**: *Ex. 32:35; Num. 11:1, 33, 14:40-45, 21:6, 25:9; 2 Sam. 24:1, 15.* **Enemies of Israel**: *1 Sam. 5:6, 7:10.* **Nadab, etc**: *Lev. 10:2.* **The spies**: *Num. 14:37.* **Korah**, etc: *Num. 18:31, 35.* **Aaron and Miriam**: *Num. 12:9-10.* **Five kings**: *Josh. 10:25.* **Abimelech**: *Judg. 9:56.* **Men of Beth-Shemesh**: *1 Sam. 6:19.* **Saul**: *1 Sam. 31:6.* **Uzzah**: *2 Sam. 6:7.* **Saul's**

family: *2 Sam. 21:1.* **Sennacherib**: *2 Kings 19:28, 35, 37.*

ANOINTING OF THE HOLY SPIRIT, THE

Is from God. *2 Cor. 1:21.*

That Christ should receive.

Foretold. *Ps. 45:7; Is. 61:1; Dan. 9:24.*

Fulfilled. *Lk. 4:18, 21; Acts 4:27; Acts 10:38; Heb. 1:9.*

God preserves those who receive. *Ps. 18:50, 20:6, Ps. 89:20-23.*

The saints receive. *Is. 61:3; 1 Jn. 2:20.*

Is abiding in the saints. *1 Jn. 2:27.*

Guides into all truth. *1 Jn. 2:27.*

Typified:*Ex. 40:13-15; Lev. 8:12. 1 Sam. 16:13; 1 Kings 19:16.*

ANTICHRIST, THE

Denies the Father and the Son. *1 Jn. 2:22.*

Denies the incarnation of Christ. *1 Jn. 4:3; 2 Jn. verse 7.*

Spirit of, prevalent in the Apostolic times. *1 Jn. 2:18.*

Deceit, a characteristic of. *2 Jn. verse 7.*

Is described. *Dan. 7:8; 2 Thess. 2:8-9.*

APOSTATES

Are described. *Deut. 13:13; Heb. 3:12.*

Persecution tends to produce. *Mat. 24:9-10; Lk. 8:13.*

A worldly spirit tends to produce. *2 Tim. 4:10.*

Never belonged to Christ. *1 Jn. 2:19.*

The saints do not become. *Ps. 44:18-19; Heb. 6:9, 10:39.*

It is impossible to restore. *Heb. 6:4-6.*

Guilt and punishment of.*Zeph. 1:4-6; Heb. 10:25-31, 39; 2 Pet. 2:17, 20-22.*

Cautions against becoming. *Heb. 3:12; 2 Pet. 3:17.*

Will abound in the latter days. *Mat. 24:12; 2 Thess. 2:3; 1 Tim. 4:1-3.*

Some examples. **Amaziah**: *2 Chron. 25:14, 27.* **Professed**

disciples: *Jn. 6:66.* **Hymeneus and Alexander**: *1 Tim. 1:19-20.*

APOSTLES, THE

Christ pre-eminently is called 'The Apostle'. *Heb. 3:1.*

Ordained by Christ. *Mk. 3:14; Jn. 15:16.*

Received their title from Christ. *Lk. 6:13.*

Called by

God. *1 Cor. 1:1, 12:28; Gal. 1:1, 15-16.*

Christ. *Mat. 10:1. Mk. 3:13; Acts 20:24; Rom. 1:5.*

The Holy Spirit. *Acts 13:2, 4.*

Were not learned men. *Acts 4:13.*

Selected from obscure positions. *Mat. 4:18.*

Sent first to the house of Israel. *Mat. 10:5-6; Lk. 24:47; Acts 13:46.*

Sent to preach the gospel to all nations. *Mat. 28:19-20; Mk. 16:15; 2 Tim.1:11.*

Christ always present with. *Mat. 28:20.*

Warned against a timid profession of Christ. *Mat. 10:27-33.*

The Holy Spirit given to. *Jn. 20:22; Acts 2:1-4, 9:17.*

Guided by the Spirit into all truth. *Jn. 14:26; Jn. 15:26, 16:13.*

Instructed by the Spirit to answer adversaries. *Mat. 10:19-20; Lk. 12:11-12.*

Specially devoted to the office of the ministry. *Acts 6:4, 20:27.*

Humility urged upon. *Mat. 20:26-27; Mk. 9:33-37; Lk. 22:24-30.*

Self-denial urged upon. *Mat. 10:37-39.*

Mutual love urged upon. *Jn. 15:17.*

Equal authority given to each of. *Mat. 16:19 with Mat. 18:18; 2 Cor. 11:5.*

Were not of the world. *Jn. 15:19, 17:16.*

Were hated by the world. *Mat. 10:22, 24:9; Jn. 15:18.*

Persecutions and sufferings of. *Mat. 10:16, 18; Lk. 21:16; Jn. 15:20, 16:2.*

Saw Christ in the flesh. *Lk. 1:2; Acts 1:22; 1 Cor. 9:1, 15:8-9; 1 Jn. 1:1.*

Witnesses of the resurrection and ascension of Christ. *Lk. 24:33-41, 51;*

Acts 1:2-9, 10:40-41; 1 Cor. 15:8.
Empowered to work miracles.
Mat. 10:1, 8; Mk. 16:20; Lk. 9:1; Acts 2:43.

ASCENSION OF CHRIST, THE
Prophecies concerning. Ps. 24:7, 68:18
with Eph. 4:7-8.
Foretold by himself. Jn. 6:62, 7:33,
14:28, 16:5, 20:17.
Forty days after his resurrection.
Acts 1:3.
Is described. Acts 1:9.
From the Mount of Olives. Lk. 24:50
with Mk. 11:1; Acts 1:12.
While blessing his disciples. Lk. 24:50.
When he had atoned for sin.
Heb. 9:12, 10:12.
Was triumphant. Ps. 68:18.
Was to supreme power and
dignity. Lk. 24:26; Eph. 1:20-21; 1 Pet. 3:22.
As the Forerunner of his people.
Heb. 6:20.
To intercede. Rom. 8:34; Heb. 9:24.
To send the Holy Spirit. Jn. 16:7,
Acts 2:33
To receive gifts for men. Ps. 68:18
with Eph. 4:8, 11.
To prepare a place for his people.
Jn. 14:2.
His second coming will be in like
manner as. Acts 1:10-11.
Typified. Lev. 16:15, 23:13 with Heb. 6:20;
Heb. 9:7, 9, 12.

ASSURANCE
Produced by faith. Eph. 3:12; 2 Tim. 1:12;
Heb. 10:22.
Made full by hope. Heb. 6:11, 19.
Confirmed by love. 1 Jn. 3:14, 19, 4:18.
Is the effect of righteousness.
Is. 32:17.
Is abundant in our understanding
of the gospel. Col. 2:2; 1 Thess. 1:5.
The saints privileged to have, from
Their election. Ps. 4:3; 1 Thess. 1:4.
Their redemption. Job 19:25.
Their adoption. Rom. 8:16; 1 Jn. 3:2.
Their salvation. Is. 12:2.
Eternal life. 1 Jn. 5:13.

The unchangeable love of God.
Rom. 8:38-39.
Union with God and Christ.
1 Cor. 6:15; 2 Cor. 13:5; Eph. 5:30; 1 Jn. 2:5,
4:13.
Peace with God by Christ. Rom. 5:1.
Preservation. Ps. 3:6, 8, 27:3-5, 46:1-3.
Answers to prayer. 1 Jn. 3:22, 5:14-15.
Continuing in grace. Phil. 1:6.
Comfort in affliction. Ps. 73:26;
Lk. 4:18-19; 2 Cor. 4:8-10, 16-18.
Support in death. Ps. 23:4.
A glorious resurrection. Job 19:26;
Ps. 17:15; Phil. 3:21; 1 Jn. 3:2.
A kingdom. Heb. 12:28; Rev. 5:10.
A crown. 2 Tim. 4:7-8; Jos. 1:12.
Give diligence to attain to.
2 Pet. 1:10-11.
Strive to maintain. Heb. 3:14, 18.
Confident hope in God restores.
Ps. 42:11.

Two examples. **David**: Ps. 23:4, 73:24-26.
Paul: 2 Tim. 1:12, 4:18.

ATONEMENT, THE
Explained. Rom. 5:8-11; 2 Cor. 5:18-19;
Gal. 1:4; 1 Jn. 2:2, 4:10.
Foreordained. Rom. 3:25 (See
margin); 1 Pet. 1:11, 20; Rev. 13:8.
Foretold. Is. 53:4-6, 8-12. Dan. 9:24-27;
Zech. 13:1, 7; Jn. 11:50-51.
Effected by Christ alone. Jn. 1:29, 36;
Acts 4:10, 12; 1 Thess. 1:10; 1 Tim. 2:5-6.
Heb. 2:9; 1 Pet. 2:24.
Was voluntary. Ps. 40:6-8 with
Heb. 10:5-9; Jn. 10:11, 15, 17-18.
Shows the grace and mercy of
God. Rom. 8:32; Eph. 2:4-5, 7; 1 Tim. 2:4;
Heb. 2:9.
Love of God. Rom. 5:8; 1 Jn. 4:9-10.
Love of Christ. Jn. 15:13; Gal. 2:20;
Eph. 8:2, 25; Rev. 1:5.
Reconciles the justice and mercy
of God. Is. 45:21; Rom. 3:25-26.
Necessity for. Lk. 19:10; Heb. 9:22.
Made only once. Heb. 7:27, 9:24-28,
10:10, 12, 14; 1 Pet. 3:18.
Acceptable to God. Eph. 5:2.

Reconciliation with God effected by. *Rom. 5:10; 2 Cor. 5:18-20; Eph. 2:13-16; Col. 1:20-22; Heb. 2:17; 1 Pet. 3:18.*

Access to God by. *Heb. 10:19-20.*

Remission of sins by. *Jn. 1:29; Rom. 3:25; Eph. 1:7; 1 Jn. 1:7; Rev. 1:5.*

Justification by. *Rom. 5:9; 2 Cor. 5:21.*

Sanctification by. *2 Cor. 5:15; Eph. 5:26-27; Titus 2:14; Heb. 10:10; Heb. 13:12.*

Redemption by. *Mat. 20:28; 1 Tim. 2:6; Heb. 9:12; Rev. 5:9.*

Has delivered the saints from

The power of sin. *Rom. 8:3; 1 Pet. 1:18-19.*

The power of the world. *Gal. 1:4; Gal. 6:14.*

The power of the devil. *Col. 2:15;*

Heb. 2:14-15.

The saints glorify God for. *1 Cor. 6:20; Gal. 2:20; Phil. 1:20-21.*

The saints rejoice in God for. *Rom. 5:11.*

The saints praise God for. *Rev. 5:9-13.*

Faith in, is indispensable. *Rom. 3:25; Gal. 3:13-14.*

Commemorated in the Lord's Supper. *Mat. 26:26-28; 1 Cor. 11:23-26.*

Ministers should fully set forth. *Acts 5:29-31, 42; 1 Cor. 15:3; 2 Cor. 5:18-21.*

Typified. *Gen. 4:4 with Heb. 11:4; Gen. 22:2 with Heb. 11:17, 19; Ex. 12:5, 11, 14 with 1 Cor. 5:7; Ex. 24:8 with Heb. 9:20; Lev. 16:30, 34 with Heb. 9:7, 12, 28; Lev. 17:11 with Heb. 9:22.*

B

BACKSLIDING

Is turning from God. *1 Kings 11:9.*

Is leaving our first love. *Rev. 2:4.*

Is departing from the simplicity of the gospel. *2 Cor. 11:3; Gal. 3:1-3, 5:4-7.*

God is displeased at. *Ps. 78:57, 59.*

Warnings against. *Ps. 85:8; 1 Cor. 10:12.*

Guilt and consequences of. *Num. 14:43; Ps. 125:5; Is. 59:2, 9-11; Jer. 5:6, 8:5, 13, 15:6; Lk. 9:62.*

Brings its own punishment. *Prov. 14:14; Jer. 2:19.*

A haughty spirit leads to. *Prov. 16:18.*

Proneness to. *Prov. 24:16; Hos. 11:7.*

Is liable to continue and increase. *Jer. 8:5, 14:7.*

Exhortations to return from. *2 Chron. 30:6; Is. 31:6; Jer. 3:12, 14, 22; Hos. 6:1.*

Pray to be restored from. *Ps. 80:3, 85:4; Lam. 5:21.*

Punishment of tempting others to the sin of. *Prov. 28:10; Mat. 18:6.*

Not hopeless. *Ps. 37:24; Prov. 24:16.*

Endeavour to bring back those guilty of. *Gal. 6:1; Jas. 5:19-20.*

Sin of, to be confessed. *Is. 59:12-14; Jer. 3:13-14; Jer. 14:7-9.*

Pardon of, promised. *2 Chron. 7:14;*

Jer. 3:12, 31:20, Jer. 36:3.

Healing of, promised. *Jer. 3:22; Hos. 14:4.*

Afflictions sent to heal. *Hos. 5:15.*

Blessedness of those who keep from. *Prov. 28:14; Is. 26:3-4; Col. 1:21-23.*

Is hateful to the saints. *Ps. 101:3.*

Some examples. **Israel:** *Ex. 32:8; Neh. 9:26; Jer. 3:11; Hos. 4:16.* **Saul:** *1 Sam. 15:11.* **Solomon:** *1 Kings 11:3-4.* **Peter:** *Mat. 26:70-74.*

BAPTISM

As administered by John. *Mat. 3:5-12; Jn. 3:23; Acts 13:24, 19:4.*

Sanctioned in Christ's submission to it. *Mat. 3:13-15; Lk. 3:21.*

Adopted by Christ. *Jn. 3:22, 4:1-2.*

Appointed an ordinance of the Christian Church. *Mat.28:19-20; Mk. 16:15-16.*

To be administered in the name of the Father, the Son, and the Holy Spirit. *Mat. 28:19.*

Water, the outward and visible sign in. *Acts 8:36; Acts 10:47.*

Regeneration, the inward and

spiritual grace of. *Jn. 3:3, 5-6;
Rom. 6:3, 4, 11.*
Remission of sins, signified by.
Acts 2:38, 22:16.
Unity of the Church effected by.
1 Cor. 12:13; Gal. 3:27-28.
Confession of sin necessary to.
Mat. 3:6.
Repentance necessary to. *Acts 2:38.*
Faith necessary to. *Acts 8:37, 18:8.*
There is only one. *Eph. 4:5.*
Administered to
Individuals. *Acts 8:38, 9:18.*
Households. *Acts 16:15; 1 Cor. 1:16.*
An emblem of the influence of
the Holy Spirit. *Mat. 3:11; Titus 3:5.*
Typified. *1 Cor. 10:2; 1 Pet. 3:20-21.*

BAPTISM WITH THE HOLY SPIRIT
Foretold. *Ezek. 36:25.*
Is through Christ. *Titus 3:6.*
Christ administered. *Mat. 3:11; Jn. 1:33.*
Promised to the saints. *Acts 1:5,
2:38-39, 11:16.*
All saints partake of. *1 Cor. 12:13.*
Necessity for. *Jn. 3:5; Acts 19:2-6.*
Renews and cleanses the soul.
Titus 3:5; 1 Pet. 3:20-21.
The Word of God is instrumental
in. *Acts 10:44; Eph. 5:26.*
Typified. *Acts 2:1-4.*

BLASPHEMY
Christ was charged with. *Mat. 10:25;
Lk. 22:64-65; 1 Pet. 4:14.*
Charges were laid against Christ.
Mat. 9:2-3, 26:64-65; Jn. 10:33, 36.
Charged upon the saints. *Acts 6:11, 13.*
Proceeds from the heart. *Mat. 15:19.*
Forbidden. *Ex. 20:7; Col. 3:8.*
The wicked are addicted to. *Ps. 74:18;
Is. 52:5; 2 Tim. 3:2; Rev. 16:11, 21.*
Idolatry counted as. *Is. 65:7;
Ezek. 20:27-28.*
Hypocrisy counted as. *Rev. 2:9.*
The saints grieved to hear.
Ps. 44:15-16, 74:10, 18, 22.
Give no occasion for. *2 Sam. 12:14;
1 Tim. 6:1.*

Against the Holy Spirit, is unpar-
donable. *Mat. 12:31-32; Mk. 3:28-30;
Lk. 12:10.*
Connected with folly and pride.
2 Kings 19:22; Ps. 74:18.
Punishment of. *Lev. 24:16; Is. 65:7;
Ezek. 20:27-33, 35:11-12.*

Some examples. The **Danite:**
Lev. 24:11. **Sennacharib:** *2 Kings 19:4, 10,
22.* **The Jews:** *Lk. 22:65.* **Hymeneus:**
1 Tim. 1:20.

BLESSED, THE
Whom God chooses. *Ps. 65:4; Eph. 1:3-4.*
Whom God calls. *Is. 51:2; Rev. 19:9.*
Who know Christ. *Mat. 16:16-17.*
Who know the gospel. *Ps. 89:15.*
Who are not offended at Christ.
Mat. 11:6.
Who believe. *Lk. 1:45; Gal. 3:9.*
Whose sins are forgiven. *Ps. 32:1;
Rom. 4:7.*
To whom God imputes righteous-
ness without works. *Rom. 4:6-9.*
Whom God chastens. *Job 5:17;
Ps. 94:12.*
Who suffer for Christ. *Lk. 6:22.*
Who have the Lord as their God.
Ps. 144:15.
Who trust in God. *Ps. 2:12, 34:8, 40:4,
84:12; Jer. 17:7.*
Who fear God. *Ps. 112:1, 128:1, 4.*
Who hear and keep the Word of
God. *Ps. 119:2; Jas. 1:25; Mat. 13:16;
Lk. 11:28; Rev. 1:3, 22:7.*
Who delight in the command-
ments of God. *Ps. 112:1.*
Who keep the commandments
of God. *Rev. 22:14.*
Who wait for the Lord. *Is. 30:18.*
Whose strength is in the Lord.
Ps. 84:5.
Who hunger and thirst after
righteousness. *Mat. 5:6.*
Who frequent the house of God.
Ps. 65:4, 84:4.
Who avoid the wicked. *Ps. 1:1.*
Who endure temptation. *Jas. 1:12.*

Who watch against sin. *Rev. 16:15.*
Who rebuke sinners. *Prov. 24:25.*
Who watch for the Lord. *Lk. 12:37.*
Who die in the Lord. *Rev. 14:13.*
Who have a part in the first resurrection. *Rev. 20:6.*
Who favour the saints. *Gen. 12:3. Ruth 2:19.*
The undefiled. *Ps. 119:1.*
The pure in heart. *Mat. 5:8.*
The just. *Ps. 106:3; Prov. 10:6.*
The children of the just. *Prov. 20:7.*
The righteous. *Ps. 5:12.*
The generation of the upright. *Ps. 112:2.*
The faithful. *Prov. 28:20.*
The poor in spirit. *Mat. 5:3.*
The meek. *Mat. 5:5.*
The merciful. *Mat. 5:7.*
The bountiful. *Deut. 15:10; Ps. 41:1; Prov. 22:9; Lk. 14:13-14.*
The peace-makers. *Mat. 5:9.*
Holy mourners. *Mat. 5:4; Lk. 6:21.*
The saints at the Judgement Day. *Mat. 25:34.*
Who will eat bread in the kingdom of God. *Lk. 14:15. Rev. 19:9.*

BLINDNESS, SPIRITUAL

Explained. *Jn. 1:5; 1 Cor. 2:14.*
The effect of sin. *Mat. 6:23; Jn. 3:19-20.*
Unbelief the effect of. *2 Cor. 4:3-4.*
Uncharitableness is a proof of. *1 Jn. 2:9, 11.*
A work of the devil. *2 Cor. 4:4.*
Leads to all evil. *Eph. 4:17-19.*
Is inconsistent with communion with God. *1 Jn. 1:6-7.*
Of ministers, fatal to themselves and their people. *Mat. 15:14.*
The wicked are in. *Ps. 82:5; Jer. 5:21.*
The self-righteous are in. *Mat. 23:19, 26; Rev. 3:17.*
The wicked are wilfully guilty of. *Is. 26:11; Rom. 1:19-21.*
Judicially inflicted. *Ps. 69:23; Is. 29:10, 44:18; Mat. 13:13-14; Jn. 12:40.*
Pray for the removal of. *Ps. 13:3, 119:18.*
Christ appointed to remove. *Is. 42:7;*
Lk. 4:18; Jn. 8:12, 9:39; 2 Cor. 3:14, 4:6.
Christ appoints his ministers to remove. *Mat. 5:14; Acts 26:18.*
The saints are delivered from. *Jn. 8:12; Eph. 5:8; Col. 1:13; 1 Thess. 5:4-5; 1 Pet. 2:9.*
Removal of, illustrated. *Mat. 11:5; Jn. 9:7, 11, 25; Acts 9:18; Rev. 3:18.*

Some examples. **Israel:** *Rom. 11:25; 2 Cor. 3:15.* **Scribes and Pharisees:** *Mat. 23:16, 24.* **Church of Laodicea:** *Rev. 3:17.*

BOLDNESS, HOLY

Christ set an example of. *Jn. 7:26.*
Is through faith in Christ. *Eph. 3:12; Heb. 10:19.*
A characteristic of the saints. *Prov. 28:1.*
Produced by
　A trust in God. *Is. 50:7.*
　The fear of God. *Acts 5:29.*
　Faithfulness toward God. *1 Tim. 3:13.*
Express your trust in God with. *Heb. 13:6.*
Have, in prayer. *Eph. 3:12; Heb. 4:16.*
The saints will have, in the Judgement. *1 Jn. 4:17.*
Exhortation to. *Josh. 1:7; 2 Chron. 19:11; Jer. 1:8; Ezek. 3:9.*
Pray for. *Acts 4:29; Eph. 6:19-20.*
Ministers should show, in
　Faithfulness to their people. *2 Cor. 7:4, 10:1.*
　Preaching. *Acts 4:31; Phil. 1:14.*
　Reproving sin. *Is. 58:1; Mic. 3:8.*
　The face of opposition. *Acts 13:46; 1 Thess. 2:2.*
Some examples. **Abraham:** *Gen. 18:22-32.* **Jacob:** *Gen. 32:24-29.* **Moses:** *Ex. 32:31-32, 33:18.* **Aaron:** *Num. 16:47-48.* **David:** *1 Sam. 17:45.* **Elijah:** *1 Kings 18:15, 18.* **Nehemiah:** *Neh. 6:11.* **Shadrach:** *Dan. 3:17-18.* **Daniel:** *Dan. 6:10.* **Joseph:** *Mk. 15:43.* **Peter and John:** *Acts 4:8-13.* **Stephen:** *Acts 7:51.* **Paul:** *Acts 9:27, 29, 19:8.* **Barnabas:** *Acts 14:3.* **Apollos:** *Acts 18:26.*

BONDAGE, SPIRITUAL

Is to the devil. *1 Tim. 3:7; 2 Tim. 2:25.*
Is to the fear of death. *Heb. 2:14-15.*
Is to sin. *Jn. 8:34; Acts 8:23; Rom. 6:16; Rom. 7:23; 2 Pet. 2:19.*
Deliverance from, promised. *Is. 61:1-2, 42:6-7; Lk. 4:18.*
Christ delivers from. *Lk. 4:18, 21; Jn. 8:36; Rom. 7:24-25; Eph. 4:8.*
The gospel is the instrument of deliverance from. *Jn. 8:32; Rom. 8:2.*
The saints are delivered from. *Rom. 6:18, 22.*

Deliverance from, illustrated. *Deut. 4:20.*
Typified. Israel in Egypt. *Ex. 1:13-14*

BUSY-BODIES

Fools are. *Prov. 20:3.*
The idle are. *2 Thess. 3:11; 1 Tim. 5:13.*
Are mischievous tale-bearers. *1 Tim. 5:13.*
Bring mischief on themselves. *2 Kings 14:10. Prov. 26:17.*
Christians must not be. *1 Pet. 4:15.*

C

CALL OF GOD, THE

By Christ. *Is. 55:6; Rom. 1:6.*
By his Spirit. *Rev. 22:17.*
By his works. *Ps. 19:2-3; Rom. 1:20.*
By his ministers. *Jer. 35:15; 2 Cor. 5:20.*
By his gospel. *2 Thess. 2:14.*
Is from out of darkness. *1 Pet. 2:9.*
Addressed to all. *Is. 45:22; Mat. 20:16.*
Most reject. *Prov. 1:24; Mat. 20:16.*
Effective for the saints. *Ps. 110:3; Acts 13:48; 1 Cor. 1:24.*

To the saints, is
Of grace. *Gal. 1:15; 2 Tim. 1:9.*
According to the purpose of God. *Rom. 8:28, 9:11, 23-24.*
High. *Phil. 3:14.*
Holy. *2 Tim. 1:9.*
Heavenly. *Heb. 3:1.*
To fellowship with Christ. *1 Cor. 1:9.*
To holiness. *1 Thess. 4:7.*
To liberty. *Gal. 5:13.*
To peace. *1 Cor. 7:15; Col. 3:15.*
To glory and virtue. *2 Pet. 1:3.*
To the eternal glory of Christ. *2 Thess. 2:14; 1 Pet. 5:10.*
To eternal life. *1 Tim. 6:12.*
Partakers of, justified. *Rom. 8:30.*
Walk worthy of. *Eph. 4:1.*
Blessedness of receiving. *Rev. 19:9.*
Praise God for. *1 Pet. 2:9.*
Illustrated. *Prov. 9:3-4. Mat. 23:3-9.*

Rejection of, leads to
Judicial blindness. *Is. 6:9 with Acts 28:24-27; Rom. 11:8-10.*
Delusion. *Is. 66:4; 2 Thess. 2:10-11.*
Withdrawal of the means of grace. *Jer. 26:4-6; Acts 13:46, 18:6; Rev. 2:5.*
Temporal judgements. *Is. 28:12; Jer. 6:16, 19, 35:17; Zech. 7:12-14.*
Exclusion from the benefits of the gospel. *Lk. 12:24.*
Rejection by God. *Prov. 1:24-32; Jer. 6:19, 30.*
Condemnation. *Jn. 12:48; Heb. 2:1-3, 12:25.*
Destruction. *Prov. 29:1; Mat. 22:3-7.*

CARE, TOO MUCH

About earthly things, is forbidden. *Mat. 6:25; Lk. 12:22, 29; Jn. 6:27.*
God's providential goodness should keep us from. *Mat. 6:26, 28, 30; Lk. 22:35.*
God's promises should keep us from. *Heb. 13:5.*
Trust in God should free us from. *Jer. 17:7-8; Dan. 3:16.*
Should be cast on God. *Ps. 37:5, 55:22; Prov. 16:3; 1 Pet. 5:7.*
Is an obstruction to the gospel. *Mat. 12:22; Lk. 8:14, 14:18-20.*
Be without. *1 Cor. 7:32; Phil. 4:6.*

Is unbecoming in the saints. *2 Tim. 2:4.*
Uselessness of. *Mat. 6:27; Lk. 12:25-26.*
Vanity of. *Ps. 39:6; Eccl. 4:8.*
Warning against. *Lk. 21:34.*
Sent as a punishment to the wicked. *Ezek. 4:16, 12:19.*

Some examples. **Martha**: *Lk. 10:41.* **Persons who offered to follow Christ** *Lk. 9:57, etc.*

CHARACTER OF THE SAINTS

Attentive to Christ's voice. *Jn. 10:3-4.*
Blameless and harmless. *Phil. 2:15.*
Bold. *Prov. 28:1.*
Contrite. *Is. 57:15, 66:2.*
Devout. *Acts 8:2, 22:12.*
Faithful. *Rev. 17:14.*
Fearing God. *Mal. 3:16; Acts 10:2.*
Following Christ. *Jn. 10:4, 27.*
Godly. *Ps. 4:3; 2 Pet. 2:9.*
Guileless. *Jn. 1:47.*
Holy. *Deut. 7:6, 14:2; 2 Col. 3:12.*
Humble. *Ps. 34:2; 1 Pet. 5:5.*
Hungering after righteousness. *Mat. 5:6.*
Just. *Gen. 6:9; Hab. 2:4; Lk. 2:25.*
Led by the Spirit. *Rom. 8:14.*
Generous. *Is. 32:8; 2 Cor. 9:13.*
Loving. *Col. 1:4; 1 Thess. 4:9.*
Lowly. *Prov. 16:19.*
Loathing themselves. *Ezek. 20:43.*
Meek. *Is. 29:19; Mat. 5:5.*
Merciful. *Ps. 37:26; Mat. 5:7.*
New creatures. *2 Cor. 5:17; Eph. 2:10.*
Obedient. *Rom. 16:19; 1 Pet. 1:14.*
Poor in spirit. *Mat. 5:3.*
Prudent. *Prov. 16:21.*
Pure in heart. *Mat. 5:8; 1 Jn. 3:3.*
Righteous. *Is. 60:21; Lk. 1:6.*
Sincere. *2 Cor. 1:12, 2:17.*
Steadfast. *Acts 2:42; Col. 2:5.*
Taught by God. *Is. 54:13; 1 Jn. 2:27.*
True. *2 Cor. 6:8.*
Undefiled. *Ps. 119:1.*
Upright. *1 Kings 3:6; Ps. 15:2.*
Watchful. *Lk. 12:37.*
Zealous for good works. *Titus 2:14.*

CHARACTER OF THE WICKED, THE

Abominable. *Rev. 21:8.*
Alienated from God. *Eph. 4:18; Col. 1:21.*
Blasphemous. *Lk. 22:65; Rev. 16:9.*
Blinded. *2 Cor. 4:4; Eph. 4:18.*
Boastful. *Ps. 10:3, 49:6.*
Conspiring against the saints. *Neh. 4:8, 6:2; Ps. 38:12.*
Covetous. *Mic. 2:2; Rom. 1:29.*
Deceitful. *Ps. 5:6; Rom. 3:13.*
Delighting in the iniquity of others. *Prov 2:14; Rom. 1:32.*
Despising the saints. *Neh. 2:19, 4:2; 2 Tim. 3:3-4.*
Destructive. *Is. 59:7.*
Disobedient. *Neh. 9:26; Titus 3:3; 1 Pet. 2:7.*
Enticing to evil. *Prov. 1:10-14; 2 Tim. 3:6.*
Envious. *Neh. 2:10; Titus 3:3.*
Fearful. *Prov. 28:1; Rev. 21:8.*
Fierce. *Prov. 16:29; 2 Tim. 3:3.*
Foolish. *Deut. 32:6; Ps. 5:5.*
Forgetting God. *Job 8:13.*
Fraudulent. *Ps. 37:21; Mic. 6:11.*
Glorying in their shame. *Phil. 3:19.*
Hard hearted. *Ezek. 3:7.*
Hating the light. *Job 24:13; Jn. 3:20.*
Headstrong and high-minded. *2 Tim. 3:4.*
Hostile to God. *Rom. 8:7; Col. 1:21.*
Hypocritical. *Is. 29:13; 2 Tim. 3:5.*
Ignorant of God. *Hos. 4:1; 2 Thess. 1:8.*
Impudent. *Ezek. 2:4.*
Infidel. *Ps. 10:4, 14:1.*
Loathsome. *Prov. 13:5.*
Lovers of pleasure more than God. *2 Tim. 3:4.*
Lying. *Ps. 58:3, 62:4; Is. 59:4.*
Mischievous. *Prov. 24:8; Mic. 7:3.*
Murderous. *Ps. 10:8, 94:6; Rom. 1:29.*
Obstinate. *Prov. 21:8; Is. 57:17.*
Perverse. *Deut 32:5.*
Prayerless. *Job 21:15; Ps. 53:4.*
Persecuting. *Ps. 69:26, 109:16.*
Proud. *Ps. 59:12; Obad. verse 3; 2 Tim. 3:2.*
Rejoicing in the afflictions of the saints. *Ps. 35:15.*
Reprobate. *2 Cor. 13:5; 2 Tim. 3:8; Titus 1:16.*
Selfish. *2 Tim. 3:2.*
Sensual. *Phil. 3:19; Jude verse 19.*

Sold under sin. *1 Kings 21:20; 2 Kings 17:17.*

Stubborn. *Ezek. 2:4.*

Stiff-necked. *Ex. 33:5; Acts 7:51.*

Uncircumcised in heart. *Jer. 9:26; Acts 7:51.*

Unjust. *Prov. 11:7; Is. 26:10.*

Unmerciful. *Rom. 1:31.*

Ungodly. *Prov. 16:27.*

Unholy. *2 Tim. 3:2.*

Unprofitable. *Mat. 25:30; Rom. 3:12.*

Unruly. *Titus 1:10.*

Unthankful. *Lk. 6:35; 2 Tim. 3:2.*

Perverse. *Acts 2:40.*

Unwise. *Deut. 32:6.*

CHARITY

Encouraged. *Col. 3:14.* (See Love towards Man)

Explained. *1 Cor. 13:4-7.*

CHASTITY, SEXUAL

Commanded. *Ex. 20:14; Prov. 31:3; Acts. 15:20; Rom. 13:13; Col. 3:5; 1 Thess. 4:3.*

Required in look. *Job 31:1; Mat. 5:28.*

Required in heart. *Prov. 6:25.*

Required in speech. *Eph. 5:3.*

Keep the body in. *1 Cor. 6:13, 15-18.*

Preserved by wisdom. *Prov. 2:10-11, 16, 7:1-5.*

The saints are kept in. *Eccles. 7:26.*

Advantages of. *1 Pet. 3:1-2.*

Shun those devoid of. *1 Cor. 5:11; 1 Pet. 4:3.*

The wicked are devoid of. *Rom. 1:29; Eph. 4:19; 2 Pet. 2:14; Jude verse 8.*

Temptation to deviate from, dangerous. *2 Sam. 11:2-4.*

Consequences of associating with those devoid of. *Prov. 5:3-11, 7:25-27, 22:14.*

Lack of, excludes from heaven. *Gal. 5:19-21.*

Drunkenness is destructive of. *Prov. 23:31-33.*

Breach of, punished. *1 Cor. 3:16-17; Eph. 5:5-6; Heb. 13:4; Rev. 22:15.*

Motives for. *1 Cor. 6:19; 1 Thess. 4:7.*

Some examples. **Abimelech**: *Gen. 20:4-5, 26:10-11.* **Joseph**: *Gen. 39:7-10.* **Ruth**: *Ruth 3:10-11.* **Boaz**: *Ruth 3:13.*

CHILDREN

Christ is an example to. *Lk. 2:51; Jn. 19:26-27.*

Are a gift from God. *Gen. 33:5; Ps. 127:3.*

Are capable of glorifying God. *Ps. 8:2, 148:12-13; Mat. 21:15-16.*

Should be

Brought to Christ. *Mk. 10:13-16.*

Brought early to the house of God. *1 Sam. 1:24.*

Instructed in the ways of God. *Deut. 31:12-13; Prov. 22:6.*

Fairly corrected. *Prov. 22:15, 29:17.*

Should

Obey God. *Deut. 30:2.*

Fear God. *Prov. 24:21.*

Remember God. *Eccl. 12:1.*

Attend to parental teaching. *Prov. 1:8-9.*

Honour their parents. *Ex. 20:12; Heb. 12:9.*

Respect their parents. *Lev. 19:3.*

Obey their parents. *Prov. 6:20; Eph. 6:1.*

Take care of their parents. *1 Tim. 5:4.*

Honour the elderly. *Lev. 19:32; 1 Pet. 5:5.*

Not imitate bad parents. *Ezek. 20:18.*

CHILDREN, GOOD

The Lord is with. *1 Sam. 3:19.*

Know the Scriptures. *2 Tim. 3:15.*

Observe the Law of God. *Prov. 28:7.*

Their obedience to parents is well pleasing to God. *Col. 3:20.*

Partake of the promises of God. *Acts 2:39.*

Will be blessed. *Prov. 3:1-4; Eph. 6:2-3.*

Show love to their parents. *Gen. 46:29.*

Obey their parents. *Gen. 28:7, 47:30.*

Attend to parental teaching. *Prov. 13:1.*

Take care of parents. *Gen. 45:9-11, 47:12.*

Make their parents' hearts glad. *Prov. 10:1, 29:17.*

Honour the elderly. *Job 32:6-7.*

Used as a motive for submission

to God. *Heb. 12:9.*
Character of, illustrative of
conversion. *Mat. 18:3.*
Illustrative of a teachable spirit.
Mat. 18:4.

Some examples. **Isaac:** *Gen. 22:6-10.*
Joseph: *Gen. 45:9, 46:29.* **Jephthah's
daughter:** *Judg. 11:34, 36.* **Samson:**
Judg. 13:24. **Samuel:** *1 Sam. 3:19.*
Obadiah: *1 Kings 18:12.* **Josiah:**
2 Chron. 34:3. **Esther:** *Esth. 2:20.* **Job:**
Job 29:4. **David:** *1 Sam. 17:20; Ps. 71:5.*
Daniel: *Dan. 1:6.* **John the Baptist:**
Lk. 1:80. **The children in the Temple:**
Mat. 21:15-16. **Timothy:** *2 Tim. 3:15.*

CHILDREN, WICKED
Do not know God. *1 Sam. 2:12.*
Are void of understanding. *Prov. 7:7.*
Are proud. *Is. 3:5.*
With regard to parents
Do not listen to them. *1 Sam. 2:25.*
Despise them. *Prov. 15:5, 20; Ezek. 22:7.*
Curse them. *Prov. 30:11.*
Bring reproach on them. *Prov. 19:26.*
Are a calamity to them. *Prov. 19:13.*
Are a grief to them. *Prov. 17:25.*
Despise their elders. *Job 19:18.*
Punishment of, for
Treating their parents with
contempt. *Deut. 27:16.*
Disobeying their parents.
Deut. 21:21.
Mocking their parents. *Prov. 30:17.*
Cursing their parents. *Ex. 21:17
with Mk. 7:10.*
Hitting their parents. *Ex. 21:15.*
Mocking the saints. *2 Kings 2:23-24.*
Gluttony and drunkenness.
Deut. 21:20-21.
Their guilt in robbing their parents.
Prov. 28:24.

Some examples. **Esau:** *Gen. 26:34-35.*
Sons of Eli: *1 Sam. 2:12, 17.* **Sons of
Samuel:** *1 Sam. 8:3.* **Absolom:**
2 Sam. 15:10. **Adonijah:** *1 Kings 1:5-6.*
Children at Bethel: *2 Kings 2:23.*

Adrammelech and Sharezer:
2 Kings 19:37.

CHRIST IS GOD
As Jehovah. *Is. 40:3 with Mat. 3:3.*
As Jehovah of glory. *Ps. 24:7, 10, with
1 Cor. 2:8; Jas. 2:1.*
As Jehovah our Righteousness.
Jer. 23:5, 8, with 1 Cor. 1:30.
As Jehovah, above all. *Ps. 97:9 with
Jn. 3:31.*
As Jehovah, the First and the Last.
*Is. 44:6 with Rev. 1:17; Is. 48:12-16 with
Rev. 22:13.*
As Jehovah's Fellow and Equal.
Zech. 13:7; Phil. 2:6.
As Jehovah of hosts. *Is. 6:1-3 with
Jn. 12:41; Is. 8:13-14 with 1 Pet. 2.8.*
As Jehovah of David. *Ps. 110:1 with
Mat. 22:42-45.*
As Jehovah the Shepherd. *Is. 40:10-
11; Heb. 13:20.*
As Jehovah, for whose glory all
things were created. *Prov. 16:4 with
Col. 1:16.*
As Jehovah the Messenger of the
covenant. *Mal. 3:1 with Lk. 2:27.*
Invoked as Jehovah. *Joel 2:32 with
1 Cor. 1:2.*
As the Eternal God and Creator.
Ps. 102:24-27 with Heb. 1:8, 10-12.
As the Mighty God. *Is. 9:6.*
As the great God and Saviour. *Hos.
1:7 with Titus 2:13.*
As God over all. *Rom. 9:5.*
As the true God. *Jer. 10:10 with 1 Jn. 5:20.*
As God the Word. *Jn. 1:1.*
As God the Judge. *Eccl. 12:14 with
1 Cor. 4:5; 2 Cor. 5:10; 2 Tim. 4:1.*
As Emmanuel. *Is. 7:14 with Mat. 1:23.*
As King of kings and Lord of
lords. *Dan. 10:17 with Rev. 1:5; Rev. 17:14.*
As the Holy One. *1 Sam. 2:2 with
Acts 3:14.*
As the Lord from heaven.
1 Cor. 15:47.
As Lord of the Sabbath. *Gen. 2:3
with Mat. 12:8.*
As Lord of all. *Acts 10:36; Rom. 10:11-13.*

As Son of God. *Mat. 26:63-67.*
As the Only-Begotten Son of the Father. *Jn. 1:14, 18, 3:16, 18; 1 Jn. 4:9.*
His blood is called the blood of God. *Acts 20:28.*
As one with the Father. *Jn. 10:30, 38, 12:45, 14:7-10, 17:10.*
As sending the Spirit, equally with the Father. *Jn. 14:16 with Jn. 15:26.*
As entitled to equal honour with the Father. *Jn. 5:23.*
As owner of all things, equally with the Father. *Jn. 16:15.*
As unrestricted by the law of the Sabbath, equally with the Father. *Jn. 5:17.*
As the Source of grace, equally with the Father. *1 Thess. 3:11; 2 Thess. 2:16-17.*
As unsearchable, equally with the Father. *Prov. 30:4; Mat 11:27.*
As Creator of all things. *Is. 40:28; Jn. 1:3; Col. 1:16.*
As Supporter and Preserver of all things. *Neh. 9:6 with Col. 1:17; Heb. 1:3.*
As possessed of the fullness of the Godhead. *Col. 2:9.*
As raising the dead. *Jn. 5:21, 6:40, 54.*
As raising himself from the dead. *Jn. 2:19, 21, 10:18.*
As Eternal. *Is. 9:6; Mic. 5:2; Jn. 1:1; Col. 1:17; Heb. 1:8-10; Rev. 1:8.*
As Omnipresent (Present everywhere). *Mat. 18:20, 28:20; Jn. 3:13.*
As Omnipotent (All powerful). *Ps. 45:3; Phil. 3:21; Rev. 1:8.*
As Omniscient (All knowing). *Jn. 18:30, 21:17.*
As discerning the thoughts of the heart. *1 Kings 8:39 with Lk. 5:22; Ezek. 11:5 with Jn. 2:24-25; Rev. 2:23.*
As unchangeable. *Mal. 3:6 with Heb. 1:12; Heb. 13:8.*
As having power to forgive sins. *Col. 3:13 with Mk. 2:7, 10.*
As Giver of pastors to the Church. *Jer. 3:15 with Eph. 4:11-13.*
As Husband of the Church. *Is. 54:5 with Eph. 5:25-32; Is. 62:5 with Rev. 21:2, 9.*

As the object of divine worship. *Acts 7:59; 2 Cor. 12:8-9; Heb. 1:6; Rev. 5:12.*
As the object of faith. *Ps. 2:12 with 1 Pet. 2:6; Jer. 17:5, 7 with Jn. 14:1.*
As God, he redeems and purifies the Church for himself. *Rev. 5:9 with Titus 2:14.*
As God, he presents the Church to himself. *Eph. 5:27 with Jude verses 24-25.*
The saints live for him as God. *Rom. 6:11 and Gal. 2:19 with 2 Cor. 5:15.*
Acknowledged by his Apostles. *Jn. 20:28.*
Acknowledged by Old Testament saints. *Gen. 17:1 with Gen. 48:15-16; Gen. 32:24-30 with Hos. 12:3-5; Judg. 6:22-24; Judg. 12:31-32; Job 19:25-27.*

CHRIST, THE MEDIATOR

By virtue of his atonement. *Eph. 2:13-18; Heb.9:15, 12:24.*
The only One between God and man. *1 Tim. 2:5.*
Of the gospel-covenant. *Heb. 8:6, 12:24.*

Typified. **Moses**: *Deut. 5:5; Gal. 3:19.* **Aaron**: *Num. 16:48.* **Melchizedek**: *Heb. 7:1-6.*

CHRIST, THE HIGH PRIEST

Appointed and called by God. *Heb. 3:1-2, 5:4-5.*
After the order of Melchizedek. *Ps. 110:4 with Heb. 5:6; Heb. 6:20, 7:15, 17.*
Superior to Aaron and the Levitical priests. *Heb. 7:11, 16, 22, 8:1-2, 6.*
Consecrated with an oath. *Heb. 7:20-21.*
Has an unchangeable priesthood. *Heb. 7:23, 28.*
Is of unblemished purity. *Heb. 7:26, 28.*
Faithful. *Heb. 3:2.*
Needed no sacrifice for himself. *Heb. 7:27.*

Offered himself as a sacrifice. *Heb. 9:14, 26.*

His sacrifice was superior to all others. *Heb. 9:13-14, 23.*

Offered his sacrifice only once. *Heb. 7:27.*

Made reconciliation. *Heb. 2:17.*

Obtained redemption for us. *Heb. 9:12.*

Entered into heaven. *Heb. 4:14, 10:12.*

Sympathises with the saints. *Heb. 2:18, 4:15.*

Intercedes. *Heb. 7:25, 9:24.*

Blesses. *Num. 6:23-26 with Acts 3:26.*

Is on his throne. *Zech. 6:13.*

Appointment of, an encouragement to steadfastness. *Heb. 4:14.*

Typified. **Melchisedek**: *Gen. 14:18-20.* **Aaron**, etc: *Ex. 40:12-15;*

CHRIST, THE PROPHET

Foretold. *Deut. 18:15, 18; Is. 52:7; Nahum 1:15.*

Anointed with the Holy Spirit. *Is. 42:1; 61:1 with Lk. 4:18; Jn. 3:34.*

Alone knows and reveals God. *Mat. 11:27; Jn. 3:2, 13-14, 17:6, 14, 26; Heb. 1:1-2.*

Declared his doctrine to be that of the Father. *Jn. 8:26, 28, 12:49-50, 14:10, 24, 15:15, 17:8, 16.*

Preached the gospel, and worked miracles. *Mat. 4:23, 11:5; Lk. 4:43.*

Foretold things to come. *Mat. 24:3-35; Lk. 19:41-44.*

Faithful to his trust. *Lk. 4:43; Jn. 17:8; Heb. 3:2; Rev. 1:5, 3:14.*

Abounded in wisdom. *Lk. 2:40, 47, 52; Col. 2:3.*

Mighty in deed and word. *Mat. 13:54; Mk. 1:27; Lk. 4:32; Jn. 7:46.*

Meek and not self-glorying in his teaching. *Is. 42:2; Mat. 12:17-20.*

God commands us to hear. *Deut. 18:15; Acts 3:22.*

God will severely visit our neglect of. *Deut. 18:19; Acts 3:23; Heb. 2:3.*

Typified. **Moses**: *Deut. 18:15.* **Jonah**: *Mat. 12:40.*

CHRIST, THE KING

Foretold. *Num. 24:17; Ps. 2:6, 45:1-17; Is. 9:7; Jer. 23:5; Mic. 5:2.*

Glorious. *Ps. 24:7-10; 1 Cor. 2:8; Jas. 2:1.*

Supreme. *Ps. 2:9, 89:27; Rev. 1:5, 19:16.*

Sits at the throne of God. *Rev. 3:21.*

Sits on the throne of David. *Is. 9:7; Ezek. 37:24-25; Lk. 1:32; Acts 2:30.*

Is King of Zion. *Ps. 2:6; Is. 52:7; Zech. 9:9; Mat. 21:5; Jn. 12:12-15.*

Has a righteous kingdom. *Ps. 45:6 with Heb. 1:9; Is. 32:1; Jer. 23:5.*

Has an everlasting kingdom. *Dan. 2:44, 7:14; Lk. 1:33.*

Has a universal kingdom. *Ps. 2:8, 72:8; Zech. 14:9; Rev. 11:15.*

His kingdom is not of this world. *Jn. 18:36.*

The saints, the subjects of. *Col. 1:13; Rev. 15:3.*

The saints receive a kingdom from. *Lk. 22: 29-30; Heb. 12:28.*

Acknowledged by
  The wise men from the East. *Mat. 2:2.*
  Nathanael. *Jn. 1:49.*
  His followers. *Lk. 19:38; Jn. 12:13.*

Declared by himself. *Mat. 25:34; Jn. 18:37.*

Written on his cross. *Jn. 19:19.*

The Jews will testify to. *Hos. 3:5.*

The saints will behold. *Is. 33:17; Rev. 22:3-4.*

Kings will offer homage to. *Ps. 72:10; Is. 49:7.*

Will overcome all his enemies. *Ps. 110:1; Mk. 12:36; 1 Cor. 15:25; Rev. 17:14.*

Typified. **Melchizedek**: *Gen. 14:18.* **David**: *1 Sam. 16:1, 12, 13 with Lk. 1:32.* **Solomon**: *1 Chron. 28:6-7.*

CHRIST, THE SHEPHERD

Foretold. *Gen. 49:24; Is. 40:11; Ezek. 34:23, 37:24.*

The Chief. *1 Pet. 5:4.*
The good. *Jn. 10:11, 14.*
The great. *Mic. 5:4; Heb. 13:20.*
His sheep
He knows. *Jn. 10:14, 27.*
He calls. *Jn. 10:3.*
He gathers. *Is. 40:11; Jn. 10:16.*
He guides. *Ps. 23:3; Jn. 10:3-4.*
He feeds. *Ps. 23:1-2; Jn. 10:9.*
He cherishes tenderly. *Is. 40:11.*
He protects and preserves.
Jer. 31:10; Ezek. 34:10; Zech. 9:16; Jn. 10:28.
He laid down his life for.
Zech. 13:7; Mat. 26:31; Jn. 10:11, 15; Acts 20:28.
He gives eternal life to.
Jn. 10:28.
Typified. **Joseph** *Gen. 41:47.*
David: *1 Sam. 16:11.*

CHRIST, THE HEAD OF THE CHURCH

Predicted. *Ps. 118:22 with Mat. 21:42.*
Appointed by God. *Eph. 1:22.*
Declared by himself. *Mat. 21:42.*
As his mystical body. *Eph. 4:12, 15, 5:23.*
Has the pre-eminence in all things. *1 Cor. 11:3; Eph. 1:22; Col. 1:18.*
Commissioned his Apostles.
Mat. 10:1, 7; Mat. 28:19.
Instituted the sacraments.
Mat. 28:19; Lk. 22:19-20.
Imparts gifts. *Ps. 68:18 with Eph. 4:8.*
The saints are complete in. *Col. 2:10.*
Perverters of the truth do not hold. *Col. 2:18-19.*

CHRIST, CHARACTER OF

Altogether lovely. *Song 5:16.*
Holy. *Lk. 1:35; Acts 4:27; Rev. 3:7.*
Righteous. *Is. 53:1; Heb. 1:9.*
Good. *Acts 10:38.*
Faithful. *Is. 11:5; 1 Thess. 5:24.*
True. *Jn. 1:14, 7:18; 1 Jn. 5:20.*
Just. *Zech. 9:9; Jn. 5:30; Acts 22:14.*
Sinless. *Jn. 8:46; 2 Cor. 5:21.*
Spotless. *1 Pet. 1:19.*
Innocent. *Mat. 27:4.*

Harmless. *Heb. 7:26.*
Resisting temptation. *Mat. 4:1-10.*
Obedient to God the Father.
Ps. 40:8; Jn. 4:34, 15:10.
Without guile. *Is. 53:9; 1 Pet. 2:22.*
Zealous. *Lk. 2:49; Jn. 2:17, 8:29.*
Meek. *Is. 53:7; Zech. 9:9; Mat. 11:29.*
Lowly in heart. *Mat. 11:29.*
Merciful. *Heb. 2:17.*
Patient. *Is. 53:7; Mat. 27:14.*
Longsuffering. *1 Tim. 1:16.*
Compassionate. *Is. 40:11; Lk. 19:41.*
Benevolent. *Mat. 4:23-24; Acts 10:38.*
Loving. *Jn. 13:1, 15:13.*
Self-denying. *Mat. 8:20; 2 Cor. 8:9.*
Humble. *Lk. 22:27; Phil. 2:8.*
Resigned. *Lk. 22:42.*
Forgiving. *Lk. 23:34.*
Subject to his parents. *Lk. 2:51.*
The saints are conformed to.
Rom. 8:29.

CHURCH, THE

Belongs to God. *1 Tim. 3:15.*
The body of Christ. *Eph. 1:23; Col. 1:24.*
Christ, the foundation-stone of.
1 Cor. 3:11; Eph. 2:20; 1 Pet. 2:4, 6.
Christ, the head of. *Eph. 1:22, 5:23.*
Loved by Christ. *Song 7:10; Eph. 5:25.*
Purchased by the blood of Christ.
Acts 20:28; Eph. 5:25; Heb. 9:12.
Sanctified and cleansed by Christ.
1 Cor. 6:11; Eph. 5:26-27.
Subject to Christ. *Rom. 7:4; Eph. 5:24.*
The object of the grace of God.
Is. 27:3; 2 Cor. 8:1.
Displays the wisdom of God.
Eph. 3:10.
Shows forth the praises of God.
Is. 60:6.
God defends. *Ps. 89:18. Is. 4:5. Is. 49:25; Mat. 16:18.*
God provides ministers for.
Jer. 3:15; Eph. 4:11-12.
Glory to be ascribed to God by.
Eph. 3:21.
Elect. *1 Pet. 5:13.*
Glorious. *Ps. 35:13; Eph. 5:27.*
Clothed in righteousness. *Rev. 19:8.*

Believers continually added to, by the Lord. *Acts 2:47, 5:14, 11:24.*
Unity of. *Rom. 12:5; 1 Cor. 10:17, 12:12; Gal. 3:28.*
The saints baptised into, by one Spirit. *1 Cor. 12:13.*
Ministers commanded to feed. *Acts 20:28.*
Is edified by the Word. *1 Cor. 14:4, 13; Eph. 4:15-16.*
The wicked persecute. *Acts 8:1-3; 1 Thess. 2:14-15.*
Not to be despised. *1 Cor. 11:22.*
Defiling of, will be punished. *1 Cor. 3:17.*
Extent of, predicted. *Is. 2:2; Ezek. 17:22-24; Dan. 2:34-35.*

COMMANDMENTS, THE TEN
Spoken by God. *Ex. 20:1; Deut. 5:4, 22.*
Written by God. *Ex. 32:16, 34:1, 28; Deut. 4:13, Deut. 10:4.*
Enumerated. *Ex. 20:3-17.*
Summed up by Christ. *Mat. 22:35-40.*
Law of, is spiritual. *Mat. 5:28; Rom. 7:14.* (See Law of God)

COMMUNION WITH GOD
Is communion with the Father. *1 Jn. 1:3.*
Is communion with the Son. *1 Cor. 1:9; 1 Jn. 1:3; Rev. 3:20.*
Is communion with the Holy Spirit. *1 Cor. 12:13; 2 Cor. 13:14; Phil. 2:1.*
Reconciliation must precede. *Amos 3:3.*
Holiness essential to. *2 Cor. 6:14-16.*
Promised to the obedient. *Jn. 14:23.*
The saints
  Desire. *Ps. 42:1; Phil. 1:23.*
  Have, in meditation. *Ps. 63:5-6.*
  Have, in prayer. *Phil. 4:6; Heb. 4:16.*
  Have, in the Lord's Supper. *1 Cor. 10:16.*
  Should always enjoy. *Ps. 16:8; Jn. 14:16-18.*

Some examples. **Enoch**: *Gen. 5:24.*
Noah: *Gen. 6:9.* **Abraham**: *Gen. 18:33.* **Jacob**: *Gen. 32:24-29.*
Moses: *Ex. 33:11,23.*

COMMUNION OF SAINTS, THE
According to the prayer of Christ. *Jn. 17:20-21.*
Is with
  God. *1 Jn. 1:3.*
  The saints in heaven. *Heb. 12:22-24.*
  Each other. *Gal. 2:9; 1 Jn. 1:3, 7.*
God marks with his approval. *Mal. 3:16.*
Christ is present in. *Mat. 18:20.*
In public and social worship. *Ps. 34:3, 55:14; Acts 1:14; Heb. 10:25.*
In the Lord's Supper. *1 Cor. 10:17.*
In holy conversation. *Mal. 3:16.*
In prayer for each other. *2 Cor. 1:11; Eph. 6:18.*
In exhortation. *Col. 3:16; Heb. 10:25.*
In mutual comfort and edification. *1 Thess. 4:18, 5:11.*
In mutual sympathy and kindness. *Rom. 12:15; Eph. 4:32.*
Delight of. *Ps. 16:3, 42:4, 133:1-3; Rom. 15:32.*
Exhortation to. *Eph. 4:1-3.*
Opposed to communion with the wicked. *2 Cor. 6:14-17; Eph. 5:11.*

Some examples. **Jonathan**: *1 Sam. 23:16.* **David**: *Ps. 119:63.* **Daniel**: *Dan. 2:17-18.* **The Apostles**: *Acts 1:14.*
The early Church: *Acts 2:42, 5:12.*
Paul: *Acts 20:36-38.*

COMMUNION OF THE LORD'S SUPPER
Prefigured. *Ex. 12:21-28; 1 Cor. 5:7-8.*
Instituted. *Mat. 26:26. 1 Cor. 11:23.*
Object of. *Lk. 22:19. 1 Cor. 11:24, 26.*
Is the communion of the body and blood of Christ. *1 Cor. 10:16.*
Both bread and wine are necessary to be received. *Mat. 26:27; 1 Cor. 11:26.*
Self-examination commanded

before partaking of. *1 Cor. 11:28, 31.*
Newness of heart and life
necessary to the worthy partaking of. *1 Cor. 5:7-8.*
Partakers of, should be wholly
separate to God. *1 Cor. 10:21.*
Was continually partaken of, by
the early Church. *Acts 2:42, 20:7.*

Unworthy partakers of
Are guilty of the body and
blood of Christ. *1 Cor. 11:27.*
Do not discern the Lord's body.
1 Cor. 11:29.
Are visited with judgements.
1 Cor. 11:30.

COMPASSION AND SYMPATHY
Christ set an example of. *Lk. 19:41-42.*
Exhortation to. *Rom. 12:15; 1 Pet. 3:8.*

Exercised towards
The afflicted. *Job 6:14; Heb. 13:3.*
The chastened. *Is. 22:4; Jer. 9:1.*
Enemies. *Ps. 35:13.*
The poor. *Prov. 19:17.*
The weak. *2 Cor. 11:29; Gal. 6:2.*
The saints. *1 Cor. 12:25-26.*
Inseparable from love to God.
1 Jn. 3:17.

Motives
The compassion of God.
Mat. 18:27, 33.
The sense of our infirmities.
Heb. 5:2.
The wicked made to feel, for the
saints. *Ps. 106:46.*
Promise to those who show.
Prov. 19:17.
Illustrated. *Lk. 10:33, 15:20.*

Some examples. **Pharaoh's
daughter**: *Ex. 2:6.* **Shobi**, *etc:
2 Sam. 17:27-29.* **Elijah**: *1 Kings 17:18-19.*
Nehemiah: *Neh. 1:4.* **Job's friends**:
Job 2:11. **Job**: *Job 30:25.* **David**: *Ps. 35:13-
14.* **Jews**: *Jn. 11:19.* **Paul**: *1 Cor. 9:22.*

COMPASSION AND SYMPATHY
OF CHRIST, THE
Necessary for his priestly office.

Heb. 5:2 with verse 7.

Is manifested for the
Weary and heavy-laden.
Mat. 11:28-30.
Weak in faith. *Is. 40:11, 42:3 with
Mat. 12:20.*
Tempted. *Heb. 2:18.*
Afflicted. *Lk. 7:13. Jn. 11:33, 35.*
Diseased. *Mat. 14:14; Mk. 1:41.*
Poor. *Mk. 8:2.*
Perishing sinners. *Mat. 9:36; Lk. 19:41.*
An encouragement to prayer.
Heb. 4:15.
The saints should imitate. *1 Pet. 3:8.*

CONDEMNATION
The sentence of God against sin.
Mat. 25:41.
Universal, caused by the offence
of Adam. *Rom. 5:12, 16, 18.*
Inseparable consequence of sin.
Prov. 12:2; Rom. 6:23.

Increased by
Impenitence. *Mat. 11:20-24.*
Unbelief. *Jn. 3:18-19.*
Pride. *1 Tim. 3:6.*
Oppression. *Jas. 5:1-5.*
Hypocrisy. *Mat. 23:14.*
Conscience testifies to the justice
of. *Job 9:20; Rom. 2:1; Titus 3:11.*
The law testifies to the justice of.
Rom. 3:19.
Is according to men's deserts.
Mat. 12:37; 2 Cor. 11:15.
The saints are delivered from, by
Christ. *Jn. 3:18, 5:24; Rom. 8:1, 33- 34.*
Of the wicked, an example.
2 Pet. 2:6; Jude verse 7.
Chastisement is designed to
rescue us from. *1 Cor. 11:32.*
Apostates ordained unto. *Jude verse 4.*
Unbelievers remain under. *Jn. 3:18, 36.*
The law is the ministration of.
2 Cor. 3:9.

CONDUCT, CHRISTIAN
Believing God. *Mk. 11:22; Jn. 14:1.*
Fearing God. *Eccl. 12:13; 1 Pet. 2:17.*
Loving God. *Deut. 6:5; Mat. 22:37.*

Following God. *Eph. 5:1; 1 Pet. 1:15.*
Obeying God. *Eccl. 12:13; Lk. 1:6.*
Rejoicing in God. *Ps. 33:1; Hab. 3:18.*
Believing in Christ. *Jn. 6:29; Gal. 2:20.*
Loving Christ. *Jn. 21:15; Eph. 6:24.*
Following the example of Christ.
Jn. 13 15; 1 Pet. 2:21-24.
Obeying Christ. *Jn. 14:21, 15:14.*

Living
For Christ. *Rom. 14:8; 2 Cor. 5:15.*
Godly in Christ Jesus. *2 Tim. 3:12.*
Unto righteousness. *Rom. 6:18;*
1 Pet. 2:24.
Soberly, righteously, and godly.
Titus 2:12.

Walking
Worthy of God. *1 Thess. 2:12.*
Worthy of the Lord. *Col. 1:10.*
In the Spirit. *Gal. 5:25.*
After the Spirit. *Rom. 8:1.*
In newness of life. *Rom. 6:4.*
Worthy of our vocation. *Eph. 4:1.*
As children of light. *Eph. 5:8.*
Abstaining from all appearance of
evil. *1 Thess. 5:22.*
Rejoicing in Christ. *Phil. 3:1, 4:4.*
Loving one another. *Jn. 15:12; Rom.*
12:10; 1 Cor. 13:3; Eph. 5:2; Heb. 13:1.
Striving for the faith. *Phil. 1:27;*
Jude verse 3.
Putting away all sin. *1 Cor. 5:7; Heb. 12:1.*
Perfecting holiness. *Mat. 5:48;*
2 Cor. 7:1; 2 Tim. 3:17.
Hating defilement. *Jude verse 23.*
Following after what is good.
Phil. 4:8; 1 Thess. 5:15; 1 Tim. 6:11.
Overcoming the world. *1 Jn. 5:4-5.*
Adorning the gospel. *Phil. 1:27;*
Titus 2:10.
Showing a good example.
1 Tim. 4:12; 1 Pet. 2:12.
Abounding in the work of the
Lord. *1 Cor. 15:58; 2 Cor. 8:7; 1 Thess. 4:1.*
Shunning the wicked. *Ps. 1:1;*
2 Thess. 3:6.
Controlling the body. *1 Cor. 9:27; Col. 3:5.*
Subduing the temper. *Eph. 4:26;*
Jas. 1:19.
Submitting to injuries. *Mat. 5:39-41;*

1 Cor. 6:7.
Forgiving injuries. *Mat. 6:14;*
Rom. 12:20.
Living peaceably with all. *Rom. 12:18;*
Heb. 12:14.
Visiting the afflicted. *Mat. 25:36; Jas. 1:27.*
Treating others as we would like
to be treated. *Mat. 7:12; Lk. 6:31.*
Sympathising with others.
Rom. 12:15; 1 Thess. 5:14.
Honouring others. *Ps. 15:4;*
Rom. 12:10.
Fulfilling domestic duties. *Eph. 6:1-*
8; 1 Pet. 3:1-7.
Submitting to the authorities.
Rom. 13:1-7.
Being generous in our giving to
others. *Acts 20:35; Rom. 12:13.*
Being contented. *Phil. 4:11; Heb. 13:5.*
The blessedness of maintaining.
Ps. 1:1-3, 19:9-11, 50:23; Mat. 5:3-12; Jn.
15:10.

CONFESSING CHRIST
Influences of the Holy Spirit
necessary to. *1 Cor. 12:3; 1 Jn. 4:2.*
A test of being saints. *1 Jn. 2:23, 4:2-3.*
An evidence of union with God.
1 Jn. 4:15.
Necessary to salvation. *Rom. 10:9-10.*
Ensures his confessing us. *Mat. 10:32.*
The fear of man prevents. *Jn. 7:13,*
12:42-43.
Persecution should not prevent
us from. *Mk. 8:35; 2 Tim. 2:12.*
Must be connected with faith.
Rom. 10:9.
Consequences of not doing.
Mat. 10:33.

Some examples. **Nathanael**: *Jn. 1:49.*
Peter: *Jn. 6:68-69. Acts 2:22-36.* **A man
born blind**: *Jn. 9:25, 33.* **Martha**:
Jn. 11:27. **Peter and John**: *Acts 4:7-12.*
The apostles: *Acts 5:29-32, 42.*
Stephen: *Acts 7:52, 59.* **Paul**: *Acts 9:29.*
Timothy: *1 Tim. 6:12;* **John**: *Rev. 1:9.*
The church in Pergamos: *Rev. 2:13.*
Martyrs: *Rev. 20:4.*

CONFESSION OF SIN

God requires. *Lev. 5:5; Hos. 5:15.*
God regards. *Job 33:27-28; Dan. 9:20, etc.*
Exhortations to. *Josh. 7:19; Jer. 3:13.*
Promises to. *Lev. 26:40-42; Prov. 28:13.*

Should be accompanied with
Submission to punishment.
Lev. 26:41; Neh.9:33.
Prayer for forgiveness. *2 Sam.
24:10; Ps. 25:11, Ps. 51:1; Jer. 14:7-9, 21.*
Self-abasement. *Is. 64:5-6; Jer. 3:25.*
Godly sorrow. *Ps. 38:18; Lam. 1:20.*
Forsaking sin. *Prov. 28:13.*
Restitution. *Num. 5:6-7.*

Should be full and unreserved.
Ps. 32:5, 51:3, 106:6.
Followed by pardon. *Ps. 32:5; 1 Jn. 1:9.*
Illustrated. *Lk. 15:21, 18:13.*

Some examples. **Aaron:** *Num. 12:11.*
Israelites: *Num. 21:6-7. 1 Sam. 7:6, 12:19.*
Saul: *1 Sam. 15:24.* **David**: *2 Sam. 24:10.*
Ezra: *Ezra 9:6.* **Nehemiah**: *Neh. 1:6-7.*
Levites: *Neh. 9:4, 33, 34.* **Job**: *Job 7:20.*
Daniel: *Dan. 9:4.* **Peter**: *Lk. 5:8.* **A dying
thief**: *Lk. 23:41.*

CONSCIENCE, THE

Witnesses in man. *Prov. 20:27;
Rom. 2:15.*
Accuses of sin. *Gen. 42:21; 1 Sam. 24:5;
Mat. 27:3; Lk. 9:7.*
We must have the approval of.
Job 27:6; Acts 24:16; Rom. 9:1, 14:22.
The blood of Christ alone can
purify. *Heb. 9:14, 10:2-10, 22.*
Keep the faith in purity of.
1 Tim. 1:19, 3:9.
Of the saints, pure and good.
Heb. 13:18; 1 Pet. 3:16, 21.
Submit to authority and. *Rom. 13:5.*
Suffer patiently for. *1 Pet. 2:19.*
Testimony of, a source of joy.
2 Cor. 1:12; 1 Jn. 3:21.
Of others, not to be offended.
Rom. 14:1; 1 Cor. 10:28-32.
Ministers should commend
themselves to their people's.
2 Cor. 4:2, 5:11.

Of the wicked, a seared. *1 Tim. 4:2.*
Of the wicked, a defiled. *Titus 1:15.*
Without spiritual illumination, a
false guide. *Acts 23:1 with Acts 26:9.*

CONTEMPT

Sin of. *Job 31:13-14; Prov. 12:21.*
Folly of. *Prov. 11:12.*
A characteristic of the wicked.
Prov. 18:3; 2 Tim. 3:3.

Forbidden towards
Parents. *Prov. 23:22.*
Christ's little ones. *Mat. 18:10.*
Weak brothers. *Rom. 14:3.*
Young ministers. *1 Cor. 16:11.*
Believing masters. *1 Tim. 6:2.*
The poor. *Jas. 2:1-3.*

Self-righteousness prompts to.
Is. 65:5; Lk. 18:9, 11.
Pride and prosperity lend
themselves to. *Ps. 123:4.*
Masters should give no occasion
for. *1 Tim. 4:12.*
Of ministers, is a despising of
God. *Lk. 10:16; 1 Thess. 4:8.*

Towards the church
Often turned into respect. *Is. 60:14.*
Often punished. *Ezek. 28:26.*

To be met with patience.
1 Sam. 10:27.
Causes the saints to cry to God.
Neh. 4:4;. Ps. 123:3.

The wicked show, towards
Christ. *Ps. 22:6; Is. 53:3; Mat.27:29.*
The saints. *Ps. 119:141; 1 Cor. 4:10.*
Authorities. *2 Pet. 2:10; Jude verse 8.*
Parents. *Prov. 15:3, 20.*
The afflicted. *Job 19:18.*
The poor. *Ps. 14:6. Eccl. 9:16.*

The saints are sometimes guilty
of. *Jas. 2:6.*

Some examples. **Hagar**: *Gen. 16:4.*
Children of Belial: *1 Sam. 10:27.*
Nabal: *1 Sam. 25:10-11.*
Michal: *2 Sam. 6:16.* **Sanballat**, etc:
Neh. 2:19, 4:2-3. **False teachers**:
2 Cor. 10:10.

CONTENTMENT
With godliness is great gain.
Ps. 37:16; 1 Tim. 6:6.
The saints should show
In their respective callings.
1 Cor. 7:20.
With appointed wages. *Lk. 3:14.*
With whatever they possess.
Heb. 13:5.
With food and clothing. *1 Tim. 6:8.*
God's promises should lead to.
Heb. 13:5.
The wicked lack. *Is. 5:8.*

Some examples. **Barzillai:**
2 Sam. 19:33-37. **Shunammite:** *2 Kings 4:13.* **David:** *Ps. 16:6.* **Agur:** *Prov. 30:8-9.*
Paul: *Phil. 4:11-12.*

CONVERSION
By God. *1 Kings 18:37; Jn. 6:44; Acts 21:19.*
By Christ. *Acts 3:26; Rom. 15:18.*
By the power of the Holy Spirit.
Prov. 1:23.
Is of grace. *Acts 11:21 with verse 23.*
Follows repentance. *Acts 3:19, 26:20.*
Is the result of faith. *Acts 11:21.*
Through the instrumentality of
The Scriptures. *Ps. 19:7; 2 Tim. 3:15.*
Ministers. *Acts 26:18. 1 Thess. 1:9.*
Self-examination. *Ps. 119:59; Lam. 3:40.*
Affliction. *Ps. 78:34.*
Of sinners, a cause of joy
To God. *Ezek. 18:23; Lk. 15:32.*
To the saints. *Acts 15:3; Gal. 1:23-24.*
Is necessary. *Mat. 18:3.*
Commanded. *Job 36:10.*
Exhortations to. *Prov. 1:23; Is. 31:6, 55:7; Jer. 3:7; Ezek. 33:11.*
Promises connected with. *Neh. 1:9; Is. 1:27; Jer. 3:14; Ezek. 18:27.*
Pray for. *Ps. 80:7, 85:4; Jer. 31:18; Lam. 5:21.*
Is accompanied by confession of sin, and prayer. *1 Kings 8:35.*
The danger of neglecting. *Ps. 7:12; Jer. 44:5, 11; Ezek. 3:19.*
The duty of leading sinners to.
Ps. 51:13.
Encouragement for leading

sinners to. *Dan. 12:3; Jas. 5:19-20.*
Of Gentiles, predicted. *Is. 2:2, 11:10, 60:5, 66:12.*
Of Israel, predicted. *Ezek. 36:25-27; Rom. 11:26.*

COUNSELS AND PURPOSES OF GOD, THE
Are great. *Jer. 32:19.*
Are wonderful. *Is. 28:29.*
Are immutable. *Ps. 33:11; Prov. 19:21; Jer. 4:28; Rom. 9:11; Heb. 6:17.*
Are sovereign. *Is. 40:13-14; Dan. 4:35.*
Are eternal. *Eph. 3:11.*
Are faithfulness and truth. *Is. 25:1.*
None can disannul or hinder.
Job 42:2; Is. 14:27.
Will be performed. *Is. 14:24, 46:11.*
The sufferings and death of Christ were according to. *Acts 2:23, 4:28.*
The saints are called and saved according to. *Rom. 8:28; 2 Tim. 1. 9.*
The union of all saints in Christ is according to. *Eph. 1:9-10.*
The works of God are according to. *Eph. 1:11.*
Should be declared by ministers.
Acts 20:27.
Attend to. *Jer. 49:20; 50:45.*
Secret, not to be searched into.
Deut. 29:29; Mat. 24:36; Acts 1:7.
The wicked
Do not understand. *Mic. 4:12.*
Despise. *Is. 5:19.*
Reject. *Lk. 7:30.*

COURTS OF JUSTICE
Have authority from God. *Rom. 13:1-5.*
Superior court
Held first by Moses alone in the wilderness. *Ex.18:13-20.*
Consisted subsequently of priests and Levites. *Deut. 17:9 with Mal. 2:7.*
Presided over by the governor or the high priest. *Deut. 17:12; Judg. 4:4- 5.*

Held at the seat of government.
Deut. 17:8.
Decided on all appeals and difficult cases. Ex. 18:26; Deut. 1:17, 17:8-9.
Decisions of, conclusive.
Deut. 17:10-11.

Lower courts

In all cities. Deut. 16:18; 2 Chron. 19:5-7.
Held at the gates. Gen. 34:20; Deut. 16:18; Deut. 21:19; Job 5:4.
Judges of, appointed by the governor. Ex. 18:21, 25; Deut. 1:9-15; 2 Sam. 15:3.
All minor cases decided by.
Ex. 18:26; 2 Sam. 15:4.
All transfers of property made before. Gen. 23:17-20; Ruth 4:1-2
Re-established by Jehoshaphat.
2 Chron. 19:5-10.
Re-established by Ezra. Ezra 7:25.

Sanhedrin, or Court of the Seventy

Probably derived from the seventy elders appointed by Moses. Ex. 24:9; Num. 11:16-17, 24-30.
Mentioned in the latter part of sacred history. Lk. 22:66; Jn. 11:47; Acts 5:27.
Consisted of the chief priests, etc. Mat. 26:57, 69.
Presided over by the High Priest. Mat. 26:62-66.
Sat in the High Priest's palace.
Mat. 26:57-58.

While the Romans were Judea

Presided over by the governor or deputy. Mat. 27:2, 11; Acts 18:12.
Place of, called the Hall of Judgement. Jn. 18:28, 33; Jn. 19:9.
Never interfered in any dispute about minor matters, or about religion. Acts 18:14-15.
Could alone award the death penalty. Jn. 18:31.
Never examined their own citizens using torture. Acts 22:25-29.
Appeals from, were made to the Emperor. Acts 25:11; Acts 28:32, 28:19.

Generally held in the morning.
Jer. 21:12; Mat. 27:1; Lk. 22:66; Acts 5:21.
Sometimes held in synagogues.
Mat. 10:17; Acts 22:19, 26:11. Jas. 2:2.
(Greek)

Provided with

Judges. Deut. 16:18.
Officers. Deut. 16:18; Mat. 5:25.
Tormentors and executioners.
Mat. 18:34.

The judges

Were called elders. Deut. 25:7; 1 Sam. 16:4.
Were called magistrates. Lk. 12:58.
Often rode on white donkeys.
Judg. 5:10.
To judge righteously. Lev. 19:15; Deut. 1:16.
To judge without respect of persons. Ex. 23:3, 6; Lev. 19:15; Deut. 1:17; Prov. 22:22.
To investigate every case. Deut. 19:18.
Not to take bribes. Ex. 23:8; Deut. 16:19.
To judge as for God. 2 Chron. 19:6, 7, 9.
To decide according to law.
Ezek. 44:24.
To promote peace. Zech. 8:16.
Sat on the judgement-seat while hearing cases. Ex. 18:13; Judg. 8:10; Is. 28:6; Mat. 27:19.
Examined the parties concerned. Acts 24:8.
Conferred together before giving judgement. Acts 5:34-40, 25:12, 26:30-31.
Pronounced the judgement of the court. Mat. 26:65-66; Lk. 23:24; Acts 5:40.
Both the accusers and accused were required to appear before.
Deut. 25:1; Acts 25:16.

Cases in, were opened by

The complainant. 1 Kings 3:17-21; Acts 16:19-21.
An advocate. Acts 24:1.

The accused

Stood before the judge. *Num. 35:12; Mat. 27:11.*

Were permitted to plead their own cause. *1 Kings 3:22; Acts 24:10; Acts 26:1.*

Might have advocates. *Prov. 31:8-9; Is. 1:17.*

Were exhorted to confess. *Josh. 7:19.*

Were examined on oath. *Lev. 5:1; Mat. 26:63.*

Were sometimes examined under torture. *Acts 22:24, 29.*

Were sometimes treated with insults. *Mat. 26:67. Jn. 18:22-23. Acts 23:2-3.*

The evidence of two or more witnesses was required. *Deut. 17:6, 19:15; Jn. 8:17; 2 Cor. 13:1.*

Witnesses sometimes laid their hands on the criminal's head before punishment. *Lev. 24:14.*

False witnesses received the punishment of the accused. *Deut. 19:19.*

Corruption and bribery were often practised. *Is. 10:1; Amos 5:12, 8:6.*

The judgement of

Was not given till the accused was heard. *Jn. 7:51.*

Was recorded in writing. *Is. 10:1* (See margin).

Was immediately executed. *Deut. 25:2; Josh. 7:25; Mk. 15:15-20.*

Witnesses led the execution. *Deut. 17:7; Acts 7:58.*

Allusions to. *Job 5:4; Ps. 127:5; Mat. 5:22.*

Illustrative of the last judgement. *Mat. 19:28; Rom. 14:10; 1 Cor. 6:12.*

COVENANT, THE

Christ, the substance of. *Is. 42:6, 49:8.*

Christ, the Mediator of. *Heb. 8:6, 9:15, 12:24.*

Christ, the Messenger of. *Mal. 3:1.*

Made with

Abraham. *Gen. 15:7-18, 17:2-14; Lk. 1:72-75; Acts 3:25; Gal. 3:16.*

Isaac. *Gen. 17:19, 21, 26:3-4.*

Jacob. *Gen. 28:13-14 with 1 Chron. 16:16-17.*

Israel. *Ex. 6:4; Acts 3:25.*

David. *2 Sam. 23:5; Ps. 89:3-4.*

Renewed under the gospel. *Jer. 31:31-33; Rom. 11:27; Heb. 8:8-10, 13.*

Fulfilled in Christ. *Lk. 1:68-79.*

Confirmed in Christ. *Gal. 3:17.*

Ratified by the blood of Christ. *Heb. 9:11-14, 16-23.*

Is a covenant of peace. *Is. 54:9-10; Ezek. 34:25, 37:26.*

Is unalterable. *Ps. 89:34; Is. 54:10, 69:21; Gal. 8:17.*

Is everlasting. *Ps. 111:9; Is. 55:3, 81:8; Ezek. 16:60-63; Heb. 13:20.*

All the saints are interested in. *Ps. 25:14, 89:29-37; Heb. 8:10.*

The wicked have no interest in. *Eph. 2:12.*

Blessings connected with. *Is. 56:4-7; Heb. 8:10-12.*

God is faithful to. *Deut. 7:9; 1 Kings 8:23; Neh. 1:5; Dan. 9:4.*

God is ever mindful of. *Ps. 105:8; Ps. 111:5; Lk. 1:72.*

Be mindful of. *1 Chron. 16:15.*

Caution against forgetting. *Deut. 4:23.*

Plead, in prayer. *Ps. 74:20; Jer. 14:21.*

Punishment for despising. *Heb. 10:29-30.*

COVETOUSNESS

Comes from the heart. *Mk. 7:22-23.*

Engrosses the heart. *Ezek. 33:31; 2 Pet. 2:14.*

Is idolatry. *Eph. 5:5; Col. 3:5.*

Love of money is the root of all kinds of evil. *1 Tim. 6:10.*

Is never satisfied. *Eccl. 5:10; Hab. 2:5.*

Is vanity. *Ps. 39:6; Eccl. 4:8.*

Is inconsistent

In the saints. *Eph. 5:8; Heb. 13:5.*

Especially in ministers. *1 Tim. 3:3.*

Leads to

Injustice and oppression. *Prov. 28:20; Mic. 2:2.*

Foolish and hurtful lusts. *1 Tim. 6:9.*
A departure from the faith.
1 Tim. 6:10.
Lying. *2 Kings 5:22-25.*
Murder. *Prov. 1:18-19; Ezek. 22:12.*
Theft. *Josh. 7:21.*
Poverty. *Prov. 28:22.*
Misery. *1 Tim. 6:10.*
Domestic affliction. *Prov. 15:27.*
Abhorred by God. *Ps. 10:3.*
Forbidden. *Ex.20:17.*
A characteristic of the wicked.
Rom. 1:29.
A characteristic of the slothful.
Prov. 21:26.
Only commended by the wicked.
Ps. 10:3.
Hated by the saints. *Ex. 18:21; Acts 20:33.*
To be mortified by the saints. *Col. 3:5.*
Woe denounced against. *Is. 5:8;*
Hab. 2:9.
The punishment of. *Job 20:15; Is. 57:17;*
Jer. 22:17-19; Mic. 2:2-3.

Excludes from heaven. *1 Cor. 6:10;*
Eph. 5:5.
Beware of. *Lk. 12:15.*
Avoid those guilty of. *1 Cor. 5:11.*
Pray against. *Ps. 119:36.*
The reward of those who hate.
Prov. 28:16.
Will abound in the last days.
2 Tim. 3:2; 2 Pet. 2:1-3.

Some examples. **Laban**: *Gen. 31:41.*
Achan: *Josh. 7:21.* **Eli's sons**: *1 Sam.
2:12-14.* **Samuel's sons**: *1 Sam. 8:3.*
Saul: *1 Sam. 15:9, 19.* **Ahab**: *1 Kings 21:2,*
etc. **Gehazi**: *2 Kings 5:20-24.***Noble-
men among the Jews**: *Neh. 5:7; Is. 1:23.*
Jewish priests: *Is. 56:11; Jer. 6:13.*
Babylon: *Jer. 51:13.* **A rich young
man**: *Mat. 19:22.* **Judas Iscariot**:
Mat. 26:14-15;. Jn. 12:6. **The Pharisees**:
Lk. 16:14. **Ananias**, etc: *Acts 5:1-10.*
Demetrius: *Acts 19:27.* **Felix**:
Acts 24:26. **Balaam**: *Num. 22:21;*
2 Pet. 2:15 with Jude verse 11.

D

DEATH, SPIRITUAL

Alienation from God is. *Eph. 4:18.*
A worldly mind means. *Rom. 8:6.*
Walking in trespasses and sins is.
Eph. 2:1; Col. 2:13.
Spiritual ignorance is. *Is. 9:2; Mat. 4:
16; Lk. 1:79; Eph. 4:18.*
Unbelief is. *Jn. 6:53; 1 Jn. 5:12.*
Living in pleasure is. *1 Tim. 5:6.*
Hypocrisy is. *Rev. 3:1-2.*
Is a consequence of the Fall.
Rom. 5:15.
Is the state of all men by nature.
Mat. 8:22; Jn. 5:25; Rom. 6:13.
The fruit of, is dead works. *Heb. 6:1,
9:14.*
A call to arise from. *Eph. 5:14.*
Deliverance from, is through
Christ. *Jn. 5:24-25; Eph. 2:5; 1 Jn. 5:12.*
The saints are raised from. *Rom. 6:13.*
Love of the brothers is a proof of
being raised from. *1 Jn. 3:14.*

Illustrated. *Ezek. 37:2-3; Lk. 15:24.*

DEATH, NATURAL

By Adam. *Gen. 3:19; 1 Cor. 15:21-22.*
Consequence of sin. *Gen. 2:17;*
Rom. 5:12.
Is the lot of all. *Eccl. 8:8; Heb. 9:27.*
Ordered by God. *Deut. 32:39; Job 14:5.*
Puts an end to earthly projects.
Eccl. 9:10.
Strips of earthly possessions.
Job 1:21; 1 Tim. 6:7.
Levels all ranks. *Job 1:21, 3:17-19.*
Conquered by Christ. *Rom. 6:9;*
Rev. 1:18.
Abolished by Christ. *2 Tim. 1:10.*
Will finally be destroyed by
Christ. *Hos. 13:14; 1 Cor. 15:26.*
Christ delivers from the fear of.
Heb. 2:15.
Regard, as at hand. *Job 14:1-2;*
Ps. 39:4-5, 90:9; 1 Pet. 1:24.

Prepare for. *2 Kings 20:1.*
Pray to be prepared for. *Ps. 39:4, 13, 90:12.*
Consideration of, a motive for diligence. *Eccl. 9:10; Jn. 9:4.*
When averted for a season, it is a motive for increased devotion. *Ps. 56:12-13, 116:7-9, 118:17; Is. 38:20.*
Enoch and Elijah were exempt from. *Gen. 5:24 with Heb. 11:5; 2 Kings 2:11.*
All will be raised from. *Acts 24:15.*
None subject to, in heaven. *Lk. 20:36; Rev. 21:4.*
Illustrates the change produced in conversion. *Rom. 6:2; Col. 2:20.*

Is described as
A sleep. *Deut. 31:16; Jn. 11:11.*
The earthly house of this tabernacle being dissolved. *2 Cor. 5:1.*
Putting off this tabernacle. *2 Pet. 1:14.*
God requiring the soul. *Lk. 12:20.*
Going along the way from which there is no return. *Job 16:22.*
Gathering to our people. *Gen. 49:33.*
Going down into silence. *Ps. 115:17.*
Yielding up the spirit. *Acts 5:10.*
Returning to the dust. *Gen. 3:19; Ps. 104:29.*
Being cut down. *Job 14:2.*
Fleeing as a shadow. *Job 14:2.*
Departing. *Phil. 1:23.*

DEATH, ETERNAL
The necessary consequence of sin. *Rom. 6:16, 21, 8:13; Jas. 1:15.*
The wages of sin is. *Rom. 6:23.*
Is the portion of the wicked. *Mat. 25:41, 46; Rom. 1:32.*
The way to, is described. *Mat. 7:13.*
Self-righteousness leads to. *Prov. 14:12.*
God alone can inflict. *Mat. 10:28; Jas. 4:12.*

Is described as
Banishment from God. *2 Thess. 1:9.*
Society with the devil, etc. *Mat. 25:41.*
A lake of fire. *Rev. 19:20, 21:8.*

A place where the worm does not die. *Mk. 9:44.*
Outer darkness. *Mat. 25:30.*
A mist of darkness forever. *2 Pet. 2:17.*
Indignation, wrath, etc. *Rom. 2:8-9.*

Is called
Destruction. *Rom. 9:22; 2 Thess. 1:9.*
Perishing. *2 Pet. 2:12.*
The wrath to come. *1 Thess. 1:10.*
The second death. *Rev. 2:11.*
A resurrection to condemnation. *Jn. 6:29.*
A resurrection to shame, etc. *Dan. 12:2.*
Condemnation to hell. *Mat. 23:33.*
Everlasting punishment. *Mat. 25:46.*
Will be inflicted by Christ. *Mat. 25:33, 41; 2 Thess. 1:7-8.*
Christ, the only, way of escape from. *Jn. 3:16, 8:51.*
The saints will escape. *Rev. 2:11, 21:27.*
Strive to preserve others from. *Jas. 5:20.*
Illustrated. *Lk. 16:23-26.*

DEATH OF CHRIST, THE
Foretold. *Ps. 22:1-31; Is. 53:8; Dan. 9:26; Zech. 13:7.*
Appointed by God. *Is. 53:6, 10; Acts 2:23.*
Necessary for the redemption of man. *Lk. 24:46; Jn. 12:24; Acts 17:3.*
Acceptable, as a sacrifice to God. *Mat. 20:28; Eph. 5:2; 1 Thess. 5:10.*
Was voluntary. *Is. 53:12; Mat. 26:53; Jn. 10:17-18.*
Was undeserved. *Is. 53:9.*

Mode of
Foretold by Christ. *Mat. 20:18-19; Jn. 12:32-33.*
Prefigured. *Num. 21:8 with Jn. 3:14.*
Shameful. *Heb. 12:2.*
Accursed. *Deut. 21:23; Gal. 3:13.*
In humility. *Phil. 2:8.*
A stumbling-block to the Jews. *1 Cor. 1:23.*

Foolishness to the Gentiles.
1 Cor. 1:18, 23.
Demanded by the Jews.
Mat. 27:22-23.
Inflicted by the Gentiles.
Mat. 27:26-35.
In the company of criminals.
Is. 53:12 with Mat. 27:38.
Accompanied by supernatural
signs. *Mat. 27:45, 51-53.*
Emblematic of the death unto
sin. *Rom. 6:3-8; Gal. 2:20.*
Commemorated in the sacrament of the Lord's Supper.
Lk. 22:19-20.

DEATH OF THE SAINTS, THE

Asleep in Christ. *1 Cor. 15:18;
1 Thess. 4:14.*
Is blessed. *Rev. 14:13.*
Is gain. *Phil. 1:21.*
Is full of
  Faith. *Heb. 11:13.*
  Peace. *Is. 57:2.*
  Hope. *Prov. 14:32.*
Is sometimes desired. *Lk. 2:29.*
Is waited for. *Job 14:14.*
Is met with resignation.
Gen. 50:24; Josh. 23:14; 1 Kings 2:2.
Is met without fear. *Ps. 23:4.*
Is precious in God's sight. *Ps. 116:15.*
God preserves them during.
Ps. 48:14.
God is with them in. *Ps. 23:4.*
Removes them from coming evil.
2 Kings 22:20; Is. 57:1.
Leads to
  Rest. *Job 3:17; Rev. 14:13.*
  Comfort. *Lk. 16:25.*
  Christ's presence. *2 Cor. 5:8; Phil. 1:23.*
  A crown of life. *2 Tim. 4:8; Rev. 2:10.*
  A joyful resurrection. *Is. 26:19;
  Dan. 12:2.*
Disregarded by the wicked. *Is. 57:1.*
Survivors are consoled. *1 Thess. 4:13.*
The wicked wish theirs to
resemble believers. *Num. 23:10.*
Illustrated. *Lk. 16:22.*

Some examples. **Abraham**:
Gen. 25:8. **Isaac**: *Gen. 35:29.* **Jacob**:
Gen. 49:33. **Aaron**: *Num. 20:28.* **Moses**:
Deut. 34:5. **Joshua**: *Josh. 24:29.* **Elisha**:
2 Kings 13:14, 20. **One of the thieves**:
Lk. 23:43. **Dorcas**: *Acts 9:37.*

DEATH OF THE WICKED, THE

Is in their sins. *Ezek. 3:19; Jn. 8:21.*
Is without hope. *Prov. 11:7.*
Is sometimes without fear. *Jer. 34:5
with 2 Chron. 36:11-13.*
Is frequently sudden and
unexpected. *Job 21:13, 23; Job 27:21;
Prov. 29:1.*
Is frequently marked with terror.
Job 18:11-15, 27:19-21; Ps. 73:19.
Punishment follows. *Is. 14:9; Acts 1:25.*
The remembrance of them
perishes in. *Job 18:17; Ps. 34:16; Prov. 10:7.*
God has no pleasure in. *Ezek. 18:23, 32.*
Is like the death of beasts. *Ps. 49:14.*
Illustrated. *Lk. 12:20, 16:22-23.*

Some examples. **Korah**, etc:
Num. 16:32. **Absolom**: *2 Sam. 18:9-10.*
Ahab: *1 Kings 22:34.* **Jezebel**:
2 Kings 9:33. **Athaliah**: *2 Chron. 23:15.*
Haman: *Esther 7:10.* **Belshazzar**:
Dan. 5:30. **Judas**: *Mat. 27:5 with Acts 1:18.*
Ananias, etc: *Acts 5:5, 9, 10.* **Herod**:
Acts 12:23.

DECEIT

Is falsehood. *Ps. 119:118.*
The tongue is the instrument of.
Rom. 3:13.
Comes from the heart. *Mk. 7:22.*
Is characteristic of the heart.
Jer. 17:9.
God abhors. *Ps. 5:6.*
Is forbidden. *Prov. 24:28; 1 Pet. 3:10.*
Christ was perfectly free from.
Is. 53:9 with 1 Pet. 2:22.
The saints
  Must be free from. *Ps. 24:4;
  Zeph. 3:13; Rev. 14:5.*
  Keep their tongues from. *Job 27:4.*
  Avoid. *Job 31:5.*

Shun those addicted to. *Ps. 101:7.*
Pray for deliverance from those who use. *Ps. 43:1, 120:2.*
Are delivered from those who use. *Ps. 72:14.*
Should beware of those who teach such. *Eph. 5:6; Col. 2:8.*
Should lay aside such, when seeking the truth. *1 Pet. 2:1.*
Ministers should certainly lay aside such. *2 Cor. 4:2; 1 Thess. 2:3.*

The wicked
Are full of. *Rom. 1:29.*
Devise. *Ps. 35:20, 38:12; Prov. 12:5.*
Utter. *Ps. 10:7, 36:3.*
Work hard in their. *Prov. 11:18.*
Increase in. *2 Tim. 3:13.*
Use, even to each other. *Jer. 9:5.*
Use for their own ends. *Jer. 37:9-13; Obad. verse 7.*
Delight in. *Prov. 20:17.*

False teachers
Are workers of. *2 Cor. 11:13.*
Preach it. *Jer. 14:14, 23:26.*
Impose on others by. *Rom. 16:18; Eph. 4:14.*
Take pleasure in. *2 Pet. 2:13.*
Hypocrites devise. *Job 15:35.*
Hypocrites practise. *Hos. 11:12.*
False witnesses use. *Prov. 12:17.*
A characteristic of AntiChrist. *2 Jn. 7.*
A characteristic of the Apostacy. *2 Thess. 2:10.*

Evil of
Keeps from a knowledge of God. *Jer. 9:6.*
Keeps from turning to God. *Jer. 8:5.*
Leads to pride and oppression. *Jer. 5:27-28.*
Leads to lying. *Prov. 11:25.*
Is often accompanied by fraud and injustice. *Ps. 10:7, 43:1.*
Hatred often concealed by. *Prov. 26:24, 26.*
The folly of fools is. *Prov. 14:8.*
The kisses of an enemy are. *Prov. 27:6.*
The blessedness of being free from. *Ps. 24:4-5, 32:2.*
The punishment of. *Ps. 55:23; Jer. 9:7-9.*

Some examples. **The devil**: *Gen. 3:1, 4-5.* **Rebecca and Jacob**: *Gen. 27:9, 19.* **Laban**: *Gen. 31:7.* **Joseph's brothers**: *Gen. 37:31-32.* **Pharaoh**: *Ex. 8:29.* **David**: *1 Sam. 21:13.* **Job's friends**: *Job 6:15.* **Doeg**: *Ps. 52:2* compared with the title. **Herod**: *Mat. 2:8.* **Pharisees**: *Mat. 22:16.* **Chief Priests**: *Mk. 14:1.* **A lawyer**: *Lk. 10:25.*

DECISION
Necessary for the service of God. *Lk. 9:62.*
Exhortations to. *Josh. 24:14-15.*

Shown in
Seeking God with the heart. *2 Chron. 15:12.*
Keeping the commandments of God. *Neh. 10:29.*
Being on the Lord's side. *Ex. 32:26.*
Following God fully. *Num. 14:24, 32:12.*
Serving God. *Is. 56:6.*
Loving God perfectly. *Deut. 6:5.*
The blessedness of. *Josh. 1:7.*

Opposed to
A divided service. *Mat. 6:24.*
Double-mindedness. *Jas. 1:8.*
Halting between two opinions. *1 Kings 18:21.*
Not making the heart right. *Ps. 78:8, 37*

Some examples. **Abraham**: *Heb. 11:8.* **Moses**: *Ex. 32:26.* **Caleb**: *Num. 13:30.* **Joshua**: *Josh. 24:15.* **Ruth**: *Ruth 1:16.* **Asa**: *2 Chron. 15:8.* **David**: *Ps. 17:3.* **Peter**: *Jn. 6:68.* **Paul**: *Acts 21:13.*

DELIGHTING IN GOD
Commanded. *Ps. 37:4.*
Reconciliation leads to. *Job 22:21, 26.*
Observing the Sabbath leads to. *Is. 58:13-14.*

The saints experience, in
Communion with God. *Song. 2:3.*
The Law of God. *Ps. 1:2, 119:24-35.*
The goodness of God. *Neh. 9:25.*
The comforts of God. *Ps. 94:19.*
Hypocrites
Pretend to. *Is. 58:2.*
In their hearts despise. *Job 27:10; Jer. 6:10.*
Promises to. *Ps. 37:4.*
The blessedness of. *Ps. 112:1.*

DENIAL OF CHRIST
In doctrine. *Mk. 8:38; 2 Tim. 1:8.*
In practice. *Phil. 3:18-19; Titus 1:16.*
A characteristic of false teachers. *2 Pet. 2:1; Jude verse 4.*
Is the spirit of Antichrist. *1 Jn. 2:22-23, 4:3.*
Christ will deny those guilty of. *Mat. 10:33; 2 Tim. 2:12.*
Leads to destruction. *2 Pet. 2:1; Jude verses 4, 15.*

Some examples. **Peter**: *Mat. 26:69-75.*
The Jews: *Jn. 18:40. Acts 3:13-14.*

DESPAIR
Produced in the wicked by divine judgements. *Deut. 28:34, 67; Rev. 9:6, 16:10.*
Leads to
Continuing in sin. *Jer. 2:25, 18:12.*
Blasphemy. *Is. 8:21; Rev. 16:10-11.*
Will seize upon the wicked at the appearing of Christ. *Rev. 6:16.*
The saints sometimes tempted to. *Job 7:6; Lam. 3:18.*
The saints enabled to overcome. *2 Cor. 4:8-9.*
Trust in God, a preservative against. *Ps. 42:5, 11.*

Some examples. **Cain**: *Gen. 4:13-14.*
Ahithophel, *2 Sam. 17:23.* **Judah**: *Mat. 27:5.*

DEVIL, THE
Sinned against God. *2 Pet. 2:4; 1 Jn. 3:8.*
Was cast out of heaven. *Lk. 10:18.*
Was cast down to hell. *2 Pet. 2:4; Jude verse 6.*
Is the author of the Fall. *Gen 3:1, 6, 14, 24.*
Tempted Christ. *Mat. 4:3-10.*
Perverts the Scriptures. *Mat. 4:6 with Ps. 91:11-12.*
Opposes God's work. *Zech. 3:1; 1 Thess. 2:18.*
Hinders the gospel. *Mat. 13:19; 2 Cor. 4:4.*
Works lying wonders. *2 Thess. 2:9; Rev. 16:14.*
Assumes the form of an angel of light. *2 Cor. 11:14.*
The wicked
Are the children of. *Mat. 13:38; Acts 13:10; 1 Jn. 3:10.*
Turn aside after. *1 Tim. 5:15.*
Fulfil the lusts of. *Jn. 8:44.*
Are possessed by. *Lk. 22:3; Acts 5:3; Eph. 2:2.*
Are blinded by. *2 Cor. 4:4.*
Are deceived by. *1 Kings 22:21-22; Rev. 20:7-8.*
Are ensnared by. *1 Tim. 3:7; 2 Tim. 2:26.*
Are troubled by. *1 Sam. 10:14.*
Are punished, together with. *Mat. 25:41.*
The saints
Are afflicted by, only so far as God permits. *Job 1:12, 2:4-7.*
Are tempted by. *1 Chron. 21:1; 1 Thess. 3:5.*
Are sifted by. *Lk. 22:31.*
Should resist. *Jas. 4:7; 1 Pet. 5:9.*
Should be armed against. *Eph. 6:11-16.*
Should be watchful against. *2 Cor. 2:11.*
Overcome. *1 Jn. 2:13; Rev. 12:11.*
Will finally triumph over. *Rom. 16:20.*
The saints triumph over, in Christ
Is predicted. *Gen. 3:15; Ps. 68:18.*
In resisting his temptations. *Mat. 4:11*
In casting out the spirits of. *Lk. 11:20, 13:32.*

In empowering his disciples to cast them out. *Mat 10:1; Mk. 16:17.*

In destroying the works of. *1 Jn. 3:8.*

Completed by his death. *Col. 2:15; Heb. 2:14.*

Illustrated. *Lk. 11:21-22.*

Character of,

Presumptuous. *Job 1:6; Mat. 4:5-6.*

Proud. *1 Tim. 3:6.*

Powerful. *Eph. 2:2, 6:12.*

Wicked. *1 Jn. 2:13.*

Malignant. *Job 1:9, 2:4.*

Subtle. *Gen. 3:1 with 2 Cor. 11:3.*

Deceitful. *2 Cor. 11:14; Eph. 6:11.*

Fierce and cruel. *Lk. 8:29, 9:38, 42; 1 Pet. 5:8.*

Active in doing evil. *Job 1:7, 2:2.*

Cowardly. *Jas. 4:7.*

The Apostasy is of. *2 Thess. 2:9; 1 Tim. 4:1.*

Will be condemned at the Judgement. *Jude verse 6; Rev. 20:10.*

Everlasting fire is prepared for. *Mat. 25:41.*

Compared with. **A fowler**: *Ps. 91:3.* **Birds**: *Mat. 13:4.* **A sower of tares**: *Mat. 13:25, 28.* **A wolf**: *Jn. 10:12.* **A roaring lion**: *1 Pet. 5:8.*

DEVOTION TO GOD

A characteristic of the saints. *Ps. 119:38.*

Christ an example of. *Jn. 4:34, 17:4.*

Grounded upon

The mercies of God. *Rom. 12:1.*

The goodness of God. *1 Sam. 12:24.*

The call of God. *1 Thess. 2:12.*

The death of Christ. *2 Cor. 5:15.*

Our creation. *Ps. 86:9.*

Our preservation. *Is. 46:4.*

Our redemption. *1 Cor. 6:19-20.*

Should be

With our spirit. *1 Cor. 6:20. 1 Pet. 4:6.*

With our bodies. *Rom. 12:1; 1 Cor. 6:20.*

With our members. *Rom. 6:12-13.*

With our substance. *Ex. 22:29; Prov. 3:9.*

Unreserved. *Mat. 6:24; Lk. 14:33.*

Abounding. *1 Thess. 4:1.*

Persevering. *Lk. 1:74-75; Lk. 9:62.*

In life and death. *Rom. 14:8; Phil. 1:20*

Should be shown in

Loving God. *Deut. 6:5; Lk. 10:27.*

Serving God. *1 Sam. 12:24; Rom. 12:11.*

Walking worthy of God. *1 Thess. 2:12.*

Doing all for God's glory. *1 Cor. 10:31.*

Bearing the cross. *Mk. 8:34.*

Self-denial. *Mk. 8:34.*

Living for Christ. *2 Cor. 5:15.*

Giving up all for Christ. *Mat. 19:21; 28, 29.*

Lack of, condemned. *Rev. 3:16.*

Some examples. **Joshua**: *Josh. 24:15.* **Peter, Andrew, James, John**: *Mat. 4:20-22.* **Joanna**: *etc: Lk. 8:3.* **Paul**: *Phil. 1:21.* **Timothy**: *Phil. 2:19-22.* **Epaphroditus**: *Phil. 2:30.*

DILIGENCE

Christ is an example. *Mk. 1:35; Lk. 2:49.*

Required by God in

Seeking him. *1 Chron. 22:19; Heb. 11:6.*

Obeying him. *Deut. 6:17, 11:13.*

Listening to him. *Is. 55:2.*

Striving after perfection. *Phil. 3:13-14.*

Cultivating Christian grace. *2 Pet. 1:5.*

Keeping the soul. *Deut. 4:9.*

Keeping the heart. *Prov. 4:23.*

Labours of love. *Heb. 6:10-12.*

Following every good work. *1 Tim. 5:10.*

Guarding against defilement. *Heb. 12:15.*

Seeking to be found spotless. *2 Pet. 3:14.*

Making our calling and election sure. *2 Pet. 1:10.*

Self-examination. *Ps. 77:6.*

Lawful business. *Prov. 27:22; Eccl. 9:10.*

Teaching the faith. *2 Tim. 4:2; Jude verse 3.*

Instructing children. *Deut. 6:7, 11:19.*

Discharging official duties.
Deut. 19:18.
The saints should abound in.
2 Cor. 8:7.
In the service of God
  Should be persevered in.
  Gal. 6:9.
  Is not in vain. *1 Cor. 15:58.*
  Preserves us from evil.
  Ex. 15:26.
  Leads to assured hope.
  Heb. 6:11.
God rewards. *Deut. 11:14; Heb. 11:6.*
In temporal matters, leads to
  Favour. *Prov. 11:27.*
  Prosperity. *Prov. 10:4, 13:4.*
  Honour. *Prov. 12:24, 22:29.*
Illustrated. *Prov. 6:6-8.*

Some examples. **Jacob**:
Gen. 31:40. **Ruth**: *Ruth 2:17.* **Heze-
kiah**: *2 Chron. 31:21.* **Nehemiah**, etc:
Neh. 4:6. **The Psalmist**: *Ps. 119:60.*
The apostles: *Acts 5:42.* **Apollos**:
Acts 18:25. **Titus**: *2 Cor. 8:22.* **Paul**: *1
Thess. 2:9.* **Onesiphorus**: *2 Tim. 1:17.*

**DISCIPLINE OF THE CHURCH,
THE**
Ministers are authorised to
establish. *Mat. 16:19, 18:18.*
Consists of
  Maintaining sound doctrine.
  1 Tim.1:3; Titus 1:13.
  Ordering its affairs. *1 Cor. 11:34;
  Titus 1:5.*
  Rebuking offenders. *1 Tim. 5:20;
  2 Tim. 4:2.*
  Removing obstinate offend-
  ers. *1 Cor. 5:3-5, 13; 1 Tim. 1:20.*
Should be submitted to.
Heb. 13:17.
Is for edification. *2 Cor. 10:8;
2 Cor. 13:10.*
Decency and order, the objects
of. *1 Cor. 14:40.*
The exercise of, should be in
the spirit of love. *2 Cor. 2:6-8.*

DISOBEDIENCE, TO GOD
Provokes his anger. *Ps. 78:10, 40.
Is. 3:8.*
Forfeits his favour. *1 Sam. 13:14.*
Forfeits his promised blessings.
Josh. 5:6; 1 Sam. 2:30; Jer. 18:10.
Brings a curse. *Deut. 11:28;
Deut. 28:15 etc.*
A characteristic of the wicked.
Eph. 5:6; Titus 1:16; Titus 3: 3.
The wicked persevere in.
Jer. 22:21.
Guilt is illustrated. *Jer. 35:14 etc.*
Men are prone to excuse
themselves. *Gen. 3:12-13.*
Will be punished. *Is. 42:24-25;
Heb. 2:2.*
Men will acknowledge that the
punishment of, is fair. *Neh. 9:32-33;
Dan. 9:10-11, 14.*
Warnings against. *1 Sam. 12:15;
Jer. 12:17.*
The bitter results of, illustrated.
Jer. 9:13, 15.

Some examples. **Adam and Eve**:
Gen. 3:6, 11. **Pharaoh**: *Ex. 5:2.*
Nadab, etc: *Lev. 10:1.* **Moses**, etc:
Num. 20. 8, 11, 24. **Saul**: *1 Sam. 28:18.*
A prophet: *1 Kings 13:20-23.* **Israel**:
2 Kings 18:9-12. **Jonah**: *Jonah 1:2-3.*

DIVISIONS
Are forbidden in the Church.
1 Cor. 1:10.
Are condemned in the Church.
1 Cor. 1:11-13, 18.
Are unbecoming in the Church.
1 Cor. 11:24-25.
Are contrary to the
  Unity of Christ. *1 Cor. 1:13, 12:13.*
  Desire of Christ. *Jn. 17:21-23.*
  Purpose of Christ. *Jn. 10:16.*
  Spirit of the early Church.
  1 Cor. 11:16.
Are proof of a worldly spirit.
1 Cor. 3:3.
Avoid those who cause.
Rom. 16:17.
Evil of, illustrated. *Mat. 12:25.*

DIVORCE
The law of marriage is against. *Gen. 2:24; Mat. 19:6.*

Permitted
By the Law of Moses. *Deut. 24:1.*
On account of the hardness of men's hearts. *Mat. 19:8.*
Often sought by the Jews. *Mic. 2:9; Mal. 2:14.*
Sought on slight grounds. *Mat. 5:31; Mat. 19:3.*
Not allowed for those who falsely accused their wives. *Deut. 22:18-19.*

Women
Could obtain. *Prov. 2:17 with Mk. 10:12.*
Could marry again under the Law of Moses. *Deut. 24:2.*
Responsible for their vows afterwards. *Num. 30:9.*
Re-married, could not return to the first husband. *Deut. 24:3-4; Jer. 3:1.*
Abandonement bring affliction. *Is. 54:4, 6.*
Priests were not to marry divorced women. *Lev. 21:14.*
Of maidservants was regulated by law. *Ex. 21:7, 11.*
Of female captives was regulated by law. *Deut. 21:13-14.*

Was forced on those who had idolatrous wives. *Ezra 10:2-17; Neh. 13:23, 30.*
The Jews were condemned for their love of. *Mal. 2: 14-16.*
Was forbidden by Christ except in the case of adultery. *Mat.5:32, 19:9.*
The prohibition of, offended the Jews. *Mat. 19:10.*
Illustrative of God's casting away the Jewish Church. *Is. 50:1; Jer. 3:8.*

DOCTRINES OF THE GOSPEL, THE
Are from God. *Jn. 7:16; Acts 13:12.*
Are taught by Scripture. *2 Tim. 3:16.*
Are godly. *1 Tim. 6:3; Titus 1:1.*

Immorality is condemned by. *1 Tim. 1:9-11.*
Lead to fellowship with the Father and the Son. *1 Jn. 1:3; 2 Jn. verse 9.*
Lead to holiness. *Rom. 6:17-22; Titus 2:12.*
Bring no reproach on. *1 Tim. 6:1; Titus 2:5.*

Ministers should
Be nourished by. *1 Tim. 4:6.*
Attend to. *1 Tim. 4:13, 16.*
Hold, in sincerity. *1 Cor. 2:17. Titus 2:7.*
Hold, steadfastly. *2 Tim. 1:13; Titus 1:9.*
Continue in. *1 Tim. 4:16.*
Speak things that are suitable for. *Titus 2:1.*

The saints obey from the heart. *Rom. 6:17.*
The saints abide in. *Acts 2:42; 2 Jn. verse 9.*
A faithful walk adorns. *Titus 2:10.*
The obedience of saints leads to surer knowledge of. *Jn. 7:17.*

Those who oppose are
Proud. *1 Tim. 6:3-4.*
Ignorant. *1 Tim. 6:4.*
Obsessed with questions about other things. *1 Tim. 6:4.*
Not to be received. *2 Jn. verse 10.*
To be avoided. *Rom.16:17.*

Not endured by the wicked. *2 Tim. 4:3.*

DOCTRINES, FALSE
Are a hindrance to growth in grace. *Eph. 4:14.*
Are destructive to faith. *2 Tim. 2:18.*
Are hateful to God. *Rev. 2:14-15.*
Are unprofitable and useless. *Titus 3:9; Heb. 13:9.*

Should be avoided by
Ministers. *1 Tim. 1:4, 6:20.*
The saints. *Eph.4:14; Col. 2:8.*
All men. *Jer. 23:16, 29:8.*

The wicked love. *2 Tim. 4:3-4.*
The wicked are given up to believe. *2 Thess. 2:11.*

Teachers of
Not to be accepted. *2 Jn. verse 10.*
Should be avoided. *Rom. 16:17-18.*

Bring reproach on the true faith. *Acts 20:30; 2 Pet. 2:2.*
Speak perverse things. *Acts 20:30.*
Attract many. *Acts 20:30; 2 Pet. 2:2.*
Deceive many. *Mat. 24:5.*
Will abound in the latter days. *1 Tim. 4:1.*
Pervert the gospel of Christ. *Gal. 1:6-7*
Will be exposed. *2 Tim. 3:9.*

Teachers of, are described as
Cruel. *Acts 20:29.*
Deceitful. *2 Cor. 11:13.*
Covetous. *Titus 1:11; 2 Pet. 2:3.*
Ungodly. *Jude verses 4, 8.*
Proud and ignorant. *1 Tim. 6:3-4.*
Corrupt and reprobate. *2 Tim. 3:8.*
Are tested by Scripture. *Is. 8:20; 1 Jn. 4:1.*
Are cursed for their false teaching. *Gal. 1:8-9.*
The punishment of those who teach. *Mic. 3:6-7; 2 Pet. 2:1, 3.*

DRUNKENNESS
Forbidden. *Eph. 5:18.*
A caution against. *Lk. 21:34.*
Is a work of the flesh. *Gal. 5:21.*
Is debasing. *Is. 28:8.*
Is inflaming. *Is. 5:11.*
Overburdens the heart. *Lk. 21:34.*
Takes away the heart. *Hos. 4:11.*

Leads to
Poverty. *Prov. 21:17, 23:21.*
Strife. *Prov. 23:29-30.*
Woe and sorrow. *Prov. 23:29-30.*
Error. *Is. 28:7.*
Contempt of God's works. *Is. 5:12.*
Scorning. *Hos. 7:5.*
Rioting and waywardness. *Rom. 13:13.*
The wicked are addicted to. *Dan. 5:1-4.*
False teachers are often addicted to. *Is. 56:12.*
The folly of yielding to. *Prov. 20:1.*
Avoid drunkards. *Prov. 23:20; 1 Cor. 5:11.*

Denunciations against
Those given to. *Is. 5:11-12, 28:1-3.*
Those who encourage. *Hab. 2:15.*
Their exclusion from heaven. *1 Cor. 6:10; Gal. 5:21.*
Their punishment. *Deut. 21:20-21; Joel 1:5-6; Amos 6:7; Mat. 24:49-51.*

Some examples. **Noah**: *Gen. 9:21.* **Nabal**: *1 Sam. 25:36.* **Uriah**: *2 Sam. 11:13.* **Elah**: *1 Kings 16:9-10.* **Benhadad**: *1 Kings 20:16.* **Belshazzar**: *Dan. 5:4.* **The Corinthians**: *1 Cor. 11:21-22.*

E

EARLY RISING
Christ set an example of. *Mk. 1:35; Lk. 21:38; Jn. 8:2.*

Required for
Redeeming the time. *Eph. 5:16.*
Devotion. *Ps. 5:3, 59:16, 63:1, 88:13; Is. 26:9.*
Communion with Christ. *Song 7:12.*
Executing God's commands. *Gen. 22:3.*
Discharge of daily duties. *Prov. 31:15.*
Neglect of, leads to poverty. *Prov. 6:9-11.*

Practised by the wicked, for
Deceit. *Prov. 27:14.*
Drunkenness. *Is. 5:11.*
Corrupting their deeds. *Zeph. 3:7.*
Executing evil plans. *Mic. 2:1.*
Illustrates spiritual diligence. *Rom. 13:11-12.*

Some examples. **Abraham**: *Gen. 19:27.* **Isaac**, etc: *Gen. 26:31.* **Jacob**: *Gen. 28:18.* **Joshua**, etc: *Josh. 3:1.* **Gideon**: *Judg. 6:38.* **Samuel**: *1 Sam. 15:12.* **David**: *1 Sam. 17:20.* **The servant of Elisha**: *2 Kings 6:15.*

Mary, *etc: Mk. 16:2.* **The apostles**: *Acts 5:21.*

EDIFICATION
Is described. *Eph. 4:12-16.*
Is the object of
The ministerial office. *Eph. 4:11-12.*
Ministerial gifts. *1 Cor. 14:3-5, 12.*
Ministerial authority. *2 Cor. 10:8, 13:10.*
The Church's union in Christ. *Eph. 4:16.*
The gospel, the instrument of. *Acts 20:32.*
Love leads to. *1 Cor. 8:1.*
Exhortation to. *Jude verses 20-21.*
Mutual, commanded. *Rom. 14:19; 1 Thess. 5:11.*
All to be done for. *2 Cor. 12:19; Eph. 4:29.*
Use self-denial to promote, in others. *1 Cor. 10:23, 33.*
The peace of the Church depends on. *Acts 9:31.*
Foolish questions are opposed to. *1 Tim. 1:4.*

ELECTION (SEE ALSO PREDESTINATION)
Of Christ, as Messiah. *Is. 42:1; 1 Pet. 2:6.*
Of good angels. *1 Tim. 5:21.*
Of Israel. *Deut. 7:6; Is. 45:4.*
Of ministers. *Lk. 6:13; Acts 9:15.*
Of churches. *1 Pet. 5:13.*
Of the saints, is
Of God. *1 Thess. 1:4; Titus 1:1.*
By Christ. *Jn. 13:18, 15:16.*
In Christ. *Eph. 1:4.*
Personal. *Mat. 20:16 with Jn. 6:44; Acts 22:14; 2 Jn. verse 13.*
According to the purpose of God. *Rom. 9:11; Eph. 1:11.*
According to the foreknowledge of God. *Rom. 8:29; 1 Pet. 1:2.*
Eternal. *Eph. 1:4.*
Sovereign. *Rom. 9:15-16; 1 Cor. 1:27; Eph. 1:11.*
Irrespective of merit. *Rom. 9:11.*
Of grace. *Rom. 11:5.*
Recorded in heaven. *Lk. 10:20.*
For the glory of God. *Eph. 1:6.*
Through faith. *2 Thess. 2:13.*
Through sanctification of the Spirit. *1 Pet. 1:2; 2 Thess. 2:13.*
To adoption. *Eph. 1:5.*
To salvation. *2 Thess. 2:13.*
To conformity with Christ. *Rom. 8:29.*
To good works. *Eph. 2:10.*
To spiritual warfare. *2 Tim. 2:4.*
To eternal glory. *Rom. 9:23.*
Ensures for the saints
Effectual calling. *Rom. 8:30.*
Divine teaching. *Jn. 17:6.*
Belief in Christ. *Acts 13:48.*
Acceptance with God. *Rom. 11:7.*
Protection. *Mk. 13:20.*
Vindication of their wrongs. *Lk. 18:7.*
Working of all things for good. *Rom. 8:28.*
Blessedness. *Ps. 33:12, 65:4.*
The inheritance. *Is. 65:9; 1 Pet. 1:4-5.*
Should lead to the cultivation of graces. *Col. 3:12.*
Should be evidenced by diligence. *2 Pet. 1:10.*
The saints may have assurance of. *1 Thess. 1:4.*

Some examples. **Isaac**: *Gen. 21:12.* **Abra(ha)m**: *Neh. 9:7.* **Zerubbabel**: *Hag. 2:23.* **The apostles**: *Jn. 13:18, 15:19.* **Jacob**: *Rom. 9:12-13.* **Rufus**: *Rom. 16:13.* **Paul**: *Gal. 1:15.*

EMBLEMS OF THE HOLY SPIRIT, THE
Water. *Jn. 3:5, 7:38-39.*
Cleansing. *Ezek. 16:9, 36:25; Eph. 5:26; Heb. 10:22.*
Fertilising. *Ps. 1:3; Is. 27:3, 6, 44:3-4, 58:11.*
Refreshing. *Ps. 46:4; Is. 41:17-18.*
Abundant. *Jn. 7:37-38.*
Freely given. *Is. 55:1; Jn. 4:14; Rev. 22:17.*
Fire. *Mat. 3:11.*
Purifying. *Is. 4:4; Mal. 3:2-3.*
Illuminating. *Ex. 13:21; Ps. 78:14.*
Searching. *Zeph. 1:12 with 1 Cor. 2:10.*
Wind. *Song 4:16.*

Independent. *Jn. 3:8; 1 Cor. 12:11.*
Powerful. *1 Kings 19:11 with Acts 2:2.*
Sensible in its effects. *Jn. 3:8.*
Reviving. *Ezek. 37:9-10, 14.*
Oil. *Ps. 45:7.*
  Healing. *Is. 1:6; Lk. 10:34; Rev. 3:18.*
  Comforting. *Is. 61:3; Heb. 1:9.*
  Illuminating. *Zech. 4:2-3, 11-14;*
  Mat. 25:3-4; 1 Jn. 2:20, 27.
  Consecrating. *Ex. 29:7, 30:30; Is. 61:1.*
Rain and dew. *Ps. 72:6.*
  Fertilising. *Ezek. 34:26-27;Hos. 6:3,*
  10:12, 14:5.
  Refreshing. *Ps. 68:9; Is. 18:4.*
  Abundant. *Ps. 133:3.*
  Imperceptible. *2 Sam. 17:12 with*
  Mk. 4:26-28.
A dove. *Mat. 3:16.*
  Gentle. *Mat. 10:16 with Gal. 5:22.*
A voice. *Is. 6:8.*
  Speaking. *Mat. 10:20.*
  Guiding. *Is. 30:21 with Jn. 16:13.*
  Warning. *Heb. 3:7-11.*
A seal. *Rev. 7:2.*
  Impressing. *Job 38:14 with 2 Cor. 3:18.*
  Securing. *Eph. 1:13-14, 4:30.*
  Authenticating. *Jn. 6:27; 2 Cor. 1:22.*
Forked tongues. *Acts 2:3, 6:11.*

ENEMIES

Christ prayed for hIs. *Lk. 23:34.*
The lives of, to be spared.
1 Sam. 24:10; 2 Sam. 16:10-11.
The goods of, to be taken care of.
Ex. 23:4-5.
Should be
  Loved. *Mat. 5:44.*
  Prayed for. *Mat. 5:44; Acts 7:60.*
  Assisted. *Prov. 25:21 with Rom. 12:20.*
  Overcome by kindness.
  1 Sam. 26:21; Prov. 25:22 with Rom. 12:20.
Do not rejoice at the misfortunes
of. *Job 31:29.*
Do not rejoice at the failings of.
Prov. 24:17.
Do not desire the death of.
1 Kings 3:11.
Do not curse them. *Job 31:30.*
Are affectionately concerned for.

Ps. 35:13.
Their friendship is deceitful.
2 Sam. 20:9-10; Prov. 26:26, 27:6. Mat.26:48-49.
God defends us against. *Ps. 59:9, 61:3.*
God delivered us from. *1 Sam. 12:11;*
Ezra 8:31; Ps. 18:48.
Made to be at peace with the
saints. *Prov. 16:7.*
Pray for deliverance from.
1 Sam. 12:10; Ps. 17:9, 59:1, 64:1.
Of the saints, God will destroy.
Ps. 60:12.
Praise God for deliverance from.
Ps. 136:24.

ENVY

Is forbidden. *Prov. 3:31; Rom. 13:13.*
Is produced by foolish disputa-
tions. *1 Tim. 6:4.*
Becomes excited by the good
deeds of others. *Eccl. 4:4.*
Is a work of the flesh. *Gal. 5:21; Jas. 4:5.*
Is harmful to the envious. *Job 5:2;*
Prov. 14:30.
None can stand before. *Prov. 27:4.*
A proof of a worldly mind.
1 Cor. 3:1, 3.
Inconsistent with the gospel. *Jas. 3:14.*
Hinders growth in grace. *1 Pet. 2:1-2.*
The wicked
  Are full of. *Rom. 1:29.*
  Live in. *Tit. 3:3.*
Leads to every evil work. *Jas. 3:16.*
Prosperity should not excite.
Ps. 37:1, 35, 73:3, 17-20.
The punishment of. *Ps. 106:16-17;*
Is. 26:11.

Some examples. **Cain:** *Gen. 4:5.*
The Philistines: *Gen. 26:14.* **Laban's**
sons: *Gen 31:1.* **Joseph's brothers:**
Gen. 37:11. **Joshua:** *Num. 11:28-29.*
Aaron, *etc: Num. 12:2.* **Korah,** *etc: Num.*
16:3 with Ps. 106:16. **Saul:** *1 Sam. 18:8.*
Sanballat, *etc: Neh. 2:10.* **Haman:**
Esth. 5:13. **The Edomites:** *Ezek. 35:11.*
Princes of Babylon: *Dan. 6:3-4.*
The Chief Priests: *Mk. 15:10.*
The Jews: *Acts 13:45, 17:5.*

EXAMPLE OF CHRIST, THE
Is perfect. *Heb. 7:26.*
Conformity to, required in
Holiness. *1 Pet. 1:15-16 with Rom. 1:6.*
Righteousness. *1 Jn. 2:6.*
Purity. *1 Jn. 3:3.*
Love. *Jn. 13:34; Eph. 5:2; 1 Jn. 3:16.*
Humility. *Lk. 22:27; Phil. 2:5, 7.*
Meekness. *Mat.11:29.*
Lowliness of heart. *Mat. 11:29.*
Obedience. *Jn. 15:10.*
Self-denial. *Mat.16:24. Rom. 15:3.*
Ministering to others. *Mat. 20:28; Jn. 13:14-15.*
Benevolence. *Acts 20:35; 2 Cor. 8:7, 9.*
Forgiving injuries. *Col. 3:13.*
Overcoming sin. *1 Pet. 4:1.*
Overcoming the world. *Jn. 16:33 with 1 Jn. 5:4.*
Being not of the world. *Jn. 17:16.*
Being without guile. *1 Pet. 2:21-22.*
Suffering wrongfully. *1 Pet. 2:21-23.*
Suffering for righteousness. *Heb. 12:3-4.*
The saints are predestined to follow. *Rom. 8:29.*
Conformity to, is progressive. *2 Cor. 3:18.*

EXCELLENCE AND GLORY OF CHRIST, THE
As God. *Jn. 1:1-5; Phil. 2:6, 9, 10.*
As the Son of God. *Mat. 3:17; Heb. 1:6, 8.*
As one with the Father. *Jn. 10:30, 38.*
As the First-born. *Col. 1:15, 18.*
As the First-begotten. *Heb. 1:6.*
As Lord of lords, etc. *Rev. 17:14.*
As the image of God. *Col. 1:15; Heb. 1:3.*
As Creator. *Jn. 1:3; Col. 1:16; Heb. 1:2.*
As the Blessed of God. *Ps. 45:2.*
As Mediator. *1 Tim. 2:5; Heb. 8:6.*
As Prophet. *Deut. 18:15-16 with Acts 3:22.*
As Priest. *Ps. 110:4; Heb. 4:15.*
As King. *Is. 6:1-5 with Jn. 12:41.*
As Judge. *Mat. 16:27, 25:31-33.*
As Shepherd. *Is. 40:10-11; Jn. 10:11, 14.*
As Head of the Church. *Eph. 1:22.*
As the true Light. *Lk. 1:78-79; Jn. 1:4, 9.*
As the foundation of the Church. *Is. 28:16.*
As the way. *Jn. 14:6; Heb. 10:19-20.*
As the truth. *Jn. 14:6; 1 Jn. 5:20; Rev. 3:7.*
As the life. *Jn. 14:6, 11:25; Col. 3:4; 1 Jn. 5:11.*
As incarnate. *Jn. 1:14.*
By his words. *Lk. 4:22; Jn. 7:46.*
By his works. *Mat. 13:54; Jn. 2:11.*
In his sinless perfection. *Heb. 7:26-28.*
In the fullness of his grace and truth. *Ps. 45:2 with Jn. 1:14.*
In his transfiguration. *Mat. 17:2 with 2 Pet. 1:16-18.*
In his exaltation. *Acts 7:55-56; Eph. 1:21.*
In the calling of the Gentiles. *Ps. 72:17; Jn. 12:21, 23.*
In the restoration of the Jews. *Ps. 102:16.*
In his triumph. *Is. 63:1-3 with Rev. 19:11, 16.*
Followed his sufferings. *1 Pet. 1:10-11*
Followed his resurrection. *1 Pet. 1:21.*
Is unchangeable. *Heb. 1:10-12.*
Is incomparable. *Song 5:10; Phil. 2:9.*
Imparted to the saints. *Jn. 17:22; 2 Cor. 3:18.*
Celebrated by the redeemed. *Rev. 5:8-14; Rev. 7:9-12.*
Revealed in the gospel. *Is. 40:5.*
The saints will rejoice at the revelation of. *1 Pet. 4:13.*
The saints will behold, in heaven. *Jn. 17:24.*

EXCELLENCE AND GLORY OF THE CHURCH, THE
Derived from God. *Is. 28:5.*
Derived from Christ. *Is. 60:1; Lk. 2:39.*
Result from the favour of God. *Is. 43:4.*
God delights in. *Ps. 45:11; Is. 62:3-5.*
The saints delight in. *Is. 66:11.*
Consist in its
Being the seat of God's worship. *Ps. 96:6.*
Being the temple of God. *1 Cor. 3:16-17; Eph. 2:21-22.*
Being the body of Christ. *Eph. 1:22-23.*
Being the bride of Christ.

Ps. 45:13-14; Rev. 19:7-8; Rev. 21:2.
Being established. Ps. 48:8; Is. 33:20.
Having an eminent position.
Ps. 48:2; Is. 2:2.
Graces of character. Song 2:14.
Perfection of beauty. Ps. 50:2.
Members being righteous. Is. 60:21;
Rev. 19- 8.

Strength and defence. Ps. 48:12-13.
Sanctification. Eph. 5:26-27.
**Augmented by the increase of its
members.** Is. 49:18, 60:4-14.
Are abundant. Is. 66:11.
Sin obscures. Lam. 2:14-15.

F

FAITH
Is the substance of things hoped
for. Heb. 11:1.
Is the evidence of things not
seen. Heb. 11:1.
Commanded. Mk. 11:22; 1 Jn. 3:23.
The objects of, are
God. Mk. 11:22; Jn. 14:1.
Christ. Jn. 6:29, 14:1. Acts 20:21.
The writings of Moses. Jn. 5:46;
Acts 24:14.
The writings of the prophets.
2 Chron. 20:20; Acts 26:27.
The gospel. Mk. 1:15.
The promise of God. Rom. 4:21;
Heb. 11:13.
In Christ, is
The gift of God. Rom. 12:3; Eph. 2:8;
Eph. 6:23; Phil. 1:29.
The work of God. Acts 11:21; 1 Cor. 2:5.
Precious. 2 Pet. 1:1.
Most holy. Jude verse 20.
Fruitful. 1 Thess. 1:3.
Accompanied by repentance.
Mk. 1:15; Lk. 24:47.
Followed by conversion.
Acts 11:21.
Christ is the Author and Finisher
of. Heb. 12:2.
Is a gift of the Holy Spirit. 1 Cor. 12:9.
17; 1 Cor. 3:5.
Through it, comes
Remission of sins. Acts 10:43;
Rom. 3:25.
Justification. Acts 13:39; Rom. 3:21-22,
28, 30; Rom. 5:1; Gal. 2:16.
Salvation. Mk. 16:16; Acts 16:31.
Sanctification. Acts 15:9; Acts

26:18.
Spiritual light. Jn. 12:36, 46.
Spiritual life. Jn. 20:31; Gal. 2:20.
Eternal life. Jn. 3:15-16, 6:40, 47.
Rest in heaven. Heb. 4:3.
Edification. 1 Tim. 1:4; Jude verse 20.
Preservation. 1 Pet. 1:5.
Adoption. Jn. 1:12; Gal. 3:26.
Access to God. Rom. 5:2; Eph. 3:12.
Inheritance of the promises.
Gal. 3:22; Heb. 6:12.
The gift of the Holy Spirit.
Acts 11:15-17; Gal. 3:14; Eph. 1:13.
It is impossible to please God
without. Heb. 11:6.
Justification is by, of grace.
Rom. 4:16.
Essential for a profitable
reception of the gospel. Heb. 4:2.
Necessary in Christian warfare.
1 Tim. 1:18-19; 1 Tim. 6:12.
The gospel is effective in those
who have. 1 Thess. 2:13.
Excludes self-justification.
Rom. 10:3-4.
Excludes boasting. Rom. 3:27.
Works by love. Gal. 5:6; 1 Tim. 1:5;
Philem. Verse 5.
Produces
Hope. Rom. 5:2.
Joy. Acts 16:34; 1 Pet. 1:8.
Peace. Rom. 15:13.
Confidence. Is. 28:16 with 1 Pet. 2:6.
Boldness in preaching. Ps 116:10
with 2 Cor. 4:13.
Christ is precious to those who
have. 1 Pet. 2:7.
Christ dwells in the heart by. Eph. 3:17.

Necessary in prayer. *Mat. 21:22; Jas. 1:6.*
Those who are not Christ's do not possess. *Jn. 10:26-27.*
An evidence of the new birth.
1 Jn. 5:1.

By it, the saints
  Live. *Gal. 2:20.*
  Stand. *Rom. 11:20; 2 Cor. 1:24.*
  Walk. *Rom. 4:12; 2 Cor. 5:7.*
  Obtain a good report. *Heb. 11:2.*
  Overcome the world. *1 Jn. 5:4-5.*
  Resist the devil. *1 Pet. 5:9.*
  Overcome the devil. *Eph. 6:16.*
  Are supported. *Ps. 27:13; 1 Tim. 4:10.*
The saints die in. *Heb. 11:13.*

The saints should
  Be full of. *Acts 6:5, 11:24.*
  Be sincere in. *1 Tim. 1:5; 2 Tim. 1:5.*
  Abound in. *2 Cor. 8:7.*
  Continue in. *Acts 14:22; Col. 1:23.*
  Be strong in. *Rom. 4:20.*
  Stand fast in. *1 Cor. 16:13.*
  Be grounded and settled in.
  Col. 1:23.
  Hold, with a good conscience.
  1 Tim. 1:19.
  Pray for the increase of. *Lk. 17:5.*
  Have full assurance of. *2 Tim. 1:12; Heb. 10:22.*
True, evidenced by its fruits.
Jas. 2:21-25.
Without fruits, is dead. *Jas. 2:17, 20, 26.*
Examine whether they are in the.
2 Cor. 13:5.
All difficulties are overcome by.
Mat. 17:20, 21:21; Mk. 9:23.
All things should be done in.
Rom. 14:22.
Whatsoever is not of, is sin.
Rom. 14:23.
Often tested by affliction. *1 Pet. 1:6-7.*
Trial of, works patience. *Jas. 1:3.*
The wicked often profess. *Acts 8:13, 21.*
The wicked are destitute of.
Jn. 10:25, 12:37; Acts 19:9; 2 Thess. 3:2.

Protection of, illustrated. **A shield**:
Eph. 6:16. **A breastplate**: *1 Thess. 5:8.*

Some examples. **Abel**: *Gen. 4:2-8; Heb. 11:4.* **Enoch**: *Gen. 5:21-24; Heb. 11:5.* **Noah**: *Gen. 6:13-22; Heb. 11:7.* **Abraham**: *Gen. 12:1-4, 15:1-6; Heb. 11:8, 17.* **Isaac**: *Gen. 27:27-29; Heb. 11:20.* **Jacob**: *Gen. chapters 48-49; Heb. 11:21.* **Joseph**: *Gen. 50:22-26; Heb. 11:22.* **Moses**: *Ex. 2:10-14; Heb. 11:24.* **Rahab**: *Josh. 2:8-21; Heb. 11:31.* **Caleb**: *Num. 13:30.* **Gideon**, etc: *Heb. 11:32-33, 39.* **Job**: *Job 19:25.* **Shadrach**, etc: *Dan. 3:17.* **Daniel**: *Dan. 6:10, 23.* **Peter**: *Mat. 16:16.* **A woman who was a sinner**: *Lk. 7:50.* **Nathanael**: *Jn. 1:49.* **Some Samaritans**: *Jn. 4:39.* **Martha**: *Jn. 11:27.* **The disciples**: *Jn. 16:30.* **Thomas**: *Jn. 20:28.* **Stephen**: *Acts 6:5.* **Some priests**: *Acts 6:7.* **An Ethiopian**: *Acts 8:37.* **Barnabas**: *Acts 11:24.* **Sergius Paulus**: *Acts 13:12.* **The Philippian jailor**: *Acts 16:31, 34.* **The Romans**: *Rom. 1:8.* **The Colossians**: *Col. 1:4.* **The Thessalonians**: *1 Thess. 1:3.* **Lois**: *2 Tim. 1:5.* **Paul**: *2 Tim. 4:7.*

FAITHFULNESS
Is a characteristic of the saints.
Eph. 1:1; Col. 1:2; 1 Tim. 6:2; Rev. 17:14.

Shown in
  The service of God. *Mat. 21:45.*
  Declaring the word of God.
  Jer. 23:28; Cor. 2:17; 2 Cor. 4:2.
  The care of dedicated things.
  2 Chron. 31:12.
  Helping the brothers. *3 Jn. verse 5.*
  Administering justice. *Deut. 1:16.*
  Bearing witness. *Prov. 14:5.*
  Reproving others. *Prov. 27:6; Ps. 141:5.*
  Situations of trust. *2 Kings 12:15; Neh. 13:13; Acts 6:1-3.*
  Doing work. *2 Chron. 34:12.*
  Keeping secrets. *Prov. 11:13.*
  Conveying messages. *Prov. 13:17, 25:13.*
  All things. *1 Tim. 3:11.*
  The smallest matters. *Lk. 16:10-12.*
Should be to death. *Rev. 2:10.*
The mercy of God towards us,

designed to lead to. *1 Cor. 7:25.*
Especially required in
Ministers. *1 Cor. 4:2; 2 Tim. 2:2.*
The wives of ministers. *1 Tim. 3:11.*
The children of ministers. *Titus 1:6.*
Difficulty of finding. *Prov. 20:6.*
The wicked are devoid of. *Ps. 5:9.*
Associate with those who show.
Ps. 101:6.
The blessedness of. *1 Sam. 26:23;*
Prov. 28:20.
The blessedness of, illustrated.
Mat. 24:45-46, 25:21, 23.

Some examples. **Joseph:** *Gen. 39:22-23.*
Moses: *Num. 12:7 with Heb. 3:2, 5.*
David: *1 Sam. 22:14.* **Hananiah:**
Neh. 7:2. **Abraham:** *Neh. 9:8; Gal. 3:9.*
Daniel: *Dan. 6:4.* **Paul:** *Acts 20:20, 27.*
Timothy: *1 Cor. 4:17.* **Tychicus:**
Eph. 6:21. **Epaphras:** *Col. 1:7.*
Onesimus: *Col 4:9.* **Silvanus** (Silas):
1 Pet. 5:12. **Antipas:** *Rev. 2:13.*

FAITHFULNESS OF GOD, THE
Is part of his character. *Is. 49:7;*
1 Cor. 1:9; 1 Thess. 5:24.
Declared to be
Great. *Lam. 3:23.*
Established. *Ps. 89:2.*
Incomparable. *Ps. 89:8.*
Unfailing. *Ps. 89:33; 2 Tim. 2:13.*
Infinite. *Ps. 36:5.*
Everlasting. *Ps. 119:90, 146:6.*
Should be pleaded in prayer.
Ps. 143:1.
Should be proclaimed. *Ps. 40:10;*
Ps. 89:1.
Is manifested
In his counsels. *Is. 25:1.*
In the affliction of his saints.
Ps. 119:75.
In fulfilling his promises.
1 Kings 8:20; Ps. 132:11; Mic. 7:20;
Heb. 10:23.
In keeping his covenant.
Deut. 7:9; Ps. 111:5.
In his testimonies. *Ps. 119:138.*
In executing his judgements.

Jer. 23:20, 51:29.
In forgiving sins. *1 Jn. 1:9.*
To his saints. *Ps. 89:24; 2 Thess. 3:3.*
The saints are encouraged to
depend on. *1 Pet. 4:19.*
Should be magnified. *Ps. 89:5, 92:2.*

FALL OF MAN, THE
By the disobedience of Adam.
Gen. 3:6, 11-12 with Rom. 5:12, 15, 19.
Through temptation of the devil.
Gen. 3:1-5; 2 Cor. 11:3; 1 Tim. 2:14.
Man in consequence of,
Is made in the image of Adam.
Gen. 5:3 with 1 Cor. 15:48-49.
Is born in sin. *Job 25:4; Ps. 51:5;*
Is. 48:8; Jn. 3:6.
Is a child of the devil. *Mat. 13:38;*
Jn. 8:44; 1 Jn. 3:8, 10.
Is a child of wrath. *Eph. 2:3.*
Is evil in heart. *Gen. 6:5; Gen. 8:21;*
Jer. 16:12; Mat. 15:19.
Is blinded in his heart. *Eph. 4:18.*
Is corrupt and perverse in his
ways. *Gen. 6:12; Ps. 10:5; Rom. 3:12-16.*
Is depraved in his mind. *Rom.*
8:5-7; Eph. 4:17; Col. 1:21; Titus 1:15.
Is without understanding.
Ps. 14:2-3 with Rom. 3:11; Rom. 1:31.
Does not receive the things of
God. *1 Cor. 2:14.*
Comes short of God's glory.
Rom. 3:23.
Is defiled in conscience.
Titus 1:15; Heb. 10:22.
Is stubborn. *Job 11:12.*
Is estranged from God. *Gen. 3:8;*
Ps. 58:3; Eph. 4:18; Col. 1:21.
Is in bondage to sin. *Rom. 6:19, 7:5,*
23. Gal. 5:17; Titus 3:3.
Is in bondage to the devil.
2 Tim. 2:26; Heb. 2:14-15.
Is constant in doing evil. *Ps. 10:5;*
2 Pet. 2:14.
Is conscious of guilt. *Gen. 3:7-8, 10.*
Is unrighteous. *Eccl. 7:20; Rom. 3:10.*
Is abominable. *Job 15:16; Ps. 14:3.*
Turns to his own way. *Is. 53:6.*
Loves darkness. *Jn. 3:19.*

Is corrupt, etc. in speech.
Rom. 3:13-14.
Is destructive. *Rom. 3:15-16.*
Is devoid of the fear of God.
Rom. 3:18.
Is totally depraved. *Gen. 6:5; Rom. 7:18.*
Is dead in sin. *Eph. 2:1; Col. 2:13.*
All men partake of the effects of.
Kings 8:46; Gal. 3:22; 1 Jn. 1:8; 1 Jn. 5:19.
Punishment consequent upon
Banishment from paradise.
Gen. 3:24.
Condemnation to labour and
sorrow. *Gen. 3:16, 19; Job 5:6-7.*
Temporal death. *Gen. 3:19;*
Rom. 5:12; 1 Cor. 15:22.
Eternal death. *Job 21:30; Rom. 5:18,*
21, 6:23.
Cannot be remedied by man.
Prov. 20:9; Jer. 2:22, 13:23.
Remedy for, is provided by God.
Gen. 3:15.

FAMILIES
Of the saints are blessed. *Ps. 128:3, 6.*
Should
Be taught the Scriptures.
Deut. 4:9-10.
Worship God together. *1 Cor. 16, 19.*
Be duly regulated. *Prov. 31:27;*
1 Tim. 3:4, 5, 12.
Live in unity. *Gen. 45:24; Ps. 133:1.*
Live in mutual forbearance.
Gen. 50:17-21; Mat. 18:21-22.
Rejoice together before God.
Deut. 14:26.
Deceivers and liars should be
removed from. *Ps. 101:7.*
Are warned against departing
from God. *Deut. 29:18.*
The punishment of the irreli-
gious. *Jer. 10:25.*

Some examples of good families.
Abraham: *Gen. 18:19.* **Jacob**: *Gen. 35:2.*
Joshua: *Josh. 24:15.* **David**: *2 Sam. 6:20.*
Job: *Job 1:5.* **Lazarus of Bethany**:
Jn. 11:1-5. **Cornelius**: *Acts 10:2, 33.*
Lydia: *Acts 16:15.* **Philippian jailor**:

Acts 16:31-34. **Crispus**: *Acts 18:8.*
Lois: *2 Tim. 1:5.*

FASTING
Its true spirit is explained.
Is. 58:6-7.
Not to be made a subject of
display. *Mat. 6:16-18.*
Should be for God. *Zech. 7:5;*
Mat. 6:18.
For the chastening of the soul.
Ps. 69:10.
For the humbling of the soul.
Ps. 35:13.
Was observed on occasions of
The judgements of God.
Joel 1:14, 2:12
Public calamities. *2 Sam. 1:12.*
Afflictions in the Church. *Lk. 5:33-35.*
Afflictions in others. *Ps. 35:13;*
Dan. 6:18.
Private afflictions. *2 Sam. 12:16.*
Approaching danger. *Esther 4:16.*
The ordination of ministers.
Acts 13:3, 14:23.
Accompanied by
Prayer. *Ezra 8. 23; Dan. 9:3.*
Confession of sin. *1 Sam. 7:6;*
Neh. 9:1-2.
Mourning. *Joel 2:12.*
Humiliation. *Deut. 9:18; Neh. 9. 1.*
Promises connected with. *Is. 58:8-12;*
Mat. 6:18.
Of hypocrites
Described. *Is. 58:4-5.*
Ostentatious. *Mat. 6:16.*
Boasted of, before God. *Lk. 18:12.*
Rejected. *Is. 58:3; Jer. 14:12.*

Special examples. **Our Lord
Jesus**: *Mat. 4:2.* **Moses**: *Ex. 34:28;*
Deut. 9:9, 18. **Elijah**: *1 Kings 19:8.*

National examples. **Israel**:
Judg. 20:26; Ezra 8:21; Esth. 4:3, 16; Jer. 36:9.
Men of Jabesh-Gilead: *1 Sam. 31:13.*
The Ninevites: *Jonah 3:5-8.*

Examples of some of the saints.
David: *2 Sam. 12:16; Ps. 109:24.*

Nehemiah: *Neh. 1:4.* **Esther**: *Esth. 4:16.*
Daniel: *Dan. 9:3.* **Some disciples of John**: *Mat. 9:14.* **Anna**: *Lk. 2:37.*
Cornelius: *Acts 10:30.* **Some early Christians**: *Acts 13:2.* **Apostles**:
2 Cor. 6:5. **Paul**: *Acts 27:21; 2 Cor. 11:27.*

Some examples of the wicked.
The elders of Jezreel: *1 Kings 21:12.*
Ahab: *1 Kings 21:27.* **The Pharisees**:
Mk. 2:18; Lk. 18:12.

FATHERLESS, THE
Find mercy in God. *Hos. 14:3*
God will
Be a father to. *Ps. 68:5.*
Be a helper of. *Ps. 10:14.*
Hear the cry of. *Ex. 22:23.*
Execute the judgement of.
Deut. 10:18; Ps. 10:18.
Punish those who oppress.
Ex. 22:24; Is. 10:1-3; Mal 3:5.
Punish those who refuse judgement. *Jer. 5:28-29.*
Visit, in affliction. *Jas. 1:27.*
Let them share in our blessings.
Deut. 14:29.
Defend them. *Ps. 82:3; Is. 1:17.*
Do them no wrong in judgement.
Deut. 24:17.
Do not defraud them. *Prov. 23:10.*
Do not afflict them. *Ex. 22:22.*
Do not oppress them. *Zech. 7:10.*
Do no violence to them. *Jer. 22:3.*
The blessedness of taking care of them. *Deut. 14:29; Job 29:12-13; Jer. 7:6-7.*
The wicked
Rob. *Is. 10:2.*
Overwhelm. *Job 6:27.*
Vex. *Ezra 22:7.*
Oppress. *Job 24:3.*
Murder. *Ps. 94:6.*
Do not judge on their behalf.
Is. 1:23; Jer. 5:28.
A curse on those who oppress.
Deut. 27:19.
Promises concerning. *Jer. 49:11.*
A type of Zion in affliction. *Lam. 5:3.*

Some examples. **Lot**: *Gen. 11:27-28.*
Daughters of Zelophehad:
Num. 27:1-5. **Jotham**: *Judg. 9:16-21.*
Mephibosheth: *2 Sam. 9:3.* **Joash**:
2 Kings 11:1-12. **Esther**: *Esth. 2:7.*

FAVOUR OF GOD, THE
Christ the special object of. *Lk. 2:52.*
Is the source of
Mercy. *Is. 60:10.*
Spiritual life. *Ps. 30:5.*
Spiritual wisdom leads to.
Prov. 8:35.
Mercy and truth lead to. *Prov. 3:3-4.*
The saints
Obtain. *Prov. 12:2.*
Are encompassed by. *Ps. 5:12.*
Are strengthened by. *Ps. 30:7.*
Are victorious through. *Ps. 44:3.*
Are preserved through. *Job 10:12.*
Are exalted in. *Ps. 89:17.*
Are sometimes tempted to doubt. *Ps. 77:7.*
Domestic blessings can be traced to. *Prov. 18:22.*
Disappointed enemies are an assured evidence for the. *Ps. 41:11.*
Given, in answer to prayer.
Job 33:26.
Pray for. *Ps. 106:4, 119:58.*
Plead in prayer. *Ex. 33:13. Num. 11:15.*
Favours should be acknowledged.
Ps. 85:1.
The wicked
Are uninfluenced by. *Is. 26:10.*
Do not obtain. *Is. 27:11; Jer. 16:13.*

Some examples. **Naphtali**:
Deut. 33:23. **Samuel**: *1 Sam. 2:26.* **Job**:
Job 10:12. **The virgin Mary**: *Lk. 1:28, 30.*
David: *Acts 7:46.*

FEAR, GODLY
God is the object of. *Is. 8:13.*
God is the author of. *Jer. 32:39-40.*
Searching the Scriptures gives us an understanding of. *Prov. 2:3-5.*
Is described as
Hatred of evil. *Prov. 8:13.*

Wisdom. *Job 28:28; Ps. 111:10.*
A treasure to the saints.
Prov. 15:16; Is. 33:6.
A fountain of life. *Prov. 14:27.*
Sanctifying. *Ps. 19:9.*
Filial and reverent. *Heb. 12:9, 28.*
Commanded. *Deut. 13:4; Ps. 22:23;*
Eccl. 12:13; 1 Pet. 2:17.

Motives for:
The holiness of God. *Rev. 15:4.*
The greatness of God. *Deut. 10:12, 17.*
The goodness of God. *1 Sam. 12, 24.*
The forgiveness of God. *Ps. 130:4.*
The wonderful works of God.
Josh. 4:23-24.
The judgements of God. *Rev. 14:7.*
A characteristic of the saints. *Mk. 3:16.*
Should accompany the joy of the
saints. *Ps. 2:11.*

Necessary for
The worship of God. *Ps. 5:7, 89:7.*
The service of God. *Ps. 2:11;*
Heb. 12:29.
The avoiding of sin. *Ex. 20:20.*
Righteous government.
2 Sam. 23:3.
The impartial administration of
justice. *2 Chron. 19:6-9.*
Perfecting holiness. *2 Cor. 7:1.*

Those who have,
Give pleasure to God. *Ps. 147:11.*
Are pitied by God. *Ps. 103:13.*
Are accepted by God. *Acts 10:35.*
Receive mercy from God.
Ps. 103:11, 17; Lk. 1:50.
Are blessed. *Ps. 112:1, 115:13.*
Confide in God. *Ps. 115:11; Prov. 14:26.*
Depart from evil. *Prov. 16:6.*
Speak together of holy things.
Mal. 3:16.
Should not fear man. *Is. 8:12-13;*
Mat. 10:28.
Desires of, are fulfilled by God.
Ps. 145:19.
Days of, are prolonged.
Prov. 10:27.

Should be
Prayed for. *Ps. 86:11.*
Shown in our callings. *Col. 3:22.*

Shown in giving a reason for
our hope. *1 Pet. 3:15.*
Constantly maintained.
Deut. 14:23; Josh. 4:24; Prov. 23:17.
Taught to others. *Ps. 34:11.*
Advantages of. *Prov. 15:16, 19:23;*
Eccl. 8:12-13.
The wicked are destitute of.
Ps. 36:1. Prov. 1:29; Jer. 2:19; Rom. 3:18.

Some examples. **Abraham**:
Gen. 22:12. **Joseph**: *Gen. 39:9, 42:18.*
Obadiah: *1 Kings 18:12.* **Nehemiah**:
Neh. 5:15. **Job**: *Job 1:1, 8.* **Early**
Christians: *Acts 9:31.* **Cornelius**:
Acts 10:2. **Noah**: *Heb. 11:7.*

FEAR, UNHOLY
A characteristic of the wicked.
Rev. 21:8.

Is described as
A fear of idols. *2 Kings 17:38.*
A fear of man. *1 Sam.15:24; Jn. 9:22.*
A fear of judgement. *Is. 2:19;*
Lk. 21:26; Rev 8:16-17.
A fear of future punishment.
Heb. 10:27.
Overwhelming. *Ex. 15:16; Job 15:21, 24.*
Consuming. *Ps. 73:19.*
A guilty conscience leads to.
Gen. 3:8, 10; Ps. 53:5; Prov. 28:1.
Seizes the wicked. *Job 15:24; Job 18:11.*
Surprises the hypocrite. *Is. 33:14, 18.*
The wicked are judicially filled
with. *Lev. 26:16-17; Deut. 28:65-67; Jer. 49:5.*
Will be realised. *Prov. 1:27; Prov. 10:24.*
God mocks. *Prov. 1:26.*
The saints are sometimes
tempted to. *Ps. 55:6.*
The saints are delivered from.
Prov. 1:33. Is. 14:3.
Trust in God is a preservative
from. *Ps. 27:1.*
Exhortations against. *Is. 8:12.*
Jn. 14:27.

Some examples. **Adam**: *Gen. 3:10.*
Cain: *Gen. 4:14.* **The Midianites**:
Judg. 7:21-22. **The Philistines**:

1 Sam. 14:15. **Saul**: *1 Sam. 28:5, 20.*
Adonijah's guests: *1 Kings 1:49.*
Haman: *Esther 7:6.* **Ahaz**: *Is. 7:2.*
Belshazzar: *Dan. 5:6.* **Pilate**: *Jn. 19:8.*
Felix: *Acts 24:25.*

FLATTERY
The saints should not use.
Job 32:21-22.
Ministers should not use.
1 Thess. 2:5.
The wicked use, towards
Others. *Ps. 5:9, 12:2.*
Themselves. *Ps. 36:2.*
Hypocrites use, to
God. *Ps. 78:36.*
Those in authority. *Dan. 11:34.*
False prophets and teachers use.
Ezek. 12:24 with Rom. 16:18.
Wisdom, a preservative against.
Prov. 4:5.
Worldly advantage obtained by.
Dan. 11:21, 32.
Seldom gains respect. *Prov. 28:23.*
Avoid those given over to.
Prov. 20:19.
Danger of. *Prov. 7:21-23, Prov. 29:5.*
Punishment of. *Job 17:5; Ps. 12:3.*

Some examples. **Women of Tekoah**. *2 Sam. 14:17, 20.* **Absolom**: *2 Sam. 15:2-6.* **False prophets**: *1 Kings 22:13.* **Darius' courtiers**: *Dan. 6:7.* **Some Pharisees**, *etc: Mk. 12:14.* **Tyrians**, *etc: Acts 12:22.*

FOOLS
All men are, by nature. *Titus 3:3.*
Deny God. *Ps. 14:1, 53:1.*
Blaspheme God. *Ps. 74:18.*
Reproach God. *Ps. 74:22.*
Make a mock of sin. *Prov. 14:9.*
Despise instruction. *Prov. 1:7, 15:5.*
Despise wisdom. *Prov. 1:7.*
Hate knowledge. *Prov. 1:22.*
Have no delight in understanding.
Prov. 18:2.
Make sport with evil. *Prov. 10:23.*
Walk in darkness. *Eccl. 2:14.*

Hate to depart from evil.
Prov. 13:19.
The worship of, is hateful to God.
Eccl. 5:1.
Are
Corrupt and abominable. *Ps. 14:1.*
Self-sufficient. *Prov. 12:15; Rom. 1:22.*
Self-confident. *Prov. 14:16.*
Self-deceivers. *Prov. 14:8.*
Mere professors of religion.
Mat. 25:2-12.
Full of words. *Eccl. 10:14.*
Given to meddling. *Prov. 20:3.*
Slanderers. *Prov. 10:18.*
Liars. *Prov. 10:18.*
Lazy. *Eccl. 4:5.*
Angry. *Eccl. 7:9.*
Always arguing. *Prov. 18:6.*
A grief to their parents.
Prov. 17:25; 19:13.
Come to shame. *Prov. 3:35.*
Destroy themselves by their
speech. *Prov. 10:8, 14; Eccl. 10:12.*
The company of, is ruinous.
Prov. 13:20.
The lips of, are a snare to the
soul. *Prov. 18:7.*
Cling to their folly. *Prov. 26:11, 27:22.*
Worship idols. *Jer. 10:8; Rom. 1:22-23.*
Trust in their own hearts.
Prov. 28:26.
Depend on their wealth. *Lk. 12:20.*
Hear the gospel and refuse to
obey it. *Mat. 7:26.*
Their mouths pour out folly.
Prov. 15:2.
Honour is unbecoming for.
Prov. 26:1, 8.
God takes no pleasure in. *Eccl. 5:4.*
Will not stand in the presence of
God. *Ps. 5:5.*
Avoid them. *Prov. 9:6; Prov. 14:7.*
Are exhorted to seek wisdom.
Prov. 8:5.
The punishment of. *Ps. 107:17; Prov. 19:29, 26:10.*

Some examples. **Rehoboam**:
1 Kings 12:8. **Israel**: *Jer. 4:22.*

Pharisees: *Mat. 23:17, 19.*

FORGETTING GOD

A characteristic of the wicked.
Prov. 2:17; Is. 65:11.
Backsliders are guilty of. *Jer. 3:21-22.*
Means forgetting his
   Covenant. *Deut. 4:23; 2 Kings 17:38.*
   Works. *Ps. 78:7, 11, 106:13.*
   Benefits. *Ps. 103:2, 106:7.*
   Word. *Heb. 12:5; Jas. 1:25.*
   Law. *Ps. 119:153, 176. Hos. 4:6.*
   Church. *Ps. 137:5.*
   Past deliverances. *Judg. 8:34; Ps. 78:42.*
   Power to deliver. *Is. 51:13-15.*
Encouraged by false teachers.
   Jer. 23:27.
Prosperity often leads to.
Deut. 8:12-14; Hos. 13:6.
Trials should not lead to. *Ps. 44:17-20.*
Resolve against. *Ps. 119:16, 93.*
Cautions against. *Deut. 6:12, 8:11.*
Exhortation to those guilty of.
Ps. 50:22.
   Punishment of. *Job 8:12-13; Ps. 9:17;*
Is. 17:10-11; Ezek. 23:35; Hos. 8:14.

FORGIVENESS OF INJURIES RECEIVED

Christ the example. *Lk. 23:34.*
Commanded. *Mk. 11:25; Rom. 12:19.*
To be unlimited. *Mat. 18:22; Lk. 17:4.*
A characteristic of the saints. *Ps. 7:4.*
Motives for the,
   The mercy of God. *Lk. 6:36.*
   Our need of forgiveness. *Mk. 11:25.*
   God's forgiveness of us. *Eph. 4:32.*
   Christ's forgiveness of us. *Col. 3:13.*
   A glory to the saints. *Prov. 19:11.*
Should be accompanied by
   Forbearance. *Col. 3:13.*
   Kindness. *Gen. 45:5-11; Rom. 12:20.*
   Blessing and prayer. *Mat. 5:44.*
Promises to. *Mat. 6:14; Lk. 6:37.*
No forgiveness without. *Mat. 6:15;*
Jas. 2:13.
Illustrated. *Mat. 18:23-35.*

Some examples. **Joseph**: *Gen.
50:20-21.* **David**: *1 Sam. 24:7; 2 Sam. 18:5,
19:23.*
Solomon: *1 Kings 1:53.*
Stephen: *Acts 7:60.* **Paul**: *2 Tim. 4:16.*

FORSAKING GOD

Idolaters are guilty of. *1 Sam. 8:8;
1 Kings 1 1:33.*
The wicked are guilty of. *Deut.
28:20.*
Backsliders are guilty of. *Jer. 15:6.*
Is to forsake
   His house. *2 Chron. 29:6.*
   His covenant. *Deut. 29:25;
   1 Kings 19:10; Jer. 22:9; Dan. 11:30.*
   His commandments. *Ezra 9:10.*
   His right way. *2 Pet. 2:15.*
Trusting in man is. *Jer. 17:5.*
Leads men to follow their own
devices. *Jer. 2:13.*
Prosperity tempts to. *Deut. 31:20, 32:15.*
The wickedness of. *Jer. 2:13, 5:7.*
Unreasonableness and ingrati-
tude of. *Jer. 2:5-6.*
Brings confusion. *Jer. 17:13.*
Followed by remorse. *Ezek. 6:9.*
Brings down God's wrath.
Ezra 8:22.
Provokes God to forsake men.
Judg. 10:1; 2 Chron. 15:2; 2 Chron. 24:20, 24.
Resolve against. *Josh. 24:16;
Neh. 10:21, 39.*
A curse pronounced on. *Jer. 17:5.*
Sin of, to be confessed. *Ezra 9:10.*
Warning against. *Josh. 24:20;
1 Chron. 28:9.*
The punishment of. *Deut. 28:20;
2 Kings 2:16-17; Is. 1:28; Jer. 1:16, 5:19.*

Some examples. **Balaam**: *2 Pet. 2:15.*
The Children of Israel: *1 Sam. 12:10.*
Saul: *1 Sam. 15:11.* **Ahab**: *1 Kings 18:18.*
Amon: *2 Kings 21:22.* **The kingdom
of Judah**: *2 Chron. 12:1, 5, 21:10; Is. 1:4;
Jer. 15:6.* **The kingdom of Israel**:
2 Chron. 13:11 with 2 Kings 17:7-18. **Many
disciples**: *Jn. 6:66.* **Phygellus**, *etc:
2 Tim. 1:15.*

G

GENEROSITY

Is pleasing to God. *2 Cor. 9:7; Heb. 13:16.*

God never forgets. *Heb. 6:10.*

Christ set an example of. *2 Cor. 8:9.*

Characteristic of the saints. *Ps. 112:9; Is. 32:8.*

Is unprofitable without love. *1 Cor. 13:3.*

Should be exercised

In the service of God. *Ex. 35:21-29.*

Toward the saints. *Rom. 12:13; Gal. 6:10.*

Toward servants. *Deut. 15:12-14.*

Toward the poor. *Deut. 15:11; Is. 58:7.*

Toward strangers. *Lev. 25:35.*

Toward enemies. *Prov. 25:21.*

Toward all men. *Gal. 6:10.*

In lending to those in need. *Mat. 5:42.*

In charitable giving. *Lk. 12:33.*

In relieving the destitute. *Is. 58:7.*

In forwarding missions. *Phil. 4:14-16.*

In rendering personal services. *Phil. 2:30.*

Without show. *Mat. 6:1-3.*

With simplicity. *Rom. 12:8.*

According to ability. *Deut. 16:10, 17; 1 Cor. 16:2.*

Willingly. *Ex. 25:2; 2 Cor. 8:12.*

Abundantly. *2 Cor. 8:7, 9:11-13.*

The exercise of, provokes others to. *2 Cor. 9:2.*

Labour to be able to exercise. *Acts 20:45; Eph. 4:28.*

Lack of,

Brings many a curse. *Prov. 28:27.*

A proof of not loving God. *1 Jn. 3:17.*

A proof of not having faith. *Jas. 2:14-16.*

Blessings associated with. *Ps. 41:1; Prov. 22:9; Acts 20:35.*

Promises to. *Ps. 112:9; Prov. 11:25, 28:27; Eccl. 11:1-2; Is. 58:10.*

Exhortations to. *Lk. 3:11, 11:41; Acts 20:35; 1 Cor. 16:1; 1 Tim. 6:17-18.*

Some examples. **The princes of Israel**: *Num. 7:2.* **Boaz**, *Ruth 2:16.* **David**: *2 Sam. 9:7, 10.* **Barzillai**, *etc: 2 Sam. 17:28.* **Araunah**: *2 Sam. 24:22-23.* **A Shunammite**, *2 Kings 4:8, 10.* **Judah**: *2 Chron. 24:10-11.* **Nehemiah**: *Neh. 7:70.* **The Jews**: *Neh. 7:70- 72.* **Job**: *Job 29:15-16.* **Nebuzar-Adan**: *Jer. 40:4-5.* **Joanna**: *etc: Lk. 8:3.* **Zaccheus**: *Lk. 19:8.* **Early Christians**: *Acts 2:45.* **Barnabas**: *Acts 4:36-37.* **Dorcas**: *Acts 9:36.* **Cornelius**: *Acts 10:2.* **The Church at Antioch**: *Acts 11:29-30.* **Lydia**: *Acts 16:15.* **Paul**: *Acts 20:34.* **The people of Melita (Malta):** *Acts 28:2.* **Stephanas**, *etc: 1 Cor. 16:17.*

Examples of very generous giving. **The Israelites**: *Ex. 36:5.* **A poor widow**: *Mk. 12:42.* **The churches of Macedonia**: *2 Cor. 8:1-5.* **The Philippian Church**: *Phil. 4:15-16.*

GIFTS OF GOD, THE

All blessings are. *Jas. 1:17; 2 Pet. 1:3.*

Are dispensed according to his will. *Eccl. 2:26; Dan. 2:21; Rom. 12:6; 1 Cor. 7:7.*

Are free and abundant. *Num. 14:8; Rom. 8:32.*

Spiritual gifts.

Christ is the chief of them. *Is. 42:6, 55:4; Jn. 3:16, 4:10, 6:32-33.*

Are through Christ. *Ps. 68:18 with Eph. 4:7-8. Jn. 6:27.*

The Holy Spirit. *Lk. 11:13; Acts 8:20.*

Grace. *Ps. 84:11; Jas. 4:6.*

Wisdom. *Prov. 2:6; Jas. 1:5.*

Repentance. *Acts 11:8.*

Faith. *Eph. 2:8; Phil. 1:29.*

Righteousness. *Rom. 5:16-17.*

Strength and power. *Ps. 68:35.*

A new heart. *Ezek. 11:19.*
Peace. *Ps. 29:11.*
Rest. *Mat. 11:28; 2 Thess. 1:7.*
Glory. *Ps. 84:11; Jn. 17:22.*
Eternal life. *Rom. 6:23.*
Not recalled by God. *Rom. 11:29.*
To be used for mutual profit.
1 Pet. 4:10.
Pray for. *Mat. 7:7, 11; Jn. 16:23-24.*
Acknowledge. *Ps. 4:7; Ps. 21:2.*
Temporal gifts.
Life. *Is. 42:5.*
Food and clothing. *Mat. 6: 25-33.*
Rain and fruitful seasons. *Gen. 27:28;*
Lev. 26:4-5; Is. 30:23.
Wisdom. *2 Chron. 1:12.*
Peace. *Lev. 26:6; 1 Chron. 22:9.*
All good things. *Ps. 34:10; 1 Tim. 6:17.*
To be used and enjoyed. *Eccl.*
3:13, 5:19-20; 1 Tim. 4:4-5.
Should cause us to remember
God. *Deut. 8:18.*
All creatures partake of. *Ps. 136:25,*
145:15-16.
Pray for. *Zech. 10:1; Mat. 6:11.*
Illustrated. *Mat. 25:15-30.*

GIFT OF THE HOLY SPIRIT, THE
From the Father. *Neh. 9:20; Lk. 11:13.*
From the Son. *Jn. 20:22.*
To Christ without measure. *Jn. 3:34.*
Given
According to promise. *Acts 2:38-39.*
Upon the exaltation of Christ.
Ps. 68:18; Jn. 7:39.
Through the intercession of
Christ. *Jn. 14:16.*
In answer to prayer. *Lk. 11:13;*
Eph. 1:16-17.
For instruction. *Neh. 9:20.*
For the comfort of the saints.
Jn. 14:16.
To those who repent and
believe. *Acts 2:38.*
To those who obey God. *Acts 5:32.*
To the Gentiles. *Acts 10:44-45, 11:17,*
15:8.
Is abundant. *Ps. 68:9; Jn. 7:38-39.*
Is permanent. *Is. 59:21; Hag. 2:5;*

1 Pet. 4:14.
Is fruitful. *Is. 32:15.*
Received through faith. *Gal. 3:14.*
An evidence of union with Christ.
1 Jn. 3:24, 4:13.
A guarantee of the inheritance of
the saints. *2 Cor. 1:22; 2 Cor. 5:5; Eph. 1:14.*
A pledge of the continued favour
of God. *Ezek. 39:29.*

GLORIFYING GOD
Is commanded. *1 Chron. 16:28;*
Ps. 22:23; Is. 42:12.
Is due to him. *1 Chron. 16:29.*
For his
Holiness. *Ps. 99:9; Rev. 15: 4.*
Mercy and truth. *Ps. 115:1; Rom. 15:9.*
Faithfulness and truth. *Is. 25:1.*
Wonderful works. *Mat. 15:31;*
Acts 4:21.
Judgements. *Is. 25:3; Ezek. 28:22;*
Rev. 14:7.
Deliverances. *Ps. 50:15.*
Grace towards others. *Acts 11:18;*
2 Cor. 9:13; Gal 1:24.
Obligation of the saints to the.
1 Cor. 6:20.
Is acceptable through Christ.
Phil. 1:11; 1 Pet. 4:11.
Christ is an example of. *Jn. 17:4.*
Accomplished by
Relying on his promises.
Rom. 4:20.
Praising him. *Ps. 50:23.*
Doing all for him. *1 Cor. 10:31.*
Dying for him. *Jn. 21:19.*
Confessing Christ. *Phil. 3:11.*
Suffering for Christ. *1 Pet. 4:14, 16.*
Glorifying Christ. *Acts 19:17;*
2 Thess. 1:12.
Bringing forth the fruits of
righteousness. *Jn. 15:8; Phil. 1:11.*
Patience in affliction. *Is. 24:15.*
Faithfulness. *1 Pet. 4:11.*
Required in body and spirit.
1 Cor. 6:20.
Will be universal. *Ps. 86:9; Rev. 5:13.*
The saints should
Resolve on. *Ps. 69:30, 118:28.*

Be united in. *Ps. 34:3; Rom. 15:6.*

Persevere in. *Ps. 86:12.*

All the blessings of God are designed to lead to. *Is. 60:21, 61:3.*

The holy example of the saints may lead others to. *Mat. 5:16; 1 Pet. 2:12.*

All, by nature, fail in. *Rom. 3:23.*

The wicked are averse to. *Dan. 5:23; Rom. 1:21.*

The punishment for not doing so. *Dan. 5:23, 30; Mal. 2:2; Acts 12:23; Rom. 1:21.*

Heavenly hosts are engaged in. *Rev. 4:11.*

Some examples. **Abraham**: *Rom. 4:20.* **David**: *Ps. 57:5.* **The multitude**: *Mat. 9:8, 15:31.* **The virgin Mary**: *Lk. 1:46.* **Angels**: *Lk. 2:14.* **Shepherds**: *Lk. 2:20.* **A paralysed man**: *Lk. 5:25.* **A woman with an infirmity**: *Lk. 13:13.* **A leper**: *Lk. 17:15.* **A blind man**: *Lk. 18:43.* **A centurion**: *Lk. 23:47.* **The Church at Jerusalem**: *Acts 11:18.* **The Gentiles at Antioch**: *Acts 13:48.* **Paul**: *Rom. 11:36.*

GLORY

God is, to his people. *Ps. 3:3; Zech. 2:5.*

Christ is, to his people. *Is. 60:1; Lk. 2:32.*

The gospel is ordained to be, to the saints. *1 Cor. 2:7.*

Of the gospel, exceeds that of the Law. *2 Cor. 3:9-10.*

The joy of the saints is full of. *1 Pet. 1:8.*

Spiritual,

Is given by God. *Ps. 84:11.*

Is given by Christ. *Jn. 17:22.*

Is the work of the Holy Spirit. *2 Cor. 3:18.*

Eternal,

Is procured by the death of Christ. *Heb. 2:10.*

Accompanies salvation by Christ. *2 Tim. 2:10.*

Is inherited by the saints. *1 Sam. 2:8; Ps. 73:24; Prov. 3:35; Col. 3:4; 1 Pet. 5:10.*

The saints are called to. *2 Thess. 2:14; 1 Pet. 5:10.*

The saints are prepared beforehand for. *Rom. 9:23.*

Is enhanced by present afflictions. *2 Cor. 4:17.*

Present afflictions are not worthy to be compared with. *Rom. 8:18.*

Of the Church, will be rich and abundant. *Is. 60:11-13.*

The bodies of the saints will be raised in. *1 Cor. 15:43; Phil. 3:21.*

The saints will be the, of their ministers. *1 Thess. 2:19-20.*

Afflictions of ministers are, to the saints. *Eph. 3:13.*

Temporal,

Is given by God. *Dan. 2:37.*

Passes away. *1 Pet. 1:24.*

The devil tries to seduce us with. *Mat. 4:8.*

Of hypocrites, is turned to shame. *Hos. 4:7.*

Do not seek, from man. *Mat. 6:2; 1 Thess. 2:6.*

Of the wicked,

Is in their shame. *Phil. 3:19.*

Ends in their destruction. *Is. 5:14.*

GLORY OF GOD, THE

Shown in Christ. *Jn. 1:14; 2 Cor. 4:6; Heb. 1:3.*

Shown in

His name. *Deut. 28:58; Neh. 9:5.*

His majesty. *Job 37:22; Ps. 93:1, 104:1, 145:5, 12; Is. 2:10.*

His power. *Ex. 15:1, 6; Rom. 6:4.*

His works. *Ps. 19:1, 111:3.*

His holiness. *Ex. 15:11.*

Is described as

Great. *Ps. 138:5.*

Eternal. *Ps. 104:31.*

Rich. *Eph. 3:16.*

Highly exalted. *Ps. 8:1, 113:4.*

Shown to

Moses. *Ex. 34:5-7 with Ex. 33:18-23.*

Stephen. *Acts 7:55.*

His Church. *Deut. 5:24; Ps. 102:16.*

Enlightens the Church. *Is 60:1-2; Rev. 21:11, 23.*

The saints desire to behold. *Ps. 63:2, 90:16.*

God is jealous of. *Is. 42:8.*

Revere. *Is. 69:19.*

Plead in prayer. *Ps. 79:9.*

Declare. *1 Chron. 16:24; Ps. 145:5, 11.*

Magnify. *Ps. 57:5.*

The earth is full of. *Is. 6:3.*

The knowledge of, will fill the earth. *Hab. 2:14.*

GLUTTONY

Christ was falsely accused of. *Mat. 11:19.*

The wicked are addicted to. *Phil. 3:19; Jude verse 12.*

Leads to

Worldly security. *Is. 22:13 with 1 Cor. 15:32; Lk. 12:19.*

Poverty. *Prov. 23:21.*

Of princes, ruinous to their people. *Eccl. 10:16-17.*

Is inconsistent in the saints. *1 Pet. 4:3.*

A warning against. *Prov. 23:2-3; Lk. 21:34; Rom. 13:13-14.*

Pray against temptation to. *Ps. 141:4.*

The punishment of. *Num. 11:33-34 with Ps. 78:31; Deut. 21:21; Amos 6:4, 7.*

The danger of, illustrated. *Lk. 12:45-46.*

Some examples. **Esau**: *Gen. 25:30-34 with Heb. 12:16-17.* **Israel**: *Num. 11:4 with Ps. 78:18.* **The sons of Eli**: *1 Sam. 2:12-17.* **Belshazzar**: *Dan. 5:1.*

GOD

Is a spirit. *Jn. 4:24; 2 Cor. 3:17.*

Is declared to be

Light. *Is. 60:19; Jas. 1:17; 1 Jn. 1:5.*

Love. *1 Jn. 4:8, 16.*

Invisible. *Job 23:8-9; Jn. 1:18, 5:37; Col. 1:15; 1 Tim. 1:17.*

Unsearchable. *Job 11:7, 37:23; Ps. 145:3; Is. 40:28; Rom. 11:33.*

Incorruptible. *Rom. 1:23.*

Eternal. *Deut. 33:27; Ps. 90:2; Rev. 4:8-10.*

Immortal. *1 Tim. 1:17, 6:16.*

Omnipotent. *Gen. 17:1; Ex. 6:3.*

Always seeing. *Ps. 139:1-6; Prov. 5:21.*

Omnipresent. *Ps. 139:7; Jer. 23:23.*

Unchanging. *Ps. 102:26-27; Jas. 1:17.*

Only-wise. *Rom. 16:27; 1 Tim. 1:17.*

Glorious. *Ex. 15:11; Ps. 145:5.*

Most High. *Ps. 83:18; Acts 7:48.*

Perfect. *Mat. 5:48.*

Holy. *Ps. 99:9; Is. 5:16.*

Just. *Deut. 32:4; Is. 45:21.*

True. *Jer. 10:10; Jn. 17:3.*

Upright. *Ps. 25:8, 92:15.*

Righteous. *Ezra 9:15; Ps. 145:17.*

Good. *Ps. 25:8, 119:68.*

Great. *2 Chron. 2:5; Ps. 86:10.*

Gracious. *Ex. 34:6; Ps. 116:5.*

Faithful. *1 Cor. 10:13; 1 Pet. 4:19.*

Merciful. *Ex. 34:6-7; Ps. 86:5.*

Long-suffering. *Num. 14:18; Mic. 7:18.*

Jealous. *Josh. 24:19; Nahum 1:2.*

Compassionate. *2 Kings 13:23.*

A consuming fire. *Heb. 12:29.*

There is none beside him. *Deut. 4:35; Is. 44:6.*

There is none before him. *Is. 43:10.*

There is none like him. *Ex. 9:14; Deut. 33:26; 2 Sam. 7:22; Is. 46:5, 9; Jer. 10:6.*

There is none good but him. *Mat. 19:17.*

He fills heaven and earth. *1 Kings 8:27; Jer. 23:24.*

He should be worshipped in spirit and in truth. *Jn. 4:24.*

GOODNESS OF GOD, THE

Is part of his character. *Ps. 25:8; Nahum 1:7; Mat. 10:17.*

He is declared to be

Great. *Neh. 9:35; Zech. 9:17.*

Rich. *Ps. 104:24; Rom. 2:4.*

Abundant. *Ex. 34:6; Ps. 33:5.*

Satisfying. *Ps. 65:4; Jer. 31:12, 14.*

Enduring. *Ps. 23:6, 52:1.*

Universal. *Ps. 145:9; Mat. 5:45.*

Is manifested

To his Church. *Ps. 31:19; Lam. 3:25.*

In doing good. *Ps. 119:68, 145:9.*

In supplying temporal needs.
Acts 14:17.

In providing for the poor.
Ps. 68:10.

In forgiving sins. *2 Chron. 30:18;*
Ps. 86:5.

Leads to repentance. *Rom. 2:4.*

Is recognised in his dealings.
Ezra 8:18; Neh. 2:18.

Pray for the manifestation of.
2 Thess. 1:11.

Do not despise. *Rom. 2:4.*

Revere. *Jer. 33:9; Hos. 3:5.*

Magnify. *Ps. 107:8; Jer. 33:11.*

Urge others to confide in. *Ps. 34:8.*

The wicked disregard. *Neh. 9:35.*

GOSPEL, THE

Is described. *Lk. 2:10-11.*

Was foretold. *Is. 41:27, 52:7 with*
Rom. 10:15; Is. 61:1-3.

Was preached under the Old
Covenant (Testament). *Heb. 4:2.*

Shows the grace of God. *Acts 11:3,*
20:32.

The knowledge of God's glory is
by. *2 Cor. 4:4, 6.*

Life and immortality are brought
to light by. *2 Tim. 1:10.*

Is the power of God to salvation.
Rom. 1:16; 1 Cor. 1:18; 1 Thess. 1:5.

Is true. *Col. 1:5.*

Is glorious. *2 Cor. 4:4.*

Is everlasting. *1 Pet. 1:25; Rev. 14:6.*

Was preached by Christ. *Mat. 4:23;*
Mk. 1:14.

Ministers have a dispensation to
preach. *1 Cor. 9:17.*

Was preached beforehand to
Abraham. *Gen. 22:18 with Gal. 3:8.*

Preached to

The Jews first. *Lk. 24:47; Acts 13:46,*
14:1, 16:3, 17:1-2, 18:4, 19:8, 28:17.

The Gentiles. *Mk. 13:10; Gal. 2:2.*

The poor. *Mat. 11:5; Lk. 4:18.*

Every creature. *Mk. 16:15; Col. 1:23.*

Must be believed. *Mk. 1:15; Heb. 4. 2.*

Brings peace. *Lk. 2:10, 14; Eph. 6:15.*

Produces hope. *Col. 1:23.*

The saints have fellowship in.
Phil. 1:5.

There is fullness of blessing in.
Rom. 15:29.

Those who receive, should

Adhere to the truth of. *Gal. 1:6-7,*
2:14.

Not be ashamed of it. *Rom. 1:16.*

Live in subjection to. *2 Cor. 9:13.*

Adjust their conversation as
suitable for. *Phil. 1:27.*

Earnestly contend for the faith
of. *Phil. 1:17, 27; Jude verse 3.*

Sacrifice friends and property
for. *Mk. 10:29.*

Sacrifice your very life for. *Mk. 8:35.*

Profession of, attended with
afflictions. *2 Tim. 1:8.*

Promises to sufferers, for the
sake of. *Mk. 8:35, 10:30.*

Be careful not to hinder. *1 Cor. 9:12.*

Is hidden to those who are lost.
2 Cor. 4:3.

Testifies to the final judgement.
Rom. 2:16.

Let the one who preaches
another gospel be accursed. *Gal. 1:8.*

The awful consequences of not
obeying. *2 Thess. 1:8-9.*

Is called, the

Dispensation of the grace of
God. *Eph. 3:2.*

Gospel of peace. *Eph. 6:15.*

Gospel of God. *Rom. 1:1;*
1 Thess. 2:8; 1 Pet. 4:17.

Gospel of Jesus Christ. *Rom. 1:9,*
16; 2 Cor. 2:12; 1 Thess. 3:2.

Gospel of the grace of God.
Acts 20:24.

Gospel of the kingdom.
Mat. 24:14.

Gospel of salvation. *Eph. 1:13.*

Glorious gospel of Christ.
2 Cor. 4:4.

Preaching of Jesus Christ.
Rom. 16:25.

Mystery of Christ. *Eph. 3:4.*

Mystery of the gospel. *Eph. 6:19.*

Word of God. *1 Thess. 2:13.*

Word of Christ. *Col. 3:16.*
Word of grace. *Acts 14:3, 20:32.*
Word of salvation. *Acts 13:26.*
Word of reconciliation. 2 *Cor. 5:19.*
Word of truth. *Eph. 1:13; 2 Cor. 6:7.*
Word of faith. *Rom. 10:8.*
Word of life. *Phil. 2:16.*
Ministration of the Spirit. *2 Cor. 3:8.*
Doctrine according to
godliness. *1 Tim. 6:3.*
Form of sound words. *2 Tim. 1:13.*
Rejection of, by many, foretold.
Is. 53:1 with Rom. 10:15-16.
Rejection of, by the Jews, has
become a means of blessing to
the Gentiles. *Rom. 11:28.*

GRACE
God is the God of all. *1 Pet. 5:10.*
God is the Giver of. *Ps. 84:11.*
God's throne is the throne of.
Heb. 4:16.
The Holy Spirit is the Spirit of.
Zech. 12:10; Heb. 10:29.
Was upon Christ. *Lk. 2:40.*
Christ spoke with. *Ps. 45:2 with Lk. 4:22.*
Christ was full of. *Jn. 1:14.*
Came through Christ. *Jn. 1:17;
Rom. 5:15.*
Given by Christ. *1 Cor. 1:4.*
Riches of, shown in God's
kindness through Christ. *Eph. 2:7.*
Glory of, shown in our accept-
ance in Christ. *Eph. 1:6.*
Is described as
Great. *Acts 4:33.*
Sovereign. *Rom. 5:21.*
Rich, *Eph. 1:7, 2:7.*
Exceeding. *2 Cor. 9:14.*
Manifold. *1 Pet. 4:10.*
All-sufficient. *2 Cor. 12:9.*
All-abundant. *Rom. 5:15, 17, 20.*
True. *1 Pet. 5:12.*
Glorious. *Eph. 1:6.*
Not in vain. *1 Cor. 15:10.*
The gospel, a declaration of.
Acts 20:24, 32.

Is the source of
Election. *Rom. 11:5.*
The call of God. *Gal. 1:15.*
Justification. *Rom. 3:24; Titus 3:7.*
Faith. *Acts 18:27.*
The forgiveness of sins. *Eph. 1:7.*
Salvation. *Acts 15:11. Eph. 2:5, 8.*
Consolation. *2 Thess. 2:16.*
Hope. *2 Thess. 2:16.*
Necessary for the service of God.
Heb. 12:28.
God's work is completed in the
saints by. *2 Thess. 1:11-12.*
The success and completion of
the work of God is attributed to.
Zech. 4:7.
The inheritance of the promises
by. *Rom. 4:16.*
Justification by, opposed to that
of works. *Rom. 4:4-5; Rom. 11:6; Gal. 5:4.*
The saints
Are heirs of. *1 Pet. 3:7.*
Are under. *Rom. 6:14.*
Receive, from Christ. *Jn. 1:16.*
Are what they are by. *1 Cor. 15:10;
2 Cor. 1:12.*
Abound in gifts of. *Acts 4:33;
2 Cor. 8:1, 9:8, 14.*
Should be established in. *Heb. 13:9.*
Should be strong in. *2 Tim. 2:1.*
Should grow in. *2 Pet. 3:18.*
Should speak with. *Eph. 4:29; Col. 4:6.*
Specially given
To ministers. *Rom. 12:3, 6;
Rom. 15:15; 1 Cor. 3:10; Gal. 2:9; Eph. 3:7.*
To the humble. *Prov. 3:34 with Jas. 4:6.*
To those who walk uprightly.
Ps. 84:11.
Gospel of, not to be received in
vain. *2 Cor. 6:1*
Pray
For yourselves. *Heb. 4:16.*
For others. *2 Cor. 13:14; Eph. 6:24.*
Beware lest you fail the work of
grace. *Heb. 12:15.*
Manifestation of, in others, a
cause of gladness. *Acts 11:23.*

Special manifestation of, at the Second Coming of Christ. *1 Pet. 1:13.*

Not to be abused. *Rom. 6:1, 15.* Antinomians (the 'No Law' false teachers) abuse. *Jude verse 4.*

H

HAPPINESS OF THE SAINTS IN THIS LIFE
Is in God. *Ps. 73:25.*
Is only found in the ways of wisdom. *Prov. 3:17-18.*
Is derived from
   The fear of God. *Ps. 128:1-2; Prov. 28:14.*
   Trust in God. *Prov. 16:20; Phil. 4:6-7.*
   Obedience to God. *Ps. 40:8; Jn. 13:17.*
   Salvation. *Deut. 33:29; Is. 12:2-3.*
   Hope in the Lord. *Ps. 146:5.*
   Hope of glory. *Rom. 5:2.*
   God being their Lord. *Ps. 144:15.*
   God being their help. *Ps. 146:5.*
   Praising God. *Ps. 135:3.*
   Their mutual love. *Ps. 133:1.*
   Divine chastening. *Job 5:17; Jas. 5:11.*
   Suffering for Christ. *2 Cor. 12:10; 1 Pet. 3:14, 4:13-14.*
   Having mercy on the poor. *Prov. 14:21.*
   Finding wisdom. *Prov. 3:13.*
   Retaining wisdom. *Prov. 3:18.*
Is abundant and satisfying. *Ps. 36:8, 63:5.*

HAPPINESS OF THE WICKED, THE
Is limited to this life. *Ps. 17:14; Lk. 16:25.*
Is short-lived. *Job 20:5.*
Is uncertain. *Lk. 12:20.*
Is vain. *Eccl. 2:1, 7:6.*
Is derived from
   Their wealth. *Job 21:13; Ps. 52:7.*
   Their power. *Job 21:7; Ps. 37:35.*
   Their worldly prosperity. *Ps. 17:14, 73:3, 4. 7.*
   Gluttony. *Is. 22:13; Hab.1:16.*
   Drunkenness. *Is. 5:11; Is. 56:12.*
   Vain pleasure. *Job 21:12; Is. 5:12.*

   Successful oppression. *Hab. 1:15.*
Marred by jealousy. *Esth. 5:13.*
Often interrupted by judgements. *Num. 11:33; Job 15:21; Ps. 73:18-20; Jer. 25:10-11.*
Leads to sorrow. *Prov. 14:13.*
Leads to recklessness. *Is. 22:13.*
Sometimes a stumbling-block to the saints. *Ps. 73:3, 16; Jer. 12:1; Hab. 1:13.*
The saints are often permitted to see the end of. *Ps. 73:17-20.*
Do not envy them. *Ps. 37:1.*
Woe against. *Amos 6:1; Lk. 6:25.*
Illustrated. *Ps. 37:35-36; Lk. 12:16-20, 16:19, 25.*

Some examples. **Israel**: *Num. 11:33.* **Haman**: *Esth. 5:9-11.* **Belshazzar**: *Dan. 5:1.* **Herod**: *Acts 12:21-23.*

HATRED
Is forbidden. *Lev. 19:17; Col. 3:8.*
Is murder. *1 Jn. 3:15.*
Is a work of the flesh. *Gal. 5:20.*
Is often cloaked by deceit. *Prov. 10:18, 26:26.*
Leads to deceit. *Prov. 26:24-25.*
Stirs up strife. *Prov. 10:12.*
Embitters life. *Prov. 15:17.*
Is inconsistent with
   The knowledge of God. *1 Jn. 2:9, 11.*
   The love of God. *1 Jn. 4:20.*
Liars are prone to. *Prov. 26:28.*
The wicked show,
   Towards God. *Rom. 1:30.*
   Towards the saints. *Ps. 25:19; Prov. 29:10.*
   Towards each other. *Titus 3:3.*

Christ experienced. *Ps. 35:19 with Jn. 15:25.*

The saints should
Expect. *Mat. 10:22.*
Not marvel at. *1 Jn. 3:13.*
Return good for. *Ex. 23:5; Mat. 5:44.*
Not rejoice in the calamities of those who show. *Job 31:29-30; Ps. 35:13-14.*
Give no cause for. *Prov. 25:17.*
The punishment of. *Ps. 34:21, 44:7, 89:23; Amos 1:11.*

We should show, against
False ways. *Ps. 119:104, 128.*
Lying. *Ps. 119:163.*
Evil. *Ps. 97:10; Prov. 8:13.*
Backsliding. *Ps. 101:3.*
Hatred and opposition to God. *Ps. 139: 21-22.*

Some examples. **Cain**: *Gen. 4:5, 8.*
Esau: *Gen. 27:41.* **Joseph's brothers**: *Gen. 37:4.* **Men of Gilead**: *Judg. 11:7.*
Saul: *1 Sam. 18:8-9.* **Ahab**: *1 Kings 22:8.*
Haman. *Esth. 3:5-6.* **Enemies of the Jews**: *Esth. 9:1, 5; Ezek. 35:5-6.*
Chaldeans: *Dan. 3:12.* **Enemies of Daniel**: *Dan. 6:4-15.* **Herodias**: *Mat. 14:3, 8.* **The Jews**: *Acts 23:12, 14.*

HATRED TOWARDS CHRIST
Is without cause. *Ps. 69:4 with Jn. 15:25.*
Is on account of his testimony against the world. *Jn. 7:7.*
Involves
Hatred to the Father. *Jn. 15:23-24.*
Hatred to his people. *Jn. 15:18.*
The punishment of. *Ps. 2:2, 9, 21:8.*
No escape for those who persevere in. *1 Cor. 15:25; Heb. 10:29-31.*
Illustrated. *Lk. 19:12-14, 17.*
Some examples. **The Chief Priests**, etc: *Mat. 27:1-2; Lk. 22:5.* **The Jews**: *Mat. 27:22-23.* **The Scribes**, etc: *Mk. 11:18; Lk. 11:53-54.*

HEART, THE
Issues of life proceed from. *Prov. 4:23.*

God
Tests. *1 Chron. 29:17; Jer. 12:3.*
Knows. *Ps. 44:21; Jer. 20:12.*
Searches. *1 Chron. 28:9; Jer. 17:10.*
Understands the thoughts of. *1 Chron. 28:9; Ps. 139:2.*
Ponders. *Prov. 21:2, 24:12.*
Influences. *1 Sam. 10:26; Ezra 6:22, 7:27; Prov. 21:1; Jer. 20:9.*
Creates a new. *Ezra 36:26.*
Prepares. *1 Chron. 29:18; Prov. 16:1.*
Opens. *Acts 16:14.*
Enlightens. *2 Cor. 4:6.*
Strengthens. *Ps. 27:14.*
Establishes. *Ps. 112:8; 1 Thess. 3:13.*

Should be
Prepared for God. *1 Sam. 7:3.*
Given to God. *Prov. 23:26.*
Perfect before God. *1 Kings 8:61.*
Applied to wisdom. *Ps. 90:12; Prov. 2:2.*
Guided in the right way. *Prov. 23:19.*
Purified. *Jas. 4:8.*
Single. *Eph. 6:5; Col. 3:22.*
Tender. *Eph. 4:32.*
Kept with diligence. *Prov. 4:23.*

We should
Believe with. *Acts 8:37; Rom. 10:10.*
Serve God with all our. *Deut. 11:13.*
Keep God's statutes with all. *Deut. 26:16.*
Walk before God with all. *1 Kings 2:4.*
Trust in God with all. *Prov. 3:5.*
Love God with all. *Mat. 22:37.*
Return to God with all. *Deut. 30:2.*
Do the will of God from. *Eph. 6:6.*
Sanctify God in. *1 Pet. 3:15.*
No one can cleanse. *Prov. 20:9.*
Faith, the means of purifying. *Acts 15:9.*
Renewal of, promised under the gospel. *Ezek. 11:19, 36:26; Heb. 3:10.*
When broken and contrite, is not despised by God. *Ps. 51:17.*

Pray that it may be
Cleansed. *Ps. 51:10.*
Inclined to God's testimonies. *Ps. 119:36.*

Blameless in God's statutes.
Ps. 119:80.
United to fear God. Ps. 86:11.
Directed into the love of God.
2 Thess. 3:5.
Do not harden against God.
Ps. 95:8 with Heb. 4:7.
Do not harden against the poor.
Deut. 15:7.
Do not regard iniquity in. Ps. 66:18.
Take heed lest it be deceived.
Deut. 11:16.
Know the plague of. 1 Kings 8:38.
The one who trusts in, is a fool.
Prov. 28:26.

HEART, THE CHARACTER OF THE RENEWED
It is
Inclined to seek God. 2 Chron. 11:16.
Prepared to seek God. 2 Chron. 19:3;
Ezra 7:10; Ps. 10:17.
Fixed on God. Ps. 57:7, 112:7.
Joyful in God. 1 Sam. 2:1; Zech. 10:7.
Perfect with God. 1 Kings 8:61; Ps. 102:2.
Upright. Ps. 97:11, 125:4.
Clean. Ps. 73:1.
Pure. Ps. 24:4; Mat. 5:8.
Tender. 1 Sam. 24:5; 2 Kings 22:19.
Single and sincere. Acts 2:46; Heb. 10:22.
Honest and good. Lk. 8:15.
Broken, contrite. Ps. 34:18, 51:17.
Obedient. Ps 119:112; Rom. 6:17.
Filled with the Law of God. Ps. 40:8,
119:11.
Awed by the Word of God.
Ps. 119:161.
Filled with the fear of God. Jer. 32:40.
Meditative. Ps. 4:4, 77:6.
Circumcised. Deut. 30:6; Rom. 2:29.
Without fear. Ps. 27:3.
Desirous of God. Ps. 84:2.
Enlarged. Ps. 119:32; 2 Cor. 6:11.
Faithful to God. Neh. 9:8.
Confident in God. Ps. 112:7.
Sympathetic. Jer. 4:19; Lam. 3:51.
Prayerful. 1 Sam. 1:13; Ps. 27:8.
Inclined to obedience. Ps. 119:112.
Wholly devoted to God. Ps. 9:1,

119:10, 69, 145.
Zealous. 2 Chron. 17:6; Jer. 20:9.
Wise. Prov. 10:8, 14:33, 23:15.
A treasury of good. Mat. 12:35.

HEART, THE CHARACTER OF THE UNREGENERATED
It is
Hateful to God. Prov. 6:16, 18; Prov. 11:20.
Full of evil. Eccl. 9:3.
Full of evil desires and ideas.
Gen. 6:5, 8:21; Prov. 6:18.
Full of vain thoughts. Jer. 4:14.
Fully set on doing evil. Eccl. 8:11.
Desperately wicked. Jer. 17:9.
Far from God. Is. 29:13 with Mat. 15:8.
Not perfect with God. 1 Kings 15:3;
Prov. 6:18; Acts 8:21.
Not prepared to seek God.
2 Chron. 12:14.
A treasury of evil. Mat. 12:35; Mk. 7:21.
Darkened. Rom. 1:21.
Prone to error. Ps. 95:10.
Prone to depart from God.
Deut. 29:18; Jer. 17:5.
Impenitent. Rom. 2:5.
Unbelieving. Heb. 3:12.
Blind. Eph. 4:18.
Uncircumcised. Lev. 26:41; Acts 7:51.
Of little worth. Prov. 10:20.
Deceitful. Jer. 17:9.
Deceived. Is. 44:20; Jas. 1:26.
Divided. Hos. 10:2.
Double. 1 Chron. 12:33; Ps. 12:2.
Hard. Ezek. 3:7; Mk. 10:5; Rom. 2:5.
Haughty. Prov. 18:12; Jer. 48:29.
Influenced by the devil. Jn. 13:2.
Worldly. Rom. 8:7.
Covetous. Jer. 22:17; 2 Pet. 2:14.
Despiteful. Ezek. 25:15.
Ensnaring. Eccl. 7:26.
Foolish. Prov. 12:23, 22:15.
Obstinate. Ps. 101:4; Prov. 6:14, 17:20.
Fretful against the Lord. Prov. 19:3.
Idolatrous. Ezra 14:3-4.
Mad. Eccl. 9:3.
Mischievous. Ps. 28:3, 140:2.
Proud. Ps. 101:5; Jer. 49:16.
Rebellious. Jer. 6:23.

Perverse. *Prov. 12:8.*
Stiff. *Ezek. 2:4.*
Stony. *Ezek. 11:19, 36:26.*
Stubborn. *Is. 10:12, 46:12.*
Elated by sensual indulgence. *Hos. 13:6.*
Elated by prosperity. *2 Chron. 26:16; Dan. 5:20.*
Often devising destruction. *Prov. 24:2.*
Often judicially stupefied. *Is. 6:10; Acts 28:26-27.*
Often judicially hardened. *Ex. 4:21; Josh. 11:20.*

HEAVEN

Created by God. *Gen. 1:1 Rev. 10:6.*
Everlasting. *Ps. 89:29; 2 Cor. 5:1.*
Immeasurable. *Jer. 31:37.*
High. *Ps. 103:11; Is. 57:15.*
God's dwelling place. *1 Kings 8:30; Mat. 6:9.*
God's throne. *Is. 66:1 with Acts 7:49.*

God

Is the Lord of. *Dan. 5:23; Mat. 11:26.*
Reigns in. *Ps. 11:4, 135:6; Dan. 4:35.*
Fills. *1 Kings 8:27; Jer. 23:24.*
Answers his people from. *1 Chron. 21:26; 2 Chron. 7:14; Neh. 9:27; Ps. 20:6.*
Sends his judgements from. *Gen. 19:24; 1 Sam. 2:10; Dan. 4:13-14; Rom. 1:18.*

Christ

As Mediator, entered into. *Acts 3:21; Heb. 6:20; Heb. 9:12, 24.*
Is all-powerful in. *Mat. 28:18; 1 Pet. 3:22.*

Angels are in. *Mat. 18:10; Mk. 24:36.*
Names of the saints are written in. *Lk. 10:20; Heb. 12:23.*
The saints receive their reward in. *Mat. 5:12; 1 Pet. 1:4.*
Repentance brings about joy in. *Lk. 15:7.*
Lay up treasure in. *Mat. 6:20; Lk. 12:33.*
Flesh and blood cannot inherit. *1 Cor. 15:50.*
The happiness of, is described. *Rev. 7:16-17.*

Is called

A full barn. *Mat. 3:12.*
The kingdom of Christ and of God. *Eph. 5:5.*
The Father's house. *Jn. 14:2.*
A heavenly country. *Heb. 11:16.*
A rest. *Heb. 4:9.*
Paradise. *2 Cor. 12:2, 4.*
The wicked are excluded from. *Gal. 5:21; Eph. 5:5; Rev. 22:15.*
Enoch and Elijah were translated into. *Gen. 5:24 with Heb. 11:5;.2 Kings 2:11.*

HEEDFULNESS

Commanded. *Ex.23:13; Prov.4:25-27.*

Is necessary

In the care of the soul. *Deut. 4:9.*
In the house and worship of God. *Eccl. 5:1.*
In what we hear. *Mk. 4:24.*
In how we hear. *Lk. 8:18.*
In keeping God's commandments. *Josh. 22:5.*
For conduct. *Eph. 5:15.*
For speech. *Prov. 13:3; Jas. 1:19.*
In worldly company. *Ps. 39:1; Col. 4:5.*
In giving judgement. *1 Chron. 19:6, 7.*
Against sin. *Heb.12:15-16.*
Against unbelief. *Heb. 3:12.*
Against idolatry. *Deut. 4:15-16.*
Against false christs and false prophets. *Mat. 24:4-5, 23-24.*
Against false teachers. *Phil. 3:2; Col. 2:8; 2 Pet. 3:16-17.*
Against presumption. *1 Cor. 10:12.*
Promises to. *1 Kings 2:4. 1 Chron. 22:13.*

HELL

A place of torment. *Lk. 16:23; Rev 14:10-11.*

Is described as

Everlasting punishment. *Mat. 25:46.*
Everlasting fire. *Mat. 25:41.*
Everlasting burnings. *Is. 33:14.*
A furnace of fire. *Mat. 13:42, 50.*
A lake of fire. *Rev. 20:15.*
Fire and brimstone. *Rev. 14:10.*
Unquenchable fire. *Mat. 3:12.*
Devouring fire. *Is. 33:14.*

Prepared for the devil, etc. *Mat. 25:41.*
Devils are confined in, until the
Day of Judgement. *2 Pet. 2:4;
Jude verse 6.*
The punishment of, is eternal.
Is. 33:14; Rev. 20:10.
The wicked will be turned into.
Ps. 9:17.
Human power cannot preserve
from. *Ezek. 32:27.*
The body suffers in. *Mat. 5:29, 10:28.*
The soul suffers in. *Mat. 10:28.*
The wise will avoid. *Prov. 15:24.*
Endeavour to keep others from.
Prov. 23:14; Jude verse 23.
The society of the wicked leads
to. *Prov. 5:5, 9:18.*
The beast, false prophet, and the
devil will be cast into. *Rev. 19:20, 20:10.*
The powers of, cannot prevail
against the Church. *Mat. 16:18.*
Illustrated. *Is. 30:33.*

HOLINESS
Commanded. *Lev. 11:45, 20:7.*
Christ
Desires this, for his people.
Jn. 17:17.
Effects, in his people. *Eph. 5:25-27.*
An example of. *Heb. 7:26; 1 Pet. 2:21-22.*
The character of God is the
standard of. *Lev. 19:2 with 1 Pet. 1:15-16.*
The character of Christ is the
standard of. *Rom. 8:29; 1 Jn. 2:6.*
The gospel is the way of. *Is. 35:8.*
Is necessary for the worship of
God. *Ps. 24:3-4.*
None will see God without.
Heb. 12:14.
The saints
Elected to. *Rom. 8:29; Eph. 1:4.*
Called to. *1 Thess. 4:7; 2 Tim. 1:9.*
New, are created in. *Eph. 4:24.*
Possess. *1 Cor. 3:17; Heb. 3:1.*
Have their fruit in. *Rom. 6:22.*
Should follow after. *Heb. 12:14.*
Should serve God in. *Lk. 1:74-75.*
Should yield their members as
instruments of. *Rom. 6:13, 19.*

Should present their bodies to
God in. *Rom. 12:1.*
Should lives their lives in.
1 Pet. 1:15; 2 Pet. 3:11.
Should continue in. *Lk. 1:75.*
Should seek perfection in. *2 Cor. 7:1.*
Will be presented to God in.
Col. 1:22; 1 Thess. 3:13.
Will continue in, forever. *Rev. 22:11.*
The behaviour of older women
should be suitable, in. *Titus 2:3.*
A promise to women who
continue in. *1 Tim. 2:15.*
Promised to the Church. *Is. 35:8.
Obad. verse 17. Zech. 14:20-21.*
Adorns the Church. *Ps. 93:5.*
The Church is the beauty of.
1 Chron. 16:29; Ps. 29:2.
The Word of God is the means of
producing. *Jn. 17:17; 2 Tim. 3:16-17.*
Is the result of
The manifestation of God's
grace. *Titus 2:3, 11-12.*
Subjection to God. *Rom. 6:22.*
Union with Christ. *Jn. 15:4-5.*
Required in prayer. *1 Tim. 2:8.*
Ministers should
Possess. *Titus 1:8.*
Avoid everything inconsistent
with. *Lev. 21:6; Is. 52:11.*
Be examples of. *1 Tim. 4:12.*
Exhort to. *Heb. 12:14; 1 Pet. 1:14-16.*
Motives for:
The glory of God. *Jn. 15:8; Phil. 1:11.*
The mercies of God. *Rom. 12:1-2.*
The dissolution of all things.
2 Pet. 3:11.
Chastisements are intended to
produce, in the saints. *Heb. 12:10.*
Should lead to separation from
the wicked. *Num. 16:21, 26; 2 Cor. 6:17-18.*
Hypocrites pretend to have. *Is. 65:5.*
The wicked are without. *1 Tim. 1:9;
2 Tim. 3:2.*
Some examples. **David:** *Ps. 86:2.*
Israel: *Jer. 2:3.* **John the Baptist:**
Mk. 6:20. **Prophets:** *Lk. 1:70.* **Paul:**
1 Thess. 2:10. **Wives of the Patriarchs**
(founding Fathers): *1 Pet. 3:5.*

HOLINESS OF GOD, THE

Is incomparable. *Ex. 15:11; 1 Sam. 2:3.*

Is shown in his

Character. *Ps. 22:3; Jn. 17:11.*

Name. *Is. 57:15; Lk. 1:49.*

Words. *Ps. 60:6; Jer. 23:9.*

Works. *Ps. 145:17.*

Kingdom. *Ps. 47:8.*

Is pledged for the fulfilment of

His promises. *Ps. 89:35.*

His judgements. *Amos 4:2.*

The saints are commanded to imitate. *Lev. 11:44 with 1 Pet. 1:15-16.*

The saints should praise. *Ps. 30:4.*

Should produce reverential fear. *Rev. 15:4.*

Requires holy service. *Josh. 24:19. Ps. 93:5.*

The heavenly hosts adore. *Is. 6:3; Rev. 4:8.*

Should be magnified. *1 Chron. 16:10; Ps. 48:1, 99:3, 5; Rev. 15:4.*

HOLY SPIRIT IS GOD, THE

As Jehovah. *Ex. 17:7 with Heb. 3:7-9; Num. 12:6 with 2 Pet. 1:21.*

As Jehovah of Hosts. *Is. 6:3, 8-10 with Acts 28:25.*

As Jehovah, Most High. *Ps. 78:17, 21 with Acts 7:51.*

Being invoked as Jehovah. *Lk. 2:26-29; Acts 4:23-25 with Acts 1:16, 20; 2 Thess. 3:5.*

As being called God. *Acts 5:3-4.*

As eternal. *Heb. 9:14.*

As omnipresent (present everywhere). *Ps. 139:7-13.*

As omniscient (knowing all things). *1 Cor. 2:10.*

As omnipotent (all-powerful). *Lk. 1:35; Rom. 15:19.*

As the Spirit of glory and of God. *1 Pet. 4:14.*

As Creator. *Gen. 1:26-27 with Job 33:4.*

As equal with, and one with, the Father. *Mat. 28:19; 2 Cor. 13:14.*

As Sovereign Disposer of all things. *Dan. 4:35 with 1 Cor. 12:6, 11.*

As Author of the new birth. *Jn. 3:5-6 with 1 Jn. 5:4.*

As raising Christ from the dead. *Acts 2:24 with 1 Pet. 3:18; Heb. 13:20 with Rom. 1:4.*

As inspiring Scripture. *2 Tim. 3:16 with 2 Pet 1:21.*

As the source of wisdom. *1 Cor. 12:8.*

As the source of miraculous power. *Mat. 12:28 with Lk. 11:20; Acts 19:11 with Rom. 15:19.*

As appointing and sending ministers. *Acts 13:2, 4 with Mat. 9:38; Acts 20:28.*

As directing where the gospel should be preached. *Acts 16:6-7, 10.*

As dwelling in the saints. *Jn. 14:17 with 1 Cor 14:25; 1 Cor. 3:16 with 1 Cor. 6:19.*

As Comforter of the Church. *Acts 9:31 with 2 Cor. 1:3.*

As sanctifying the Church. *Ezek. 37:28 with Rom. 15:16.*

As the Witness. *Heb. 10:15 with 1 Jn. 5:9.*

HOLY SPIRIT, THE COMFORTER, THE

Proceeds from the Father and the Son. *Jn. 15:26.*

Given

By the Father. *Jn. 14:16.*

By Christ. *Is. 61:3.*

Through Christ's intercession. *Jn. 14:16.*

Sent in the name of Christ. *Jn. 14:26.*

Sent by Christ from the Father. *Jn. 15:26, 16:7.*

As such he

Communicates joy to the saints. *Rom. 14:17; Gal. 5:22; 1 Thess. 1:6.*

Edifies the Church. *Acts 9:31.*

Testifies of Christ. *Jn. 15:26.*

Imparts the love of God. *Rom. 5:3-5.*

Imparts hope. *Rom. 15:13; Gal. 5:5.*

Teaches the saints. *Jn. 14:26.*

Dwells with, and is in the saints. *Jn. 14:17.*

Abides forever with the saints. *Jn. 14:16.*

Is known by the saints. *Jn. 14:17.*

The world cannot receive. *Jn. 14:17.*

HOLY SPIRIT, THE TEACHER, THE

Was promised. *Prov. 1:23.*

As the Spirit of wisdom. *Is. 11:2, 40:13-14.*

He was given

In answer to prayer. *Eph. 1:16-17.*

To the saints. *Neh. 9:20; 1 Cor. 2:12-13.*

He is needed for. *1 Cor. 2:9-10.*

As such he

Reveals the things of God. *1 Cor. 10:13.*

Reveals the things of Christ. *Jn. 16:14.*

Brings the words of Christ to remembrance. *Jn. 14:26.*

Directs us in the way of godliness. *Is. 30:21; Ezek. 36:27.*

Teaches the saints how to answer their persecutors. *Mk. 13:11; Lk. 12:12.*

Enables ministers to teach. *1 Cor. 12:8.*

Guides into all truth. *Jn. 14:26, 16:13.*

Attends to the instruction of. *Rev. 2:7, 11, 29.*

The natural man will not receive the things of. *1 Cor. 2:14.*

HOMOSEXUALITY (SODOMY)

Sodom

Was guilty of great sins and is the first reference to. *Gen. 19:47*

Was punished extensively by God. *Gen. 19:47*

Became a symbol of persecution. *Rev. 11:8*

Homosexuality

Was forbidden under the Law. *Lev. 18:6-7; Deut. 22:30*

Is called an abomination. *Lev. 18:20, 20:13*

Defiles the land. *Lev. 18:24-28*

Was the sin of Gibeah. *Judges 19:22-24*

Is called a perversion. *Deut. 23:17*

Is called a vile passion. *Romans 1:26-27*

Historical references to homosexuals

Were tolerated by King Rehoboam. *1 Kings 14:24*

Were banished by King Asa. *1 Kings 15:12*

Were banished by King Jehoshaphat. *1 Kings 22:46*

King Hilkiah destroyed their shrines. *2 Kings 23:7*

Homosexuals

Have no place in God's kingdom. *1 Cor. 6:9*

May repent and be changed. *1 Cor 6:11*

Will be punished in the Day of Judgement. *2 Pet. 2:6-9*

Will suffer eternal fire. *Jude verse 7*

HOPE

In God. *Ps. 39:7; 1 Pet. 1:21.*

In Christ. *1 Cor. 15:19; 1 Tim. 1:1.*

In God's promises. *Acts 26:6-7; Titus 1:2.*

In the mercy of God. *Ps. 33:18.*

Is a work of the Holy Spirit. *Rom. 15:13; Gal. 5:5.*

Is obtained through

Grace. *2 Thess. 2:16.*

The Word. *Ps. 119:81.*

Patience and comfort of the Scripture. *Rom. 15:4.*

The gospel. *Col. 1:5, 23.*

Faith. *Rom. 5:1-2; Gal. 5:5.*

The result of experience. *Rom. 5:4*

Is described as

Good. *2 Thess. 2:16.*

Lively. *1 Pet. 1:3.*

Sure and steadfast. *Heb. 6:19.*

Gladdening. *Prov. 10:28.*

Blessed. *Titus 2:13.*

Does not make us ashamed. *Rom. 5:5.*

Triumphs over difficulties. *Rom. 4:18.*

Is an encouragement to be bold in preaching. *2 Cor. 3:12.*

The saints

Are called to. *Eph. 4:4.*

Rejoice in. *Rom. 5:2, 12:12.*
Have all the same. *Eph. 4:4.*
Have, in death. *Prov. 14:32.*
Should abound in. *Rom. 15:13.*
Should look for the object of.
Titus 2:13.
Should not be ashamed of.
Ps. 119:116.
Should hold fast. *Heb. 3:6.*
Should not be moved from.
Col. 1:23.
Should continue in. *Ps. 71:14;*
1 Pet. 1:13.
Connected with faith and love.
1 Cor. 13:13.
The objects of:
Salvation. *1 Thess. 5:8.*
Righteousness. *Gal. 5:5.*
Christ's glorious appearing.
Titus 2:13.
The resurrection. *Acts 23:6, 24:15.*
Eternal life. *Titus 1:2, Titus 3:7.*
Glory. *Rom. 5:2; Col. 1:27.*
Leads to purity. *1 Jn. 3:3.*
Leads to patience. *Rom. 8:25;*
1 Thess. 1:3.
Seek for a full assurance of.
Heb. 6:11.
Be ready to give an answer
concerning. *1 Pet. 3:15.*
Encouragement to. *Hos. 2:15;*
Zech. 9:12.
Encourage others to. *Ps. 130:7.*
The happiness of. *Ps. 146:5.*
Life is the season of. *Eccl. 9:4;*
Is. 38:18.
The wicked have no grounds for.
Eph. 2:12.
Of the wicked, it
Resides in their worldly
possessions. *Job 31:24.*
Will make them ashamed.
Is. 20:5-6; Zech. 9:5.
Will perish. *Job 8:13, 11:20; Prov. 10:28.*
Will be extinguished at death.
Job 27:8.
Illustrated by: **An anchor**: *Heb. 6:19.*
A helmet: *1 Thess. 5:8.*

Some examples. **Abraham**:
Rom. 4:18. **David**: *Ps. 39:7.* **Paul**:
Acts 24:15. **The Thessalonians**:
1 Thess. 1:3.

HOSPITALITY
Is commanded. *Rom. 12:13; 1 Pet. 4:9.*
Is required of ministers. *1 Tim. 3:2;*
Titus 1:8.
Is a test of Christian character.
1 Tim. 5:10.
Is to be shown particularly to
Strangers. *Heb. 13:2.*
The poor. *Is. 58:7; Lk. 14:13.*
Even enemies. *2 Kings 6:22-23;*
Rom. 12:20.
Encouragement to. *Lk. 14:14; Heb. 13:2.*

Some examples. **Melchizedek**:
Gen. 14:18. **Abraham**: *Gen. 18:3-8.* **Lot**:
Gen. 19:2-3. **Laban**: *Gen. 24:31.* **Jethro**:
Ex. 2:20. **Manoah**: *Judg. 13:15.* **Samuel**:
1 Sam. 9:22. **David**: *2 Sam. 6:19.* **Barzillai**:
2 Sam. 19:32. **A Shunammite**:
2 Kings 4:8. **Nehemiah**: *Neh. 5:17.* **Job**:
Job 31:17, 32. **Zaccheus**: *Lk. 19:6.* **Some**
Samaritans: *Jn. 4:40.* **Lydia**: *Acts 16:15.*
Jason: *Acts 17:7.* **Mnason**: *Acts 21:16.*
The people of Melita (Malta):
Acts 28:2. **Publius**: *Acts 28:7.* **Gaius**:
3 Jn. verses 5-6.

HUMAN NATURE OF CHRIST, THE
Was necessary for his mediatorial
office. *1 Tim. 2:5; Heb. 2:17.*
Is proved by his
Conception in the virgin Mary's
womb. *Mat. 1:18; Lk. 1:31.*
Birth. *Mat. 1:16, 25, 2:2; Lk. 2:7, 11.*
Partaking of flesh and blood.
Jn. 1:14; Heb. 2:14.
Having a human soul. *Mat. 26:38;*
Lk. 23:46; Acts 2:31.
Circumcision. *Lk. 2:21.*
Growth in wisdom and stature.
Lk. 2:52.
Weeping. *Lk. 19:41; Jn. 11:35.*
Hungering. *Mat. 4:2, 21:18.*
Thirsting. *Jn. 4:7, 19:28.*

Sleeping. *Mat. 8:24; Mk. 4:38.*
Being subject to weariness. *Jn. 4:6.*
Being a man of sorrows. *Is. 53:3-4; Lk. 22:44; Jn. 11:33, 12:27.*
Being buffeted. *Mat. 26:67; Lk. 22:64.*
Enduring indignities. *Lk. 23:11.*
Being scourged. *Mat. 27:26; Jn. 19:1.*
Being nailed to the cross. *Ps. 22:16 with Lk. 23:33.*
Death. *Jn. 19:30.*
Side being pierced. *Jn. 19:34.*
Burial. *Mat. 27:59-60; Mk. 15:46.*
Resurrection. *Acts 3:15; 2 Tim. 2:8.*

He was like us in all things, except in sin. *Acts 3:22; Phil. 2:7-8; Heb. 2:17.*

He was without sin. *Heb. 7:26, 28; 1 Jn. 3:5.*

He was submitted to the evidence of the senses. *Lk. 24:39; Jn. 20:27; 1 Jn. 1:1-2.*

He was of the seed of
The woman. *Gen. 3:15; Is. 7:14; Jer. 31:22; Lk. 1:31; Gal. 4:4.*
Abraham. *Gen. 22:18 with Gal. 3:16; Heb. 2:16.*
David. *2 Sam. 7:12, 16; Ps. 89:35-36; Jer. 23:5; Mat. 22:42; Mk. 10:47; Acts 2:30, 13:23; Rom. 1:3.*

The genealogy of. *Mat. 1:1-17; Lk. 3:23-37.*
Affirmed by himself. *Mat. 8:20, 16:13.*
Confession of, is a test of belonging to God. *Jn. 4:2.*
Acknowledged by men. *Mk. 6:3; Jn. 7:27, 19:5; Acts 2:22.*
Denied by the Antichrist. *1 Jn. 4:3; 2 Jn. verse 7.*

HUMILITY

Necessary for the service of God. *Mic. 6:8.*
Christ is an example of. *Mat. 11:29; Jn. 13:14-15; Phil. 2:5-8.*
A characteristic of the saints. *Ps. 34:2.*

Those who have it
Are highly regarded by God. *Ps. 138:6; Is. 66:2.*
Are heard by God. *Ps. 9:12, 10:17.*

Enjoy the presence of God. *Is. 57:15.*
Are delivered by God. *Job 22:29.*
Are lifted up by God. *Jas. 4:10.*
Are exalted by God. *Lk. 14:11, 18:14.*
Are the greatest in Christ's kingdom. *Mat. 18:4.*
Receive more grace. *Prov. 3:34; Jas. 4:6.*
Are upheld in honour. *Prov. 18:12, 29:23.*

Is before honour. *Prov. 15:33.*
Leads to riches, honour, and life. *Prov. 22:4.*

The saints should
Put on. *Col. 3:12.*
Be clothed with. *1 Pet. 5:5.*
Walk with. *Eph. 4:1-2.*
Beware of false. *Col. 2:18, 23.*

Afflictions are intended to produce. *Lev. 26:41; Deut. 8:3; Lam. 3:20.*
Lack of, is to be condemned. *2 Chron. 33:23; 2 Chron. 36:12; Jer. 44:10; Dan. 5:22.*
Temporal judgements are averted by. *2 Chron. 7:14; 2 Chron. 12:6-7.*
The excellence of. *Prov. 16:19.*
The blessedness of. *Mat. 5:3.*

Some examples. **Abraham**: *Gen. 18:27.* **Jacob**: *Gen. 32:10.* **Moses**: *Ex. 3:11, 4:10.* **Joshua**: *Josh. 7:6.* **Gideon**: *Judg. 6:15.* **David**: *1 Chron. 29:14.* **Hezekiah**: *2 Chron. 32:26.* **Manasseh**: *2 Chron. 33:12.* **Josiah**: *2 Chron. 34:27.* **Job**: *Job 40:4, 42:6.* **Isaiah**: *Is. 6:5.* **Jeremiah**: *Jer. 1:6.* **John the Baptist**: *Mat. 3:14.* **A centurion**: *Mat. 8:8.* **A woman of Canaan**: *Mat. 15:27.* **Elizabeth**: *Lk. 1:43.* **Peter**: *Lk. 5:8.* **Paul**: *Acts 20:19.*

HUMILITY OF CHRIST, THE

Declared by himself. *Mat. 11:29.*
Shown in his
Taking our nature. *Phil. 2:7; Heb. 2:16.*
Birth. *Lk. 2:4-7.*
Subjection to his parents. *Lk. 2:51.*

Station in life. *Mat. 13:55; Jn. 9:29.*

Poverty. *Lk. 9:58; 2 Cor. 8. 9.*

Partaking of our infirmities.
Heb. 4:15, 5:7.

Submitting to ordinances.
Mat. 3:13-15.

Becoming a servant. *Mat. 20:28;*
Lk. 22:27; Phil. 2:7.

Associating with the despised.
Mat. 9:10-11; Lk. 15:1-2.

Refusing honours. *Jn. 5:41, 6:15.*

Entry into Jerusalem. *Zech. 9:9*
with Mat. 21:5, 7.

Washing his diciples' feet.
Jn. 13:5.

Obedience. *Jn. 6:38; Heb. 10:9.*

Submitting to suffering. *Is. 50:6,*
53:7 with Acts 8:32; Mat. 26: 37-39.

Exposing himself to reproach
and contempt. *Ps. 22:6, 69:9 with*
Rom. 15:3; Is. 53:3.

Death. *Jn. 10:15, 17-18; Phil. 2:8;*
Heb. 12:2.

The saints should imitate.
Phil. 2:5-8.

On account of, he was despised.
Mk. 6:3; Jn. 9:29.

His exaltation was the result of.
Phil. 2:9.

HUSBANDS

Should have only one wife.
Gen. 2:24; 1 Tim. 3:2, 12.

Have authority over their wives.
Gen. 3:16; 1 Cor. 11:3; Eph. 5:23.

Duty of, to their wives

To respect them. *1 Pet. 3:7.*

To love them. *Eph. 5:25, etc; Col. 3:19.*

To regard them as themselves.
Gen. 2:23 with Mat. 19:5.

To be faithful to them. *Prov. 5:19;*
Mal. 2:14-15.

To dwell with them for life.
Gen. 2:24; Mat. 19:3-9.

To comfort them. *1 Sam. 1:8.*

To consult with them. *Gen. 31:4-7.*

Not to leave them, though
unbelieving. *1 Cor. 7:11-12, 14, 16.*

Duties of, not to interfere with

their duties to Christ. *Lk. 14:26 with*
Mat. 19:29.

Examples of good wives. **Isaac's:**
Gen. 24:67. **Elkanah's:** *1 Sam. 1:4, 5.*

Examples of bad wives.
Solomon's: *1 Kings 11:1.* **Ahasuerus':**
Esth. 1:10, 11.

HYPOCRITES

God knows and detects. *Is. 29:15-16.*

Christ knew and detected.
Mat. 22:18.

God has no pleasure in. *Is. 9:17.*

Will not come before God. *Job 13:16.*

Are described as

Wilfully blind. *Mat. 23:17, 19, 26.*

Vile. *Is. 32:6.*

Self-righteous. *Is. 65:5; Lk. 18:11.*

Covetous. *Ezek. 33:31; 2 Pet. 2:3.*

Ostentatious. *Mat. 6:2, 5, 16, 23:5.*

Censorious. *Mat. 7:3-5; Lk. 13:14-15.*

Putting tradition before the
Word of God. *Mat. 15:1-3.*

Exact in minor, but neglecting
important duties. *Mat. 23:23-24.*

Having only a form of godliness. *2 Tim.3:5.*

Seeking only outward purity.
Lk. 11:39.

Professing but not practising.
Ezek. 33:31-32; Mat. 23:3; Rom. 2:17-23.

Producing only lip-worship.
Is. 29:13 with Mat. 15:8.

Glorying in appearance only.
2 Cor. 5:12.

Trusting in privileges. *Jer. 7:4; Mat. 3:9.*

Apparently zealous in the
things of God. *Is. 58:2.*

Zealous in making proselytes.
Mat. 23:15.

Devouring widows' houses.
Mat. 23:14.

Loving pre-eminence. *Mat. 23:6-7.*

Their worship is not acceptable
to God. *Is. 1:11-15, 58:3-5; Mat. 15:9.*

Joy of, but only for a moment.
Job 20:5.

Hope of, perishes. *Job 8:13, 27:8-9.*
Heap up wrath. *Job 36:13.*
Fearfulness will surprise. *Is. 33:14.*
Destroy others by their slander. *Prov. 11:9.*
When in power, they are a snare. *Job 34:30.*
Their apostasy will abound in. *1 Tim. 4:2.*
Beware of the principles of. *Lk. 12:1.*
Spirit of, hinders growth in grace. *1 Pet. 2:1.*

Woe to. *Is. 29:15; Mat. 23:13.*
The punishment of. *Job 15:34; Is. 10:6; Jer. 42:20, 22; Mat. 24:51.*
Illustrated. *Mat. 23:27-28; Lk. 11:44.*

Some examples. **Cain**: *Gen. 4:3.*
Absolom: *2 Sam. 15:7-8.* **The Jews**: *Jer. 3:10.* **The Pharisees**, etc: *Mat. 16:3.*
Judas Iscariot: *Mat. 26:49.* **The Herodians**: *Mk. 12:13, 15.* **Ananias**: *Acts 5:1-8.* **Simon**: *Acts 8:13-23.*

I

IDLENESS AND SLOTH
Forbidden. *Rom. 12:11; Heb. 6:12.*
Produce apathy. *Prov. 12:27, 26:15.*
Next to extravagance. *Prov. 18:9.*
Accompanied by conceit. *Prov. 26:16.*
Lead to
Poverty. *Prov. 10:4, 20:13.*
Need. *Prov. 20:4, 24:34.*
Hunger. *Prov. 19:15, 24:34.*
Bondage. *Prov. 12:24.*
Disappointment. *Prov. 13:4, 21:25.*
Ruin. *Prov. 24:30-31; Eccl. 10:18.*
Gossip and meddling. *1 Tim. 5:13.*
Effects of, afford instruction to others. *Prov. 24:30-32.*
A protest against. *Prov. 6:6, 9.*
False excuses for. *Prov. 20:4, 22:13.*
Illustrated. *Prov. 26:14; Mat. 25:18, 26.*

Some examples. **The watchmen**: *Is. 56:10.* **The Athenians**: *Acts 17:21.*
The Thessalonians: *2 Thess. 3:11.*

IDOLATRY
Forbidden. *Ex. 20:2-3. Deut. 5:7.*
Consists of
Making images. *Ex. 20:4; Deut. 5:8.*
Bowing down to images. *Ex. 20:5; Deut. 5:9.*
Worshipping images. *Is. 44:17; Dan. 3:5, 10, 15.*
Sacrificing to images. *Ps. 106:38; Acts 7:41.*
Worshipping other gods. *Deut. 30:17; Ps. 81:9.*
Mentioning the names of other gods. *Ex. 23:13.*
Following after other gods. *Deut. 8:19.*
Speaking in the name of other gods. *Deut. 18:20.*
Looking to other gods. *Hos. 3:1.*
Serving other gods. *Deut. 7:4; Jer. 5:19.*
Fearing other gods. *2 Kings 17:35.*
Sacrificing to other gods. *Ex. 22:20.*
Worshipping the true God with an image, etc. *Ex. 32:4-6 with Ps. 106:19-20.*
Worshipping angels. *Col. 2:18.*
Worshipping the host of heaven. *Deut. 4:19, 17:3.*
Worshipping demons. *Mat. 4:9-10; Rev. 9:20.*
Worshipping the dead. *Ps. 106:28.*
Setting up idols in the heart. *Ezek. 14:3-4.*
Covetousness. *Eph. 5:5; Col. 3:5.*
Sensuality. *Phil. 3:19.*
Is changing the glory of God into an image. *Rom. 1:23 with Acts 17:29.*
Is changing the truth of God into a lie. *Rom. 1:25 with Is. 41:20.*
Is a work of the flesh. *Gal. 5:19-20.*
Is incompatible with the service of God. *Gen. 35:2-3; Josh. 24:23; 1 Sam. 7:3; 1 Kings 18:21; 2 Cor. 6:15-16.*
Is described as
An abomination to God. *Deut. 7:25.*

Hateful to God. *Deut. 16:22; Jer. 44:4.*
Vain and foolish. *Ps. 115:4-8;*
Is. 44:19; Jer. 10:3.
Bloody. *Ezek. 23:39.*
Abominable. *1 Pet. 4:3.*
Unprofitable. *Judg. 10:14; Is. 46:7.*
Defiling. *Ezek. 20:7; Ezek. 36:18.*

Those who practise,
Forget God. *Deut. 8:19; Jer. 18:15.*
Go astray from God. *Ezek. 44:10.*
Pollute the name of God.
Ezek. 20:39.
Defile the sanctuary of God.
Ezek. 5:11.
Are estranged from God. *Ezek. 14:5.*
Forsake God. *2 Kings 22:17; Jer. 16:11.*
Hate God. *2 Chron. 19:2-3.*
Provoke God. *Deut. 31:30; Is. 65:3;*
Jer. 25:6.
Are vain in their thoughts.
Rom. 1:21.
Are ignorant and foolish.
Rom. 1:21-22.
Inflame themselves. *Is. 57:5.*
Hold fast their deceit. *Jer. 8:5.*
Are carried away by it. *1 Cor. 12:2.*
Go after it in their hearts.
Ezek. 20:16.
Are mad for it. *Jer. 50:38.*
Boast of it. *Ps. 97:7.*
Have fellowship with devils.
1 Cor. 10:20.
Ask counsel of their idols. *Hos. 4:12.*
Look to the idols for deliverance. *Is. 44:17, 45:20.*
Swear by their idols. *Amos 8:14.*
Objects of, are numerous. *1 Cor. 8:5.*

Objects of, are described as
Strange gods. *Gen. 35:2, 4; Josh. 24:20.*
Other gods. *Judg. 2:12, 17; 1 Kings 14:9.*
New gods. *Deut. 32:17; Judg. 5:8.*
Gods that cannot save. *Is. 45:20.*
Gods that have not made the heavens. *Jer. 10:11.*
No gods. *Jer. 5:7; Gal. 4:8.*
Moulded gods. *Ex. 34:17; Lev. 19:4.*
Moulded images. *Deut. 27:15;*
Is. 45:20; Hos. 11:2; Hab. 2:18.
Senseless idols. *Deut. 4:28; Ps. 115:5, 7.*

Dumb idols. *Hab. 2:18; 1 Cor. 12:2.*
Dumb stones. *Hab. 2:19.*
Stones and trees. *Jer. 3:9; Hos. 4:12.*
Abominations. *Is. 44:19; Jer. 32:34.*
Images of abomination.
Ezek. 7:20.
Idols of abomination. *Ezek. 16:36.*
Stumbling-blocks. *Ezek. 14:3.*
Teachers of lies. *Hab. 2:18.*
Wind and confusion. *Is. 41:29.*
Nothing. *Is. 41:24; 1 Cor. 8:4.*
Helpless. *Jer. 10:5.*
Vanity. *Jer. 18:15.*
Vanities of the Gentiles. *Jer. 14:22.*
Making idols for the purpose of,
is described and ridiculed. *Is. 44:10-20.*
Obstinate sinners are judicially
given up to. *Deut.4:28, 28:64; Hos.4:17.*
Warnings against. *Deut. 4:15-19.*
Exhortations to turn away from.
Ezek. 14:6, 20:7; Acts 14:15.
Renounced on conversion.
1 Thess. 1:9.

The saints should
Keep themselves from. *Josh. 23:7;*
1 Jn. 5:21.
Flee from. *1 Cor. 10:14.*
Not have anything connected
with, in their homes. *Deut. 7:26.*
Not partake in anything
connected with. *1 Cor. 10:19-20.*
Not have anything to do with
those who practise. *Josh. 23:7;*
1 Cor. 5:11.
Not make a covenant with
those who practise. *Ex. 34:12, 15;*
Deut. 7:2.
Not intermarry with those who
practise. *Ex. 34:16; Deut. 7:3.*
Testify against. *Acts 14:15, 19:26.*
Refuse to engage in, though
threatened with death. *Dan. 3:18.*
The saints are preserved by God
from. *1 Kings 19:18 with Rom. 11:4.*
The saints refuse to receive the
worship of. *Acts 10:25-26, 14:11-15.*
Angels refuse to receive the
worship of. *Rev. 22:8-9.*

Destruction of, promised.
Ezek. 36:25; Zech. 13:2.
Everything connected with, should be destroyed. *Ex. 34:13; Deut. 7:5; 2 Sam. 5:21; 2 Kings 23:14.*
A Woe denounced against. *Hab. 2:19.*
A curse pronounced on. *Deut. 27:15.*
Punishment of, leads to
Judicial death. *Deut. 17:2-5.*
Dreadful judgements that end in death. *Jer. 8:2, 16:1-11.*
Banishment. *Jer. 8:3; Hos. 8:5-8; Amos 5:26-27.*
Exclusion from heaven. *1 Cor. 6:9-10; Eph. 5:5; Rev. 22:15.*
Eternal torment. *Rev. 14:9-11, 21:8.*

Some examples. **Israel:** *Ex. 32:1; 2 Kings 17:12.* **The Philistines:** *Judg. 16:23.* **Micah:** *Judg. 17:4-5.* **Solomon:** *1 Kings 11:1-8.* **Jeroboam:** *1 Kings 12:28.* **Maachah:** *1 Kings 15:13.* **Ahab:** *1 Kings 16:31.* **Jezebel:** *1 Kings 18:19.* **Sennacharib:** *2 Kings 19:37.* **Manasseh:** *2 Kings 21:4-7.* **Amon:** *2 Kings 21:21.* **Ahaz:** *2 Chron. 28:3.* **Judah:** *Jer. 11:13.* **Belshazzar:** *Dan. 5:23.* **The people of Lystra:** *Acts 14:11-12.* **The Athenians:** *Acts 17:16.* **The Ephesians:** *Acts 19:28.*

Some examples of zeal against idolatry. **Asa:** *1 Kings 15:12.* **Josiah:** *2 Kings 23:5.* **Jehoshaphat:** *2 Chron. 17:6.* **Israel:** *2 Chron. 31:1.* **Manasseh:** *2 Chron. 33:15.*

IGNORANCE TOWARDS GOD
Ignorance of Christ is. *Jn. 8:19.*
Evidenced by
A lack of love. *1 Jn. 4:8.*
Not keeping his commands. *1 Jn. 2:4.*
Living in sin. *Titus 1:16; 1 Jn. 3:6.*
Leads to
Error. *Mat. 22:29.*
Idolatry. *Is. 44:19; Acts 17:29-30.*
Alienation from God. *Eph. 4:18.*

Sinful lusts. *1 Thess. 4:5; 1 Pet. 1:14.*
Persecuting the saints. *Jn. 15:21; Jn. 16:3.*
Is no excuse for sin. *Lev. 4:2; Lk. 12:48.*
The wicked are in a state of. *Jer. 9:3; Jn. 15:21, 17:25; Acts 17:30.*
The wicked choose. *Job 21:14; Rom. 1:28.*
The punishment of. *Ps. 79:6; 2 Thess. 1:8.*
Ministers should
Have compassion on those in. *Heb. 5:2.*
Labour to remove. *Acts 17:23.*
Some examples. **Pharaoh:** *Ex. 5:2.* **The Israelites:** *Ps. 95:10; Is. 1:3.* **False prophets:** *Is. 56:10-11.* **The Jews,** *Lk. 23:34.* **Nicodemus:** *Jn. 3:10.* **The Gentiles:** *Gal. 4:8.* **Paul:** *1 Tim. 1:13.*

INDUSTRY
Is commanded. *Eph. 4:28; 1 Thess. 4:11.*
Was required of man in his state of innocence. *Gen. 2:15.*
Was required of man after the Fall. *Gen. 3:23.*
Was to be suspended on the Sabbath. *Ex. 20:10.*
Characteristic of godly women. *Prov. 31:13, etc.*
Early rising necessary for. *Prov. 31:15.*
Necessary to supply
Our own needs. *Acts 20:34; 1 Thess. 2:9.*
The needs of others. *Acts 20:35; Eph. 4:28.*
The lazy are devoid of. *Prov. 24:30-31.*
Leads to
An increase in possessions. *Prov. 13:11.*
The affection of relatives. *Prov. 31:28.*
A general commendation. *Prov. 31:31.*
Illustrated. *Prov. 6:6-8.*

Some examples. **Rachel:** *Gen. 29:9.* **Jacob:** *Gen. 31:6.* **Jethro's daughters:**

Ex. 2:16. **Ruth**: *Ruth 2:2-3.* **Jeroboam**:
1 Kings 11:28. **David**: *1 Sam. 16:11.*
Jewish Elders: *Ezra 6:14-15.* **Dorcas**:
Acts 9:39. **Paul**: *Acts 18:3; 1 Cor. 4:12.*

INDWELLING OF THE HOLY SPIRIT, THE

In his Church, as his temple.
1 Cor. 3:16.
In the body of the saints, as his
temple. *1 Cor. 6:19; 2 Cor. 6:16.*
Promised to the saints. *Ezek. 36:27.*
The saints enjoy. *Is. 63:11; 2 Tim. 1:14.*
The saints are full of. *Acts 6:5; Eph. 5:18.*
Is the means of
Giving life. *Rom. 8:11.*
Guiding. *Jn. 16:13; Gal. 5:18.*
Making fruitful. *Gal. 5:22.*
A proof of being Christ's. *Rom. 8:9.*
A proof of adoption. *Rom. 8:15; Gal. 4:6.*
Is abiding. *1 Jn. 2:27.*
Those who do not have
Are sensual. *Jude verse 19.*
Are without Christ. *Rom. 8:9.*
Is opposed by the worldly nature.
Gal. 5:17.

INGRATITUDE

A characteristic of the wicked.
Ps. 38:20; 2 Tim. 3:2.
Often shown
By relatives. *Job 19:14.*
By servants. *Job 19:15-16.*
To benefactors. *Ps. 109:5; Eccl. 9:15.*
To friends in distress. *Ps. 38:11.*
The saints avoid the guilt of. *Ps. 7:4-5.*
Should be met with
Prayer. *Ps. 35:12-13, 109:4.*
Faithfulness. *Gen. 31:38-42.*
Persevering love. *2 Cor. 12:15.*
The punishment of. *Prov. 17:13;
Jer. 18:20-21.*

Some examples. **Laban**: *Gen. 31:6-7.*
The Chief Butler: *Gen. 40:23.* **Israel**:
Ex. 17:4. **The men of Keilah**: *1 Sam.
23:5, 12.* **Saul**: *1 Sam. 24:17.* **Nabal**:
1 Sam. 25:5-11, 21. **Absolom**: *2 Sam. 15:6.*
Joash: *2 Chron. 24:22.*

INGRATITUDE TO GOD

A characteristic of the wicked.
Rom. 1:21.
Is inexcusable. *Is. 1:2-3; Rom. 1:21.*
Is unreasonable. *Jer. 2:5-6, 31; Mic. 6:2, 3.*
The stupidity of. *Deut. 32:6.*
The guilt of. *Ps. 106:7, 21; Jer. 2:11-13.*
Prosperity is likely to produce.
Deut. 31:20, 32:15; Jer. 5:7-11.
Warnings against. *Deut. 8:11-14;
1 Sam. 12:24-25.*
The punishment of. *Neh. 9:20-27;
Hos. 2:8-9.*
Illustrated. *Is. 5:1-7; Ezra 16:1-15.*

Some examples. **Israel**: *Deut. 32:18.*
Saul: *1 Sam. 15:17-19.* **David**:
2 Sam. 12:7-9. **Nebuchadnezzar**:
Dan. 5:18-21. **Lepers**: *Lk. 17:17-18.*

INJUSTICE

Forbidden. *Lev. 19:15, 35. Deut. 16:19.*
Specially to be avoided towards
The poor. *Ex. 23:6; Prov. 22:16.*
The stranger and fatherless.
Ex. 22:21-22; Deut. 24:17; Jer. 22:3.
Servants. *Job 31:13-14.*
Of the least kind, is condemned.
Lk. 16:10.
God
Takes note of. *Eccl. 5:8.*
Does not approve of. *Lam. 3:35-36.*
Abominates. *Prov. 17:15, 20:10.*
Hears the cry of those who
suffer. *Jas. 5:4.*
Is provoked to avenge. *Ps. 12:5.*
Brings a curse. *Deut. 27:17, 19.*
A bad example leads to. *Ex. 23:2.*
Intemperance leads to. *Prov. 31:5.*
Covetousness leads to. *Jer. 6:13.*
The saints should
Hate. *Prov. 29:27.*
Testify against. *Ps. 58:1-2; Mic. 3:8-9.*
Bear, patiently. *1 Cor. 6:7.*
Take no vengeance for. *Mat. 5:39.*
The wicked
Deal with. *Is. 26:10.*
Judge with. *Ps. 82:2; Eccl. 3:16; Hab. 1:4.*

Practise without shame. *Jer. 6:13, 15; Zeph. 3:5.*

The punishment of. *Prov. 11:7, 28:8; Amos 5:11-12; Amos 8:5-8; 1 Thess. 4:6.*

Some examples. **Potiphar**: *Gen. 39:20.* **The sons of Samuel**: *1 Sam. 8:3.* **Ahab**: *1 Kings 21:10, 15-16.* **The Jews**: *Is. 59:14.* **The Princes**, etc: *Dan. 6:4.* **Judas Iscariot**: *Mat. 27:4.* **Pilate**: *Mat. 27:24-26.* **Priests**, etc: *Acts 4:3.* **Festus**: *Acts 24:27.*

INSPIRATION OF THE HOLY SPIRIT, THE

Foretold. *Joel 2:28 with Acts 2:16-18.*

All Scripture is given by. *2 Tim. 3:16; 2 Pet. 1:21.*

The purpose of:

To reveal future events. *Acts 1:16, 28:25.*

To reveal the mysteries of God. *Amos 3:7; 1 Cor. 2:10.*

To give power to ministers. *Mic. 3:8; Acts 1:8.*

To direct ministers. *Ezek. 3:24-27; Acts 11:12; Acts 13:2.*

To control ministers. *Acts 16:6.*

To testify against sin. *2 Kings 17:13; Neh. 9:30; Mic. 3:8; Jn. 16:8-9.*

Modes of:

Varied. *Heb. 1:1.*

By secret impulse. *Judg. 13:25; 2 Pet. 1:21.*

By a voice. *Is. 6:8; Acts 8:29; Rev. 1:10.*

By visions. *Num. 12:6; Ezek. 11:24.*

By dreams. *Num. 12:6; Dan. 7:1.*

Necessary for prophesying. *Num. 11:25-27; 2 Chron. 20:14-17.*

Is irresistible. *Amos 3:8.*

Despisers of, are punished. *2 Chron. 36:15-16; Zech. 7:12.*

J

JEWS, THE

Descendants of Abraham. *Ps. 105:6; Jn. 8:33; Rom. 9:7.*

The people of God. *Deut. 32:9; 2 Sam. 7:24; Is. 51:16.*

Separated for God. *Ex. 33:16; Num. 23:9; Deut. 4:34.*

Beloved, for their fathers' sake. *Deut. 4:37, 10:15 with Rom. 11:28.*

Christ descended from. *Jn. 4:22; Rom. 9:5.*

The objects of

God's love. *Deut. 7:8, 23:5; Jer. 31:3.*

God's choice. *Deut. 7:6.*

God's protection. *Ps. 105:15; Zech. 2:8.*

The covenant was established with. *Ex. 6:4, 24:6-8, 34:27.*

Promises concerning, made to

Abraham. *Gen. 12:1-3, 13:14-17, 15:18, 17:7-8.*

Isaac. *Gen. 26:2-5, 24.*

Jacob. *Gen. 18. 12-15, 35:9-12.*

Themselves. *Ex. 6:7-8, 19:5-6; Deut. 26:18-19.*

Privileges of. *Ps. 76:1-2; Rom. 3:1-2, 9:4-5.*

Punished for

Idolatry. *Is. 65:3-7.*

Unbelief. *Rom. 11:20.*

Breaking the covenant. *Is. 24:5; Jer. 11:10.*

Transgressing the Law. *Is. 1:4, 7, 24:5-6.*

Changing the ordinances. *Is. 24:5.*

Killing the prophets. *Mat. 23:37-38.*

Charging on themselves the blood of Christ. *Mat. 27:25.*

Scattered among the nations. *Deut. 28:64; Ezek. 6:8, 36:19.*

Despised by the nations. *Ezek. 36:3.*

Their country trodden under foot by the Gentiles. *Deut. 28:49-52; Lk. 21:24.*

Their houses were left desolate. *Mat. 24:38.*

Deprived of civil and religious

privileges. *Hos. 3:4.*

Denunciations against those who

Cursed. *Gen. 27:29; Num. 24:9.*

Contended with. *Is. 41:11, 49:25.*

Oppressed. *Is. 49:26, 51:21-23.*

Hated. *Ps. 129:5; Ezek. 35:5-6.*

Aggravated the afflictions of. *Zech. 1:14-15.*

Slaughtered. *Ps. 79:1-7; Ezek. 35:5-6.*

God was mindful of. *Ps. 98:3; Is. 49:15-16.*

Christ was sent to. *Mat. 15:24, 21:37; Acts 3:20, 22, 26.*

Compassion of Christ to. *Mat. 23:37; Lk. 19:41.*

The gospel was preached to, first. *Mat. 10:6; Lk. 24:47; Acts 1:8.*

The blessedness of blessing. *Gen. 27:29.*

The blessedness of favouring. *Gen. 12:3; Ps. 122:6.*

Pray urgently for. *Ps. 122:8; Is. 62:1, 6-7; Jer. 31:7; Rom. 10:1.*

The saints remember. *Ps. 102:14, 137:5; Jer. 51:50.*

Promises concerning:

The pouring out of the Spirit upon them. *Ezek. 39:29; Zech. 12:10.*

The removal of their blindness. *Rom. 11:25; 2 Cor. 3:14-16.*

Their return and seeking after God. *Hos. 3:5.*

Their humiliation for the rejection of Christ. *Zech. 12:10.*

The pardon of sin. *Is. 44:22; Rom. 11:27.*

Salvation. *Is. 59:20 with Rom. 11:26.*

Sanctification. *Jer. 33:8; Ezek. 36:25; Zech. 12:1, 9.*

Joy occasioned by the conversion of. *Is. 44:23, 49:13, 52:8-9, 66:10.*

Made a blessing to the Gentiles by their conversion. *Is. 2:1-5, 60:5, 66:19; Rom. 11:12, 15.*

The re-union of. *Jer. 3:18; Is. 11:11-12; Ezek. 37:16-17, 20-22; Hos. 1:11; Mic. 2:12.*

Restoration to their own land. *Is. 11:15-16, 14:1-3, 27:12-13; Jer. 16:14-15; Ezek. 36:24, 37:21, 25, 39:25, 28; Lk. 21:24.*

The Gentiles are assisting in their restoration. *Is. 49:22-23, 60:10, 14, 61:4-6.*

The subjection of the Gentiles to. *Is. 60:11-12, 14.*

The future glory of. *Is. 60:19, 62:3-4; Zeph. 3:19-20; Zech. 2:5.*

The future prosperity of. *Is. 60:6-7, 9, 17, 61:4-6; Hos. 14:5-6.*

That Christ will appear among. *Is. 59:20; Zech. 14:4.*

That Christ will dwell among. *Ezek. 43:7, 9; Zech. 2:11.*

That Christ will reign over. *Is. 9:7; Ezek. 34:23, 37:24-25.*

The conversion of, is illustrated. *Ezek. 37:1-14; Rom. 11:24.*

JOY OF GOD OVER HIS PEOPLE, THE

Greatness of, is described. *Zeph. 3:17.*

On account of their

Repentance. *Lk. 15:7, 10.*

Faith. *Heb. 11:5-6.*

Fear of him. *Ps. 147:11.*

Praying to him. *Prov. 15:8.*

Hoping in his mercy. *Ps. 147:11.*

Meekness. *Ps. 149:4.*

Uprightness. *1 Chron. 29:17; Prov. 11:20.*

Leads him to

Prosper them. *Deut. 30:9.*

Do them good. *Deut. 28:63; Jer. 32:41.*

Deliver them. *2 Sam. 22:20.*

Comfort them. *Is. 65:19.*

Give them an inheritance. *Num. 14:8.*

Illustrated. *Is. 62:5. Lk. 15:23-24.*

An example in **Solomon**: *1 Kings 10:9.*

JOY

God gives. *Eccl. 2:26; Ps. 4:7.*

Christ was appointed to give. *Is. 61:3.*

Is a fruit of the Spirit. *Gal. 5:22.*

The gospel is good news of. *Lk. 2:10-11.*

God's Word brings. *Neh. 8:12; Jer. 15:16.*

The gospel, to be received with.

1 Thess. 1:6.

Promised to the saints. Ps. 132:16; Is. 35:10, 55:12, 56:7.

Prepared for the saints. Ps. 97:11.

Enjoined to the saints. Ps. 32:11; Phil. 3:1.

The fullness of, in God's presence. Ps. 16:11.

The futility of seeking, in earthly things. Eccl. 2:10-11, 11:8.

Experienced by

Believers. Lk. 24:52; Acts 16:34.

Peace-makers. Prov. 12:20.

The just. Prov. 21:15.

The wise, and discreet. Prov. 15:23.

Parents of good children. Prov. 23:24.

Increased in the meek. Is. 29:19.

Of the saints, is

In God. Ps. 89:16, 149:2; Hab. 3:18; Rom. 5:11.

In Christ. Lk. 1:47; Phil. 3:3.

In the Holy Spirit. Rom. 14:17.

Found in their election. Lk. 10:20.

Found in their salvation. Ps. 21:1; Is. 61:10.

For deliverance from bondage. Ps. 105:43; Jer. 31:10-13.

For the manifestation of goodness. 2 Chron. 7:10.

For temporal blessings. Joel 2:23-24.

For supplies of grace. Is. 12:3.

For divine protection. Ps. 5:11, 16:8-9.

For divine support. Ps. 28:7, 63:7.

For the victory of Christ. Jn. 16:33.

For the hope of glory. Rom. 5:2.

For the success of the gospel. Acts 15:3.

Of the saints, should be

Great. Zech. 9:9; Acts 8:8.

Abundant. 2 Cor. 8:2.

Exceeding. Ps. 21:6, 68:3.

Animated. Ps. 32:11; Lk. 6:23.

Unspeakable. 1 Pet. 1:8.

Full of glory. 1 Pet. 1:8.

Constant. 2 Cor. 6:10; Phil. 4:4.

For evermore. 1 Thess. 5:16.

With awe. Ps. 2:11.

In hope. Rom. 12:12.

In sorrow. 2 Cor. 6:10.

Under trials. Jas. 1:2; 1 Pet. 1:6.

Under persecutions. Mat. 5:11-12; Lk. 6:22-23; Heb. 10:34.

Under calamities. Hab. 3:17-18.

Expressed in hymns. Eph. 5:19; Jas. 5:13.

The afflictions of the saints is succeeded by. Ps. 30:5, 126:5; Is. 35:10; Jn. 16:20.

Pray for the restoration of. Ps. 51:8, 12, 85:6.

Promote, in the afflicted. Job 29:13.

Of the saints, made full by

The favour of God. Acts 2:28.

Faith in Christ. Rom. 15:13.

Abiding in Christ. Jn. 15:10-11.

The word of Christ. Jn. 17:13.

Answers to prayer. Jn. 16:24.

The communion of the saints. 2 Tim. 1:4; 1 Jn. 1:3-4; 2 Jn. verse 12.

The saints should bring, to their ministers. Phil. 2:2; Philem. verse 20.

Ministers should

Esteem their people as their. Phil. 4:1; 1 Thess. 2:20.

Promote, among their people. 2 Cor. 1:24; Phil. 1:25.

Pray for, for their people. Rom. 15:13.

Have, in the faith and holiness of their people. 2 Cor. 7:4; 1 Thess. 3:9; 3 Jn. verse 4.

Come to their people with. Rom. 15:32.

Finish their course with. Acts 20:24.

Desire to render an account with. Phil. 2:16; Heb. 13:17.

Serve God with. Ps. 100:2.

Generosity in God's service should cause. 1 Chron. 29:9, 17.

Is strengthening to the saints. Neh. 8:10.

The saints should engage in all religious services with. Ezra 6:22; Ps. 42:4.

The saints should have, in all their undertakings. Deut. 12:18.

The saints will be presented to

God with exceeding. *1 Pet. 4:13 with Jude verse 24.*

The coming of Christ will bring to the saints exceeding. *1 Pet. 4:13.*

Will be the final reward of the saints at the Day of Judgement. *Mat. 25:21.*

Of the wicked
Is derived from earthly pleasures. *Eccl. 2:10, 11:9.*
Is derived from folly. *Prov. 15:21.*
Is delusive. *Prov. 14:13.*
Is short-lived. *Job 20:5; Eccl. 7:6.*
Should be turned into mourning. *Jas. 4:9.*
Will be taken away. *Is. 16:10.*

Holy joy is illustrated. *Is. 9:3; Mat. 13:44.*

Some examples. **Hannah:** *1 Sam. 2:1.* **David:** *1 Chron. 29:9.* **The Wisemen:** *Mat. 2:10.* **The virgin Mary:** *Lk. 1:47.* **Zaccheus:** *Lk. 19:6.* **Some converts:** *Acts 2:46, Acts 13:52.* **Peter,** etc: *Acts 5:41.* **Samaritans:** *Acts 8:8.* **Philippian jailor:** *Acts 16:34.*

JUDGEMENT, THE
Predicted in the Old Testament. *1 Chron. 16:33; Ps. 9:7, 96:13; Eccl. 3:17.*

A first principle of the gospel. *Heb. 6:2.*

A day has been appointed for. *Acts 17:31; Rom. 2:16.*

The time of, is unknown to us. *Mk. 13:32.*

Is called the
Day of wrath. *Rom. 2:5; Rev. 6:17.*
The revelation of the righteous judgement of God. *Rom. 2:5.*
The day of judgement and perdition of ungodly men. *2 Pet. 3:7.*
The day of destruction. *Job 21:30.*
The judgement of the great day. *Jude verse 6.*

Will be administered by Christ. *Jn. 5: 22, 27; Acts 10:42; Rom. 14:10; 2 Cor. 5 10.*

The saints will sit with Christ in. *1 Cor. 6:2; Rev. 20:4.*

Will take place at the coming of Christ. *Mat. 25:31; 2 Tim. 4:1.*

For the nations, by the law of conscience. *Rom. 2:12, 14-15.*

For the Jews, by the Law of Moses. *Rom. 2:12.*

For Christians, by the gospel. *Jas. 2:12.*

Will involve
All nations. *Mat. 25:32.*
All men. *Heb. 9:27, 12:23.*
The small and the great. *Rev. 20:12.*
The righteous and the wicked. *Eccl. 3:17.*
The living and the dead. *2 Tim. 4:1; 1 Pet. 4:5.*

Will be in righteousness. *Ps. 98. 9; Acts 17:31.*

The books will be opened at. *Dan. 7:10.*

Will be of all
Actions. *Eccl. 11:9; Eccl. 12:14; Rev. 20:13.*
Words. *Mat. 12:36-37; Jude verse 15.*
Thoughts. *Eccl. 12:14; 1 Cor. 4:5.*

None, by nature, can stand in. *Ps. 130:3, 143:2; Rom.3:19.*

The saints will, through Christ, be enabled to stand in. *Rom. 8:33-34.*

Christ will acknowledge the saints at. *Mat. 25:34-40. Rev. 3:5.*

Perfect love will give boldness in. *1 Jn. 4:17.*

The saints will be rewarded at. *2 Tim. 4:8; Rev. 11:18.*

The wicked will be condemned in. *Mat. 7:22-23, 25:41.*

The final punishment of the wicked will succeed. *Mat. 13:40-42, 25:46.*

The word of Christ will be a witness against the wicked in. *Jn. 12:48.*

The certainty of, is a motive for
Repentance. *Acts 17:30-31.*
Faith. *Is. 28:16-17.*
Holiness. *2 Cor. 5:9-10; 2 Pet. 3:11, 14.*
Prayer and watchfulness. *Mk. 13:33.*
Warn the wicked of. *Acts 24:25; 2 Cor. 5:11.*
The wicked dread. *Acts 24:25;*

Heb. 10:27.
Neglected advantages increase condemnation at. *Mat. 11:20-24; Lk. 11:31-32.*
Devils will be condemned at. *2 Pet. 2:4; Jude verse 6.*

JUDGEMENTS
Are from God. *Deut. 32:39; Job 12:23; Amos 3:6; Mic. 6:9.*
Different kinds of:
Blotting out the name. *Deut. 29:20.*
Abandonment by God. *Hos. 4:17.*
Cursing men's blessings. *Mal. 2:2.*
Pestilence. *Deut. 28:21-22; Amos 4:10.*
Enemies. *2 Sam. 24:13.*
Famine. *Deut. 28:38-40; Amos 4:7-9.*
A famine of hearing the Word. *Amos 8:11.*
The sword. *Ex. 22:24; Jer. 19:7.*
Captivity. *Deut. 28:41; Ezek. 39:23.*
Continued sorrows. *Ps. 32:10, 78:32-33; Ezek. 24:23.*
Desolation. *Ezek. 33:29; Joel 3:19.*
Destruction. *Job 31:3; Ps. 34:16; Prov. 2:22; Is. 11:4.*
Inflicted upon
Nations. *Gen. 15:14; Jer. 51:20-21.*
Individuals. *Deut. 29:20; Jer. 23:34.*
False gods. *Ex. 12:12; Num. 33:4.*
The posterity of sinners. *Ex. 20:5; Ps. 37:28; Lam. 5:7.*
All the enemies of the saints. *Jer. 30:16.*
Sent for correction. *Job 37:13; Jer. 30:11.*
Sent for the deliverance of the saints. *Ex. 6:6.*
Are sent, as punishment for
Disobedience to God. *Lev. 26:14-16; 2 Chron. 7:19-20.*
Despising the warnings of God. *2 Chron. 36:16; Prov. 1:24-31; Jer. 44:4-6.*
Murmuring against God. *Num. 14:29.*
Idolatry. *2 Kings 22:17; Jer. 16:18.*
Iniquity. *Is. 26:21; Ezek. 24:13-14.*
Persecuting the saints. *Deut. 32:43.*
The sins of rulers. *1 Chron. 21:2, 12.*
Manifest the righteous character

of God. *Ex. 9:14-16; Ezek. 39:21; Dan. 9:14.*
Are in all the earth. *1 Chron. 16:14.*
Are frequently tempered with mercy. *Jer. 4:27, 5:10, 15-18; Amos 9:8.*
Should lead to
Humiliation. *Josh. 7:6; 2 Chron. 12:6; Lam. 3:1-20; Joel 1:13; Jonah 3:5-6.*
Prayer. *2 Chron. 20:9.*
Contrition. *Neh. 1:4; Esth. 4:3; Is. 22:12.*
Learning righteousness. *Is. 26:9.*
Should be a warning to others. *Lk. 13:35.*
May be averted by
Humiliation. *Ex. 33:3-4, 14; 2 Chron. 7:14.*
Prayer. *Judg. 3:9-11; 2 Chron. 7:13-14.*
Forsaking iniquity. *Jer. 18:7-8.*
Turning to God. *Deut. 30:1-3.*
The saints
Are preserved during. *Job 5:19-20; Ps. 91:7; Is. 26:20; Ezek. 9:6; Rev. 7:3.*
Are provided for, during. *Gen. 47:12; Ps. 33:19, 37:19.*
Pray for those under. *Ex. 32:11-13; Num. 11:2; Dan. 9:3.*
Sympathise with those under. *Jer. 9:1, 13:17; Lam. 3:48.*
Acknowledge the justice of. *2 Sam. 24:17; Ezra 9:13; Neh. 9:33; Jer. 14:7.*
Some examples of former judgements. **The old world**: *Gen. 6:7, 17.* **Sodom**, etc: *Gen. 19:24.* **Egypt**: *Ex. 9:14.* **Israel**: *Num. 14:29, 35, 21:6.* **The people of Ashdod**: *1 Sam. 5:6.* **The people of Bethshemesh**: *1 Sam. 6:19.* **The Amalakites**: *1 Sam. 15:3.*

Some examples of individual judgements. **Cain**: *Gen. 4:11-12.* **Canaan**: *Gen. 9:25.* **Korah**, etc: *Num. 16:33-35.* **Achan**: *Josh. 7:25.* **Hophni**, etc: *1 Sam. 2:34.* **Saul**: *1 Sam. 15:23.* **Uzzah**: *2 Sam. 6:7.* **Jeroboam**: *1 Kings 13:4.* **Ahab**: *1 Kings 22:38.* **Gehazi**: *2 Kings 5:27.* **Jezebel**: *2 Kings 9:35.* **Nebuchadnezzar**: *Dan. 4:31.* **Belshazzar**: *Dan. 5:30.* **Zacharias**: *Lk. 1:20.* **Ananias**, etc: *Acts 5:1-10.*

Herod: *Acts 12:23.* **Elymas**: *Acts 13:11.*

Some examples of preservation during judgement. **Noah**: *Gen. 7:1, 16.* **Lot**: *Gen. 19:15-17.* **Joseph**, etc: *Gen. 45:7.* **Elijah**: *1 Kings 17:9.* **Elisha**, etc: *2 Kings 4:38-41.*
A Shunammite: *2 Kings 8:1-2.*

JUSTICE

Commanded. *Deut. 16:20; Is. 56:1.*
Christ, an example of. *Ps. 98:9; Is. 11:4; Jer. 23:5.*
Specially required in rulers. *2 Sam. 23:3; Ezek. 45:9.*
To be done
  While judgement is executed. *Deut. 16:18; Jer. 21:12.*
  In buying and selling. *Lev. 19:36; Deut. 25:15.*
  To the poor. *Prov. 29:14; Prov. 31:9.*
  To the fatherless and widows. *Is. 1:17.*
  To servants. *Col. 4:1.*
Gifts pervert the course of. *Ex. 23:8.*
God
  Requires. *Mic. 6:8.*
  Sets the highest value on. *Prov. 21:3.*
  Delights in. *Prov. 11:1.*
  Gives wisdom to execute. *1 Kings 3:11-12; Prov. 2:8-9.*
  Is displeased with the lack of. *Eccl. 5:8.*
Brings its own reward. *Jer. 22:15.*
The saints should
  Study the principles of. *Phil. 4:8.*
  Receive instruction in. *Prov. 1:3.*
  Pray for wisdom to execute. *1 Kings 3:9.*
  Always do. *Ps. 119:121; Ezek. 18:8-9.*
  Take pleasure in doing. *Prov. 21:15.*
  Teach others to do. *Gen. 18:19.*
Promises to. *Is. 33:15-16. Jer. 7:5, 7.*
The wicked
  Scorn. *Prov. 19:28.*
  Abhor. *Mic. 3:9.*
  Do not call for. *Is. 59:4.*
  Banish. *Is. 59:14.*

Pass over. *Lk. 11:42.*
Afflict those who act with. *Job 12:4; Amos 5:12.*

Some examples. **Moses**: *Num. 16:15.* **Samuel**: *1 Sam. 12:4.* **David**: *2 Sam. 8:15.* **Solomon**: *1 Kings 3:16-27.* **Josiah**: *Jer. 22:15.*
Joseph: *Lk. 23:50-51.* **The apostles**: *1 Thess. 2:10.*

JUSTICE OF GOD, THE

Is part of his character. *Deut. 32:4; Is. 45:21.*
Is declared to be
  Abundant. *Job 37:23.*
  Incomparable. *Job 4:17.*
  Incorruptible. *Deut. 10:17; 2 Chron. 19:7.*
  Impartial. *2 Chron. 19:7; Jer. 32:19.*
  Unfailing. *Zeph. 3:5.*
  Undeviating. *Job 8:3, 34:12.*
  Without respect of persons. *Rom. 2:11; Col. 3:25; 1 Pet. 1:17.*
  The habitation of his throne. *Ps. 89:14.*
Not to be sinned against. *Jer. 50:7.*
Denied by the ungodly. *Ezek. 33:17, 20.*
Shown in
  Forgiving sins. *1 Jn. 1:9.*
  Redemption. *Rom. 3:26.*
  His government. *Ps. 9:4; Jer. 9:24.*
  His judgements. *Gen. 18:25; Rev. 19:2.*
  All his ways. *Ezek. 18:25, 29.*
  The final judgement. *Acts 17:31.*
Acknowledge. *Ps. 51:4 with Rom. 3:4.*
Magnify. *Ps. 98:9, 99:3-4.*

JUSTIFICATION BEFORE GOD

Is promised in Christ. *Is. 45:25, 53:11.*
Is an act of God. *Is. 50:8; Rom. 8:33.*

Under the Law

Requires perfect (but impossible) obedience. *Lev. 18:5 with Rom. 10:5; Rom. 2:13; Jas. 2:10.*

Man cannot attain to. *Job 9:2-3, 20. Job 25:4. Ps. 130:3, 143:2 with Rom. 3:20, 9:31-32.*

Under the gospel,

Is not of works. *Acts 13:39; Rom. 8:3; Gal. 2:6, 3:11.*

Is not of faith and works together. *Acts 15:1-29; Rom. 3:28, 11:6; Gal. 2:14-21, 5:4.*

Is by faith alone. *Jn. 5:24; Acts 13:39; Rom. 3:30, 5:1; Gal.2:16.*

Is of grace. *Rom. 3:24, 4:16, 5:17-21.*

In the name of Christ. *1 Cor. 6:11.*

By the imputing of Christ's righteousness. *Is. 61:10; Jer. 23:6; Rom. 3:22, 5:18; 1 Cor. 1:30; 2 Cor. 5:21.*

By the blood of Christ. *Rom. 5:9.*

By the resurrection of Christ. *Rom. 4:25; 1 Cor. 15:17.*

The blessedness of. *Ps. 32:1-2 with Rom. 4:6-8.*

Sets free from condemnation. *Is. 50:8-9, 54:17 with Rom. 8:33-34.*

Entitles the saints to an inheritance. *Titus 3:7.*

Ensures glorification. *Rom. 8. 30.*

The wicked will not attain to. *Ex. 23:7.*

By faith,

It was revealed under the old dispensation. *Hab. 2:4 with Rom. 1:17.*

It excludes boasting. *Rom. 3:27, 4:2; 1 Cor. 1:29, 31.*

It does not make void the Law. *Rom. 3:30-31;. 1 Cor. 9:21.*

Typified. *Zech. 3:4-5.*

Illustrated. *Lk. 18:14.*

Two examples. **Abraham**: *Gen. 15:6.* **Paul**: *Phil. 3:8-9.*

K

KINGS

God chooses. *Deut. 17:15; 1 Chron. 28:4-6.*

God ordains. *Rom. 13:1.*

God anoints. *1 Sam. 16:12; 2 Sam. 12:7.*

Are set up by God. *1 Sam. 12:13; Dan. 2:21.*

Are removed by God. *1 Kings 11:11; Dan. 2:21.*

Christ is the Prince of. *Rev. 1:5.*

Christ is the King of. *Rev. 17:14.*

Reigns under the direction of Christ. *Prov. 8:15.*

Are supreme judges of the nations. *1 Sam. 8:5.*

Resistance to, is resistance to the ordinance of God. *Rom. 13:2.*

Have the power to enforce their commands. *Eccl. 8:4.*

Their numerous subjects are their honour. *Prov. 14:28.*

Are not saved by their armies. *Ps. 33:16.*

Are dependant on the land. *Eccl. 5:9.*

Should

Fear God. *Deut. 17:19.*

Serve Christ. *Ps. 2:10-12.*

Keep the Law of God. *1 Kings 2:3.*

Study the Scriptures. *Deut. 17:19.*

Promote the interests of the Church. *Ezra 1:2-4, 6:1-12.*

Nourish the Church. *Is. 49:23.*

Rule in the fear of God. *2 Sam. 23:3.*

Maintain the cause of the poor and oppressed. *Prov. 31:8-9.*

Investigate all matters. *Prov. 25:2.*

Not pervert judgement. *Prov. 31:5.*

Prolong their reign by hating covetousness. *Prov. 28:16.*

Their throne is established in righteousness and justice. *Prov. 16:12, 29:14.*

Are specially warned about

Impurity. *Prov. 31:3.*

Lying. *Prov. 17:7.*

Listening to lies. *Prov. 29:12.*

Excesses. *Prov. 31:4-5.*

The gospel to be preached to. *Acts 9:15, 26:27-28.*

Without understanding, they become oppressors. *Prov. 28:16.*

Are often reproved by God. *1 Chron. 16:21.*

Judgements upon, when opposed to Christ. *Ps. 2:2, 5. 9.*

Good kings

Regard God as their strength. *Ps. 99:4.*

Speak righteously. *Prov. 16:10.*

Love righteous lips. *Prov. 16:13.*

Hate wickedness. *Prov. 16:12.*

Dismiss evil severely. *Prov. 20:8.*

Punish the wicked. *Prov. 20:26.*

Favour the wise. *Prov. 14:35.*

Honour the diligent. *Prov. 22:29.*

Befriend the good. *Prov. 22:11.*

Are pacified by submission. *Prov. 16:14, 25:15.*

Evil counsellors should be removed from. *2 Chron. 22:3-4 with Prov. 25:5.*

Do not curse them, even in your thoughts. *Ex. 22:28; Eccl. 10:20.*

Do not speak evil of. *Job 34:18; 2 Pet. 2:10.*

Pay tribute to. *Mat. 22:21; Rom. 13:6-7.*

Do not be presumptuous before. *Prov. 25:6.*

Should be

Honoured. *Rom. 13:7; 1 Pet. 2:17.*

Feared. *Prov. 24:21.*

Revered. *1 Sam. 24:8; 1 Kings 1:23, 31.*

Obeyed. *Rom. 13:1, 5; 1 Pet. 2:13.*

Prayed for. *1 Tim. 2:1-2.*

The folly of resisting. *Prov. 19:12, 20:2.*

The punishment for resisting the lawful authority of. *Rom. 13:2.*

Guilt and danger of raising the hand against. *1 Sam. 28:9; 2 Sam. 1:14.*

Those who walk after the flesh despise. *2 Pet. 2:10; Jude verse 8.*

Examples of good kings. **David**: *2 Sam. 8:15.* **Asa**: *1 Kings 15:11.* **Jehoshaphat**: *1 Kings 22:43.* **Amaziah,** etc: *2 Kings 15:3.* **Uzziah**, etc: *2 Kings 15:34.* **Hezekiah**: *2 Kings 18:3.* **Josiah**: *2 Kings 22:2.* **Manasseh**: *2 Chron. 33:12-16.*

L

LANGUAGES

Of all mankind were just one at first. *Gen. 11:1, 6.*

Called

Speech. *Mk. 14:70; Acts 14:11.*

Tongues *Acts 1:19. Rev. 5:9.*

The confusion of:

As a punishment for pride and presumption, etc. *Gen. 11:2-6.*

The origin of all the varieties in. *Gen. 11:7.*

Scattered mankind over the earth. *Gen. 11:8-9.*

Divided mankind into separate nations. *Gen. 10:5, 20, 31.*

A great variety of, spoken by men. *1 Cor. 14:10.*

Ancient kingdoms often took in nations of different. *Esther 1:22; Dan. 3:4, 6:25.*

Different languages mentioned:

Hebrew. *2 Kings 18:28; Acts 26:14.*

Chaldean. *Dan. 1:4.*

Aramaic. *2 Kings 18:26; Ezra 4:7.*

Greek. *Acts 21:37.*

Latin. *Lk. 23:38.*

Lycaonian. *Acts 14:11.*

Arabic, etc. *Acts 2:11.*

Egyptian. *Ps. 81:5, 114:1; Acts 2:10.*

Of some nations are very difficult. *Ezra 3:5-6.*

The term 'barbarian' was applied to those who spoke a strange. *1 Cor. 14:11.*

Different kinds of tongues

A gift of the Holy Spirit. *1 Cor. 12:10.*

Promised. *Mk. 16:17.*

Given on the day of Pentecost. *Acts 2:3-4.*

Followed receiving the gospel. *Acts 10:44-46.*

Conferred by laying on of the apostles' hands. *Acts 8:17-18, 19:6.*

Necessary for the spread of the gospel. *Acts 2:7-11.*

A sign to unbelievers. *1 Cor. 14:22.*

Sometimes abused. *1 Cor. 14:2-12, 23.*

The interpretation of tongues

The antiquity of engaging persons for. *Gen. 42:23.*

Was a gift of the Holy Spirit. *1 Cor. 12:10.*

Was very important in the early Church. *1 Cor. 14:5, 13, 27-28.*

The Jews were punished by being given up to a people of a strange. *Deut. 28:49; Is. 28:11; Jer. 5:15.*

LAW OF GOD, THE

Is absolute and perpetual. *Mat. 5:18.*

Was given

To Adam. *Gen. 2:16-17 with Rom. 5:12-14.*

To Noah. *Gen. 9:6.*

To the Israelites. *Ex. 20:2, etc; Ps. 75:5.*

Through Moses. *Ex. 31:18; Jn. 7:19.*

Through the ministry of angels. *Acts 7:53; Gal. 3:19; Heb. 2:2.*

Is described as

Pure. *Ps. 19:8.*

Spiritual. *Rom. 7:14.*

Holy, just, and good. *Rom. 7:12.*

Exceedingly broad. *Ps. 119:96.*

Perfect. *Ps. 19:7. Rom. 12:2.*

Truth. *Ps. 119:142.*

Not grievous. *1 Jn. 5:3.*

Requires the obedience of the heart. *Ps. 51:6; Mat.5:28, 22:37.*

Requires perfect obedience. *Deut. 27:26; Gal. 3:10; Jas. 2:10.*

Love is the fulfilling of. *Rom. 13:8, 10; Gal. 5:14; Jas. 2:8.*

It is man's duty to keep. *Eccl. 12:13.*

Man, by nature, is not in subjection to. *Rom. 7:5; Rom. 8:7.*

Man cannot render perfect obedience to. *1 Kings 8:46; Eccl. 7:20; Rom. 3:10.*

Sin is a transgression of. *1 Jn. 3:4.*

All men have transgressed. *Rom. 3:9, 19.*

Man cannot be justified by. *Acts 13:39; Rom. 3:20, 28; Gal. 2:16; Gal. 3:11.*

Gives the knowledge of sin. *Rom. 3:20, 7:7.*

Works wrath. *Rom. 4:15.*

Our conscience testifies to. *Rom. 2:15.*

Is designed to lead to Christ. *Gal. 3:24.*

Obedience to,

Is a characteristic of the saints. *Rev. 12:17.*

Is a test of love. *1 Jn. 5:3.*

Is of first importance. *1 Cor. 7:19.*

Blessedness of keeping. *Ps. 119:1; Mat. 5:19; 1 Jn. 3:22, 24; Rev. 22:14.*

Christ

Came to fulfil. *Mat. 5:17.*

Magnified. *Is. 42:21.*

Explained. *Mat. 7:12, 22:37-40.*

The love of, produces peace. *Ps. 119:165.*

The saints

Are free from bondage to. *Rom. 6:14, 7:4, 6; Gal. 3:13.*

Are free from the curse of. *Gal. 3:13.*

Have, written on their hearts. *Jer. 31:33 with Heb. 8:10.*

Love. *Ps. 119:97, 113.*

Delight in. *Ps. 119:77; Rom. 7:22.*

Prepare their hearts to seek. *Ezra 7:10.*

Pledge themselves to walk in. *Neh. 10:29.*

Keep. *Ps. 119:55.*

Pray to understand. *Ps. 119:18.*

Pray for power to keep. *Ps. 119:34.*

Should remember. *Mal. 4:4.*

Should make, the subject of their conversation. *Ex. 13:9.*

Lament over the violation of, by others. *Ps. 119:136.*

The wicked

Despise. *Amos 2:4.*

Forget. *Hos. 4:6.*

Forsake. *2 Chron. 12:1; Jer. 9:13.*
Refuse to hear. *Is. 30:9; Jer. 6:19.*
Refuse to walk in. *Ps. 78:10.*
Cast away. *Is. 5:24.*
Is the rule of life to the saints.
1 Cor. 9:21; Gal. 5:13-14.
Is the rule of the judgement.
Rom. 2:12.
To be used lawfully. *1 Tim. 1:8.*
Established by faith. *Rom. 3:31.*
Punishment for disobeying.
Neh. 9:26-27; Is. 65:11-13; Jer. 9:13-16.

LIBERTY, CHRISTIAN
Foretold. *Is. 42:7. Is. 61:1.*
Conferred
By God. *Col. 1:13.*
By Christ. *Gal. 4:3-5, 5:1.*
By the Holy Spirit. *Rom. 8:15;*
2 Cor. 3:17.
Through the gospel. *Jn. 8:32.*
Confirmed by Christ. *Jn. 8:36.*
Proclaimed by Christ. *Is. 61:1; Lk. 4:18.*
The service of Christ is. *1 Cor. 7:22.*
Is freedom from
The law. *Rom. 7:6, 8:2.*
The curse of the law. *Gal. 3:13.*
The fear of death. *Heb. 2:15.*
Sin. *Rom. 6:7, 18.*
Corruption. *Rom. 8:21.*
Bondage of man. *1 Cor. 9:19.*
Jewish ordinances. *Gal. 4:3; Col 2:20.*
Called the glorious liberty of the
children of God. *Rom. 8:21.*
The saints are called to. *Gal. 5:13.*
The saints should
Praise God for. *Ps. 116:16-17.*
Assert. *1 Cor. 10:29.*
Walk in. *Ps. 119:45.*
Stand fast in. *Gal. 2:5, 5:1,*
Not abuse. *Gal. 5:13; 1 Pet. 2:16.*
Not offend others by. *1 Cor. 8:9,*
10:29, 32.
The gospel is the law of. *Jn. 1:25;*
Jas. 2:12.
False teachers
Promise to others. *2 Pet. 2:19.*
Abuse. *Jude verse 4.*
Try to destroy. *Gal. 2:4.*

The wicked are devoid of. *Jn. 8:34*
with Rom. 6:2:20.
Typified. *Lev. 25:10-17; Gal. 4:22-26, 31.*

LIFE, NATURAL
God is the Author of. *Gen. 2:7;*
Acts 17:28.
God preserves. *Ps. 36:6, 66:9.*
Is in the hand of God. *Job 12:10;*
Dan. 5:23.
Forfeited by sin. *Gen. 2:17; Gen. 3:17-19.*
Of others, not to be taken away.
Ex. 20:13.
Is described as
Vain. *Eccl. 6:12.*
Limited. *Job 7:1, 14:5.*
Short. *Job 14:1; Ps. 89:47.*
Uncertain. *Jas. 4:13-15.*
Full of trouble. *Job 14:1.*
God's lovingkindness is better
than. *Ps. 63:3.*
The value of. *Job 2:4; Mat. 6:25.*
Preserved by discretion. *Prov. 13:3.*
Sometimes prolonged, in answer
to prayer. *Is. 38:2-5; Jas. 5:15.*
Obedience to God tends to
prolong. *Deut. 30:20.*
Obedience to parents tends to
prolong. *Ex. 20:12; Prov. 4:10.*
The cares and pleasures of, are
dangerous. *Lk. 8:14, 21:34; 2 Tim. 2:4.*
The saints have true enjoyment
of. *Ps. 128:2; 1 Tim. 4:8.*
Of the saints is specially pro-
tected by God. *Job 2:6; Acts 18:10;*
1 Pet. 3:13.
Of the wicked is not specially
protected by God. *Job 36:6; Ps. 78:50.*
The wicked have their portion of
good, during. *Ps. 17:14; Lk. 6:24;*
Lk. 16:25.
Should be spent in
The fear of God. *1 Pet. 1:17.*
The service of God. *Lk. 1:75.*
Living for God. *Rom. 14:8; Phil. 1:21.*
Peace. *Rom. 12:18; 1 Tim. 2:2.*
Doing good. *Eccl. 3:12.*
All due care should be taken of.
Mat. 10 23; Acts 27:34.

Should be laid down, if necessary, for Christ. *Mat. 10:39; Lk. 14:26; Acts 20:24.*

Should be laid down, if necessary, for the brothers. *Rom. 16:4; 1 Jn. 3:16.*

Be thankful for

The preservation of. *Ps. 103:4; Jn. 2:6.*

The supply of its needs. *Gen. 48:15.*

The dissatisfied despise. *Eccl. 2:17.*

We do not know what is good for us in. *Eccl. 6:12.*

Do not be over-anxious to provide for its needs. *Mat. 6:25.*

The enjoyment of, does not consist in the amount of possessions. *Lk. 12:15.*

Is compared with

An eagle swooping to its prey. *Job 9:26.*

A pilgrimage. *Gen. 47:9.*

A tale that is told. *Ps. 90:9.*

A swift runner. *Job 9:25.*

A swift ship. *Job 9:26.*

A hand-breadth. *Ps. 39:5.*

A shepherd's tent removed. *Is. 38:12.*

A dream. *Ps. 73:20.*

A sleep. *Ps. 90:5.*

A vapour. *Jas. 4:14.*

A shadow. *Eccl. 6:12.*

A thread cut by the weaver. *Is. 38:12.*

A weaver's shuttle. *Job 7:6.*

A flower. *Job 14:2.*

Grass. *1 Pet. 1:24.*

Water spilled on the ground. *2 Sam. 14:14.*

The wind. *Job 7:7.*

The brevity of, should lead to spiritual improvement. *Deut. 32:29; Ps. 90:12.*

Is sometimes judicially shortened. *1 Sam. 2:32-33; Job 36:16.*

Was miraculously restored by Christ. *Mat. 9:18, 25; Lk. 7:15, 22; Jn. 11:43.*

LIFE, SPIRITUAL

God is the Author of. *Ps. 36:9; Col. 2:13.*

Christ is the Author of. *Jn. 5:21, 25, 6:33, 51-53, 14:6; 1 Jn. 4:9.*

The Holy Spirit is the Author of. *Ezek. 37:14 with Rom. 8:9-13.*

The Word of God is the instrument of. *Is. 55:3; 2 Cor. 3:6; 1 Pet. 4:6.*

Is hidden with Christ. *Col. 3:3.*

The fear of God is. *Prov. 14:27, 19:23.*

Spiritual-mindedness is. *Rom. 8:6.*

Is maintained by

Christ. *Jn. 6:57; 1 Cor. 10:3-4.*

Faith. *Gal. 2:20.*

The Word of God. *Deut. 8:3 with Mat. 4:4.*

Prayer. *Ps. 69:32.*

Has its origin in the new birth. *Jn. 3:3-8.*

Has its infancy. *Lk. 10:21; 1 Cor. 3:1-2; 1 Jn. 2:12.*

Has its youth. *1 Jn. 2:13-14.*

Has its maturity. *Eph. 4:13; 1 Jn. 2:13-14.*

Is described as

A life for God. *Rom. 6:31. Gal. 2:19.*

A life according to God. *1 Pet. 4:6.*

Newness of life. *Rom. 6:4.*

Living in the Spirit. *Gal. 5:25.*

Revived by God. *Ps. 85:6; Hos. 6:2.*

Evidenced by love of the brothers. *1 Jn. 3:14.*

All the saints have. *Eph. 2:1, 5; Col. 2:13.*

Should animate the services of the saints. *Rom. 12:1; 1 Cor. 14:15.*

The saints praise God for. *Ps. 119:175.*

Seek to grow in. *Eph. 4:15; 1 Pet. 2:2.*

Pray for an increase in. *Ps. 119:25, 143:11.*

The wicked are alienated from. *Eph. 4:18.*

Lovers of pleasure are destitute of. *1 Tim. 5:6.*

Hypocrites are destitute of. *Jude verse 12; Rev. 3:1.*

Illustrated. *Ezek. 37:9-10; Lk. 15:24.*

LIFE, ETERNAL

Christ is. *1 Jn. 1:2, 5:20.*

Is revealed by Christ. *Jn. 6:68; 2 Tim. 1:10.*

To know God and Christ is. *Jn. 17:3.*

Is given

By God. *Ps. 133:3; Rom. 6:23.*
By Christ. *Jn. 6:27, 10:28.*
In Christ. *1 Jn. 5:11.*
Through Christ. *Rom. 5:21; Rom. 6:23.*
To all given to Christ. *Jn. 17:2.*
To those who believe in God.
Jn. 5:24.
To those who believe in Christ.
Jn. 3:15-16, 6:40, 47.
To those who hate life for
Christ. *Jn. 12:25.*
In answer to prayer. *Ps. 21:4.*
Revealed in the Scriptures. *Jn. 5:39.*

Results from

Drinking the water of life. *Jn. 4:14.*
Eating the bread of life. *Jn. 6:50-58.*
Eating of the tree of life. *Rev. 2:7.*
Those who are ordained to,
believe the gospel. *Acts 13:48.*

The saints

Have promises of. *1 Tim. 4:8;
2 Tim. 1:1; Titus 1:2; 1 Jn. 2:25.*
Have hope of. *Titus 1:2, Titus 3:7.*
May have assurance of. *2 Cor. 5:1;
1 Jn. 5:13.*
Will reap, through the Spirit.
Gal. 6:8.
Will inherit. *Mat. 19:29.*
Look for the mercy of God for.
Jude verse 21.
Should lay hold of. *1 Tim. 6:12, 19.*
Are preserved to. *Jn. 10:28-29.*
Will rise to. *Dan. 12:2; Jn. 5:29.*
Will go into. *Mat. 25:46.*
Will reign in. *Dan. 7:18; Rom. 5:17.*
The self-righteous think they will
inherit, by good works. *Mk. 10:17.*
Cannot be inherited by good
works. *Rom. 2:7 with Rom. 3:10-19.*

The wicked

Do not have. *1 Jn. 3:15.*
Judge themselves unworthy of.
Acts 13:46.
An exhortation to seek. *Jn. 6:27.*

LONGSUFFERING OF GOD, THE

Is part of his character. *Ex. 34:6;
Num. 14:18; Ps. 86:15.*

Salvation, the object of. *2 Pet. 3:15.*
Comes through Christ's interces-
sion. *Lk. 13:8.*
Should lead to repentance.
Rom. 2:4; 2 Pet. 3:9.
An encouragement to repent.
Joel 2:13.
Shown in the forgiveness of sins.
Rom. 3:25.

Exercised toward

His people. *Is. 30:18; Ezek. 20:17.*
The wicked. *Rom. 9:22; 1 Pet. 3:20.*
Plead in prayer. *Jer. 15:15.*
Limits set to. *Gen. 6:3; Jer. 44:22.*

The wicked

Abuse. *Eccl. 8:11; Mat. 24:48-49.*
Despise. *Rom. 2:4.*
Are punished for despising.
Neh. 9:30; Mat.24:48-51; Rom. 2:5.
Illustrated. *Lk. 13:6-9.*

Some examples. **Manasseh**: *2
Chron. 33:10-13.* **Israel**: *Ps. 78:38; Is. 48:9.*
Jerusalem: *Mat. 23:37.* **Paul**: *1 Tim. 1:16.*

LOVE OF GOD, THE

Is part of his character. *2 Cor. 13:11.*
Christ is the special object of.
Jn. 15:9, 17:26.
Christ abides in. *Jn. 15:10.*

Is described as

Sovereign. *Deut. 7:8, 10:15.*
Great. *Eph. 2:4.*
Abiding. *Zeph. 3:17.*
Unfailing. *Is. 49:15-16.*
Inalienable. *Rom. 8:39.*
Constraining. *Hos. 11:4.*
Everlasting. *Jer. 31:3.*
Irrespective of merit. *Deut. 7:7;
Job 7:17.*

Is manifested towards

Perishing sinners. *Jn. 3:16; Titus 3:4.*
The saints. *Jn. 16:27, 17:23; 2 Thess.
2:16; 1 Jn. 4:16.*
The destitute. *Deut. 10:18.*
A cheerful giver. *2 Cor. 9:7.*

Shown in

The giving of Christ. *Jn. 3:16.*
The sending of Christ. *1 Jn. 4:9.*

Christ's dying for us while we were yet sinners. *Rom. 5:8; 1 Jn. 4:10.*
Election. *Mal. 1:2-3; Rom. 9:11-13.*
Adoption. *1 Jn. 3:1.*
Redemption. *Is. 43:3-4, 63:9.*
Freeness of salvation. *Titus 3:4-7.*
Forgiving sin. *Is. 38:17.*
Making souls alive. *Eph. 2:4-5.*
Drawing us to himself. *Hos. 11:4.*
Temporal blessings. *Deut. 7:13.*
Chastisements. *Heb. 12:6.*
Defeating evil counsels. *Deut. 23:5.*
Shed abroad in the heart by the Holy Spirit. *Rom. 5:5.*
The saints know and believe. *1 Jn. 4:16.*
The saints should abide in. *Jude verse 21.*

Perfected in the saints
By obedience. *1 Jn. 2:5.*
By brotherly love. *1 Jn. 4:12.*
The source of our love for him. *1 Jn. 4:19.*
To be sought in prayer. *2 Cor. 13:14.*

LOVE OF CHRIST, THE
To the Father. *Ps. 91:14; Jn. 14 31.*
To the Church. *Song 4:8-9, 5:1; Jn. 15:9; Eph. 5:25.*
To those who love him. *Prov. 8:17; Jn. 14:21.*

Is manifested in his
Coming to seek the lost. *Lk. 19:10.*
Praying for his enemies. *Lk. 23:34.*
Giving himself for us. *Gal. 2:20.*
Dying for us. *Jn. 15:13. 1 Jn. 3:16.*
Washing away our sins. *Rev. 1:5.*
Interceding for us. *Heb. 7:25, 9:24.*
Sending the Spirit. *Ps. 68:18; Jn. 16:7.*
Rebukes and chastisements. *Rev. 3:19.*
Surpasses knowledge. *Eph. 3:19.*
Is to be imitated. *Jn. 13:34, 15:12; Eph. 5:2; 1 Jn. 3:16.*

To the saints, is
Unquenchable. *Song 8:7.*
Constraining. *2 Cor. 5:14.*

Unchangeable. *Jn. 13:1.*
Indissovable. *Rom. 8:35.*
Obedient saints abide in. *Jn. 15:10.*
The saints obtain victory through. *Rom. 8:37.*
Is the banner over his saints. *Song 2:4.*
Is the ground of his saints' love for him. *Lk. 7:47.*
To the saints, will be acknowledged, even by enemies. *Rev. 3:9.*
Illustrated. *Mat. 18:11-13.*

Some examples of Christ's love toward – **Peter:** *Lk. 22:32, 61.* **Lazarus,** etc: *Jn. 11:5, 36.* **Christ's apostles:** *Jn. 13:1, 34.* **John:** *Jn. 13:23.*

LOVE TOWARDS GOD
Commanded. *Deut. 11:1; Josh. 22:5.*
The first great commandment. *Mat. 22:38.*
With all the heart. *Deut. 6:5 with Mat. 22:37.*
Better than all sacrifices. *Mk. 12:33.*
Produced by
The Holy Spirit. *Gal. 5:22; 2 Thess. 3:5.*
God's love toward us. *1 Jn. 4:19.*
Answers to prayer. *Ps. 116:1.*
Shown by Christ. *Jn. 14:31.*
A characteristic of the saints. *Ps. 5:11.*
Should produce
Joy. *Ps. 5:11.*
Love to the saints. *1 Jn. 5:1.*
A hatred of sin. *Ps. 97:10.*
Obedience to God. *Deut. 30:20; 1 Jn. 5:3.*
Is perfected in obedience. *1 Jn. 2:5.*
When perfected, gives boldness. *1 Jn. 4:17-18.*
God is faithful to those who have. *Deut. 7:9.*
Those who have,
Are known by him. *1 Cor. 8:3.*
Are preserved by him. *Ps. 145:20.*
Are delivered by him. *Ps. 91:14.*
Partake of his mercy. *Ex. 20:6; Deut. 7:9.*

Have all things working for their good. *Rom. 8:28.*
Persevere in. *Jude verse 21.*
Exhort one another to. *Ps. 31:23.*
Pray for. *2 Thess. 3:5.*
Love for the world is a proof of not having. *1 Jn. 2:15.*
Those who do not love others are without. *1 Jn. 4:20.*
Hypocrites are without. *Lk. 11:42; Jn. 5:42.*
The uncharitable are without. *1 Jn. 3:17.*
God tests the sincerity of. *Deut. 13:3.*
Promises connected with. *Deut. 11:13-15; Ps. 69:36; Is. 56:6-7; Jas. 1:12.*

LOVE TOWARDS CHRIST

Shown by God. *Mat. 17:5; Jn. 5:20.*
Shown by the saints. *1 Pet. 1:8.*
His personal excellence is deserving of. *Song 5:9-16.*
His love to us is a motive for. *2 Cor. 5:14.*

Is manifested in
Seeking him. *Song 3:2.*
Obeying him. *Jn. 14:15, 21, 23.*
Ministering to him. *Mat. 27:55 with Mat. 25:40.*
Preferring him to all others. *Mat. 10:37.*
Taking up the cross for him. *Mat. 10:38.*
A characteristic of the saints. *Song 1:4.*
An evidence of adoption. *Jn. 8:42.*
Should be
Sincere. *Eph. 6:24.*
With the soul. *Song 1:7.*
In proportion to our mercies. *Lk. 7:47.*
Supreme. *Mat. 10:37.*
Ardent. *Song 2:5, 8:6.*
Unquenchable. *Song 8:7.*
Even to death. *Acts 21:13; Rev. 12:11.*
Promises to. *2 Tim. 4:8; Jas. 1:12.*
An increase in, should be prayed for. *Phil. 1:9.*
Pray for grace to those who have. *Eph. 6:24.*

Those who have
Are loved by the Father. *Jn. 14:21, 23, 16:27.*
Are loved by Christ. *Prov. 8:17; Jn. 14:21.*
Enjoy communion with God and Christ. *Jn. 14:23.*
A decrease in, is rebuked. *Rev. 2:4.*
A lack of, is denounced. *1 Cor. 16:22.*
The wicked are destitute of. *Ps. 35:19 with Jn. 15:18, 25.*

Some examples. **Joseph of Arimathaea**: *Mat. 27:57-60.* **A penitent woman**: *Lk. 7:47.* **Certain women**: *Lk. 23:28.* **Thomas**: *Jn. 11:16.* **Mary Magdalene**: *Jn. 20:11.* **Peter**: *Jn. 21:15-17.* **Paul**: *Act 21:13.*

LOVE TO OTHERS

Is of God. *1 Jn. 4:7.*
Is commanded by God. *1 Jn. 4:21.*
Is commanded by Christ. *Jn. 13:34, 15:12; 1 Jn. 3:23.*
Follows the example of Christ. *Jn. 13:34, 15:12; Eph. 5:2.*
Is taught by God. *1 Thess. 4:9.*
Faith works by. *Gal. 5:6.*
A fruit of the Spirit. *Gal. 5:22; Col. 1:8.*
Purity of heart leads to. *1 Pet. 1:22.*
Explained. *1 Cor. 13:4-7.*
Is an active principle. *1 Thess. 1:3; Heb. 6:10.*
Is an abiding principle. *1 Cor. 13:8, 13.*
Is the second great Commandment. *Mat. 22:37-39.*
Is the end of the Commandments. *1 Tim. 1:5.*
Supernatural gifts are nothing without. *1 Cor. 13:1-2.*
The greatest sacrifices are nothing without. *1 Cor. 13:3.*
Especially enjoined upon ministers. *1 Tim. 4:12; 2 Tim. 2:22.*
The saints should
Put on. *Col. 3:14.*
Follow after. *1 Cor. 14:1.*
Abound in. *Phil. 1:9; 1 Thess. 3:12.*
Continue in. *1 Tim. 2:15; Heb. 13:1.*

Provoke each other to. *2 Cor. 8:7; 2 Cor. 9:2; Heb. 10:24.*

Be sincere in. *Rom. 12:9; 2 Cor. 6:6, 8:8; 1 Jn. 3:18.*

Be fair-minded in. *1 Cor. 10:24; 1 Cor. 13:5; Phil. 2:4.*

Be fervent in. *1 Pet. 1:22, 4:8.*

Should be connected with brotherly-kindness. *Rom. 12:10; 2 Pet. 1:7.*

Should be with a pure heart. *1 Pet. 1:22.*

All things should be done with. *1 Cor. 16:14.*

Should be shown toward

The saints. *1 Pet. 2:17; 1 Jn. 5:1.*

Ministers. *1 Thess. 5:13.*

Our families. *Eph. 5:25; Titus 2:4.*

Fellow countrymen. *Ex. 32:32; Rom. 9:2-3, 10:1.*

Strangers. *Lev. 19:34; Deut. 10:19.*

Enemies. *Ex. 23:4-5; 2 Kings 6:22; Mat. 5:44; Rom. 12:14, 20; 1 Pet. 3:9.*

Everybody. *Gal. 6:10.*

Should be shown in

Ministering to the needs of others. *Mat. 25:35; Heb. 6:10.*

Loving each other. *Gal. 5:13.*

Relieving strangers. *Lev. 25:35; Mat. 25:35.*

Clothing the naked. *Is. 58:7; Mat. 25:36.*

Visiting the sick, etc. *Job 31:16-22; Jas. 1:27.*

Sympathising. *Rom. 12:15; 1 Cor. 12:26.*

Supporting the weak. *Gal. 6:2; 1 Thess. 5:14.*

Covering the faults of others. *Prov. 10:12 with 1 Pet. 4:8.*

Forgiving injuries. *Eph. 4:32; Col. 3:13.*

Forbearing. *Eph. 4:2.*

Rebuking. *Lev. 19:17; Mat. 18:16.*

Necessary for true happiness. *Prov. 15:17.*

The love of God is a motive for. *Jn. 13:14; 1 Jn. 4:11.*

Is an evidence of

Being in the light. *1 Jn. 2:10.*

Discipleship with Christ. *Jn. 13:35.*

Spiritual life. *1 Jn. 3:14.*

Is the fulfilling of the Law. *Rom. 13:8-10; Gal. 5:14; Jas. 2:8.*

Love for self is the measure of. *Mk. 12:33.*

Is good and pleasant. *Ps. 133:1-2.*

In a bond of union. *Col. 2:2.*

In the bond of perfection. *Col. 3:14.*

Hypocrites are devoid of. *1 Jn. 2:9, 11; 1 Jn. 4:20.*

The wicked are devoid of. *1 Jn. 3:10.*

Some examples. **Joseph**: *Gen. 45:15.* **Moses**: *Heb. 11:25.* **Ruth**: *Ruth 1:16-17.* **Jonathan**, etc: *1 Sam. 20:17, 41-42.* **Obadiah**: *1 Kings 18:4.* **A centurion**: *Lk. 7:5.* **The early Church**: *Acts 2:46; Heb. 10:33-34.* **Lydia**: *Acts 16:15.* **Aquila**, etc: *Rom. 16:3-4.* **Paul**: *2 Cor. 6:11-12.* **Epaphroditus**: *Phil. 2:25-26, 30.* **The Philippians**: *Phil. 4:15-19.* **The Colossians**: *Col. 1:4.* **The Thessalonians**: *1 Thess. 3:6.* **Onesiphorus**: *2 Tim. 1:16-18.* **Philemon**: *Philem. verses 7-9.*

LOVING-KINDNESS OF GOD, THE

Is through Christ. *Eph. 2:7; Titus 3:4-6.*

Is described as

Great. *Neh. 9:17.*

Excellent. *Ps. 36:7.*

Good. *Ps. 69:16.*

Marvellous. *Ps. 17:7. Ps. 31:21.*

Multitude of. *Is. 63:7.*

Everlasting. *Is. 54:8.*

Merciful. *Ps. 117:2.*

Better than life. *Ps. 63:3.*

A consideration of the God's dealings gives a knowledge of. *Ps. 107:43.*

The saints

Are betrothed in. *Hos. 2:19.*

Are drawn by. *Jer. 31:3.*

Are preserved by. *Ps. 40:11.*

Are made alive afterwards. *Ps. 119:88.*

Are comforted by. *Ps. 119:76.*

Look for mercy through. *Ps. 51:1.*

Receive mercy through. *Is. 54:8.*
Are heard according to. *Ps. 119:149.*
Are ever mindful of. *Ps. 26:3. Ps. 49:9.*
Should expect, in affliction.
Ps. 42:7-8.
Crowned with. *Ps. 103:4.*
Never utterly taken from the
saints. *Ps. 89:33; Is. 54:10.*
Former manifestations of, to be
pleaded for in prayer. *Ps. 26:6, 89:49.*
Pray for the
The display of. *Ps. 17:7, 143:8.*
The continuing of. *Ps. 36:10.*
The extension of. *Gen. 24:12;*
2 Sam. 2:6.
Praise God for. *Ps. 92:2, 138:2.*
Proclaim, to others. *Ps. 40:10.*

LYING

Is forbidden. *Lev. 19:11; Col. 3:9.*
Is hateful to God. *Prov. 6:16-19.*
Is an abomination to God. *Prov. 12:22.*
Is a hindrance to prayer. *Is. 59:2-3.*
The devil is the father of. *Jn. 8:44.*
The devil incites men to.
1 Kings 22:22; Acts 5:3.
The saints
Hate. *Ps. 119:163; Prov. 13:5.*
Avoid. *Is. 83:8; Zeph. 3:13.*
Have no respect for those who
practise. *Ps. 40:4.*
Reject those who practise. *Ps. 101:7.*
Pray to be preserved from.
Ps. 119:29; Prov. 30:8.
Unbecoming in rulers.
Prov. 17:7.
The evil of rulers listening to.
Prov. 29:12.
False prophets are addicted to.
Jer. 23:14; Ezek. 22:28.
False witnesses are addicted to.
Prov. 14:5, 25.
Antinomians (those showing no

respect for God's Law) are guilty
of. *1 Jn. 1:6, 2:4.*
Hypocrites are addicted to. *Hos. 11:12.*
Hypocrites are a seed of. *Is. 57:4.*
The wicked
Are addicted to, from their
infancy. *Ps. 58:3.*
Love. *Ps. 52:3.*
Delight in. *Ps. 62:4.*
Seek after. *Ps. 4:2.*
Prepare their tongues for. *Jer. 9:3, 5.*
Bring, forth. *Ps. 7:14.*
Give heed to. *Prov. 17:4.*
A characteristic of the Apostacy.
2 Thess. 2:9; 1 Tim. 4:2.
Leads to
Hatred. *Prov. 26:28.*
Love of impure speech.
Prov. 17:4.
Often accompanied by gross
crimes. *Hos. 4:1-2.*
The folly of concealing hatred by.
Prov. 10:18.
The stupidity of getting rich by.
Prov. 21:6.
Will be detected. *Prov. 12:19.*
Poverty is preferable to. *Prov. 19:22.*
Excludes from heaven. *Rev. 21:27, 22:15.*
Those who are guilty of, will be
cast into hell. *Rev. 21:8.*
Punishment for. *Ps. 5:6, 120:3-4;*
Prov. 19:5; Jer. 50:36.

Some examples. **The devil**: *Gen. 3:4.*
Cain: *Gen. 4:9.* **Sarah**: *Gen. 18:15.*
Jacob: *Gen. 27:19.* **Joseph's brothers**:
Gen. 37:31-32. **Gibeonites**: *Josh. 9:9-13.*
Samson: *Judg. 16:10.* **Saul**: *1 Sam. 15:13.*
Michal: *1 Sam. 19:14.* **David**: *Sam. 21:2.*
A prophet of Bethel:
1 Kings 13:18. **Gehazi**: *2 Kings 5:22.* **Job's**
friends: *Job 13:4.* **Ninevites**: *Nah. 3:1.*
Peter: *Mat. 26:72.* **Ananias**, etc: *Acts 5:5.*
Cretans: *Titus 1:12.*

M

MAGISTRATES

Are appointed by God. *Rom. 13:1.*
Are ministers of God will. *Rom. 13:4, 6.*
The purpose of their appointment. *Rom. 13:4; 1 Pet. 2:14.*
Are not a terror to the good, but to the bad. *Rom. 13:3.*
Should be wisely selected and appointed. *Ex. 18:21; Ezra 7:25.*
Should be prayed for. *1 Tim. 2:1-2.*

Should
   Rule in the fear of God.
   2 Sam. 23:3; 2 Chron. 19:7.
   Know the law of God. *Ezra 7:25.*
   Be faithful to the Sovereign.
   Dan. 6:4.
   Enforce the laws. *Ezra 7:26.*
   Hate covetousness. *Ex. 18:21.*
   Not take bribes. *Ex. 23:8; Deut. 16:19.*
   Defend the poor, etc. *Job 29:12, 16.*
   Judge for God, not for man.
   2 Chron. 19:6.
   Judge righteously. *Deut. 1:16, 16:18, 25:1.*
   Be impartial. *Ex. 23:6; Deut. 1:17.*
   Be diligent in ruling. *Rom. 12:8.*
Subjection to the authority is enforced. *Rom. 13:1; 1 Pet. 2:13-14.*
Wicked magistrates are illustrated. *Prov. 28:15.*

Some examples of good magistrates. **Joseph**: *Gen. 41:46.* **Gideon**: *Judg. 8:35.* **Samuel**: *1 Sam. 12:3-4; Ezra 10:1-9.* **Nehemiah**: *Neh. 3:15.* **Job**: *Job 29:16.* **Daniel**: *Dan. 6:3.*

Some examples of bad magistrates. **The sons of Samuel**: *1 Sam. 8:3.* **Pontius Pilate**: *Mat. 27:24, 26.* **The magistrates in Philippi**: *Acts 16:22-23.* **Gallio**: *Acts 18:16-17.* **Felix**: *Acts 24:26.*

MALICE

Forbidden. *1 Cor. 14:20; Col. 3:8.*
A hindrance to growth in grace. *1 Pet. 2:1-2.*
Incompatible with the worship of God. *1 Cor. 5:7-8.*
Christian liberty not to be made a cloak for. *1 Pet. 2:16.*
The saints avoid. *Job 31:29-30; Ps. 35:12-14.*

The wicked
   Speak with. *3 Jn. verse 10.*
   Live in. *Titus 3:3.*
   Plan in. *Ps. 7:14.*
   Are full of. *Rom. 1:29.*
   Treat the saints with. *Ps. 83:3; Mat. 22:6.*
Pray for those who injure you through. *Mat. 5:44.*
Brings its own punishment. *Ps. 7:15-16.*
God repays. *Ps. 10:14; Ezek. 36:5.*
The punishment of. *Amos 1:11-12. Obad. verses 10-15.*

Some examples. **Cain**: *Gen. 4:5.* **Esau**: *Gen. 27:41.* **Joseph's brothers**: *Gen. 37:19-20.* **Saul**: *1 Sam. 18:9-11.* **Sanballat**, etc: *Neh. 2:10.* **Haman**: *Esth. 3:5-6.* **Edomites**: *Ezek. 35:5.* **Presidents**, etc: *Dan. 6:4-9.* **Herodias**: *Mk. 6:19.* **Scribes**, etc:, *Mk. 11:18. Lk. 11:54.* **Diotrephes**: *3 Jn. verse 10.*

MARRIAGE

Was divinely instituted. *Gen. 2:24.*
A covenant relationship. *Mal. 2:4.*

Designed for
   The happiness of mankind.
   Gen. 2:18.
   Increasing mankind. *Gen. 1:28, 9:1.*
   Raising up a godly seed. *Mal. 2:15.*
   The preventing of fornication.
   1 Cor. 7:2.
   Expectation of the promised seed of the woman as an incentive to, at an early age.
   Gen. 3:15 with Gen. 4:1 (see margin).

Lawful in all things. *1 Cor. 7:2, 28; 1 Tim. 5:14.*

Honourable for all. *Heb. 13:4.*

Should be only with the Lord's people. *1 Cor. 7:39.*

Expressed by

Joining together. *Mat. 19:6.*

Declaring an affinity. *1 Kings 3:1.*

Taking to wife. *Ex. 2:1.*

Giving daughters to sons, and sons to daughters. *Deut. 7:3; Ezra 9:12.*

Indissoluble during the married life of the parties concerned. *Mat. 19:6; Rom. 7:2-3; 1 Cor. 7:39.*

The early and unfortunate introduction of polygamy. *Gen. 4:19.*

Contracted with near relatives in the patriarchal age. *Gen. 20:12, 24:24, 28:2.*

Often arranged by parents for their children. *Gen. 24:49-51, 34:6, 8.*

Should be with the consent of the parents. *Gen. 28:8; Judg. 14:2-3.*

Consent of the parties necessary to. *Gen. 24:57-58; 1 Sam. 18:20, 25:41.*

Parents have the right to refuse to give their children in. *Ex. 22:17; Deut. 7:3.*

The Jews

Were forbidden to marry their close relatives. *Lev. 18:6.*

Were forbidden to marry idolaters. *Deut. 7:3, 4; Josh. 23:12; Ezra 9:11-12.*

Often married foreigners. *1 Kings 11:1; Neh. 13:23.*

Were sometimes guilty of polygamy. *1 King 11:1, 3.*

Were careful in arranging marriages for their children. *Gen. 24:2-3, 28:1-2.*

Betrothed themselves beforehand. *Deut. 20:7; Judg. 14:5, 7 with verse 8; Mat. 1:18.*

Were sometime contracted when young. *Prov. 2:17; Joel 1:8.*

Were often contracted within their own tribe. *Ex. 2:1; Num. 36:6-13; Lk. 1:5, 27.*

Were obliged to contract with the wife of a brother who died without children. *Deut. 25:5; Mat. 22:24.*

Considered being debarred from, a reproach. *Is. 4:1.*

Considered being debarred from, a cause of grief. *Judg. 11:38.*

Were often punished by being debarred from. *Jer. 7:34, 16:9, 25:10.*

Were allowed divorce from, because of the hardness of their hearts. *Deut. 24:1 with Mat. 19:7-8.*

Were exempt from going to war immediately after. *Deut. 20:7.*

A priest was not allowed to marry a divorced or improper woman. *Lev. 21:7.*

The High Priest could not marry a widow, or a divorcée, or an unbelieving woman. *Lev. 21:14.*

A declaration of marriage took place at the gate, and before witnesses. *Ruth 4:1, 10- 11.*

Methods of searching for a wife in. *Gen. 24:3-4, 34:6, 8; 1 Sam. 25:39-40.*

The oldest daughters were usually given in, before the younger. *Gen. 29:26.*

A dowry was given to the woman's parents beforehand (unlike many places in the world today). *Gen. 29:18, 34:12; 1 Sam. 18:27-28; Hos. 3:2.*

Was celebrated

With great rejoicing. *Jer. 33:11; Jn. 3:29.*

With feasting. *Gen. 29:22; Judg. 14:10; Mat. 22:2-3; Jn. 2:1-10.*

For seven days. *Judg. 14:12.*

A benediction was pronounced after. *Gen. 24:60; Ruth 4:11-12.*

The bride

Received presents before. *Gen. 24:53.*

Was given a handmaid at. *Gen. 24:59, 29:24, 29.*

Was adorned with jewels for. *Is. 49:18, 61:10.*

Was beautifully clothed. Ps. 45:13-14.
Was attended by her brides-
maids. Ps. 45:9.
Stood to the right of the
bridegroom. Ps. 45:9.
Was called to forget her father's
house. Ps. 45:10.

The bridegroom
Was also adorned with
ornaments. Is. 61:10.
Was attended by many friends.
Judg. 14:11; Jn. 3:29.
Was presented with gifts. Ps. 45:12.
Was crowned with garlands.
Song 3:11.
Rejoiced over his bride. Is. 62:5.
Returned with the bride to his
house at night. Mat. 25:1-6.
Garments were provided for
guests at. Mat. 22:12.
Infidelity on the part of either of
the engaged couple was pun-
ished as if already married.
Deut. 22:23-24; Mat. 1:19.

An illustration of
God's union with the Jewish
nation. Is. 54:5; Jer. 3:14; Hos. 2:19-20.
Christ's union with his Church.
Eph. 6:23-24, 32.

MARTYRDOM
Is death endured for the Word of
God and testimony of Christ.
Rev. 6:9, 20:4.

The saints
Are forewarned of. Mat. 10:21, 24:9;
Jn. 16:2.
Should not be afraid of.
Mat. 10:28; Rev. 2:10.
Should be prepared for.
Mat. 16:24-25; Acts 21:13.
Should resist sin to. Heb. 12:4.
The reward of. Rev. 2:10, 6:11.
Inflicted at the instigation of
the devil. Rev. 2:10, 13.
The Apostasy is guilty of
inflicting. Rev. 17:6, 18:24.
Of the saints, will be avenged.
Lk. 11:50-51; Rev. 18:20-24.

Some examples. **Abel:** Gen. 4:8 with
1 Jn. 3:12. **Prophets and saints of
old:** 1 Kings 18:4. 1 Kings 19:10. Lk. 11:50-
51. Heb. 11:37. **Urijah:** Jer. 26:23. **John
the Baptist:** Mk. 6:27. **Peter:** Jn. 21:18-
19. **Stephen:** Acts 7:58. **Early Christians:** Acts 9:1 with Acts 22:4, 26:10.
James: Acts 12:2. **Antipas:** Rev. 2:13.

MASTERS
Their authority is established.
Col. 3:22; 1 Pet. 2:18.
Christ set an example to. Jn. 13:14.
Should, with their households,
Worship God. Gen. 35:3.
Fear God. Acts 10:2.
Serve God. Josh. 24:15.
Observe the Sabbath. Ex. 20:10;
Deut. 5:12-14.
Put away idols. Gen. 35:2.
Should select faithful servants.
Gen. 24:2; Ps. 101:6-7.
Should receive faithful advice
from their servants. 2 Kings 5:13-14.
Their duties towards servants:
To act justly. Job 31:13, 15; Col. 4:1.
To deal with them in the fear of
God. Eph. 6:9; Col. 4:1.
To esteem them highly, if
fellow-believers. Philem. verse 16.
To take care of them in
sickness. Lk. 7:3.
To refrain from threatening
them. Eph. 6:9.
Not to defraud them. Gen. 31:7.
Not to keep back their wages.
Lev. 19:13; Deut. 24:15.
Not to rule over them severely.
Lev. 25:43; Deut. 24:14.
Benevolent, are blessed. Deut. 15:18.
Unjust, are denounced. Jer. 22:13.
Jas. 5:4.

Some examples of good masters.
Abraham: Gen. 18:19. **Jacob:** Gen. 35:2.
Joshua: Josh. 24:15. **David:** 2 Sam. 6:20.
A Centurion: Lk. 7:2-3. **Cornelius:**
Acts 10:2.

Some examples of bad masters.
Egyptians: *Ex.1:13-14.*
Nabal: *1 Sam. 25:17.*
The Amalakites: *1 Sam. 30:13.*

MEEKNESS
Christ set an example of. *Ps. 45:4;*
Mat. 11:29, 21:5; 2 Cor. 10:1.
A fruit of the Spirit. *Gal. 5:22-23.*
The saints should
Seek. *Zeph. 2:3.*
Put on. *Col. 3:12-13.*
Receive the Word of God with.
Jas. 1:21.
Show, in behaviour. *Jas. 3:13.*
Answer for their hope with.
1 Pet. 3:15.
Show, to all men. *Titus 3:2.*
Restore the erring with. *Gal. 6:1.*
Is precious in the sight of God.
1 Pet. 3:4.
Ministers should
Follow after. *1 Tim. 6:11.*
Instruct opponents with.
2 Tim. 2:24-25.
Urge, on their people. *Titus 3:1-2.*
A characteristic of wisdom. *Jas. 3:17.*
Necessary for the Christian walk.
Eph. 4:1-2.
Those who are gifted with,
Are preserved. *Ps. 76:9.*
Are exalted. *Ps. 147:6.*
Are guided and taught. *Ps. 25:9.*
Are richly provided for. *Ps. 22:26.*
Are beautified with salvation.
Ps. 149:4.
Increase their joy. *Is. 29:19.*
Will inherit the earth. *Ps. 37:11.*
The gospel must be preached to
those who oppose. *Is. 61:1.*
The blessedness of. *Mat. 5:5.*

Some examples. **Moses**: *Num. 12:3.*
David: *2 Sam. 16:9-12.* **Paul**: *1 Thess. 2:7.*

MERCY
Is after the example of God. *Lk. 6:36.*
Is recommended. *Hos. 12:6; Col. 3:12.*
To be engraved on the heart. *Prov. 3:3.*

A characteristic of the saints.
Ps. 37:26; Is. 57:1.
Should be shown
With cheerfulness. *Rom. 12:8.*
To our brothers. *Zech. 7:9.*
To the poor. *Prov. 14:31; Dan. 4:27.*
To the animals. *Prov. 12:10.*
Upholds the throne of kings.
Prov. 20:28.
Is beneficial to those who
exercise. *Prov. 11:17.*
The blessedness of showing.
Prov. 14:21; Mat. 5:7.
Hypocrites are devoid of. *Mat. 23:23.*
Denunciations against those
devoid of. *Hos. 4:1, 3; Jas. 2:13.*

MERCY OF GOD, THE
Is part of his character. *Ex. 34:6-7;*
Ps. 62:12; Jonah 4:2; 2 Cor. 1:3.
Is described as
Great. *Num. 14:18; Is. 54:7.*
Rich. *Eph. 2:4.*
Manifold. *Neh. 9:27; Lam. 3:32.*
Plentiful. *Ps. 86:5, 15, 103:8.*
Abundant. *1 Pet. 1:3.*
Sure. *Is. 55:3; Mic. 7:20.*
Everlasting. *1 Chron. 16:34; Ps. 89:28.*
Tender. *Ps. 25:6; Lk. 1:78.*
New every morning. *Lam. 3:23.*
High as heaven. *Ps. 36:5, 103:11.*
Filling the earth. *Ps. 119:64.*
Over all his works. *Ps. 145:9.*
Is his delight. *Mic. 7:18.*
Is manifested
In the sending of Christ. *Lk. 1:78.*
In salvation. *Titus 3:5.*
In long-suffering. *Lam. 3:22; Dan. 9:9.*
To his people. *Deut. 32:43;*
1 Kings 8:23.
To those who that fear him.
Ps. 103:17; Lk. 1:50.
To returning backsliders. *Jer. 3:12;*
Joel 2:13.
To repentant sinners. *Prov. 28:13;*
Is. 55:7.
To the afflicted. *Is. 49:13, 54:7.*
To the fatherless. *Hos. 14:3.*
To whomever he will. *Hos. 2:23*

with Rom. 9:15, 18.

With everlasting kindness.
Is. 54:8.

A ground of hope. *Ps. 130:7, 147:11.*

A ground of trust. *Ps. 52:8.*

Should be

Sought for ourselves. *Ps. 6:2.*

Sought for others. *Gal. 6:16;*
1 Tim. 1:2; 2 Tim. 1:18.

Pleaded for in prayer. *Ps. 6:4, 25:6, 51:1.*

Rejoiced in. *Ps. 31:7.*

Magnified. *1 Chron. 16:34; Ps. 115:1,*
118:1-4, 29; Jer. 33:11.

Typified in the Mercy Seat. *Ex. 25:17.*

Some examples. **Lot**: *Gen. 19:16, 19.*
Epaphroditus: *Phil. 2:27.* **Paul**:
1 Tim. 1:13.

MINISTERS (PASTORS, ELDERS)

Are called by God. *Ex. 28:1 with Heb 5:4.*

Are qualified by God. *2 Cor. 3:5-6.*

Are commissioned by Christ.
Mat. 28:19.

Are sent by the Holy Spirit. *Acts 13:2, 4.*

Have authority from God.
2 Cor. 10:8, 13:10.

Their authority is for edification.
2 Cor. 10:8, 13:10.

Separated for the gospel. *Rom. 1:1.*

Entrusted with the gospel. *1 Thess. 2:4.*

Are described as

Ambassadors for Christ. *2 Cor. 5:20.*

Ministers of Christ. *1 Cor. 4:1.*

Stewards of the mysteries of
God. *Cor. 4:1.*

Defenders of the faith. *Phil. 1:7.*

Specially protected by God. *2 Cor. 1:10.*

The necessity for. *Rom. 10:14.*

The excellence of. *Rom. 10:15.*

The labours of, are in vain without
God's blessing. *1 Cor. 3:7, 15:10.*

Compared with earthen vessels.
2 Cor. 4:7

Should be

Pure. *Is. 52:11. 1 Tim. 3:9.*

Holy. *Lev. 21:6. Titus 1:8.*

Humble. *Acts 20:19.*

Patient. *2 Cor. 6:4; 2 Tim. 2:24.*

Blameless. *1 Tim. 3:2; Titus 1:7.*

Willing. *Is. 6:8; 1 Pet. 5:2.*

Fair-minded. *2 Cor. 12:14; 1 Thess. 2:6.*

Impartial. *1 Tim. 5:21.*

Gentle. *1 Thess. 2:7; 2 Tim. 2:24.*

Devoted. *Acts 20:24; Phil. 1:20-21.*

Strong in grace. *2 Tim. 2:1.*

Self-denying. *1 Cor. 9:27.*

Serious, just, and moderate.
Titus 1:8.

Hospitable. *1 Tim. 3:2; Titus 1:8.*

Able to teach. *1 Tim. 3:2; 2 Tim. 2:24.*

Studious and meditative.
1 Tim. 4:13, 15.

Watchful. *2 Tim. 4:5.*

Prayerful. *Eph .3:14; Phil. 1:4.*

Strict in ruling their own
families. *1 Tim. 3:4, 12.*

Affectionate to their people.
Phil. 1:7; 1 Thess. 2:8, 11.

Examples to the flock. *Phil. 3:17;*
2 Thess. 3:9; 1 Tim. 4:12; 1 Pet. 5:3.

Should not be

Lords over God's heritage. *1 Pet. 5:3.*

Greedy for plenty of money.
Acts 20:23; 1 Tim. 3:3, 8; 1 Pet. 5:2.

Contentious. *1 Tim. 3:3; Titus 1:7.*

Crafty. *2 Cor. 4:2.*

Men-pleasers. *Gal. 1:10; 1 Thess. 2:4.*

Easily dispirited. *2 Cor. 4:8-9, 6:10.*

Entangled by cares. *Lk. 9:60;*
2 Tim. 2:4.

Given to wine. *1 Tim. 3:3. Titus 1:7.*

Should seek the salvation of their
flock. *1 Cor. 10:33.*

Should avoid giving unnecessary
offence. *1 Cor. 10:32-33; 2 Cor. 6:3.*

Should make full proof of their
ministry. *2 Tim. 4:5.*

Are bound to

Preach the gospel to all. *Mk. 16:15;*
1 Cor. 1:17.

Feed the Church. *Jer. 3:15; Jn. 21:15-17;*
Acts 20:28; 1 Pet. 5:2.

Build up the Church. *2 Cor. 12:19;*
Eph. 4:12.

Watch for souls. *Heb. 13:17.*

Pray for their people. *Joel 2:17;*
Col. 1:9.

Strengthen the faith of their people. *Lk. 22:32; Acts 14:22.*
Teach. *2 Tim. 2:2.*
Exhort. *Titus 1:9, 2:15.*
Warn affectionately. *Acts 20:31.*
Rebuke. *Titus 1:13, 2:15.*
Comfort. *2 Cor. 1:4-6.*
Convince those who contradict. *Titus 1:9.*
Fight the good fight. *1 Tim. 1:18; 2 Tim. 4:7.*
Endure hardness. *2 Tim. 2:3.*

Should preach
Christ crucified. *Acts 8:5, 35; 1 Cor. 2:2.*
Repentance and faith. *Lk. 20:21.*
According to the oracles of God. *1 Pet. 4:11.*
Everywhere. *Mk. 16:20; Acts 8:4.*
Not with enticing words of man's wisdom. *1 Cor. 1:17; 1 Cor. 2:1, 4.*
Not putting themselves forward. *2 Cor. 4:5.*
Without deceit. *2 Cor. 2:17, 4:2; 1 Thess. 2:3, 5.*
Fully, and without reserve. *Acts 5:20; Acts 20:20, 27; Rom. 15:19.*
With boldness. *Is. 58:1; Ezek. 2:6; Mat. 10:27-28.*
With plainness of speech. *2 Cor. 3:12.*
With zeal. *1 Thess. 2:8.*
With constancy. *Acts 6:4; 2 Tim. 4:2.*
With consistency. *2 Cor. 1:18-19.*
With great care. *1 Tim. 4:16.*
With good will and love. *Phil. 1:15-17.*
Without charge, if possible. *1 Cor. 9:18; 1 Thess. 2:9.*
Woe to those who do not preach the gospel! *1 Cor. 9:16.*

When faithful,
They prove themselves to be ministers of God. *2 Cor. 6:4.*
They thank God for his gifts to their people. *1 Cor. 1:4; Phil. 1:3; 1 Thess. 3:9.*
They glory in their people. *2 Cor. 7:4.*
They rejoice in the faith and holiness of their people. *1 Thess. 2:19-20; 1 Thess. 3:6-9.*
They commend themselves to the consciences of men. *2 Cor. 4:2.*
They are rewarded. *Mat. 24:47; 1 Pet. 5:4.*

When unfaithful,
They are described. *Is. 56:10-12; Titus 1:10-11.*
They deal treacherously with their people. *Jn. 10:12.*
They delude their flock. *Jer. 6:14.*
They seek gain. *Mic. 3:11; 2 Pet. 2:3.*
They will be punished. *Ezek. 33:6-8; Mat. 24:48-51.*

Their people are bound, to
Regard them as God's messengers. *1 Cor. 4:1; Gal. 4:14.*
Attend to their instructions. *Mal. 2:7; Mat. 23:3.*
Follow their holy example. *1 Cor. 11:1; Phil. 3:17.*
Imitate their faith. *Heb. 13:7.*
Hold them in high repute. *Phil. 2:29; 1 Thess. 5:13; 1 Tim. 5:17.*
Love them. *2 Cor. 8:7. 1 Thess. 3:6.*
Pray for them. *Rom. 15:30; 2 Cor. 1:11; Eph. 6:19; Heb. 13:18.*
Obey them. *1 Cor. 16:16; Heb. 13:17.*
Give them joy. *2 Cor. 1:14, 2 Cor. 2:3.*
Help them. *Rom. 16:9; Phil. 4:3.*
Support them. *2 Chron. 31:4; 1 Cor. 9:7-11; Gal. 6:6.*
Pray for their fruitfulness. *Mat. 9:38.*

Some examples of faithful pastors. **The eleven apostles**: *Mat. 28:18-19.* **The Seventy**: *Lk. 10:1, 17.* **Matthias**: *Acts 1:26.* **Philip**: *Acts 8:5.* **Barnabas**: *Acts 11:23.* **Simeon**, etc: *Act 13:1.* **Paul**: *Acts 28:31.* **Tychichus**: *Eph. 6:21.* **Timothy**: *Phil. 2:22.* **Epaphroditus**: *Phil. 2:25.* **Archippus**: *Col. 4:17.* **Titus**: *Titus 1:5.*

MIRACLES
The power of God is necessary for. *Jn. 3:2.*

Are described as

Marvellous things. Ps. 78:12.
Marvellous works. Is. 29:14; Ps. 105:5.
Signs and wonders. Jer. 32:21;
Jn. 4:48; 2 Cor. 12:12.

Manifest

The glory of God. Jn. 11:4.
The glory of Christ. Jn. 2:11, 11:4.
The works of God. Jn. 9:3.
Were evidences of a divine
commission. Ex. 4:1-5; Mk. 16:20.
The Messiah was expected to
perform. Mat. 11:2-3; Jn. 7:31.
Jesus was proved to be the
Messiah by. Mat. 11:4-6; Jn. 5:36; Acts 2:22.
Jesus was followed on account of.
Mat. 4:23-25; Jn. 6:2, 26.
Are a gift of the Holy Spirit.
1 Cor. 12:10.

Were performed

In the power of God. Acts 14:3,
15:12, 19:11.
By the power of Christ. Mat. 10:1.
By the power of the Holy Spirit.
Mat. 12:28; Rom. 15:19.
In the name of Christ. Mk. 16:17;
Acts 3:16, 4:30.

First preaching of the gospel was
confirmed by. Mk. 16:20; Heb. 2:4.
Those who performed them,
disclaimed all power of their own.
Acts 3:12.
Should produce faith. Jn. 2:23, 20:30-31.
Should produce obedience.
Deut. 11:1-3, 29:2-3, 9.
Were instrumental in the early
propagation of the gospel. Acts 8:6;
Rom. 15:18-19.

Faith is required in

Those who performed them.
Mat. 17:20, 21:21; Jn. 14:12; Acts 3:16, 6:8.
Those for whom they were
performed. Mat. 9:28; Mk. 9:22-24;
Acts 14:9.
Should be remembered.
1 Chron. 16:12; Ps. 105:5.
Should be told to future genera-
tions. Ex. 10:2; Judg. 6:13.
Were insufficient, of themselves,
to produce conversion. Lk. 16:31.

The wicked

Long to see them performed.
Lk. 11:29, 23:8.
Often acknowledge. Jn. 11:47;
Acts 4:16.
Do not understand. Ps. 106:7.
Do not consider. Mk. 6:52.
Forget. Neh. 9:17; Ps. 78:11.
Are proof against. Num. 14:22;
Jn. 12:37.
The guilt of those who reject the
evidence afforded by. Mat. 11:20-24;
Jn. 15:24.

MIRACLES OF CHRIST, THE

Water turned into wine. Jn. 2:6-10.
The nobleman's son healed.
Jn. 4:46-53.
The centurion's servant healed.
Mat. 8:5-13.
The miraculous draughts of fish.
Lk. 5:4-6; Jn. 21:6.
Devils cast out. Mat. 8:28-32, 9:32-33,
15:22-28, 17:14-18.
Peter's mother-in-law healed.
Mat. 8:14-15.
Lepers cleansed. Mat. 8:3; Lk. 17:14.
A paralysed man healed. Mk. 2:3-12.
A withered hand restored.
Mat. 12:10-13.
An impotent man healed. Jn. 5:5-9.
The dead were raised to life.
Mat. 9:18-19, 23-25; Lk. 7:12-15; Jn. 11:11-44.
The issue of blood stopped.
Mat. 9:20-22.
The blind received their sight.
Mat. 9:27, 30; Mk. 8:22-25; Jn. 9:1-7.
The deaf and dumb cured.
Mk. 7:32-35.
The multitude fed. Mat. 14:15-21;
Mat. 15:32-38.
Christ's walking on the sea.
Mat. 14:25-27.
Peter walking on the sea. Mat. 14:29.
The storm stilled. Mat. 23:26, 14:32.
The sudden arrival of the ship at
land. Jn. 6:21.
Tribute money. Mat. 17:27.

The woman healed of an infirmity. *Lk. 13:11-13.*
Dropsy cured. *Lk. 14:2-4.*
The fig tree that was blighted. *Mat. 21:19.*
Malchus' ear healed. *Lk. 22:50-51.*
Were performed before the messengers of John. *Lk. 7:21-22.*
Many and various diseases were healed. *Mat. 4:23-24, 14:14, 15:30; Mk. 1:34; Lk. 6:17-19.*
His resurrection. *Lk. 24:6 with Jn. 10:18.*
His appearance to his disciples when the doors were shut. *Jn. 20:19.*

MIRACLES PERFORMED BY THE SERVANTS OF GOD

Moses and Aaron:
A rod was turned into a serpent. *Ex. 4:3, 7:10.*
The rod was restored. *Ex. 4:4.*
His hand was made leprous. *Ex. 4:6.*
His hand was healed. *Ex. 4:7.*
The water was turned into blood. *Ex. 4:9, 30.*
The river was turned into blood. *Ex. 7:20.*
Frogs came out. *Ex. 8:6.*
The frogs were removed. *Ex. 8:13.*
Lice were brought. *Ex. 8:17.*
Flies were brought. *Ex. 8:21-24.*
The flies were removed. *Ex. 8:31.*
Blisters appeared on the beasts. *Ex. 9:3-6.*
Boils and blains were brought. *Ex. 9:10-11.*
Hail was brought. *Ex. 9:23.*
The hail was removed. *Ex. 9:33.*
Locusts were brought. *Ex. 10:13.*
The locusts were removed. *Ex. 10:19.*
Darkness was brought. *Ex. 10:22.*
The first-born died. *Ex. 12:29.*

The Red Sea was divided. *Ex. 14:21-22.*
The Egyptians were overwhelmed. *Ex. 14:26-28.*
The water was cleansed. *Ex. 15:25.*
The water came out of the rock in Horeb. *Ex. 17:6.*
Amalek was vanquished. *Ex. 17:11-13.*
The destruction of Korah. *Num. 16:28-32.*
Water came out of the rock in Kadesh. *Num. 20:11.*
Healing by a bronze serpent. *Num. 21:8-9.*

Joshua:
The waters of the Jordan were divided. *Josh. 3:10-17.*
The River Jordan was restored to its course. *Josh. 4:18.*
Jericho was taken. *Josh. 6:6-20.*
The sun and moon were stayed. *Josh. 10:12-14.*
The Midianites were destroyed. *Judg. 7:16-22.*

Samson:
A lion was killed. *Judg. 14:6.*
The Philistines were slain. *Judg. 14:19, 15:15.*
The gates of Gaza were carried away. *Judg. 16:3.*
Dagon's house was pulled down. *Judg. 16:30.*

Samuel:
Thunder and rain during harvest. *1 Sam. 12:18.*

A prophet of Judah:
Jeroboam's hand became withered. *1 Kings 13:4.*
The withered hand was restored. *1 Kings 13:6.*
The altar was split apart. *1 Kings 13:5.*

Elijah:
A drought was caused. *1 Kings 17:1; Jas. 5:17.*
Meal and oil were multiplied. *1 Kings 17:14-16.*

A child was restored to life. *1 Kings 17:22-23.*

The sacrifice was consumed with fire. *1 Kings 18:36, 38.*

Men were destroyed by fire. *2 Kings 1:10-12.*

Rain was brought. *1 Kings 18:41-45; Jas. 5:18.*

The waters of the River Jordan were divided. *2 Kings 2:8.*

Elisha:

The waters of the River Jordan were divided. *2 Kings 2:14.*

The waters were healed. *2 Kings 2:21-22.*

Children were torn by bears. *2 Kings 2:24.*

Oil was multiplied. *2 Kings 4:1-7.*

A child was restored to life. *2 Kings 4:32-35.*

Naaman was healed. *2 Kings 5:10, 14.*

Gehazi was struck with leprosy. *2 Kings 5:27.*

Iron was caused to float. *2 Kings 6:6.*

The Syrians were smitten with blindness. *2 Kings 6:18.*

The Syrians' sight was restored. *2 Kings 6:20.*

A man was restored to life. *2 Kings 13:21.*

Isaiah:

Hezekiah was healed. *2 Kings 20:7.*

A shadow was put back on the sundial. *2 Kings 20:11.*

The seventy disciples:

Various miracles. *Lk. 10:9, 17.*

The apostles, etc:

Many miracles. *Acts 2:43, 5:12.*

Peter:

A lame man was cured. *Acts 3:7.*

The death of Ananias. *Acts 5:5.*

The death of Sapphira. *Acts 5:10.*

The sick were healed. *Acts 5:15-16.*

Aeneas was made whole. *Acts 9:34.*

Dorcas was restored to life. *Acts 9:40.*

Stephen:

Great miracles. *Acts 6:8.*

Philip the evangelist:

Various miracles. *Acts 8:6-7, 13.*

Paul:

Elymas was smitten with blindness. *Acts 13:11.*

A lame man was cured. *Acts 14:10.*

An unclean spirit was cast out. *Acts 16:18.*

Special miracles. *Acts 19:11-12.*

Eutychus was restored to life. *Acts 20:10-12.*

The viper's bite was rendered harmless. *Acts 28:5.*

The father of Publius was healed. *Acts 28:8.*

Paul and Barnabas:

Various miracles. *Acts 14:3.*

MIRACLES THROUGH EVIL AGENTS

Were performed through the power of the devil. *2 Thess. 2:9; Rev. 16:14.*

Were performed:

In support of false religions. *Deut. 13:1-2.*

By false christs. *Mat. 24:24.*

By false prophets. *Mat. 24:24; Rev. 19:20.*

Are a mark of the Apostacy. *2 Thess. 2:3, 9; Rev. 13:13.*

Are to be disregarded. *Deut. 13:3.*

May deceive the ungodly. *2 Thess. 2:10-12; Rev. 13:14, 19:20.*

Some examples. **The magicians of Egypt:** *Ex. 7:11, 22, 8:7.* **The witch of Endor:** *1 Sam. 28:7-14.* **Simon Magus:** *Acts 8:9-11.*

MIRACULOUS GIFTS OF THE HOLY SPIRIT

Were foretold. *Is. 35:4-6; Joel 2:28-29.*

Were of different sorts. *1 Cor. 12:4-6.*

Are enumerated. *1 Cor. 12:8-10, 28.*

Christ was endued with. *Mat. 12:28.*

Were poured out on the day of Pentecost. *Acts 2:1-4.*

Communicated

During the preaching of the gospel. *Acts 10:44-46.*

With the laying on of the Apostles' hands. *Acts 8:17-18, 19:6.*

For the confirmation of the gospel. *Mk. 16:20; Acts 14:3; Rom. 15:19; Heb. 2:4.*

For the edification of the Church. *1 Cor. 12:7, 14:12-13.*

Were dispensed according to his sovereign will. *1 Cor. 12:11.*

The best should be sought after. *1 Cor. 12:31, 14:1.*

The temporary nature of. *1 Cor. 13:8.*

Should not be

Neglected. *1 Tim. 4:14; 2 Tim. 1:6.*

Despised. *1 Thess. 5:20.*

Purchased. *Acts 8:20.*

Sadly, might be possessed without saving grace. *Mat. 7:22-23; 1 Cor. 13:1-2; Heb. 6:5-6.*

Are counterfeited by Antichrist. *Mat. 24:24; 2 Thess. 2:9; Rev. 13:13-14.*

MISSIONARY WORK DONE BY MINISTERS

Is commanded. *Mat. 28:19; Mk. 16:15.*

Is warranted by predictions concerning the nations. *Is. 42:10-12, 66:19.*

Is according to the purpose of God. *Lk. 24:46-47; Gal. 1:15-16; Col. 1:25-27.*

Is directed by the Holy Spirit. *Acts 13:2.*

Is required. *Lk. 10:2; Rom. 10:14-15.*

The Holy Spirit calls to. *Acts 13:2.*

Christ engaged in. *Mat. 4:17, 23, 11:1; Mk. 1:38-39; Lk. 8:1.*

Christ sent his disciples to labour in. *Mk. 3:14, 6:7.*

Obligations to engage in. *Acts 4:19-20; Rom. 1:13-15; 1 Cor. 9:16.*

The excellence of. *Is. 52:7 with Rom. 10:15.*

Worldly concerns should not delay. *Lk. 9:59-62.*

God qualifies for. *Ex. 3:11, 18, 4:11-12, 15.*

God strengthens for. *Jer. 1:7-9.*

The guilt and danger of shrinking from. *Jonah 1:3-4.*

Requires wisdom and meekness. *Mat. 10:16.*

Be ready to engage in. *Is. 6:8.*

Aid those engaged in. *2 Cor. 11:9; 3 Jn.verses 5-8.*

Unity should exist among those engaged in. *Gal. 2:9; 1 Cor. 15:11.*

The success of,

To be prayed for. *Eph. 6:18-19; Col. 4:3.*

Is a cause of joy. *Acts 15:3.*

Is a cause of praise. *Acts 11:18, 21:19-20.*

No limit to the sphere of. *Mk. 16:15; Rev. 14:6.*

Opportunities for, not to be neglected. *1 Cor. 16:9.*

Some examples. **Noah**: *2 Pet. 2:5.* **The Levites**: *2 Chron. 17:8-9.* **Jonah**: *Jonah 3:2.* **The Seventy**: *Lk. 10:1, 17.* **The apostles**: *Mk. 6:12; Acts 13:2-5.* **Philip**: *Acts 8:5.* **Paul**, etc: *Acts 13:2-4.* **Silas**: *Acts 15:40-41.* **Timothy**: *Acts 16:3.*

MISSIONARIES, ALL CHRISTIANS ARE

After the example of Christ. *Acts 10:38.*

Women and children, as well as men. *Ps. 8:2; Prov. 31:26; Mat. 21:15-16; Phil. 4:3; 1 Tim. 5:10; Titus 2:3-5; 1 Pet. 3:1.*

The zeal of idolaters should provoke to. *Jer. 7:18.*

The zeal of hypocrites should provoke to. *Mat. 23:15.*

An imperative duty. *Judg. 5:23;. Lk. 19:40.*

The principle on which. *2 Cor. 5:14-15.*

However weak they may be. *1 Cor. 1:27.*

From their calling as saints. *Ex. 19:6; 1 Pet. 2:9.*

As faithful stewards. *1 Pet. 4:10-11.*

In youth. *Ps. 71:17, 148:12-13.*

In old age. *Deut. 32:7; Ps. 71:18.*

In the family. *Deut. 6:7; Ps. 78:5-8; Is. 38:19; 1 Cor. 7:16.*

In their dealings with the world. *Mat. 5:16; Phil. 2:15-16; 1 Pet. 2:12.*

In first giving themselves to the Lord. *2 Cor. 8:5.*

In declaring what God has done for them. *Ps. 66:16, 116:16-19.*

In hating life for Christ's sake. *Lk. 14:26.*

In openly confessing Christ. *Mat. 10:32.*

In following Christ. *Lk. 14:27, 18:22.*

In preferring Christ above all family members. *Lk. 14:26.*

In joyfully suffering for Christ. *Heb. 10:34.*

In forsaking all for Christ. *Lk. 5:11.*

In providing a holy example. *Mat. 5:16; Phil. 2:15; 1 Thess. 1:7.*

In holy speech. *1 Pet. 2:12.*

In holy boldness. *Ps. 119:46.*

In dedicating themselves to the service of God. *Josh. 24:15; Ps. 27:4.*

In devoting all their property to God. *1 Chron. 29:2-3, 14, 16; Eccl. 11:1; Mat. 6:19-20; Mk. 12:44; Lk. 12:33, 18:22, 28; Acts 2:45, 4:32-34.*

In holy living. *Ps. 37:30 with Prov. 10:31; Prov. 15:7; Eph. 4:29; Col. 4:6.*

In speaking of God and his works. *Ps. 71:24, 77:12, 119:27, 145:11-12.*

In showing forth God's praises. *Is. 43:21.*

In inviting others to accept the gospel. *Ps. 34:8; Is. 2:3; Jn. 1:46, 4:29.*

In seeking the edification of others. *Rom. 14:19, 15:2; 1 Thess. 5:11.*

In admonishing others. *1 Thess. 5:14; 2 Thess. 3:15.*

In reproving others. *Lev. 19:17; Eph. 5:11.*

In teaching and exhorting. *Ps. 34:11, 51:13; Col. 3:16; Heb. 3:13, 10:25.*

In interceding for others. *Col. 4:3; Heb. 13:18; Jas. 5:16.*

In assisting ministers in their labours. *Rom. 16:3, 9; 2 Cor. 11:9; Phil. 4:14-16. 3 Jn. verse 6.*

In giving a reason for their faith. *Ex. 12:26-27; Deut. 6:20-21; 1 Pet. 3:15.*

In encouraging the weak. *Is. 35:3-4; Rom. 14:1; Rom. 15:1; 1 Thess. 5:14.*

In visiting and relieving the poor and sick, etc. *Lev. 25:35; Ps. 112:9 with 2 Cor. 9:9; Mat. 25:36; Acts 20:35; Jas. 1:27.*

With a willing heart. *Ex. 35:29; 1 Chron. 29:9, 14.*

With a superabundance in giving. *Ex. 36:5-7; 2 Cor. 8:3.*

An encouragement to. *Prov. 11:25, 30; 1 Cor. 1:27; Jas. 5:19-20.*

The blessedness of. *Dan. 12:3.*

Illustrated. *Mat. 25:14; Lk. 19:13.*

Some examples. **Hannah**: *1 Sam. 2:1-10.* **A captive maid**: *2 Kings 6:3.* **Chief of the Fathers**, etc: *Ezra 1:5.* **Shadrach**, etc: *Dan. 3:16-18.* **The restored demon-possessed man**: *Mk. 5:20.* **The shepherds**: *Lk. 2:17.* **Anna**: *Lk. 2:38.* **Joanna**, etc: *Lk. 8:3.* **A leper**: *Lk. 17:15.* **Disciples**: *Lk. 19:37-38.* **A centurion**: *Lk. 23:47.* **Andrew**: *Jn. 1:41-42.* **Philip**: *Jn. 1:46.* **The woman of Samaria**: *Jn. 4:29.* **Barnabas**: *Acts 4:36-37.* **Persecuted saints**: *Acts 8:4, 11:19-20.* **Apollos**: *Acts 18:25.* **Aquila**, etc: *Acts 18:26.* **Various individuals**: *Rom. chapter 16.* **Onesiphorus**: *2 Tim. 1:16.* **Philemon**: *Philem. verses 1-6.*

MURDER

Is forbidden. *Ex. 20:13 with Rom. 13:9.*

Is explained by Christ. *Mat. 5:21-22.*

Hatred is the same as. *1 Jn. 3:15.*

Is a work of the flesh. *Gal. 5:21.*

Comes from the heart. *Mat. 15:19.*

Defiles the

Hands. *Is. 59:3.*

Person and garments. *Lam. 4:13-14.*

Land. *Num. 35:33; Ps. 106:38.*

Not concealed from God. *Is. 26:21; Jer. 2:34.*

Cries for vengeance. *Gen. 4:10.*

God

Abominates. *Prov. 6:16-17.*

Makes enquiry concerning. *Ps. 9:12.*

Will avenge. *Deut. 32:43; Hos. 1:4.*

Requires blood for. *Gen. 9:5; Num. 35:33; 1 Kings 2:32.*
Rejects the prayers of those guilty of. *Is. 1:15, 59:2-3.*
Curses those guilty of. *Gen. 4:11.*
The law is designed to restrain. *1 Tim. 1:9.*

The saints
Are specially warned against. *1 Pet. 4:15.*
Deplore the guilt of. *Ps. 51:14.*
Should warn others against. *Gen. 37:22; Jer. 26:15.*
Is connected with idolatry. *Ezek. 22:3-4.*

The wicked
Are full of. *Rom. 1:29.*
Devise. *Gen. 27:41, 37:18.*
Are intent on. *Jer. 22:17.*
Lie in wait to commit. *Ps. 10:8-10.*
Are swift to commit. *Prov. 1:16; Rom. 3:15.*
Perpetrate. *Job 24:14; Ezek. 22:3.*
Have their hands full of. *Is. 1:15.*
Encourage others to commit. *Prov. 1:11.*
Is a characteristic of the devil. *Jn. 8:44.*
The punishment of. *Gen. 4:12-15, 9:6; Num. 35:30; Jer. 19:4-9.*
Their punishment is not commuted under the Law. *Num. 35:31.*
Of the saints, is especially avenged. *Deut. 32:43. Mat. 22:35; Rev. 18:20, 24.* Excludes from heaven. *Gal. 5:21; Rev. 22:15.*

Some examples. **Cain**: *Gen. 4:8.* **Esau**: *Gen. 27:41.* **Joseph's brothers**: *Gen. 37:20.* **Pharaoh**: *Ex. 1:22.* **Abimelech**: *Judg. 9:5.* **The men of Shechem**: *Judg. 9:24.* **The Amalekite**: *2 Sam. 1:16.* **Rechab**: etc: *2 Sam. 4:5-7.* **David**: *2 Sam. 12:9.* **Absolom**: *2 Sam. 13:29.* **Joab**: *1 Kings 2:31-32.* **Baasha**: *1 Kings 15:27.* **Zimri**: *1 Kings 16:10.* **Jezebel**: *1 Kings 21:10.* **The Elders of Jezreel**: *1 Kings 21:13.* **Ahab**: *1 Kings 21:19.* **Hazael**: *2 Kings 8:12, 15.*

Adrammelech, etc: *2 Kings 19:37.* **Manasseh**: *2 Kings 21:16.* **Ishmael**: *Jer. 41:7.* **The Princes of Israel**: *Ezek. 11:6.* **The people of Gilead**: *Hos. 6:8.* **Various Herods**: *Mat. 2:16, 14:10; Acts 12:2.* **Herodias and her daughter**: *Mat. 14:8-11.* **The Chief Priests**: *Mat. 27:1.* **Judas**: *Mat. 27:4.* **Barabbas**: *Mk. 15:7.* **The Jews**: *Acts 7:52; 1 Thess. 2:15.*

MURMURING

Is forbidden. *1 Cor. 10:10; Phil. 2:14.*
Is against
God. *Prov. 19:3.*
The sovereignty of God. *Rom. 9:19-20.*
The service of God. *Mal. 3:14.*
Christ. *Jn. 6:41-43, 52.*
Ministers of God. *Ex. 17:3; Num. 16:41.*
Disciples of Christ. *Mk. 7:2; Lk. 5:30.*
The unreasonableness of. *Lam. 3:39.*
Is tempting God. *Ex. 17:2.*
Provokes God. *Num. 14:2, 11; Deut. 9:8, 22.*
The saints cease from. *Is. 29:23-24.*
Is characteristic of the wicked. *Jude verse 16.*
The guilt of encouraging others in their. *Num. 13:31-33 with 14:36-37.*
The punishment of. *Num. 11:1, 14:27-29, Num. 16:45-46; Ps. 106:25-26.* Illustrated. *Mat. 20:11; Lk. 15:29-30.*

Some examples. **Cain**: *Gen. 4:13-14.* **Moses**: *Ex. 5:22-23.* **The Israelites**: *Ex. 14:11; Num. 21. 5.* **Aaron**, etc: *Num. 12:1-2, 8.* **Korah**, etc: *Num. 16:3.* **Elijah**: *1 Kings 19:4.* **Job**: *Job 3:1, etc.* **Jeremiah**: *Jer. 20:14-18.* **Jonah**: *Jonah 4:8-9.* **The disciples**: *Mk. 14:4-5. Jn. 6:61.* **The Pharisees**: *Lk. 15:2, 19:7.* **The Jews**: *Jn. 6:41-43.* **The Greek speakers**: *Acts 6:1.*

MUSIC

The early invention of. *Gen. 4:21.*
Divided into
Vocal. *2 Sam. 19:35; Acts 16:25.*
Instrumental. *Dan. 6:18.*

Designed to promote joy. *Eccl. 2:8, 10.*
A vanity for all who are unsanctified. *Eccl. 2;8, 11.*
Was considered efficacious in mental disorders. *1 Sam. 16:14-17, 23.*
Effects produced on the prophets of old by. *1 Sam. 10:5-6; 2 Kings 3:15.*

Instruments of,
Cymbals. *1 Chron. 16:5; Ps. 150:5.*
Horn. *Ps. 98:6; Hos. 5:8.*
Lyre. *Dan. 3:5.*
Flute. *Dan. 3:5.*
Harp. *Ps. 137:2; Ezek.26:13.*
Organ. *Gen. 4:21; Job 21:12; Ps. 150:4.*
Pipe. *1 Kings 1:40; Is. 5:12; Jer. 48:36.*
Psaltery. *Ps. 33:2, 71:22.*
Triangular harp. *Dan. 3:5.*
Tambourine. *1 Sam. 10:5; Is. 24:8.*
Timbrel. *Ex. 15:20; Ps 68:25.*
Trumpet. *2 Kings 11:14; 2 Chron. 29:27.*
Stringed instruments. *Is. 14:11; Amos 5:23.*

Made of
Fir wood. *2 Sam. 6:5.*
Almug wood. *1 Kings 10:12.*
Brass. *1 Cor. 13:1.*
Silver. *Num. 10:2.*
The horns of animals. *Josh. 6:8.*
Many were stringed. *Ps. 33:2, 150:4.*
Some made by David. *1 Chron. 23:5; 2 Chron. 7:6.*
The Jews were famous for constructing instruments. *Amos 6:5.*
Often expensively ornamented. *Ezek. 28:13.*
A great diversity of. *Eccl. 2:8.*

Appointed to be used in the temple. *1 Chron. 16:4-6, 23:5-6,25:1; 2 Chron. 29:25.*
The custom of sending away friends with. *Gen. 31:27.*

The Jews used them,
In sacred processions. *2 Sam. 6:4-5, 15; 1 Chron. 13:6-8; 1 Chron. 15:27-28.*
At the laying of the foundation of the temple. *Ezra 3:9-10.*
At the consecration of the temple. *2 Chron. 5:11-13.*
At coronations. *2 Chron. 23:11, 13.*
At the dedication of the city walls. *Neh. 12:27-28.*
To celebrate victories. *Ex. 15:20; 1 Sam. 18:6-7.*
At religious feasts. *2 Chron. 30:21.*
For private entertainment. *Is. 5:12; Amos 6:5.*
For dancing. *Mat. 11:17; Lk. 15:25.*
In funeral ceremonies. *Mat. 9:23.*
In commemorating great men. *2 Chron. 35:25.*
In idol worship. *Dan. 3:5.*
For regulating the movements of armies. *Josh. 6:8; 1 Cor. 14:8.*
Generally put away in times of affliction. *Ps. 137:2-4; Dan. 6; 18.*

Illustrative
Of joy and gladness. *Zeph. 3:17; Eph. 5:19.*
Of heavenly joy. *Rev. 5:8-9.*
Of the cessation of calamities. *Is. 24:8-9; Rev. 18:22.*

N

NATIONS, THE
Are without God and Christ. *Eph. 2:12.*

Are described as
Ignorant. *1 Cor. 1:21; Eph. 4:18.*
Idolatrous. *Ps. 135:16; Rom. 1:23, 25.*
Worshippers of the devil. *1 Cor. 10:20.*
Cruel. *Ps. 74:20; Rom. 1:31.*
Filthy. *Ezra 6:21; Eph. 4:19, 5:12.*
Persecuting. *Ps. 2:1-2; 2 Cor. 11:26.*
Scoffing at the saints. *Ps. 79:10.*
Degradation of. *Lev. 25:44.*

Have
Evidence of the power of God. *Rom. 1:19-20.*
Evidence of the goodness of God. *Acts 14:17.*
The testimony of conscience. *Rom. 2:14-15.*
The habit of imitating evil. *2 Kings 16:3; Ezek. 11:12.*

Cautions against imitating.
Jer. 10:2. Mat. 6:7.

Knowledge of the dangers of associating with. *Ps. 106:35.*

Employed in chastening the Church. *Lev. 26:33; Jer. 49:14; Lam. 1:3; Ezek. 7:24, 25:7; Dan. 4:27; Hab. 1:5-9.*

The Church will be avenged of. *Ps. 149:7; Jer. 10:25; Obad. verse 15.*

God
   Rules over. *2 Chron. 20:6; Ps. 47:8.*
   Brings to nothing the counsels of. *Ps 33:10.*
   Will be exalted among. *Ps. 46:10, 102:15.*
   Punishes. *Ps. 44:2; Joel 3:11-13; Mic. 5:15; Hab. 3:12; Zech. 14:18.*
   Will finally judge. *Rom. 2:12-16.*

Are given to Christ. *Ps. 2:8; Dan. 7:14.*

Salvation of, is foretold. *Gen. 12:3 with al. 3:8; Is. 2:2-4; Is. 52:10; Is. 60:1-8.*

Salvation is provided for. *Acts 28:28; Rom. 15:9-12.*

The glory of God must be declared among. *1 Chron. 16:24; Ps. 96:3.*

The gospel is to be preached to. *Mat. 24:14, 28:19; Rom. 16:26; Gal. 1:16.*

The need for preaching to. *Rom. 10:14.*

The gospel is received by. *Acts 11:1, 13:48, 15:3, 23.*

Baptism is to be administered to. *Mat. 28:19.*

The Holy Spirit is poured out on. *Acts 10:44-45, 15:8.*

Praise God for the success of the gospel among. *Ps. 98:1-3; Acts 11:18.*

Pray for. *Ps. 67:2-5.*

Aid evangelism among. *2 Cor. 11:9; 3 Jn. verses 6-7.*

The conversion of, is acceptable to God. *Acts 10:35; Rom. 15:16.*

NEW BIRTH, THE

The corruption of human nature requires. *Jn. 3:6; Rom. 8:7-8.*

None can enter heaven without. *Jn. 3:3.*

Effected by
   God. *Jn. 1:13; 1 Pet. 1:3.*
   Christ. *1 Jn. 2:29.*
   The Holy Spirit. *Jn. 3:6; Titus 3:5.*

Through the instrumentality of
   The Word of God. *Jas. 1:18; 1 Pet. 1:23.*
   The resurrection of Christ. *1 Pet. 1:3.*
   The ministry of the gospel. *1 Cor. 4:15.*

Is of the will of God. *Jas. 1:18.*

Is of the mercy of God. *Titus 3:5.*

Is for the glory of God. *Is. 43:7.*

Is described as
   A new creation. *2 Cor. 5:17; Gal. 6:15; Eph. 2:10.*
   Newness of life. *Rom. 6:4.*
   A spiritual resurrection. *Rom. 6:4-6; Eph. 2:1, 5; Col. 2:12, 3:1.*
   A new heart. *Ezek. 36:26.*
   A new spirit. *Ezek. 11:19; Rom. 7:6.*
   Putting on the new man. *Eph. 4:24.*
   The inward man. *Rom. 7:22; 2 Cor. 4:16.*
   The circumcision of the heart. *Deut. 30:6 with Rom. 2:29; Col. 2:11.*
   Partaking of the divine nature. *2 Pet. 1:4.*
   The washing of regeneration. *Titus 3:5.*

All saints partake of. *1 Pet. 2:2; 1 Jn. 5:1.*

Produces
   A likeness to God. *Eph. 4:24; Col. 3:10.*
   A likeness to Christ. *Rom. 8:29.*
   A knowledge of God. *Jer. 24:7; Col. 3:10.*
   Hatred of sin. *1 Jn. 3:9; 1 Jn. 5:18.*
   Victory over the world. *1 Jn. 5:4.*
   Delight in God's Law. *Rom. 7:22.*

Evidenced by
   Faith in Christ. *1 Jn. 5:1.*
   Righteousness. *1 Jn. 2:29.*
   Brotherly love. *1 Jn. 4:7.*

Connected with adoption. *Is. 43:6-7; Jn. 1:12-13.*

The ignorant make sport of. *Jn. 3:4.*

Manner of effecting is illustrated in *Jn. 3:8.*

Preserves us from Satan's devices. *1 Jn. 5:18.*

O

OBEDIENCE TO GOD
Is commanded. *Deut. 13:4.*
Without faith, is impossible. *Heb. 11:6.*
Includes
Obeying his voice. *Ex. 19:5; Jer. 7:23.*
Obeying his law. *Deut. 11:27; Is. 42:24.*
Obeying Christ. *Ex. 23:21; 2 Cor. 10:5.*
Obeying the gospel. *Rom. 1:5, 6:17, 10:16-17.*
Keeping his commandments. *Eccl. 12:13.*
Submission to higher powers. *Rom. 13:1.*
Is better than sacrifice. *1 Sam. 15:22.*
Justification is obtained by that of Christ. *Rom. 5:19.*
Christ, an example of. *Jn. 15:10; Phil. 2:5-8; Heb. 5:8.*
Angels engaged in. *Ps. 103:20.*
A characteristic of the saints. *1 Pet. 1:14.*
The saints are elected to. *1 Pet. 1:2.*
Obligations to. *Acts 4:19-20, 5:29.*
Exhortations to. *Jer. 26:13, 38:20.*
Should be
From the heart. *Deut. 11:13; Rom. 6:17.*
With willingness. *Ps. 18:44; Is. 1:19.*
Unreserved. *Josh. 22:2-3.*
Undeviating. *Deut. 28:14.*
Constant. *Phil. 2:12.*
Resolve upon. *Ex. 24:7; Josh. 24:24.*
Confess your failure in. *Dan. 9:10.*
Prepare your heart for. *1 Sam. 7:3; Ezra 7:10.*
Pray to be taught. *Ps. 119. 35, 143:10.*
Promises to. *Ex. 23:22; 1 Sam. 12:14; Is. 1:19; Jer. 7:23.*
Will be universal in the latter days. *Dan. 7:27.*
The blessedness of. *Deut. 11:27, 28:1-13; Lk. 11:28; Jas. 1:25.*
The wicked refuse. *Ex. 5:2; Neh. 9:17.*
The punishment for refusing. *Deut. 11:28, 28:15-68; Josh. 5:6; Is. 1:20.*

Some examples. **Noah**: *Gen. 6:22.*

Abra(ha)m: *Gen. 12:1-4 with Heb. 11:8; Gen. 22:3, 12.* **The Israelites**: *Ex. 12:28, 24:7.* **Moses**: *Ex. 34:4.* **Caleb**, etc: *Num. 32:12.* **Asa**: *1 Kings 15:11.* **Elijah**: *1 Kings 17:5.* **Hezekiah**: *2 Kings 18:6.* **Josiah**: *2 Chron. 35:26.* **David**: *Ps. 119:166.* **Zerubbabel**, etc: *Hag. 1:12.* **Joseph**: *Mat. 1:24.* **The Wisemen**: *Mat. 2:12.* **Zacharias**: etc: *Lk. 1:5-6.* **Paul**: *Acts 26:19.* **The saints in Rome**: *Rom. 16:19.*

OFFENCE
Occasions of, must arise. *Mat. 18:7.*
Occasioning of, is forbidden. *1 Cor. 10:32.*
Persecution, a cause of, to mere professors of the faith. *Mat. 13:21, 24:10.*
The wicked take, at
The low station of Christ. *Mat. 13:54-57.*
Christ, as the corner-stone. *Is. 8:14 with 1 Pet. 2:8.*
Christ, as the bread of life. *Jn. 6:58-61.*
Christ crucified. *1 Cor. 1:23; Gal. 5:11.*
The righteousness of faith. *Rom. 9:32.*
The necessity of inward purity. *Mat. 15:11-12.*
The blessedness of not taking, at Christ. *Mat. 11:6.*
The saints are warned against taking. *Jn. 16:1.*
The saints should
Be without. *Phil. 1:10.*
Be careful not to give. *Ps. 73:15; Rom. 14:13; 1 Cor. 8:9.*
Have a conscience devoid of. *Acts 24:16.*
Cut off what causes, to themselves. *Mat. 5:29-30; Mk. 9:43-47.*
Not let their liberty bring, to others. *1 Cor. 8:9.*

Use self-denial rather than cause. *Rom. 14:21; 1 Cor. 8:13.*
Avoid those who cause. *Rom. 16:17.*
Reprove those who bring. *Ex. 32:21; 1 Sam. 2:24.*

Ministers should
Be careful of giving. *2 Cor. 6:3.*
Remove what causes. *Is. 57:14.*

All things that cause, will be gathered out of Christ's kingdom. *Mat. 13:41.*

Denunciation against those that cause. *Mat. 18:7; Mk. 9:42.*

The punishment for causing. *Ezek. 44:12; Mal. 2:8-9; Mat. 18:6.*

Some examples. **Aaron:** *Ex. 32:2-6.* **Balaam,** etc: *Num. 31:16 with Rev. 2:14.* **Gideon:** *Judg. 8:27.* **The sons of Eli:** *1 Sam. 2:12-17.* **Jeroboam:** *1 Kings 12:26-30.* **An old prophet:** *1 Kings 13:18-26.* **Priests:** *Mal. 2:8.* **Peter:** *Mat. 16:23.*

OFFENCES AGAINST THE HOLY SPIRIT

Exhortations against. *Eph. 4:30; 1 Thess. 5:19.*

Shown in
Tempting him. *Acts 5:9.*
Vexing him. *Is. 63:10.*
Grieving him. *Eph. 4:30.*
Quenching him. *1 Thess. 5:19.*
Lying to him. *Acts 5:3-4.*
Resisting him. *Acts 7:51.*
Undervaluing his gifts. *Acts 8:19-20.*
Insulting him. *Heb. 10:29.*
Disregarding his testimony. *Neh. 9:30.*
The blasphemy against him is unpardonable. *Mat. 12:31-32; 1 Jn. 5:16.*

OFFERINGS

To be made to God alone. *Ex. 22:20; Judg. 13:16.*
The antiquity of. *Gen. 4:3-4.*

Different kinds of;
Burnt. *Lev. 1:3-17; Ps. 66:15.*
Sin. *Lev. 4:3-35, 6:25, 10:17.*
Trespass. *Lev. 5:6-19, 6:6, 7:1.*
Peace. *Lev. 3:1-17, 7:11.*

Heave. *Ex. 29:27-28; Lev. 7:14; Num. 15:19.*
Wave. *Ex. 29:26; Lev. 7:30.*
Meat. *Lev. chapter 2 and 15:4.*
Drink. *Gen. 35:14; Ex. 29:40; Num. 15:5.*
Thank. *Lev. 7:12, 22:29; Ps. 50:14.*
Freewill. *Lev. 23:28; Deut. 16:10, 23:23.*
Incense. *Ex. 30:8; Mal. 1:11; Lk. 1:9.*
Firstfruits. *Ex.22:29; Deut.18:4.*
Tithe. *Lev. 27:30; Num. 18:21; Deut. 14:22.*
Gifts. *Ex. 35:22; Num. 7:2-88.*

Grain offfering for jealousy. *Num. 5:15.*
Personal, for redemption. *Ex. 30:13, 15*
Declared to be most holy. *Num. 18:9.*

Required to be
Perfect. *Lev. 22:21.*
The best of their kind. *Mal. 1:14.*
Offered willingly. *Lev. 22:19.*
Offered in righteousness. *Mal. 3:3.*
Offered in love and charity. *Mat. 5:23-24.*
Brought in a clean vessel. *Is. 66:20.*
Brought to the place appointed by God. *Deut. 12:6; Ps. 27:6; Heb. 9:9.*
Laid before the altar. *Mat. 5:23-24.*
Presented by the priest. *Heb. 5:1.*
Brought without delay. *Ex. 22:29-30.*
Unacceptable without gratitude. *Ps. 50:8, 14.*
Could not make the offerer perfect. *Heb. 9:9.*

Things forbidden as;
The price of fornication. *Deut. 23:18.*
The price of a dog. *Deut. 23:18.*
Whatever was blemished. *Lev. 22:20.*
Whatever was imperfect. *Lev. 22:24.*
Whatever was unclean. *Lev. 27:11, 27.*

Laid up in the temple. *2 Chron. 31:12; Neh. 10:37.*

Hezekiah prepared chambers for. *2 Chron. 31:11.*

The Jews were often
Slow in presenting. *Neh. 13:10-12.*
Defrauding God of. *Mal. 3:8.*
Prone to give the worst they had as. *Mal. 1:8, 13.*
Rejected because of sin. *Is. 1:13; Mal. 1:10.*
Abhorred on account of the

sins of the priests. *1 Sam. 2:17.*
Offering to idols their sacrifices.
Ezek. 20:28.
Encouraging strangers to offer
sacrifices as they did. *Num. 15:14-16.*
Offending under the Law,
beyond the efficacy of.
1 Sam. 3:14; Ps. 51:16.

Illustrative of
Christ's offering of himself. *Eph. 5:2.*
The conversion of the Gentiles.
Rom. 15:16.
The conversion of the Jews.
Is. 66:20.

P

PARABLES OF CHRIST, THE
Wise and foolish builders.
Mat. 7:24-27.
Children of the bride-chamber.
Mat. 9:15.
New cloth and old garment. *Mat. 9:16.*
New wine and old bottles. *Mat. 9:17.*
An unclean spirit. *Mat. 12:43.*
The sower. *Mat. 13:3, 18; Lk. 8:5, 11.*
The tares. *Mat. 13:24-30, 36-43.*
The mustard seed. *Mat. 13:31-32;
Lk. 13:19.*
Leaven. *Mat. 13:33.*
Treasure hid in a field. *Mat. 13:44.*
A pearl of great price. *Mat. 13:45-46.*
A net cast into the sea. *Mat. 13:47-50.*
It is not food that defiles.
Mat. 15:10-15.
The unmerciful servant. *Mat. 18:23-35.*
Labourers hired. *Mat. 20:1-16.*
Two sons. *Mat. 21:28-32.*
Wicked husbandmen. *Mat. 21:33-45.*
A marriage feast. *Mat. 22:2-14.*
A fig tree in leaf. *Mat. 24:32-34.*
A master on guard over his
house. *Mat. 24:43.*
Faithful, and evil servants.
Mat. 24:45-51.
Ten virgins. *Mat. 25:1-13.*
The talents. *Mat. 25:14-30.*
The kingdom, divided against
itself. *Mk. 3:24.*
A house, divided against itself.
Mk. 3:25.
A strong man armed. *Mk. 3:27;
Lk. 11:21.*
Seed growing secretly. *Mk. 4:26-29.*
A lit lamp. *Mk. 4:21. Lk. 11:33-36.*

A man going off on a far journey.
Mk. 13:34-37.
The blind leading the blind.
Lk. 6:39.
The beam and the speck. *Lk. 6:41-42.*
A tree and its fruit. *Lk. 6:43-45.*
A creditor and debtors. *Lk. 7:41-47.*
The good Samaritan. *Lk. 10:30-37.*
The persistent friend. *Lk. 11:5-9.*
The rich fool. *Lk. 12:16-21.*
Cloud and wind. *Lk. 12:54-57.*
A barren fig-tree. *Lk. 13:6-9.*
Men invited to a feast. *Lk. 14:7-11.*
The builder of a tower. *Lk. 14:28-30, 33.*
A king going to war. *Lk. 14:31-33.*
The taste of salt. *Lk. 14:34-35.*
A lost sheep. *Lk. 15:3-7.*
A lost piece of silver. *Lk. 15:8-10.*
The prodigal son and the older
brother. *Lk. 15:11-32.*
The unjust steward. *Lk. 16:1-8.*
The rich man and Lazarus.
Lk. 16:19-31.
The persistent widow. *Lk. 18:1-8.*
The Pharisee and the tax-
collector. *Lk. 18:9-14.*
The pounds. *Lk. 19:12-27.*
The Good Shepherd. *Jn. 10:1-6.*
The vine and its branches. *Jn. 15:1-5.*

PARDON
Promised. *Is. 1:18; Jer. 31:34 with
Heb. 8:12; Jer. 50:20.*
None, without the shedding of
blood. *Lev. 17:11 with Heb. 9:22.*
Legal sacrifices were ineffective
for. *Heb. 10:4.*
Outward purification was

ineffective for. *Job 9:30-31; Jer. 2:22.*
The blood of Christ alone is
effective for. *Zech. 18:1 with 1 Jn. 1:7.*
Is granted
By God alone. *Dan. 9:9; Mk. 2:7.*
By Christ. *Mk. 2:5; Lk. 7:48.*
Through Christ. *Lk. 1:69, 77; Acts 5:31, 13:38.*
Through the blood of Christ. *Mat. 26:28; Rom. 3:25; Col. 1:14.*
For the name's sake of Christ. *1 Jn. 2:12.*
According to the riches of his grace. *Eph. 1:7.*
On the exaltation of Christ. *Acts 5:31.*
Freely. *Is. 43:25.*
Readily. *Neh. 9:17; Ps. 86:5.*
Abundantly. *Is. 55:7; Rom. 5:20.*
To those who confess their sins. *2 Sam. 12:13; Ps. 32:5; 1 Jn. 1:9.*
To those who repent. *Acts 2:38.*
To those who believe. *Acts 10:43.*
Should be preached in the name
of Christ. *Lk. 24:47.*
Shows the
Compassion of God. *Mic. 7:18-19.*
Grace of God. *Rom. 5:15-16.*
Mercy of God. *Ex. 34:7; Ps. 51:1.*
Goodness of God. *2 Chron. 30:18; Ps. 86:5.*
Forbearance of God. *Rom. 3:25.*
Loving-kindness of God. *Ps. 51:1.*
Justice of God. *1 Jn. 1:9.*
Faithfulness of God. *1 Jn. 1:9.*
Expressed by
Forgiving transgression. *Ps. 32:1.*
Removing transgression. *Ps. 103:12.*
Blotting out transgression. *Is. 44:22.*
Covering sin. *Ps. 32:1.*
Blotting out sin. *Acts 3:19.*
Casting sins into the sea. *Mic. 7:19.*
Not imputing sin. *Rom. 4:8.*
Not mentioning transgression. *Ezek. 18:22.*
Remembering sins no more. *Heb. 10:17.*
All the saints enjoy. *Col. 2:13; 1 Jn. 2:12.*

The blessedness of. *Ps. 32:1 with Rom. 4:7.*
Should lead to
Returning to God. *Is. 44:22.*
Loving God. *Lk. 7:47.*
Fearing God. *Ps. 130:4.*
Praising God. *Ps. 103:2-3.*
Ministers are appointed to
proclaim. *Is. 40:1-2; 2 Cor. 5:19.*
Therefore, pray,
For yourselves. *Ps. 25:11, 18; Ps. 51:1; Mat. 6:12; Lk. 11:4.*
For others. *Jas. 5:15; 1 Jn. 5:16.*
An encouragement to pray for.
2 Chron. 7:14.
Withheld from
The unforgiving. *Mk. 11:26; Lk. 6:37.*
The unbelieving. *Jn. 8:21, 24.*
The impenitent. *Lk. 13:2-5.*
Blasphemers against the Holy
Spirit. *Mat. 12:32; Mk. 3:28-29.*
Apostates. *Heb. 10:26-27; 1 Jn. 5:16.*
Illustrated. *Lk. 7:42, 15:20-24.*

Some examples. **The Israelites**:
Num. 14:20. **David**: *2 Sam. 12:13.*
Manasseh: *2 Chron. 33:13.* **Hezekiah**:
Is. 38:17. **The paralysed man**: *Mat. 9:2.*
The penitent woman: *Lk. 7:47.*

PARENTS

Receive their children from God.
Gen. 33:5; 1 Sam. 1:27; Ps. 127:3.
Their duty to their children is
To love them. *Titus 2:4.*
To bring them to Christ.
Mat. 19:13-14.
To train them up for God.
Prov. 22:6; Eph. 6:4.
To instruct them in God's word.
Deut. 4:9, 11:19; Is. 38:19.
To tell them of God's judge-
ments. *Joel 1:3.*
To tell them of God's miracu-
lous works. *Ex.10:2; Ps. 78:4.*
To command them to obey
God. *1 Deut. 32:46; 1 Chron. 28:9.*
To bless them. *Gen. 48:15; Heb. 11:20.*

To pity them. *Ps. 103:13.*

To provide for them. *Job 42:15; Cor. 12:14; 1 Tim. 5:8.*

To rule them. *1 Tim. 3:4, 12.*

To correct them. *Prov. 13:24, 19:18, 23:13, 29:17; Heb. 12:7.*

Not to provoke them. *Eph. 6:4; Col. 3:21.*

Not to make unholy marriages for them. *Gen. 24:1-4; Gen. 28:1-2.*

Wicked children are a source of grief to. *Prov. 10:1, 17:25.*

Should pray for their children

For their spiritual welfare. *Gen. 17:18; 1 Chron. 29:19.*

When in the way of temptation. *Job 1:5.*

When sick. *2 Sam. 12:16; Mk. 5:23; Jn. 4:46, 49.*

Faithful parents

Are blessed by their children. *Prov. 31:28.*

Leave a blessing on their children. *Ps. 112:2; Prov. 11:21; Is. 65:23.*

The sins of, are visited on their children. *Ex. 20:5; Is. 14:20; Lam.5:7.*

Their negligence is severely punished. *1 Sam. 3:13.*

Wicked parents,

Instruct their children in evil. *Jer. 9:14; 1 Pet. 1:18.*

Set a bad example to their children. *Ezek. 20:18; Amos 2:4.*

Some examples of good parents. **Abraham**: *Gen. 18:19.* **Jacob**: *Gen. 44:20, 30.* **Joseph**: *Gen. 48:13-20.* **Jochebed** (the mother of Moses): *Ex. 2:2-3, 6:20.* **Manoah**: *Judg. 13:8.* **Hannah**: *1 Sam. 1:28.* **David**: *2 Sam. 18:5, 33.* **A Shunammite**: *2 Kings 4:19-20.* **Job**: *Job 1:5.* **The mother of Lemuel**: *Prov. 31:1.* **A nobleman**: *Jn. 4:49.* **Lois and Eunice**: *2 Tim. 1:5.*

Some examples of bad parents. **The mother of Micah**: *Judg. 17:3.* **Eli**: *1 Sam. 3:13.* **Saul**: *1 Sam. 20:33.* **Athaliah**:

2 Chron. 22:3. **Manasseh**: *2 Chron. 33:6.* **Herodias**: *Mk. 6:24.*

PATIENCE

God is the God of. *Rom. 15:5.*

Christ is an example of. *Is. 53:7 with Acts 8:32; Mat. 27:14.*

Encouraged. *Titus 2:2;. 2 Pet. 1:6.*

Should do its perfect work. *Jas. 1:4.*

The trials of the saints lead to. *Rom. 5:3. Jas. 1:3.*

Produces

Experience. *Rom. 5:4.*

Hope. *Rom. 15:4.*

Suffering with, for well doing, is acceptable to God. *1 Pet. 2:20.*

To be exercised in

Running the race set before us. *Heb. 12:1.*

Producing fruit. *Lk. 8:15.*

Well doing. *Rom. 2:7; Gal. 6:9.*

Waiting upon God. *Ps. 37:7, 40:1.*

Waiting upon Christ. *1 Cor. 1:7; 2 Thess. 3:5.*

Waiting for the hope of the gospel. *Rom. 8:25; Gal. 5:5.*

Waiting for God's salvation. *Lam. 3:26.*

Bearing the yoke. *Lam. 3:27.*

Tribulation. *Lk. 21:19. Rom. 12:12.*

Necessary for the inheritance of the promises. *Heb. 6:12, 10:36.*

Exercise, towards all. *1 Thess. 5:14.*

Those in authority should exercise. *Mat. 18:26; Acts 26:3.*

Ministers should follow after. *1 Tim. 6:11.*

True ministers are proved by their. *2 Cor. 6:4.*

Should be accompanied by

Godliness. *2 Pet. 1:6.*

Faith. *2 Thess. 1:4; Heb. 6:12; Rev. 13:10.*

Temperance. *2 Pet. 1:6.*

Longsuffering. *Col. 1:11.*

Joy. *Col. 1:11.*

The saints are strengthened for all. *Col. 1:11.*

Commended. *Eccl. 7:8; Rev. 2:2-3.*
Illustrated. *Jas. 5:7.*

Some examples. **Job**: *Job 1:21; Jas. 5:11.* **Simeon**: *Lk. 2:25.* **Paul**: *2 Tim. 3:10.* **Abraham**: *Heb. 6:15.* **The prophets**: *Jas. 5:10.* **John**: *Rev. 1:9.*

PEACE

God is the Author of. *Ps. 147:14; Is. 45:7; 1 Cor. 14:33.*

Results from

Heavenly wisdom. *Jas. 3:17.*
The government of Christ. *Is. 2:4.*
Praying for rulers. *1 Tim. 2:2.*
Seeking the peace of those among whom we live. *Jer. 29:7.*
Necessary to the enjoyment of life. *Ps. 34:12, 14 with 1 Pet. 3:10-11.*

God bestows, upon those who

Obey him. *Lev. 26:6.*
Please him. *Prov. 16:7.*
Accept his chastisements. *Job 5:17, 23-24.*
Is a bond of union. *Eph. 4:3.*
The fruit of righteousness should be sown in. *Jas.3:18.*
The Church should enjoy. *Ps. 125:5, 128:6; Is. 2:4; Hos. 2:18.*

The saints should

Love. *Zech. 8:19.*
Seek. *Ps. 34:14 with 1 Pet. 3:11.*
Follow. *2 Tim. 2:22.*
Follow the things that make for. *Rom. 14:19.*
Cultivate. *Ps. 120:7.*
Speak. *Esth. 10:3.*
Live in. *2 Cor. 13:11.*
Maintain, with each other. *Mk. 9:50; 1 Thess. 5:13.*
Endeavour to be at, with all men. *Rom. 12:18; Heb. 12:14.*
Pray for that of the Church. *Ps. 122:6-8.*
Exhort others to seek. *Gen. 45:24.*
Ministers should exhort on the basis of the God of. *1 Thess. 5:23; 2 Thess 3:12.*

Advantages of. *Prov. 17:1. Eccl. 4:6.*
Blessedness of. *Ps. 133:1.*
Blessedness of promoting. *Mat. 5:9.*

The wicked

Speak, hypocritically. *Ps. 28:3.*
Do not speak. *Ps. 35:20.*
Do not enjoy. *Is. 48:22; Ezek. 7:25.*
Are opposed to. *Ps. 120:7.*
Hate. *Ps. 120:6.*
Will abound in the latter days. *Is. 2:4, 11:13, 32:18.*

Some examples. **Abraham**: *Gen. 13:8-9.* **Abimelech**: *Gen. 26:29.* **Mordecai**: *Esth. 10:3.* **David**: *Ps. 120:7.*

PEACE, SPIRITUAL

God is the God of. *Rom. 15:33; 2 Cor. 13:11; 1 Thess. 5:23; Heb. 13:20.*
God ordains. *Is. 26:12.*
God speaks, to his saints. *Ps. 85:8.*
Christ is the Lord of. *2 Thess. 3:16.*
Christ is the Prince of. *Is. 9:6.*
Christ gives. *2 Thess. 3:16.*
Christ guides into the way of. *Lk. 1:79.*
Christ is our. *Eph. 2:14.*
Is through the atonement of Christ. *Is. 53:5; Eph. 2:14-15; Col. 1:20.*
Was bequeathed by Christ. *Jn. 14:27.*

Was preached

By Christ. *Eph. 2:17.*
Through Christ. *Acts 10:36.*
By ministers. *Is. 52:7 with Rom. 10:15.*
Announced by angels. *Lk. 2:14.*
Follows justification. *Rom. 5:1.*
A fruit of the Spirit. *Rom. 14, 17; Gal. 5:22.*
Divine wisdom is the way of. *Prov. 3:17.*

Accompanies

Faith. *Rom. 15:13.*
Righteousness. *Is. 32:17.*
An acquaintance with God. *Job 22:21.*
A love of God's Law. *Ps. 119:165.*
Spiritual-mindedness. *Rom. 8:6.*
Established by covenant. *Is. 54:10; Ezek. 34:25; Mal.2:5.*

Promised to

The Church. *Is. 66:12.*
The Gentiles. *Zech. 9:10.*
The saints. *Ps. 72:3, 7; Is. 55:12.*
The meek. *Ps. 37:11.*
Those who confide in God. *Is. 26:3.*
Returning backsliders. *Is. 57:18-19.*
We should love. *Zech. 8:19.*
The benediction of ministers
should be. *Num 6:26. Lk. 10:5.*

The saints

Have, in Christ. *Jn. 16:33.*
Have, with God. *Is. 27:5; Rom. 5:1.*
Enjoy. *Ps. 119:165.*
Rest in. *Ps. 4:8.*
Are blessed with. *Ps. 29:11.*
Are kept in perfect. *Is. 26:3.*
Are ruled by. *Col. 3:15.*
Kept by. *Phil. 4:7.*
Die in. *Ps. 37:37; Lk. 2:29.*
Wish, to each other. *Gal. 6:16;*
Phil. 1:2; Col. 1:2; 1 Thess. 1:1.

Of the saints,

Is great. *Ps. 119:165; Is. 54:13.*
Is abundant. *Ps. 72;7; Jer. 33:6.*
Is secure. *Job 34:29.*
Surpasses all understanding.
Phil. 4:7.
Is consummated after death.
Is. 57:2.
The gospel is good news of.
Rom. 10:15.

The wicked

Do not know the way of.
Is. 59:8; Rom. 3:17.
Do not know the things
concerning. *Lk. 19:42.*
Promise, to themselves. *Deut. 29:19.*
Are promised, by false teachers.
Jer. 6:14.
Have none. *Is. 48:22, 57:21.*
Supports believers in their trials.
Jn. 14:27, 16:33.

PERFECTION

Is of God. *Ps. 18:32, 138:8.*
All the saints have, in Christ.
1 Cor. 2:6; Phil. 3:15; Col. 2:10.
God's perfection is the standard
of. *Mat. 5:48.*

Implies,

Full devotion. *Mat. 19:21.*
Purity and holiness in speech.
Jas. 3:2.
The saints are commanded to
aim for. *Gen. 17:1; Deut. 18:13.*
The saints cannot claim. *Job 9:20;*
Phil. 3:12.
The saints should follow after.
Prov. 4:18; Phil. 3:12.
Ministers are appointed to lead
the saints on to. *Eph. 4:12; Col. 1:28.*
An exhortation to. *2 Cor. 7:1; 2 Cor. 13:11.*
The impossibility of attaining.
2 Chron. 6:36; Ps. 119:96.

The Word of God is

The rule of. *Jas. 1:25.*
Designed to lead us to.
2 Tim. 3:16-17.
Charity is the bond of. *Col. 3:14.*
Patience leads to. *Jas. 1:4.*
Pray for. *Heb. 13:20-21; 1 Pet. 5:10.*
The Church will attain to. *Jn. 17:23;*
Eph. 4:13.
The blessedness of. *Ps. 37:37; Prov. 2:21.*

PERSECUTION

Christ suffered. *Ps. 69:26; Jn. 5:16.*
Christ voluntarily submitted to.
Is. 50:6.
Christ was patient under. *Is. 53:7.*
The saints may expect. *Mk. 10:30;*
Lk. 21:12; Jn. 15:20.
The saints suffer, for the sake of
God. *Jer. 15:15.*
Of the saints is actually a
persecution of Christ. *Zech. 2:8 with*
Acts 9:4-5.
All that live a godly life in Christ,
will suffer. *2 Tim. 3:12.*

Originates in

An ignorance of God and
Christ. *Jn. 16:3.*
A hatred of God and Christ.
Jn. 15:20, 24.
Hatred of the gospel. *Mat. 13:21.*
Pride. *Ps. 10:2.*

Mistaken religious zeal. *Acts 13:50, 26:9-11.*

Is inconsistent with the spirit of the gospel. *Mat. 26:52.*

Men by nature are addicted to. *Gal. 4:29.*

Preachers of the gospel are subject to. *Gal. 5:11.*

Sometimes leads to death. *Acts 22:4.*

God does not forsake his saints under. *2 Cor. 4:9.*

God delivers them out of. *Dan. 3:25, 28; 2 Cor. 1:10; 2 Tim. 3:11.*

Believers can never be separated from Christ. *Rom. 8:35.*

Lawful means may be used to escape. *Mat. 2:13, 10:23, 12:14-15; Acts 9:23-25.*

The suffering saints should

Commit themselves to God. *1 Pet. 4:19.*

Show patience. *1 Cor. 4:12.*

Rejoice. *Mat. 5:12; 1 Pet. 4:13.*

Glorify God. *1 Pet. 4:16.*

Pray for deliverance. *Ps. 7:1, 119:86.*

Pray for those who inflict. *Mat. 5:44.*

Return a blessing for. *Rom. 12:14.*

The hope of future blessedness supports us under. *1 Cor. 15:19, 32; Heb. 10:34-35.*

The blessedness of enduring, for the sake of Christ. *Mat. 5:10; Lk. 6:22.*

Pray for those who are suffering. *2 Thess. 3:2.*

Hypocrites cannot endure. *Mk. 4:17.*

False teachers shrink from. *Gal. 6:12.*

The wicked

Are addicted to causing. *Ps. 10:2, 69:26.*

Are active in. *Ps. 143:3; Lam. 4:19.*

Encourage each other in. *Ps. 71:11.*

Rejoice in their success. *Ps. 13:4; Rev. 11:10.*

The punishment for. *Ps. 7:13; 2 Thess. 1:6.*

Illustrated. *Mat. 21:33-39.*

Some examples of the spirit of persecution. **Pharaoh**, etc: *Ex. 1:8-14.*

Saul: *1 Sam. 26:18.* **Jezebel**: *1 Kings 19:2.* **Zedekiah**, etc: *Jer. 38:4-6.* **The Chaldeans**: *Dan. 3:8, etc.* **The Pharisees**: *Mat. 12:14.* **The Jews**: *Jn. 5:16; 1 Thess. 2:15.* **Herod**: *Acts 12:1.* **The Gentiles**: *Acts 14:5.* **Paul**: *Phil. 3:6; 1 Tim. 1:13.*

Some examples of suffering through persecution. **Moses**: *Heb. 11:24-26.* **Micaiah**: *1 Kings 22:27.* **David**: *Ps. 119:161.* **Jeremiah**: *Jer. 32:2.* **Daniel**: *Dan. 6:5-17.* **Peter**, etc: *Acts 4:3.* **The Apostles**: *Acts 5:18.* **The Prophets**: *Acts 7:52.* **The early Church**: *Acts 8:1.* **Paul and Barnabas**: *Acts 3:50.* **Paul and Silas**: *Acts 16:23.* **The Hebrew saints**: *Heb. 10:33.* **The saints of old**: *Heb. 11:36.*

PERSEVERANCE

An evidence of reconciliation with God. *Col. 1:21-23.*

An evidence of belonging to Christ. *Jn. 8:31; Heb. 3:6, 14.*

A characteristic of the saints. *Prov. 4:18.*

To be manifested in

Seeking God. *1 Chron. 16:11.*

Waiting upon God. *Hos. 12:6.*

Prayer. *Rom 12:12. Eph. 6:18.*

Well doing. *Rom. 2:7; 2 Thess. 3:13.*

Continuing in the faith. *Acts 14:22; Col. 1:23; 2 Tim. 4:7.*

Holding hope securely. *Heb. 3:6.*

Is maintained through

The power of God. *Ps. 37:24; Phil. 1:6.*

The power of Christ. *Jn. 10:28.*

The intercession of Christ. *Lk. 22:31-32; Jn. 17:11.*

The fear of God. *Jer. 32:40.*

Faith. *1 Pet. 1:5.*

Promised to the saints. *Job 17:9.*

Leads to an increase in knowledge. *Jn. 8:31-32.*

In well-doing,

It leads to assurance of hope. *Heb. 6:10-11.*

It is not in vain. *1 Cor. 15:58; Gal. 6:9.*

Ministers should exhort to.

Acts 13:43, 14:22.
An encouragement to. Heb. 12:2-3.
Promises to. Mat. 10:22, 24:13; Rev. 2:26-28.
The blessedness of. Jas. 1:25.

A lack of,
   Excludes us from the benefits
   of the gospel. Heb. 6:4-6.
   Is punished. Jn. 15:6; Rom. 11:22.
   Is illustrated. Mk. 4:5, 17.

PERSONALITY OF THE HOLY SPIRIT, THE

He creates and gives life. Job 33:4.
He appoints and commissions
ministers. Is. 48:16; Acts 13:2, 20:28.
He directs ministers where to
preach. Acts 8:29, 10:19-20.
He directs ministers where not to
preach. Acts 16:6-7.
He instructs ministers what to
preach. 1 Cor. 2:13.
He spoke in, and by, the Prophets.
Acts 1:16; 1 Pet. 1:11-12; 2 Pet. 1:21.
He strives with sinners. Gen. 6:3.
He reproves. Jn. 16:8.
He comforts. Acts 9:31.
He helps us in our weaknesses.
Rom. 8:26.
He teaches. Jn. 14:26; 1 Cor. 12:3.
He guides. Jn. 16:13.
He sanctifies. Rom. 15:16; 1 Cor. 6:11.
He testifies of Christ. Jn. 15:26.
He glorifies Christ. Jn. 16:14.
He has a power of his own.
Rom. 15:13.
He searches all things. Rom. 11:33-34
with 1 Cor. 2:10-11.
He works according to his own
will. 1 Cor. 12:11.
He dwells in the saints. Jn. 14:17.
He can be grieved. Is. 63:10; Eph. 4:30.
He can be resisted. Acts 7:51.
He can be tested. Acts 5:9.

PILGRIMS AND STRANGERS

Are described. Jn. 17:16.
The saints are called to be.
  Gen. 12:1 with Acts 7:3; Lk. 14:26-27, 33.
All saints are. Ps. 39:12; 1 Pet. 1:1.

The saints confess themselves to
be. 1 Chron. 29:15; Ps. 39:12, 119:19;
Heb. 11:13.
As, the saints
Have the example of Christ
before them. Lk. 9:58.
   Are strengthened by God.
   Deut. 33:25; Ps. 84:6, 7.
   Are activated by faith. Heb. 11:9.
   Have their faces toward Zion.
   Jer. 50:5.
   Keep the promises in view.
   Heb. 11:13.
   Forsake all for Christ. Mat. 19:27.
   Look for a heavenly country.
   Heb. 11:16.
   Look for a heavenly city. Heb. 11:10.
   Pass their sojourning in fear.
   1 Pet. 1:17.
   Rejoice in the statutes of God.
   Ps. 119:54.
   Pray for direction. Ps. 43:3; Jer. 50:5.
   Have a heavenly citizenship.
   Phil. 3:20.
   Hate worldly fellowship. Ps. 120:5-6.
   Are not mindful of this world.
   Heb. 11:15.
   Are not at home in this world.
   Heb. 11:9.
   Shine as lights in the world.
   Phil. 2:15.
   Invite others to go with them.
   Num. 10:29.
   Are exposed to persecution.
   Ps. 120:5-7; Jn. 17:14.
   Should abstain from fleshly
   lusts. 1 Pet. 2:11.
   Should have their treasure in
   heaven. Mat. 6:19; Lk. 12:33; Col. 3:1-2.
   Should not be over anxious
   about worldly things. Mat. 6:25.
   Long for their pilgrimage to
   end. Ps. 55:6; 2 Cor. 5:1-8.
   Die in faith. Heb. 11:13.
The world is not worthy of them.
Heb. 11:38.
God is not ashamed to be called
their God. Heb. 11:16.
They are typified in Israel. Ex. 6:4, 12:11.

Some examples. **Abraham**: *Gen. 23:4; Acts 7:4-5.* **Jacob**: *Gen. 47:9.* **The saints of old**: *1 Chron. 29:15; Heb. 11:13, 38.* **David**: *Ps. 39:12.* **The Apostles**. *Mat. 19:27.*

POOR, THE
Are made so by God. *Job 34:19; Prov. 22:2.*

Are so by God's appointment. *1 Sam. 2:7; Job 1:21.*

Condition of, often results from
 Laziness. *Prov. 20:13.*
 Bad company. *Prov. 28:19.*
 Drunkenness and gluttony. *Prov. 23:21.*

God
 Regards, equally with the rich. *Job 34:19.*
 Does not forget. *Ps. 9:18.*
 Hears. *Ps. 69:33; Is. 41:17.*
 Maintains the rights of. *Ps. 140:12.*
 Delivers. *Job 36:15; Ps. 35:10.*
 Protects. *Ps. 12:5, 109:31.*
 Exalts. *1 Sam. 2:8; Ps. 107:41.*
 Provides for. *Ps. 68:10, 146:7.*
 Does not despise the prayers of. *Ps. 102:17.*
 Is the refuge of. *Ps. 14:6.*

Will never cease from the land. *Deut. 15:11; Zeph. 3:12; Mat. 26:11.*

May be
 Rich in faith. *Jas. 2:5.*
 Generous. *Mk. 12:42; 2 Cor. 8:2.*
 Wise. *Prov. 28:11.*
 Upright. *Prov. 19:1.*

Christ lived as one of. *Mat. 8:20.*
Christ preached to. *Lk. 4:18.*
Christ delivers. *Ps. 72:12.*
Offerings of, acceptable to God. *Mk. 12:42-44; 2 Cor. 8:2, 12.*

Should
 Rejoice in God. *Is. 29:19.*
 Hope in God. *Job 5:16.*
 Commit themselves to God. *Ps. 10:14.*
 When converted, rejoice in their exaltation. *Jas. 1:9.*

They were provided for under the Law. *Ex. 23:11; Lev. 19:9-10.*

Neglect toward, is
 A neglect of Christ. *Mat. 25:42-45.*
 Inconsistent with love to God. *1 Jn. 3:17.*
 A proof of unbelief. *Jas. 2:15-17.*

Do not rob. *Prov. 22:22.*
Do not wrong by judging against them. *Ex. 23:6.*
Do not take interest on their money. *Lev. 25:36.*
Do not harden your heart against. *Deut. 15:7.*
Do not shut your hand against. *Deut. 15:7.*
Do not rule over them with severity. *Lev. 25:39, 43.*
Do not oppress. *Deut. 24:14; Zech. 7:10.*
Do not despise. *Prov. 14:21; Jas. 2:2-4.*
Relieve. *Lev. 25:35; Mat. 19:21.*
Defend. *Ps. 82:3-4.*
Bring in justice for. *Ps. 82:3; Jer. 22:3, 16.*

Care for,
 Is characteristic of the saints. *Ps. 112:9 with 2 Cor. 9:9; Prov. 29:7.*
 Is a fruit of repentance. *Lk. 3:11.*
 Should be urged. *2 Cor. 8:7-8; Gal. 2:10.*

Give to,
 Not grudgingly. *Deut. 15:10; 2 Cor. 9:7.*
 Generously. *Deut. 14:29, 15:8, 11.*
 Cheerfully. *2 Cor. 8:12; 2 Cor. 9:7.*
 Without show. *Mat. 6:1.*
 Specially if they are Christians. *Rom. 12:13; Gal. 6:10.*

Pray for. *Ps. 74:19, 21.*

Those who are of the faith and who relieve
 Are happy. *Prov. 14:21.*
 Are blessed. *Deut. 15:10; Ps. 41:1; Prov. 22:9; Acts 20:35.*
 Have the favour of God. *Heb. 13:16.*
 Have the promises. *Prov. 28:27; Lk. 14:13-14.*

By oppressing, God is reproached. *Prov. 14:31.*
By mocking, God is reproached. *Prov. 17:5.*

The wicked

Do not care about. *Jn. 12:6.*

Oppress. *Job 24:4-10; Ezek. 18:12.*

Vex. *Ezek. 22:29.*

Do not take up the cause of. *Prov. 29:7.*

Sell. *Amos 2:6.*

Crush. *Amos 4:1.*

Tread down. *Amos 5:11.*

Grind the faces of. *Is. 3:15.*

Devour. *Hab. 3:14.*

Persecute. *Ps. 10:2.*

Defraud. *Amos 8:5-6.*

Despise the counsel of. *Ps. 14:6.*

The guilt of defrauding. *Jas. 5:4.*

Punishment for

Oppressing. *Prov. 22:16; Ezek. 22:29, 31.*

Spoiling. *Is. 3:13-15; Ezek. 18:13.*

Refusing to assist. *Job 22:7, 10; Prov. 21:13.*

Acting unjustly towards. *Job 20:19, 29; Job 22:6, 10; Is. 10:1-3; Amos 5:11-12.*

Their oppression is illustrated. *2 Sam. 12:1-6.*

Care for, is illustrated. *Lk. 10:33-35.*

Some examples. **Gideon**: *Judg. 6:15.* **Ruth**: *Ruth 2:2.* **The widow of Zarephath**: *1 Kings 17:12.* **A prophet's widow**: *2 Kings 4:2.* **The saints of old**: *Heb. 11:37.*

Examples of kindnesses to the poor. **Boaz**: *Ruth 2:14.* **Job**: *Job 29:12-16.* **Nebuzaradan**: *Jer. 39:10.* **Zaccheus**: *Lk. 19:8.* **Peter and John**: *Acts 3:6.* **Dorcas**: *Acts 9:36, 39.* **Cornelius**: *Acts 10:2.* **The Church in Antioch**: *Acts 11:29-30.* **Paul**: *Rom. 15:25.* **The churches of Macedonia and Achaia**: *Rom. 15:26; 2 Cor. 8:1-5.*

POWER OF GOD, THE

Is one of his attributes. *Ps. 62:11.*

Expressed by the

Voice of God. *Ps. 29:3, 5; Ps. 68:33.*

Finger of God. *Ex. 8:19; Ps. 8:3.*

Hand of God. *Ex. 9:3, 15; Is. 48:13.*

Arm of God. *Job 40:9; Is. 52:10.*

Thunder of his power, etc. *Job 26:14.*

Is described as

Great. *Ps. 79:11. Nahum 1:3.*

Strong. *Ps. 89:13, 136:12.*

Glorious. *Ex.15:6; Is. 63:12.*

Mighty. *Job 9:4; Ps. 89:13.*

Everlasting. *Is. 26:4; Rom. 1:20.*

Sovereign. *Rom. 9:21.*

Effective. *Is. 43:13;. Eph. 3:7.*

Irresistible. *Deut. 32:39; Dan. 4:35.*

Incomparable. *Ex. 15:11-12; Deut. 3:24; Job 40:9; Ps. 89:8.*

Unsearchable. *Job 5:9, 9:10.*

Incomprehensible. *Job 26:14; Eccl. 3:11.*

All things are possible for. *Mat. 19:26.*

Nothing is too hard for. *Gen. 18:14; Jer. 32:27.*

Can save by many or by few. *1 Sam. 14:6.*

Is the source of all strength. *1 Chron. 29:12; Ps. 68:35.*

Shown in

Creation. *Ps. 102:25; Jer. 10:12.*

Establishing and governing all things. *Ps. 65:6, 66:7.*

The miracles of Christ. *Lk. 11:20.*

The resurrection of Christ. *2 Cor. 13:4; Col. 2:12.*

The resurrection of the saints. *1 Cor. 6:14.*

Making the gospel effective. *Rom. 1:16; 1 Cor. 1:18, 24.*

Delivering his people. *Ps. 106:8.*

The destruction of the wicked. *Ex. 9:16; Rom. 9:22.*

The saints

Long for displays of. *Ps. 63:1-2.*

Have confidence in. *Jer. 20:11.*

Receive an increase of grace by. *2 Cor. 9:8.*

Are strengthened by. *Eph. 6:10; Col. 1:11.*

Are upheld by. *Ps. 37:17; Is. 41:10.*

Are supported in affliction by. *2 Cor. 6:7; 2 Tim. 1:8.*

Are delivered by. *Neh. 1:10. Dan. 3:17.*

Are exalted by. *Job 36:22.*

Are kept by, for salvation. *1 Pet. 1:5.*
Exerted on behalf of the saints.
2 Chron. 16:9.
Works in, and for the saints.
2 Cor. 13:4; Eph. 1:19, 3:20.
The faith of the saints stands in.
1 Cor. 2:5.

Should be
Acknowledged. *1 Chron. 29:11; Is. 33:13.*
Pleaded in prayer. *Ps. 79:11; Mat. 6:13.*
Feared. *Jer. 5:22; Mat. 10:28.*
Magnified. *Ps. 21:13; Jude verse 25.*
The efficiency of ministers is
through. *1 Cor. 3:6-8; Gal. 2:8; Eph. 3:7.*
Is a ground of trust. *Is. 26:4; Rom. 4:21.*
Is in the Name of Jesus. *Acts 3:16.*

The wicked
Do not know. *Mat. 22:29.*
Have against them. *Ezra 8:22.*
Will be destroyed by. *Lk. 12:5.*
The heavenly host magnify.
Rev. 4:11, 5:13, 11:17.

POWER OF CHRIST, THE

As the Son of God, is the power
of God. *Jn. 5:11-19, 10:28-30.*
As man, he is from the Father.
Acts 10:38.

Is described as
Supreme. *Eph. 1:20-21; 1 Pet. 3:22.*
Unlimited. *Mat. 28:18.*
Over all flesh. *Jn. 17:2.*
Over all things. *Jn. 3:35; Eph. 1:22.*
Glorious. *2 Thess. 1:9.*
Everlasting. *1 Tim. 6:16.*
Is able to subdue all things. *Phil. 3:21.*

Shown in
Creation. *Jn. 1:3, 10; Col. 1:16.*
Upholding all things. *Col. 1:17;*
Heb. 1:3.
Salvation. *Is. 63:1; Heb. 7:25.*
His teaching. *Mat. 7:28-29; Lk. 4:32.*
Performing miracles. *Mat. 8:27;*
Lk. 5:17.
Enabling others to work
miracles. *Mat. 10:1; Mk. 16:17-18;*
Lk. 10:17.
Forgiving sins. *Mat. 9:6; Acts 5:31.*
Giving spiritual life. *Jn. 5:21, 25-26.*

Giving eternal life. *Jn. 17:2.*
Raising the dead. *Jn. 5:28-29.*
Raising himself from the dead.
Jn. 2:19-21, 10:18.
Overcoming the world. *Jn. 16:33.*
Overcoming Satan. *Col. 2:15;*
Heb. 2:14.
Destroying the works of Satan.
1 Jn. 3:8.
Ministers should make known.
2 Pet. 1:16.

The saints are
Made willing by. *Ps. 110:3.*
Aided by. *Heb. 2:18.*
Strengthened by. *Phil. 4:13; 2 Tim. 4:17.*
Preserved by. *2 Tim. 1:12; 2 Tim. 4:18.*
Their bodies will be changed by.
Phil. 3:21.
Rests upon the saints. *2 Cor. 12:9.*
Is present in the assembly of the
saints. *1 Cor. 5:4.*
Will be especially manifested at
his Second Coming. *Mk. 13:26;*
2 Pet. 1:16.
Will subdue all power. *1 Cor. 15:24.*
The wicked will be destroyed by.
Ps. 2:9; Is. 11:4, 63:3; 2 Thess. 1:9.

POWER OF THE HOLY SPIRIT, THE

Is the power of God. *Mat. 12:28 with*
Lk. 11:20.
Christ commenced his ministry
in. *Lk. 4:14.*
Christ performed his miracles by.
Mat. 12:28.

Shown in
Creation. *Gen. 1:2; Job 26:13; Ps. 104:30.*
At the conception of Christ.
Lk. 1:35.
In raising Christ from the dead.
1 Pet. 3:18.
In giving spiritual life. *Ezek. 37:11-*
14 with Rom. 8:11.
In the performing of miracles.
Rom. 15:19.
In making the gospel effective.
1 Cor. 2:4; 1 Thess. 1:5.
In overcoming all difficulties.
Zech. 4:6-7.

Was promised by the Father. *Lk. 24:49.*
Was promised by Christ. *Acts 1:8.*

The saints
Are upheld by. *Ps. 51:12.*
Are strengthened by. *Eph. 3:16.*
Are enabled to speak the
truth boldly by. *Mic. 3:8; Acts 6:5,
10; 2 Tim. 1:7-8.*
Are helped in prayer by.
Rom. 8:26.
Abound in hope by. *Rom. 15:13.*
Qualifies ministers. *Acts 1:8.*
God's Word is the instrument
of. *Eph. 6:17.*

PRAISE
God is worthy of. *2 Sam. 22:4.*
Christ is worthy of. *Rev. 5:12.*
God is glorified by. *Ps. 22:23, 50:23.*
Is offered to Christ. *Jn. 12:13.*
Is acceptable through Christ.
Heb. 13:15.

Is due to God on account of
His majesty. *Ps. 96:1, 6; Is. 24:14.*
His glory. *Ps. 138:5; Ezek. 3:12.*
His excellence. *Ex. 15:7; Ps. 148:13.*
His greatness. *1 Chron. 16:25;
Ps. 145:3.*
His holiness. *Ex. 15:11; Is. 6:3.*
His wisdom. *Dan. 2:20; Jude verse 25.*
His power. *Ps. 21:13.*
His goodness. *Ps. 107:8, 118:1,
136:1; Jer. 33:11.*
His mercy. *2 Chron. 20:21; Ps. 89:1,
118:1-4, 136:1-26.*
His lovingkindness and truth.
Ps. 138:2.
His faithfulness and truth.
Is. 25:1.
His salvation. *Ps. 18:46; Is. 35:10,
61:10; Lk. 1:68-69.*
His wonderful works. *Ps. 89:5,
150:2; Is. 25:1.*
His consolation. *Ps. 42:5; Is. 12:1.*
His judgement. *Ps. 101:1.*
His counsel. *Ps. 16:7; Jer. 32:19.*
The fulfilling of his promises.
1 Kings 8:56.
The pardoning of sin. *Ps. 103:1-3;*

Hos. 14:2.
Spiritual health. *Ps. 103:3.*
Constant preservation. *Ps. 71:6-8.*
Deliverance. *Ps. 40:1-3, 124:6.*
Protection. *Ps. 28:7, 59:17.*
In the answering of prayer. *Ps. 28:6,
118:21.*
The hope of glory. *1 Pet. 1:3-4.*
All spiritual blessings. *Ps. 103:2;
Eph. 1:3.*
All temporal blessings. *Ps. 104:1,
14, 136:25.*
The continuing of blessings.
Ps. 68:19.

Is obligatory upon
Angels. *Ps. 103:20, 148:2.*
The saints. *Ps. 30:4, 149:5.*
The Gentiles. *Ps. 117:1 with Rom. 15:11.*
Children. *Ps. 8:2 with Mat. 21:16.*
The high and the low. *Ps. 148:1, 11.*
Young and old. *Ps. 48:1, 12.*
Small and great. *Rev. 19:5.*
Everybody. *Ps. 145:21; Is. 107:8.*
All creation. *Ps. 148:1-10, 150:6.*
Is good and beautiful. *Ps. 33:1, 147:1.*

Should be offered
With the understanding. *Ps. 47:7
with 1 Cor. 14:15.*
With the soul. *Ps. 103:1, 104:1, 35.*
With the whole heart. *Ps. 9:1, 111:1,
138:1.*
With uprightness of heart. *Ps. 119:7.*
With the lips. *Ps. 63:3, 119:171.*
With the mouth. *Ps. 51:15, 63:5.*
With joy. *Ps. 63:5. Ps. 98:4.*
With gladness. *2 Chron. 29:30; Jer. 33:11.*
With thankfulness. *1 Chron. 16:4;
Neh. 12:24; Ps. 147:7.*
Continually. *Ps. 35:28, 71:6.*
During a lifetime. *Ps. 104:33.*
More and more. *Ps. 71:14.*
Day and night. *Rev. 4:8.*
Day by day. *2 Chron. 30:21.*
For ever and ever. *Ps. 145:1-2.*
Throughout the world. *Ps. 113:3.*
In psalms and hymns, etc.
Ps. 105:2; Eph. 5:19; Col. 3:16.

In Old Testament worship, was
accompanied with musical

instruments. *1 Chron. 16:41-42; Ps. 150:3-5.*
Is part of public worship in singing. *Ps. 9:14, 100:4, 118:19-20; Heb. 2:12.*

The saints should

Show forth. *Is. 43:21; 1 Pet. 2:9.*
Be endued with the spirit of. *Is. 61:3.*
Render, under affliction. *Acts 16:25.*
Glory in. *1 Chron. 16:35.*
Triumph in. *Ps. 106:47.*
Express their joy in. *Jas. 5:13.*
Declare. *Is. 42:12.*
Invite others to. *Ps. 34:3; Ps. 95:1.*
Pray for the ability to offer.
Ps. 51:15, 119:175.
Posture must be suited to.
2 Sam. 7:18, 22; 1 Chron. 23:30; Neh. 9:5; Dan. 6:10.

Called

The fruit of the lips. *Heb. 13:15.*
The voice of praise. *Ps. 66:8.*
The voice of triumph. *Ps. 47:1.*
The voice of melody. *Is. 51:3.*
The voice of a psalm. *Ps. 98:5.*
The garment of praise. *Is. 61:3.*
The sacrifice of praise. *Heb. 13:15.*
The sacrifices of joy. *Ps. 27:6.*
The bull calves (i.e. sacrifices) of the lips. *Hos. 14:2.*
The heavenly host engage in.
Is. 6:3; Lk. 2:13; Rev. 4:9-11, 5:12.

Some examples. **Melchizedek**: *Gen. 14:20.* **Moses**, etc: *Ex. 15:1-21.* **Jethro**: *Ex. 18:10.* **The Israelites**: *1 Chron. 16:36.* **David**: *1 Chron. 29:10-13; Ps. 119:164.* **Priests and Levites**: *Ezra 3:10-11.* **Ezra**: *Neh. 8:6.* **Hezekiah**: *Is. 38:19.* **Zacharias**: *Lk. 1:64.* **The shepherds**: *Lk. 2:20.* **Simeon**: *Lk. 2:28.* **Anna**: *Lk. 2:38.* **Multitudes**: *Lk. 18:43.* **The disciples**: *Lk. 19:37-38.* **The apostles**: *Lk. 24:53.* **The first converts**: *Acts 2:47.* **A lame man**: *Acts 3:8.* **Paul and Silas**: *Acts 16:25.*

PRAYER

Is commanded. *Is. 55:6; Mat. 7:7; Phil. 4:6.*

To be offered

To God. *Ps. 5:2; Mat. 4:10.*
To Christ. *Lk. 23:32; Acts 7:59.*
To the Holy Spirit. *2 Thess. 3:5.*
Through Christ. *Eph. 2:18; Heb. 10:19.*
God hears. *Ps. 10:17, 65:2.*
God answers. *Ps. 99:6; Is. 58:9.*

Is described as

Bowing the knees. *Eph. 3:14.*
Looking up. *Ps. 5:3.*
Lifting up the soul. *Ps. 25:1.*
Lifting up the heart. *Lam. 3:41.*
Pouring out the heart. *Ps. 62:8.*
Pouring out the soul. *1 Sam. 1:15.*
Calling on the name of the Lord. *Gen. 12:8; Ps. 116:4; Acts 22:16.*
Crying to God. *Ps. 27:7, 34:6.*
Drawing near to God. *Ps. 73:28; Heb. 10:22.*
Crying to heaven. *2 Chron. 32:20.*
Beseeching the Lord. *Ex. 32:11.*
Seeking God. *Job 8:5.*
Seeking the face of the Lord. *Ps. 27:8.*
Making supplication. *Job 8:5; Jer. 36:7.*
Is acceptable through Christ.
Jn. 14:13-14, 15:16, 16:23-24.
Ascends to heaven. *2 Chron. 30:27; Rev. 5:8.*
Enlivening grace is necessary for.
Ps. 80:18.

The Holy Spirit

Is promised as a Spirit of. *Zech. 12:10.*
As the Spirit of adoption, he leads to. *Rom. 5:15; Gal. 4:6*
Helps us in our weaknesses.
Rom. 8:26.
Is an evidence of conversion.
Acts 9:11.
Of the righteous, avails much.
Jas. 5:16.
Of the upright, is a delight to God. *Prov. 15:8.*

Should be offered up

In the Holy Spirit. *Eph. 6:18; Jude verse 20.*
In faith. *Mat. 21:22; Jas. 1:6.*
In full assurance of faith. *Heb. 10:22.*
In a forgiving spirit. *Mat. 6:12.*

With the heart. *Jer. 29:13; Lam. 3:41.*
With the whole heart. *Ps. 119:58, 145.*
With preparation of heart. *Job 11:13.*
With a true heart. *Heb. 10:22.*
With the soul. *Ps. 42:4.*
With the spirit and understanding. *Jn. 4:22-24; 1 Cor. 14:15.*
With confidence in God. *Ps. 56:9, 86:7; 1 Jn. 5:14.*
With submission to God. *Lk. 22:42.*
With sincere lip. *Ps. 17:1.*
With deliberation. *Eccl. 5:2.*
With holiness. *1 Tim. 2:8.*
With humility. *2 Chron. 7:14, 33:12.*
With truth. *Ps. 145:18; Jn. 4:24.*
With the desire to be heard. *Neh. 1:6; Ps. 17:1, 55:1-2, 61:1.*
With the desire to be answered. *Ps. 27:7, 102:2, 108:6, 143:1.*
With boldness. *Heb. 4:16.*
With earnestness. *1 Thess. 3:10; Jas. 5:17.*
With urgency. *Gen. 32:26; Lk. 11:8-9, 18:1-7.*
Night and day. *1 Tim. 5:5.*
Without ceasing. *1 Thess. 5:17.*
Everywhere. *1 Tim. 2:8.*
In everything. *Phil. 4:6.*
For temporal blessings. *Gen. 28:20; Prov. 30:8; Mat. 6:11.*
For spiritual blessings. *Mat. 6:33; Col. 3:1.*
For mercy and grace to help in time of need. *Heb. 4:16.*
A model for. *Mat. 6:9-13.*
Vain repetitions in, are forbidden. *Mat. 6:7.*
Outward show with, is forbidden. *Mat. 6:5.*

Accompanied by
Repentance. *1 Kings 8:33; Jer. 36:7.*
Confession. *Neh. 1:4, 7; Dan. 9:4-11.*
Self-abasement. *Gen. 18:27.*
Weeping. *Jer. 31:9; Hos. 12:4.*
Fasting. *Neh. 1:4; Dan. 9:3; Acts 13:3.*
Watchfulness. *Lk. 21:36; 1 Pet. 4:7.*
Praise. *Ps. 66:17.*
Thanksgiving. *Phil. 4:6; Col.4:2.*

Plead in
The promises of God. *Gen. 32:9-12; Ex. 32:13; 1 Kings 8:26; Ps. 119:49.*
The covenant of God. *Jer. 14:21.*
The faithfulness of God. *Ps. 143:1.*
The mercy of God. *Ps. 51:1; Dan. 9:18.*
The righteousness of God. *Dan. 9:16.*
Rise early for. *Ps. 5:3, 119:147.*
Seek divine teaching for. *Lk. 11:1.*
Do not faint in. *Lk. 18:1.*
Continue urgently in. *Rom. 12:12.*
Avoid hindrances in. *1 Pet. 3:7.*
Suitable in affliction. *Is. 26:16; Jas. 5:13.*
Shortness of time is a motive for. *1 Pet. 4:7.*

Postures in:
Standing. *1 Kings 8:22; Mk. 11:25.*
Bowing down. *Ps. 95:6.*
Kneeling. *2 Chron. 6:13; Ps. 95:6; Lk. 22:41; Acts 20:36.*
Falling on the face. *Num. 16:22; Josh. 5:14; 1 Chron. 21:16; Mat. 26:39.*
Spreading out the hands. *Is. 1:15.*
Lifting up the hands. *Ps. 28:2; Lam. 2:19; 1 Tim. 2:8.*
The promises of God encourage us to. *Is. 65:24; Amos 5:4; Zech. 13:9.*
The promises of Christ encourage us to. *Lk. 11:9-10; Jn. 14:13-14.*
Experience of past mercies are an incentive to. *Ps. 4:1, 116:2.*

PRAYER, PRIVATE
Christ was constantly in. *Mat. 14:23, 26:36, 39; Mk. 1:35; Lk. 9:18, 29.*
Is commanded. *Mat. 6:6.*
Should be offered
At evening, morning, and noon. *Ps. 55:17.*
Day and night. *Ps. 88:1.*
Without ceasing. *1 Thess. 5:17.*
Will be heard. *Job 22:27.*
Is rewarded openly. *Mat. 6:6.*
Is an evidence of conversion. *Acts 9:11.*
Nothing should hinder. *Dan. 6:10.*

Some examples. **Lot:** *Gen. 19:20.*

Eliezer: *Gen. 24:12.* **Jacob**: *Gen. 32:9-12.*
Gideon: *Judg. 6:22, 36, 39.* **Hannah**:
1 Sam. 1:10. **David**: *2 Sam. 7:18-29.*
Hezekiah: *2 Kings 20:2.* **Isaiah**:
2 Kings 20:11. **Manasseh**: *2 Chron. 33:18-*
19. **Ezra**: *Ezra 9:5-6.* **Nehemiah**:
Neh. 2:4. **Jeremiah**: *Jer. 32:16-25.*
Daniel: *Dan. 9:3, 17.* **Jonah**: *Jonah 2:1.*
Habakkuk: *Hab. 1:2.* **Anna**: *Lk. 2:37.*
Paul: *Acts 9:11.* **Peter**: *Acts 9:40, 10:9.*
Cornelius: *Acts 10:30.*

PRAYER, SOCIAL AND FAMILY

The promise of answers to.
Mat. 18:19.
Christ promises to be present at.
Mat. 18:20.
The punishment for neglecting.
Jer. 10:25.
Some examples. **Abra(ha)m**:
Gen. 12:5, 8. **Jacob**: *Gen. 35:2-3, 7.*
Joshua: *Josh. 24:15.* **David**: *2 Sam. 6:20.*
Job: *Job 1:5.* **The disciples**: *Acts 1:13-14.*
Cornelius: *Acts 10:2.* **Paul and Silas**:
Acts 16:25. **Paul**, etc., *Acts 20:36, 21:5.*

PRAYER, PUBLIC

Is acceptable to God. *Is. 56:7.*
God promises to hear. *2 Chron. 7:14,16.*
God promises to bless in. *Ex. 20:24.*
Christ
   Sanctifies by his presence.
   Mat. 18:20.
   Attended. *Mat. 12:9; Lk. 4:16.*
   Promises answers to. *Mat. 18:19.*
Instituted the form of. *Lk. 11:2.*
Should not be made in an
unknown tongue. *1 Cor. 14:14-16.*
The saints delight in. *Ps. 42:4, 122:1.*
An exhortation to. *Heb. 10:25.*
Urge others to join in. *Ps. 95:6;*
Zech. 8:21.

Some examples. **Joshua**, etc:
Josh. 7:6-9. **David**: *1 Chron. 29:10-19.*
Solomon: *2 Chron. chapter 6.*
Jehoshaphat: etc. *2 Chron. 20:5-13.*
Jeshua, etc: *Neh. chapter 9.* **The Jews**:
Lk. 1:10. **Early Christians**: *Acts 2:46,*

4:24, 12:5, 12. **Peter**, etc: *Acts 3:1.*
Teachers and Prophets in Antioch:
Acts 13:3. **Paul**, etc: *Acts 16:16.*

PRAYER, INTERCESSORY

Christ set an example of. *Lk. 22:32,*
23:34, 17:9-24.
Commanded. *1 Tim. 2:1; Jas. 5:14, 16.*
Should be offered up for
   Kings. *1 Tim. 2:2.*
   All in authority. *1 Tim. 2:2.*
   Ministers. *2 Cor. 1:11; Phil. 1:19.*
   The Church. *Ps. 122:6; Is. 62:6-7.*
   All the saints. *Eph. 6:18.*
   Everybody. *1 Tim. 2:1.*
   Masters. *Gen. 24:12-14.*
   Servants. *Lk. 7:2-3.*
   Children. *Gen. 17:18; Mat. 15:22.*
   Friends. *Job 42:8.*
   Fellow countrymen. *Rom. 10:1.*
   The sick. *Jas. 5:14.*
   Persecutors. *Mat. 5:44.*
   Enemies among whom we live.
   Jer. 29:7.
   Those who envy us. *Num. 12:13.*
   Those who forsake us. *2 Tim. 4:16.*
   Those who murmur against
   God. *Num. 11:1-2, 14:13-19.*
By ministers for their people.
Eph. 1:16, 8:14-19; Phil. 1:4.
An encouragement to. *Jas. 5:16;*
1 Jn. 5:16.
Beneficial to the offerer. *Job 42:10.*
The sin of neglecting. *1 Sam. 12:23.*
Seek an interest in. *1 Sam. 12:19;*
Heb. 13:18.
Unavailing for the obstinately
impenitent. *Jer. 7:13-16, 14:10-11.*

Some examples. **Abraham**:
Gen. 18:23-32. **Abraham's servant**:
Gen. 24:12-14. **Moses**: *Ex. 8:12, 32:11-13.*
Samuel: *1 Sam. 7:5.* **Solomon**:
1 Kings 8:30-36. **Elisha**: *2 Kings 4:33.*
Hezekiah: *2 Chron. 30:18.* **Isaiah**:
2 Chron. 32:20. **Nehemiah**: *Neh. 1:4-11.*
David: *Ps. 25:22.* **Ezekiel**: *Ezek. 9:8.*
Daniel: *Dan. 9:3-19.* **Stephen**: *Acts 7:60.*
Peter and John: *Acts 8:15.* **The**

Church of Jerusalem: *Act 12:6.* **Paul**:
Col. 1:9-12; 2 Thess. 1:11. **Epaphras**:
Col. 4:12. **Philemon**: *Philem. verse 22.*

PRAYER, ANSWERS TO

God gives. *Ps. 99:6, 118:5, 138:3.*
Christ gives. *Jn. 4:10, 14, 14:14.*
Christ received. *Jn. 11:42; Heb. 5:7.*
Granted
Through the grace of God. *Is. 30:19.*
Sometimes immediately. *Is. 65:24;*
Dan. 9:21, 23, 10:12.
Sometimes after a delay. *Lk. 18:7.*
Sometimes differently from our
desire. *2 Cor. 12:8-9.*
Beyond expectation. *Jer. 33:3;*
Eph. 3:20.
Promised. *Is. 58:9; Jer. 29:12; Mat. 7:7.*
Promised especially in times of
trouble. *Ps. 50:15, 91:15.*
Received by those who
Seek God. *Ps. 34:4.*
Seek God with all the heart.
Jer. 29:12-13.
Wait upon God. *Ps. 40:1.*
Return to God. *2 Chron. 7:14; Job 22-*
23, 27.
Ask in faith. *Mat. 21:22; Jas. 5:15.*
Ask in the name of Christ. *Jn. 14:13.*
Ask according to God's will.
1 Jn. 5:14.
Call upon God in truth. *Ps. 145:18.*
Fear God. *Ps. 145:19.*
Set their love upon God. *Ps. 91:14-15.*
Keep God's commandments.
1 Jn. 3:22.
Call upon God under oppres-
sion. *Is. 19:20.*
Call upon God in affliction. *Ps.*
18:6, 106:44; Is. 30:19-20.
Abide in Christ. *Jn. 15:7.*
Humble themselves. *2 Chron. 7:14;*
Ps. 9:12.
Are righteous. *Ps. 34:15; Jas. 5:16.*
Are poor and needy. *Is. 41:17.*
The saints
Are assured of. *1 Jn. 5:15.*
Love God for. *Ps. 116:1.*
Bless God for. *Ps. 66:20.*

Praise God for. *Ps. 116:17, 118:21.*
A motive for continued prayer.
Ps. 116:2.
Denied to those who
Ask wrongly. *Jas. 4:3.*
Regard iniquity in their heart.
Ps. 66:18.
Live in sin. *Is. 59:2; Jn. 9:31.*
Offer unworthy service to God.
Mal. 1:7-9.
Forsake God. *Jer. 14:10, 12.*
Reject the call of God.
Prov. 1:24-25, 28.
Do not heed the Law. *Prov. 28:9;*
Zech. 7:11-13.
Are deaf to the cry of the poor.
Prov. 21:13.
Are blood-shedders. *Is. 1:15, 59:3.*
Are idolaters. *Jer. 11:11-14; Ezek. 8:15-18.*
Are wavering. *Jas. 1:6-7.*
Are hypocrites. *Job 27:8-9.*
Are proud. *Job 35:12-13.*
Are self-righteous. *Lk. 18:11-12, 14.*
Are enemies of the saints.
Ps. 18:40-41.
Cruelly oppress the saints.
Mic. 3:2-4.

Some examples. **Abraham**:
Gen. 17:20. **Lot**: *Gen. 19:19-21.*
Abraham's servant: *Gen. 24:15-27.*
Jacob: *Gen. 32:24-30.* **Israelites**:
Ex. 2:23-24.
Moses: *Ex. 17:4-6, 11-13, 32:11-14.*
Samson: *Judg. 15:18-19.* **Hannah**: *1*
Sam. 1:27. **Samuel**:
1 Sam. 7:9. **Solomon**: *1 Kings 3:9, 12.*
A man of God: *1 Kings 13:6.* **Elijah**:
1 Kings 18:36-38. Jas. 5:17-18. **Elisha**:
2 Kings 4:33-35. **Jehoahaz**: *2 Kings 13:4.*
Hezekiah: *2 Kings 19:20.* **Jabez**:
1 Chron. 4:10. **Asa**: *2 Chron. 14:11-12.*
Jehoshaphat: *2 Chron. 20:6-17.*
Manasseh: *2 Chron. 33:13, 19.* **Ezra**,
etc: *Ezra 8:21-23.* **Nehemiah**: *Neh. 4:9,*
15. **Job**: *Job 42:10.* **David**: *Ps. 18:6.*
Jeremiah: *Lam. 3:55-56.* **Daniel**:
Dan. 9:20-23. **Jonah**: *Jonah 2:2, 10.*
Zacharias: *Lk. 1:13.* **A blind man**:

Lk. 18:38, 41-43. **The thief on the cross**: *Lk. 23:42-43.* **The apostles**: *Acts 4:29-31.* **Cornelius**: *Acts 10:4, 31.* **Early Christians**: *Acts 12:5, 7.* **Paul and Silas**: *Acts 16:25-26.* **Paul**: *Acts 28:8.*

Some examples of denied prayer. **Saul**: *1 Sam. 28:15.* **The elders of Israel**: *Ezek. 20:3.* **The Pharisees**: *Mat. 23:14.*

PRECIOUSNESS OF CHRIST, THE
To God. *Mat. 3:17; 1 Pet. 2:4.*
To the saints. *Song. 5:10; Phil. 3:8; 1 Pet. 2:7.*
On account of his
Goodness and beauty. *Zech. 9:17.*
Excellence and grace. *Ps. 45:2.*
Name. *Song 1:3; Heb. 1:4.*
Atonement. *1 Pet. 1:19 with Heb. 12:24.*
Words. *Jn. 6:68.*
Promises. *2 Pet. 1:4.*
Care and tenderness. *Is. 40:11.*
As the cornerstone of the Church. *Is. 28:16 with 1 Pet. 2:6.*
As the source of all grace. *Jn. 1:14; Col. 1:19.*
Unsearchable. *Eph. 3:8.*
Illustrated. *Song 2:3, 5:10-16; Mat. 13:44-46.*

PREDESTINATION (SEE ELECTION)
Of events
Rehoboam's refusal to listen. *1 Kings 12:15.*
The choice of Judah and David. *Ps. 78:67-68.*
Those who are taken. *Mat. 24:40-41; Lk 17:34-36.*
The Crucifixion of Christ. *Acts 2:23.*
Christ's sufferings. *Acts 3:18.*
Fierce opposition to Christians. *Acts 4:28-29*
The nations' boundaries. *Acts 17:26.*
All events for good to the elect. *Rom. 8:28-30, 33.*
The elect among the dispersed

Jews. *1 Pet. 1:2.*
The sacrifice and death of Christ. *1 Pet. 1:20; Rev. 13:8.*
Of persons
The posterity of Isaac and Ishmael. *Gen. 21:12-13.*
Moses. *Exodus 9:16.*
A man destined to destruction. *1 Kings 20:42; Prov. 16:4.*
Job's troubles. *Job 23:14.*
Jeremiah the prophet. *Jer. 1:4-5.*
Jacob over Esau. *Mal. 1:2-3.*
A widow of Sarepta. *Lk. 4:25-26.*
Naaman the leper. *Lk. 4:27.*
The disciples. *Jn. 15:16, 19.*
Certain Gentiles. *Acts 13:48.*
Saul's conversion. *Acts 22:14.*
Paul the gospel preacher. *Gal. 1:15-16.*
False teachers. *Jude verse 4.*
Of Israel
God's special treasure. *Ps. 135:4.*
God's choice of. *Is. 44:1-2, 7.*
Unbelieving Israel. *Rom. 9:7-33.*
A believing remnant in Israel. *Rom. 11:5, 7-8.*
Spiritual events
The grace and mercy of God. *Ex. 33:19.*
God's love in. *Deut. 7:7-8.*
The hardening of hearts. *Josh. 11:20.*
The imparting of knowledge. *Mat. 11:25-26.*
Many are called but few are chosen. *Mat. 20:16, 24:14.*
The days will be cut short for the elect. *Mat. 24:24; Mk. 13:20.*
The mysteries of God's kingdom will harden minds. *Lk. 8:10.*
The elect are given to the Son by the Father. *Jn. 6:37, 39, 44.*
Eternal life. *Jn. 17:2, 6; Tit. 1:2.*
A knowledge of times and seasons. *Acts 1:7.*
Salvation. *Acts 2:47.*
God chooses unlikely ones. *1 Cor. 1:26-29.*

God's hidden wisdom. *1 Cor. 2:7-8.*
Chosen, predestined, adopted.
Eph. 1:4-5.
Those gathered as one in
Christ. *Eph. 1:9-11.*
Good works. *Eph. 2:10.*
God's manifold wisdom in the
Church. *Eph. 3:10-11.*
The new man. *Col. 3:10, 12.*
Is made effective by the Holy
Spirit. *1 Thess. 1:4-5.*
Chosen from the beginning.
2 Thess. 2:13-14.
A holy calling apart from works.
2 Tim. 1:9.
The firstfruits. *Jas. 1:18.*

Some examples. **The posterity of
Abraham**: *Neh. 9:7-8.* **Jacob**: *Rom. 9:12-13.* **The hardening of the Hivites**:
Josh. 11:20. **Samson and the
Philistines**: *Judg. 14:4.* **Eli's obstinate
sons**: *1 Sam. 2:22-25.* **Ahaziah**: *2 Chron.
22:7.* **Amaziah and the idolatrous
Jews**: *2 Chron. 25:20.* **Zerubbabel**: *Hag.
2:23.* **The apostles**: *Jn. 13:18, 15:19.*
Judas Iscariot: *Jn. 17:12 with Mat. 26:24.*
Rufus: *Rom. 16:13.* **Paul**: *Gal. 1:15-16.*

PRESUMPTION

A characteristic of the wicked.
2 Pet. 2:10.
A characteristic of Antichrist.
2 Thess. 2:4.
Shown in
Opposing God. *Job 16:25-26.*
Wilful commission of sin.
Rom. 1:32.
Self-righteousness. *Hos. 12:8;
Rev. 3:17.*
Spiritual pride. *Is. 65:5; Lk. 18:11.*
Esteeming our own ways right.
Prov. 12:15.
Seeking precedence. *Lk. 14:7-11.*
Planning for the future. *Lk. 12:18;
Jas. 4:13.*
Pretending to prophesy.
Deut. 18:22.
Pray to be kept from sins of. *Ps. 19:13.*

The saints avoid. *Ps. 131:1.*
The punishment for. *Num. 15:30;
Rev. 18:7-8.*
Some examples. **The builders of
Babel**: *Gen. 11:4.* **The Israelites**:
Num. 14:44. **Korah**, etc: *Num. 16:3, 7.*
The men of Bethshemesh:
1 Sam. 6:19. **Uzzah**: *2 Sam. 6:6.* **Jeroboam**: *1 Kings 13:4.* **Ben-Hadad**:
1 Kings 20:10. **Uzziah**: *2 Chron. 26:16.*
Sennacharib: *2 Chron. 32:13-14.*
Theudas: *Acts 5:36.* **Sons of Sceva**:
Acts 19, 13-14. **Diotrephes**: *3 Jn. verse 9.*

PRIDE

Is sin. *Prov. 21:4.*
Is hateful to God. *Prov. 6:16-17, 16:5.*
Is hateful to Christ. *Prov. 8:12-13.*
Often originates in
Self-righteousness. *Lk. 18:11-12.*
Religious privileges. *Zeph. 3:11.*
Unsanctified knowledge. *1 Cor. 8:1.*
Inexperience. *1 Tim. 3:6.*
Possession of power. *Lev. 26:19;
Ezek. 30:6.*
Possession of wealth. *2 Kings 20:13.*
Forbidden. *1 Sam. 2:3; Rom. 12:3, 16.*
Defiles a man. *Mk. 7:20, 22.*
Hardens the mind. *Dan. 5:20.*
The saints
Should not give way to. *Ps. 131:1.*
Do not respect, in others. *Ps. 40:4.*
Mourn over, in others. *Jer. 13:17.*
Hate, in others. *Ps. 101:5.*
A hindrance to seeking God.
Ps. 10:4; Hos. 7:10.
A hindrance to improvement.
Prov. 26:12.
A characteristic of
The devil. *1 Tim. 3:6. Ezek. 28:14-17.*
The world. *1 Jn. 2:16.*
False teachers. *1 Tim. 6:3-4.*
The wicked. *Hab. 2:4-5; Rom. 1:30.*
Comes from the heart. *Mk. 7:21-23.*
The wicked are surrounded with.
Ps. 73:6.
Leads men to
Contempt and rejection of

God's Word and his ministers. *Jer. 43:2.*

A persecuting spirit. *Ps. 10:2.*

Wrath. *Prov. 21:24.*

Disputes. *Prov. 13:10, 28:25.*

Self-deception. *Jer. 49:16; Obad. verse 3.*

Exhortation against. *Jer. 13:15.*

Is followed by

Shame. *Prov. 11:2.*

Debasement. *Prov. 29:23; Is. 28:3.*

Destruction. *Prov. 16:18, 18:12.*

Will abound in the last days. *2 Tim. 3:2.*

Woe to. *Is. 28:1, 3.*

Those who are guilty of, will be

Resisted. *Jas. 4:6.*

Brought into contempt. *Is. 23:9.*

Recompensed. *Ps. 31:23.*

Marred. *Jer. 13:9.*

Subdued. *Ex.18:11; Is. 13:11.*

Brought low. *Ps. 18:27; Is. 2:12.*

Abased. *Dan. 4:37 with Mat. 23:12.*

Scattered. *Lk. 1:51.*

Punished. *Zeph. 2:10-11. Mal. 4:1.*

Some examples. **Ahithophel**: *2 Sam. 17:23.* **Hezekiah**: *2 Chron. 32:25.* **Pharaoh**: *Neh. 9:10.* **Haman**: *Esth. 3:5.* **Moab**: *Is. 16:6.* **Tyre**: *Is. 23:9.* **Israel**: *Is. 28:1; Hos. 5:5, 9.* **Judah**: *Jer. 13:9.* **Babylon**: *Jer. 50:29, 32.* **Assyria**: *Ezek. 31:3, 10.* **Tyre**: *Ezek. chapter 28.* **Nebuchadnezzar**: *Dan. 4:30, 5:20.* **Belshazzar**: *Dan. 5:22-23.* **Edom**: *Obad. verse 3.* **The Scribes**: *Mk. 12:38-39.* **Herod**: *Acts 12:21-23.* **The Laodiceans**: *Rev. 3:17.*

PRIVILEGES OF THE SAINTS, THE

Abiding in Christ. *Jn. 15:4-5.*

Partaking of the Divine nature. *2 Pet. 1:4.*

Access to God by Christ. *Eph. 3:12.*

Being of the household of God. *Eph. 2:19.*

Membership with the Church of the firstborn. *Heb. 12:23.*

Having

Christ as their Shepherd. *Is. 40:11 with Jn. 10:14, 16.*

Christ as their Intercessor. *Rom. 8:34; Heb. 7:25; 1 Jn. 2:1.*

The promises of God. *2 Cor. 7:1-2; 2 Pet. 1:4.*

The possession of all things. *1 Cor. 3:21-22.*

All things working together for their good. *Rom. 8:28; 2 Cor. 4:15-17.*

Their names are written in the book of life. *Rev. 13:8, 20:15.*

Having God as their

King. *Ps. 5:2, 44:4; Is. 44:6.*

Glory. *Ps. 3:3; Is. 60:19.*

Salvation. *Ps. 18:2, 27:1.*

Father. *Deut. 32:6; Is. 64:8.*

Redeemer. *Ps. 19:14; Is. 43:14.*

Friend. *2 Chron. 20:7 with Jas. 2:23.*

Helper. *Ps.'33:20; Heb. 13:6.*

Keeper. *Ps. 121:4-5.*

Deliverer. *2 Sam. 22:2; Ps. 18:2.*

Strength. *Ps. 18:2; Ps. 46:1.*

Refuge. *Ps. 46:1, 11; Is. 25:4.*

Shield. *Gen. 15:1; Ps. 84:11.*

Tower. *2 Sam. 22:3; Ps. 61:3.*

Light. *Ps. 27:1; Is. 60:19.*

Guide. *Ps. 48:14; Is. 58:11.*

Lawgiver. *Neh. 9:13-14; Is. 33:22.*

Habitation. *Ps. 90:1; 91:9.*

Portion. *Ps. 73:26; Lam. 3:24.*

Union in God and Christ. *Jn. 17:21.*

Committing themselves to God. *Ps. 31:5; Acts 7:59; 2 Tim. 1:12.*

Calling upon God in trouble. *Ps. 50:15.*

Suffering for Christ. *Acts 5:41; Phil. 1:29.*

Profiting by chastisement. *Heb. 12:10-11.*

Pleading the covenant. *Jer. 14:21.*

Being secure during public calamities. *Job 5:22-23; Ps. 91:5-7.*

Interceding for others. *Gen. 18:23-33; Is. 62:7; Jas.5:16.*

PROCRASTINATION

Condemned by Christ. *Lk. 9:49-62.*

The saints avoid. *Ps. 27:8, 119:60.*

To be avoided in

Listening to God. *Ps. 95:7-8 with Heb. 3:7-8.*

Seeking God. *Is. 55:6.*

Glorifying God. *Jer. 13:16.*

Keeping God's commandments. *Ps. 119:60.*

Making offerings to God. *Ex. 22:29.*

The performance of vows. *Deut. 23:21; Eccl. 4:4.*

Motives for avoiding;

The present is the accepted time. *2 Cor. 6:2.*

The present is the best time. *Eccl. 12:1.*

The uncertainty of life. *Prov. 27:1.*

The danger of, is illustrated. *Mat. 5:25; Lk. 12:25.*

Some examples. **Lot:** *Gen. 19:16.*
Felix: *Acts 24:25.* **Agrippa:** *Acts 26:28.*

PROMISES OF GOD, THE

Are contained in the Scriptures. *Rom. 1:2.*

Are made in Christ. *Eph. 3:6; 2 Tim. 1:1.*

Made to

Christ. *Gal. 3:16, 19.*

Abraham. *Gen. 12:3, 7 with Gal. 3:16.*

Isaac. *Gen. 26:3-4.*

Jacob. *Gen. 28:14.*

David. *2 Sam. 7:12; Ps. 89:35-36.*

The Fathers. *Acts 13:32, 26:6-7.*

All who are called by God. *Acts 2:39.*

Those who love him. *Jas. 1:12, 2:5.*

Were confirmed by an oath. *Ps. 89:3-4; Heb. 6:17.*

The covenant is based on. *Heb. 8:6.*

God is faithful to. *Titus 1:2; Heb. 10:23.*

God remembers. *Ps. 105:42; Lk. 1:54-55.*

Are

Good. *1 Kings 8:56.*

Holy. *Ps. 105:42.*

Exceeding great and precious. *2 Pet. 1:4.*

Confirmed in Christ. *Rom. 15:8.*

Yes and Amen in Christ. *2 Cor. 1:20.*

Fulfilled in Christ. *2 Sam. 7:12 with Acts 13:23. Lk. 1:69-73.*

Through the righteousness of faith. *Rom. 4:13, 16.*

Obtained through faith. *Heb. 11:33.*

Given to those who believe. *Gal. 3:22.*

Inherited through faith and patience. *Heb. 6:12, 15, 10:36.*

Performed at the right time. *Jer. 33:14; Acts 7:17; Gal. 4:4.*

Not one will fail. *Josh. 23:14; 1 Kings 8:56.*

The Law does not contradict. *Gal. 3:21.*

The Law cannot annul. *Gal. 3:17.*

Subjects of;

Christ. *2 Sam. 7:12-13 with Acts 13:22-23.*

The Holy Spirit. *Acts 2:33; Eph. 1:13.*

The gospel. *Rom. 1:1-2.*

Life in Christ. *2 Tim. 1:1.*

A crown of life. *Jas. 1:12.*

Eternal life. *Titus 1:2; 1 Jn. 2:25.*

The life that now is. *1 Tim. 4:8.*

Adoption. *2 Cor. 6:18 with 2 Cor. 7:1.*

Preservation in affliction. *Is. 43:2.*

Blessing. *Deut. 1:11.*

The forgiveness of sins. *Is. 1:18; Heb. 8:12.*

Putting the Law in the heart. *Jer. 31:33 with Heb. 8:10.*

The Second Coming of Christ. *2 Pet. 3:4.*

A new heavens and a new earth. *2 Pet. 3:13.*

Entering into rest. *Josh. 22:4 with Heb. 4:1.*

Should lead to perfecting holiness. *2 Cor. 7:1.*

The inheritance of the saints is of. *Rom. 4:13; Gal. 3:18.*

The saints

Are children of. *Rom. 9:8; Gal. 4:28.*

Are heirs of. *Gal. 3:29; Heb. 6:17, 11:9.*

Do not stagger at. *Rom. 4:20.*

Have implicit confidence in. *Heb. 11:11.*

Expect God to perform. *Lk. 1:38, 45; 2 Pet. 3:13.*

Are sometimes, through

weakness, tempted to doubt. *Ps. 77:8, 10.*

Plead, in prayer. *Gen. 32:9, 12; 1 Chron. 17:23, 26; Is. 43:26.*

Should wait for the performance of. *Acts 1:4.*

Gentiles will be partakers of. *Eph. 3:6.*

Man, by nature, has no interest in. *Eph. 2:12.*

Scoffers despise. *2 Pet. 3:3-4.*

Fear, lest you come short of. *Heb. 4:1.*

PROPHECIES CONCERNING CHRIST

As the Son of God. *Ps. 2:7: fulfilled Lk. 1:32, 35.*

As the seed of the woman. *Gen. 3:15: fulfilled Gal. 4:4.*

As the seed of Abraham. *Gen. 17:7, 22:18: fulfilled Gal. 3:16.*

As the seed of Isaac. *Gen. 21:12: fulfilled Hebrews 11:17-19.*

As the seed of David. *Ps. 132:11; Jer. 23:5: fulfilled Acts 12:23; Rom 1:3.*

His coming at a set time. *Gen. 49:10; Dan. 9:24-25: fulfilled Lk. 2:1.*

His being born of a virgin. *Is. 7:14: fulfilled Mat. 1:18; Lk. 2:7; Gal. 4:4.*

His being called Immanuel. *Is. 7:14: fulfilled Mat. 1:22-23.*

His being born in Bethlehem of Judea. *Mic. 5:2: fulfilled Mat. 2:1; Lk. 2:4-6.*

Great persons coming to adore him. *Ps. 72:10: fulfilled Mat. 2:1-11.*

The slaying of the children at Bethlehem. *Jer. 31:15: fulfilled Mat. 2:16-18.*

His being called out of Egypt. *Hos. 11:1: fulfilled Mat. 2:15. ·*

His being preceded by John the Baptist. *Is. 40:3; Mal. 3:1: fulfilled Mat. 3:1, 3; Lk. 1:17.*

His being anointed with the Spirit. *Ps. 45:7; Is. 11:2, 61:1: fulfilled Mat. 3:16; Jn. 3:34; Acts 10:38.*

His being a Prophet like Moses. *Deut. 18:15-18: fulfilled Acts 3:20-22.*

His being a Priest after the order of Melchizedek. *Ps. 110:4; Zech. 6:13: fulfilled Heb. 5:5-6.*

His entering upon his public ministry. *Is. 61:1-2: fulfilled Lk. 4:16-21, 43.*

His ministry commencing in Galilee. *Is. 9:1-2: fulfilled Mat. 4:12-16, 23.*

His entering publicly into Jerusalem. *Zech. 9:9: fulfilled Mat. 21:1-5.*

His coming into the temple. *Hag. 2:7, 9; Mal. 3:1: fulfilled Mat. 21:12; Lk. 2:27-32; Jn. 2:13-16.*

His poverty. *Is. 53:2: fulfilled Mk. 6:3. Lk. 9:58.*

His meekness and lack of show. *Is. 42:2: fulfilled Mat. 12:15-16, 19.*

His tenderness and compassion. *Is. 40:11, 42:3: fulfilled Mat. 12:15, 20; Heb. 4:15.*

His being without guile. *Is. 53:9: fulfilled 1 Pet. 2:22.*

His zeal. *Ps. 69:9: fulfilled Jn. 2:17.*

His preaching in parables. *Ps. 78:2: fulfilled Mat. 13:34-35.*

His performing of miracles. *Is. 35:5-6: fulfilled Mat. 11:4-6; Jn. 11:47.*

His bearing reproach. *Ps. 22:6, 69:7, 9, 20: fulfilled Rom. 15:3.*

His being rejected by his brothers. *Ps. 69:8; Is. 53:3: fulfilled Jn. 1:11, 7:5.*

His being a stone of stumbling to the Jews. *Is. 8:14: fulfilled Rom. 9:32; 1 Pet. 2:8.*

His being hated by the Jews. *Ps. 69:4; Is. 49:7: fulfilled Jn. 15:24-25.*

His being rejected by the Jewish rulers. *Ps. 118:22: fulfilled Mat. 21:42. Jn. 7:48.*

That Jews and Gentiles would combine against him. *Ps. 2:1-2: fulfilled Lk. 23:12; Acts 4:27.*

His being betrayed by a close friend. *Ps. 41:9, 55:12-14: fulfilled Jn. 13:18, 21.*

His disciples forsaking him. *Zech. 13:7: fulfilled Mat. 26:31, 56.*

His being sold for thirty pieces of silver. *Zech. 11:12: fulfilled Mat. 26:15.*

His price being given for the potter's field. *Zech. 11:13: fulfilled Mat. 27:7.*

The intensity of his sufferings. *Ps. 22:14-15: fulfilled Lk. 22:42, 44.*

His sufferings being for others. *Is. 53:4-6, 12; Dan. 9:26: fulfilled Mat. 20:28.*

His patience and silence under suffering. *Is. 53:7: fulfilled Mat. 26:63, 27:12-14.*

His being struck on the cheek. *Mic. 5:1: fulfilled Mat. 27:30.*

His face being marred. *Is. 52:14, 53:3: fulfilled Jn. 19:5.*

His being spat on and scourged. *Is. 50:6: fulfilled Mk. 14:65; Jn. 19:1.*

His hands and feet being nailed to the cross. *Ps. 22:16: fulfilled Jn. 19:18, 20:25.*

His being forsaken by God. *Ps. 22:1: fulfilled Mat. 27:46.*

His being mocked. *Ps. 22:7-8; fulfilled Mat. 27:39-44.*

Gall and vinegar being given him to drink. *Ps. 69:21: fulfilled Mat. 27:34.*

His garments being divided up, and lots cast for them. *Ps. 22:18: fulfilled Mat. 27:35.*

His being numbered with the transgressors. *Is. 53:12: fulfilled Mk. 15:28.*

His intercession for his murderers. *Is. 53:12: fulfilled Lk. 23:34.*

His death. *Is. 53:12: fulfilled Mat. 27:50.*

That not one of his bones would be broken. *Ex. 12:46; Ps. 34:20: fulfilled Jn. 19:33, 36.*

His being pierced. *Zech. 12:10: fulfilled Jn. 19:34, 37.*

His being buried with the rich. *Is. 53:9: fulfilled Mat. 27:57-60.*

His flesh not seeing corruption. *Ps. 16:10: fulfilled Acts 2:31.*

His resurrection. *Ps. 16:10; Is. 26:19: fulfilled Lk. 24:6, 31, 34.*

His ascension. *Ps. 68:18: fulfilled Lk. 24:51; Acts 1:9.*

His sitting on the right hand of God. *Ps. 110:1: fulfilled Heb. 1:3.*

His exercising the priestly office in heaven. *Zech. 6:13: fulfilled Rom. 8:34.*

His being the chief cornerstone of the Church. *Is. 28:16: fulfilled 1 Pet. 2:6-7.*

His being King in Zion. *Ps. 2:6: fulfilled Lk. 1:32; Jn. 18:33-37.*

The conversion of the Gentiles to him. *Is. 10:10, 42:1: fulfilled Mat. 12:17, 21; Jn. 10:16; Acts 10:45, 47.*

His righteous government. *Ps. 45:6-7: fulfilled Jn. 5:30; Rev. 19:11.*

His universal dominion. *Ps. 72:8. Dan. 7:14: fulfilled Phil. 2:9, 11.*

The perpetuity of his kingdom. *Is. 9:7; Dan. 7:14: fulfilled Lk. 1:32-33.*

PROPHECY

Includes the foretelling of future events. *Gen. 49:1. Num. 24:14.*

God is the Author of. *Is. 44:7, 45:21.*

God gave through Christ. *Rev. 1:1.*

Was a gift of Christ. *Eph. 4:11; Rev. 11:3.*

Was a gift of the Holy Spirit. *1 Cor. 12:10.*

Did not come through the will of man. *2 Pet. 1:21.*

Given from the beginning. *Lk. 1:70.*

Is a sure word. *2 Pet. 1:19.*

Those who uttered,

Were raised up by God. *Amos 2:11.*

Were ordained by God. *1 Sam. 3:20; Jer. 1:5.*

Were sent by God. *2 Chron. 36:15; Jer. 7:25.*

Were sent by Christ. *Mat. 23:34.*

Were filled with the Holy Spirit. *Lk. 1:67.*

Were moved by the Holy Spirit. *2 Pet. 1:21.*

Spoke by the Holy Spirit. *Acts 1:16, 11:28, 28:25.*

Spoke in the name of the Lord. *2 Chron. 33:18; Jas. 5:10.*

Spoke with authority. *1 Kings 17:1.*

God accomplishes. *Is. 44:26; Acts 3:18.*

Christ the great subject of. *Acts 3:22-24, 10:43; 1 Pet. 1:10-11.*

Fulfilled concerning Christ. *Lk. 24:44.*

The gift of, was promised. *Joel 2:28 with Acts 2:16-17.*

Is for the benefit of all ages. *1 Pet. 1:12.*

Is as a light in a dark place. *2 Pet. 1:19.*

Is not of private interpretation. *2 Pet. 1:20.*

Do not despise. *1 Thess. 5:20.*

Give attention to. *2 Pet. 1:19.*

Receive in faith. *2 Chron. 20:20; Lk. 24:25.*
The blessedness of reading, hearing, and keeping. *Rev. 1:3, 22:7.*
The guilt of pretending to the gift of. *Jer. 14:14, 23:13-14. Ezek. 13:2-3.*

The punishment for

Not giving ear to. *Neh. 9:30.*
Adding to, or taking away from. *Rev. 22:18-19.*
Pretending to the gift of. *Deut. 18:20; Jer. 14:15, 23:15.*

The gift of, is sometimes possessed by the ungodly. *Num. 24:2-9; 1 Sam. 19:20-23; Mat. 7:22; Jn. 11:49-51; 1 Cor. 13:2.*
How it is tested. *Deut. 13:1-3, 18:22.*

PROPHETS, THE

God spoke of old by. *Hos. 12:10; Heb. 1:1*
Were the messengers of God. *2 Chron. 36:15; Is. 44:26.*
Were servants of God. *Jer. 35:15.*
Were the watchmen of Israel. *Ezek. 3:17.*

Were called

Men of God. *1 Sam. 9:6.*
Prophets of God. *Ezra 5:2.*
Holy prophets. *Lk. 1:70. Rev. 18:20, 22:6.*
Holy men of God. *2 Pet. 1:21.*
Seers. *1 Sam. 9:9.*

Were esteemed as holy men. *2 Kings 4:9.*
Women were sometimes endowed as. *Joel 2:28; Acts 21:8-9.*

God communicated

His secret things. *Amos 3:7.*
At various times and in different ways. *Heb. 1:1.*
Sometimes with an audible voice. *Num. 12:8; 1 Sam. 3:4-14; Acts 26:14-18.*
By angels. *Dan. 8:15-26; Rev. 22:8-9.*
By dreams and visions. *Num. 12:6; Joel 2:28.*

Were under the influence of the Holy Spirit while prophesying. *Lk. 1:67; 2 Pet. 1:21.*
Spoke in the name of the Lord. *2 Chron. 33:18; Ezra 5:11; Jas. 5:10.*

Frequently spoke in parables and riddles. *2 Sam. 12:1-6; Is. 5:1-7; Ezek. 17:2-10; Jn 16:25.*
Often, their actions, etc., were signs to the people. *Is. 20:2-4; Jer. 19:1, 10-11, 27:2-3, 43:9, 51:63; Ezek. 4:1-13, 5:1-4, 7:23, 12:3-7, 21:6-7, 24:1-24; Hos. 1:2-9.*
Often departed without delivering a divine communication on account of the sins of the people. *1 Sam. 28:6; Lam. 2:9; Ezek. 7:26.*

Were required

To be bold and undaunted. *Ezek. 2:6, 3:8-9.*
To be vigilant and faithful. *Ezek. 3:17-21.*
To receive with attention all God's communications. *Ezek. 3:10.*
Not to speak anything except what they received from God. *Deut. 18:20.*
To declare everything that the Lord had commanded. *Jer. 26:2.*

Sometimes they received divine communications, and uttered predictions. under great bodily and mental excitement. *Jer. 23:9; Ezek. 3:14-15; Dan. 7:28, 10:8; Hab. 3:2, 16.*
Sometimes they uttered their predictions in poetic form. *Deut. 32:44; Is. 5:1.*
Were often accompanied by music while prophesying. *1 Sam. 10:5; 2 Kings 3:15.*
Often committed their prophecies to writing. *2 Chron. 21:12; Jer. 36:2.*
Their writings were read in the synagogues every Sabbath. *Lk. 4:17; Acts 13:15.*

Their normal way of life: they were

Many in Israel. *1 Sam. 10:5; 1 Kings 18:4.*
Often trained and instructed in prophetic schools. *2 Kings 2:3, 5 with 1 Sam. 19:20.*
The sacred bards of the Jews. *Ex. 15:20-21; 1 Sam. 10:5, 10; 1 Chron. 25:1.*

Extraordinary works: they were

Specially raised up on occasions of emergency. *1 Sam. 3:19-21; Is. 6:8-9; Jer. 1:5.*

Often endued with miraculous power. *Ex. 4:1-4; 1 Kings 17:23; 2 Kings 5:3-8.*

Frequently married. *2 Kings 4:1; Ezek. 24:18.*

Dressed in a coarse dress of hair-cloth. *2 Kings 1:8; Zech. 13:4; Mat. 3:4; Rev. 11:3.*

Often leading a wandering unsettled life. *1 Kings 18:10-12; 1 Kings 19:3, 8, 15; 2 Kings 4:10.*

Simple in their way of life. *Mat. 3:4.*

The sacred chroniclers of the Jewish nation. *1 Chron. 29:29; 2 Chron. 9:29.*

The interpreters of dreams, etc. *Dan. 1:17.*

Consulted in all difficulties. *1 Sam. 9:6, 28:15. 1 Kings 14:2-4, 22:7.*

Presented with gifts by those who consulted them. *1 Sam. 9:7-8; 1 Kings 14:3.*

Sometimes they thought it right to reject presents. *2 Kings 5:15-16.*

They were sent to

Reprove the wicked, and call them to repentance. *2 Kings 17:13; 2 Chron. 24:19; Jer. 25:4-5; Jon. 3:4-10.*

Denounce the wickedness of kings. *1 Sam. 15:10, 16-19; 2 Sam. 12:7-12; 1 Kings 18:18, 21:17-22.*

Exhort to faithfulness and constancy in God's service. *2 Chron. 15:1-2, 7.*

Predict the coming, etc., of the Messiah. *Lk. 24:44; Jn. 1:45; Acts 3:24, 10:43.*

Predict the downfall of nations. *Is. 15:1, 17:1, etc; Jer. chapters 47-51.*

They felt deeply about the calamities that they predicted. *Is. 16:9-11; Jer. 9:1-7.*

The predictions of, were

Often proclaimed at the gate of the Lord's house. *Jer. 7:2.*

Proclaimed in the cities and streets. *Jer. 11:6.*

Written on tablets, and hung in some public place. *Hab. 2:2.*

Written on rolls and read to the people. *Is. 8:1; Jer. 36:2.*

Were all fulfilled. *2 Kings 10:10; Is. 44:26; Acts 3:18; Rev. 10:7.*

Of assistance to the Jews in their great national undertakings. *Ezra 5:2.*

Those mentioned in Scripture:

Enoch. *Gen. 5:21-24 with Jude verse 14.*

Noah. *Gen. 9:25-27.*

Jacob. *Gen. 49:1.*

Aaron. *Ex. 7:1.*

Moses. *Deut. 18:18.*

Miriam. *Ex. 15:20.*

Deborah. *Judg. 4:4.*

A prophet sent to Israel. *Judg. 6:8.*

A prophet sent to Eli. *1 Sam. 2:27.*

Samuel. *1 Sam. 3:20.*

David. *Ps. 16:8-11 with Acts 2:25, 30.*

Nathan. *2 Sam. 7:2; 2 Sam. 12:1; 1 Kings 1:10.*

Zadok. *2 Sam. 15:27.*

Gad. *2 Sam. 24:11; 1 Chron. 29:29.*

Abijah. *1 Kings 11:29, 12:15; 2 Chron. 9:29.*

A prophet of Judah. *1 Kings 13:1.*

Iddo. *2 Chron. 9:29, 12:15.*

Shemaiah. *1 Kings 12:22; 2 Chron. 12:7, 15.*

Azariah the son of Oded. *2 Chron. 15:2, 8.*

Hanani. *2 Chron. 16:7.*

Jehu, the son of Hanani. *1 Kings 16:1, 7, 13.*

Elijah. *1 Kings 17:1.*

Elisha. *1 Kings 19:16.*

Micaiah the son of Imlah. *1 Kings 22:7-8.*

Jonah. *2 Kings 14:25; Jonah 1:1; Mat. 12:39.*

Isaiah. *2 Kings 19:2; 2 Chron. 26:22; Is. 1:1.*

Hosea. *Hos. 1:1.*

Amos. *Amos 1:1, 7:14-15.*

Micah. *Mic. 1:1.*

Oded. *2 Chron. 28:9.*

Nahum. *Nahum 1:1.*

Joel. *Joel 1:1; Acts 2:1.6.*

Zephaniah. *Zeph. 1:1.*

Huldah. *2 Kings 22:14.*
Jeduthun. *2 Chron. 35:15.*
Jeremiah. *2 Chron. 36:12, 21; Jer. 1:1-2.*
Habakkuk. *Hab. 1:1.*
Obadiah. *Obad. verse 1.*
Ezekiel. *Ezek. 1:3.*
Daniel. *Dan. 12:11 with Mat. 24:15.*
Haggai. *Ezra 5:1, 6:14; Hag. 1:1.*
Zechariah, son of Iddo. *Ezra 5:1; Zech. 1:1.*
Malachi. *Mal. 1:1.*
One generally attached to the king's household. *2 Sam. 24:11; 2 Chron. 29:25; 2 Chron. 35:15.*
Zacharias, father of John the Baptist. *Lk. 1:67.*
Anna. *Lk. 2:36.*
Agabus. *Acts 11:28, 21:10.*
The daughters of Philip. *Acts 21:9.*
Paul. *1 Tim. 4:1.*
Peter. *2 Pet. 2:1-2.*
John. *Rev. 1:1.*

The Jews

Were required to hear and believe. *Deut. 18:15 with 2 Chron. 20:20.*
Often tried to make them speak smooth things.
1 Kings 22:13; Is. 30:10; Amos 2:12.
Persecuted them. *2 Chron. 36:16; Mat. 5:12.*
Often imprisoned them.
1 Kings 22:27; Jer. 32:2; Jer. 37:15-16.
Often killed death. *1 Kings 18:13, 19:10; Mat. 23:34-37.*
Were often left without, on account of sin. *1 Sam. 3:1; Ps. 74:9; Amos 8:11-12.*

The prophets

Were mighty through faith.
Heb. 11:32-40.
Showed great patience in suffering. *Jas. 5:10.*
God avenged all injuries done to.
2 Kings 9:7; 1 Chron. 16:21-22; Mat. 23:35-38; Lk. 11:50.
Christ was predicted to exercise the office of. *Deut. 18:15 with Acts 3:22.*
Christ exercised the office of.

Mat. Chapter 24; Mk. 10:32-34.

PROSELYTES (JEWISH)

Are described. *Esth. 8:17; Is. 56:3.*
Were required
To give up all the ungodly practices of the nations. *Ezra 6:21.*
To give up all association with other nations. *Ruth 1:16, 2:11. Ps. 45:10; Lk. 14:26.*
To be circumcised. *Gen. 17:13 with Ex. 12:48.*
To enter into a covenant to serve the Lord. *Deut. 29:10-13 with Neh. 10:28-29.*
To observe the Law of Moses, like the Jews. *Ex. 12:49.*
Their unfaithfulness will be answerable before God and punished. *Ezek. 14:7.*
Ammonites and Moabites were banned forever from holding office in the congregation. *Deut. 23:3.*
From the Egyptians and Edomites, was restricted to the third generation before holding office in the congregation.
Deut. 23:7-8.
They were entitled to all privileges. *Ex. 12:48; Is. 56:3-7.*
They attended the feasts. *Acts 2:10, 8:27.*
The Pharisees, etc., were zealous in making. *Mat. 23:15.*
Many, embraced the gospel.
Acts 6:5, 13:43.
Later, were called devout Greeks.
Jn. 12:20 with Acts 17:4.

PROTECTION

God is able to give. *1 Pet. 1:5; Jude verse 24.*
God is faithful in giving.
1 Thess. 5:23-24; 2 Thess. 3:3.
From God, is
Indispensable. *Ps. 127:1.*
Seasonable. *Ps. 46:1.*
Unfailing. *Deut. 31:6; Jn. 1:5.*
Effective. *Jn. 10:28-30; 2 Cor. 12:9.*
Uninterrupted. *Ps. 121:3.*

Encouraging *Is. 41:10, 50:7.*
Perpetual. *Ps. 121:8.*
Often comes through means inadequate in and of themselves. *Judge 7:7; 1 Sam. 17:45, 50; 2 Chron. 14:11.*

Is given to
Those who listen to God. *Prov. 1:33.*
Returning sinners. *Job 22:23, 25.*
The perfect in heart. *2 Chron. 16:9.*
The poor. *Ps. 14:6, 72:12-14.*
The oppressed. *Ps. 9:9.*
The Church. *Ps. 48:3; Zech. 2:4-5.*

Is guaranteed to the saints, in
Preserving them. *Ps. 145:20.*
Strengthening them. *2 Tim. 4:17.*
Upholding them. *Ps. 37:17, 24, 63:8.*
Guarding their feet. *1 Sam. 2:9; Prov. 3:26.*
Keeping them from evil. *2 Thess. 3:3.*
Keeping them from falling. *Jude verse 24.*
Keeping them in the way. *Ex. 23:20.*
Keeping them from temptation. *Rev. 3:10.*
Providing them with a refuge. *Prov. 14:26; Is. 4:6, 32:2.*
Defending them against their enemies. *Deut. 20:1-4, 33:27; Is. 59:19.*
Defeating the counsels of their enemies. *Is. 8:10.*
Temptation. *1 Cor. 10:13; 2 Pet. 2:9.*
Persecution. *Lk. 21:18.*
Calamities. *Ps. 57:1, 59:16.*
All dangers. *Ps. 91:3-7.*
All places. *Gen. 28:15; 2 Chron. 16:9.*
Sleep. *Ps. 3:5, 4:8; Prov. 3:24.*
Death. *Ps. 23:4.*

The saints
Acknowledge God as their. *Ps. 18:2, 62:2, 89:18.*
Pray for. *Ps. 17:5, 8; Is. 51:9.*
Praise God for. *Ps. 5:11.*

Is withdrawn from the
Disobedient. *Lev. 26:14-17.*
Backsliding. *Josh. 23:12-13; Judg. 10:13.*
Presumptuous. *Num. 14:40-45.*
Unbelieving. *Is. 7:9.*
Obstinately impenitent. *Mat. 23:38.*

Cannot be found in
Idols. *Deut. 32:37-39; Is. 46:7.*
Man. *Ps. 146:3; Is. 30:7.*
Riches. *Prov. 11:4, 28; Zeph. 1:18.*
Armies. *Josh. 11:4-8 with Ps. 33:16.*
Horses. *Ps. 33:17; Prov. 21:31.*
Is illustrated. *Deut. 32:11; Ps. 125:1-2; Prov. 18:10. Is. 25:4, 31:5; Lk. 13:14.*

Some examples. **Abraham**: *Gen. 15:1.* **Jacob**: *Gen. 48:16.* **Joseph**: *Gen. 49:23-25.* **Israel**: *Josh. 24:17.* **David**: *Ps. 18:1-2.* **Elisha**: *2 Kings 6:17.* **Shadrach**, etc: *Dan. 3:28.* **Daniel**: *Dan. 6:22.* **Peter**: *Acts 12:4-7.* **Paul**: *Acts 18:10, 26:17.*

PROVIDENCE OF GOD, THE
Is his care over his works. *Ps. 145:9.*
Is exercised in
Preserving his creatures. *Neh. 9:6; Ps. 36:6; Mat. 10:29.*
Providing for his creatures. *Ps. 104:27-28, 136:25, 147:9; Mat. 6:26.*
The special preservation of his saints. *Ps. 37:28, 91:11; Mat. 10:30.*
Prospering the saints. *Gen. 24:48, 56.*
Protecting the saints. *Ps. 91:4, 140:7.*
Delivering the saints. *Ps. 91:3; Is. 31:5.*
Leading the saints. *Deut. 8:2, 15; Is. 63:12.*
Bringing his words to pass. *Num. 26:65. Josh. 21:45; Lk. 21:32-33.*
Ordering the ways of men. *Prov. 16:9, 19:21, 20:24.*
Ordaining the conditions and circumstances of men. *1 Sam. 2:7-8; Ps. 75:6-7.*
Determining the period of human life. *Ps. 31:15, 30:5; Acts 17:26.*
Defeating wicked plans. *Ex. 15:9-11; 2 Sam. 17:14-15; Ps. 33:10.*
Overruling wicked plans for good. *Gen. 45:5-7, 50:20; Phil. 1:12.*
Preserving the course of nature. *Gen. 8:22; Job 26:10; Ps. 104:5-9.*
Directing all events. *Josh. 7:14; 1 Sam. 6:7-10, 12; Prov. 16:33; Is. 44:7; Acts 1:26.*

Ruling the elements. *Job 37:9-13; Is. 50:2; Jonah 1:4, 15; Nahum 1:4.*

Ordering the smallest details. *Mat. 10:29-30; Lk. 21:18.*

Is righteous. *Ps. 145:17; Dan. 4:37.*

Is ever watchful. *Ps. 121:4; Is. 27:3.*

Is all-pervading. *Ps. 139:1-5.*

Is sometimes dark and mysterious. *Ps. 36:6, 73:16, 77:19; Rom. 11:33.*

All things are ordered by,

For his own glory. *Is. 63:14.*

For the good of his saints. *Rom. 8:28.*

The wicked are made to promote the purposes of. *Is. 10:5-12; Acts 3:17-18.*

To be acknowledged

In prosperity. *Deut. 8:18; 1 Chron. 29:12.*

In adversity. *Job 1:21; Ps. 119:75.*

In public calamities. *Amos 3:6.*

In our daily support. *Gen. 48:15.*

In all things. *Prov. 3:6.*

Cannot be defeated. *1 Kings 22:30, 34; Prov. 21:30.*

Man's efforts come to nothing without. *Ps. 127:1-2; Prov. 21:31.*

The saints should

Trust in. *Mat. 6:33-34, 10:9, 29-31.*

Have full confidence in. *Ps. 16:8; Ps. 139:10.*

Commit their works to. *Prov. 16:3.*

Encourage themselves in. *1 Sam. 30:6.*

Pray in dependence on. *Acts 12:5.*

Pray to be guided by. *Gen. 24:12-14, 28:20-21; Acts 1:24.*

The result of depending on. *Lk. 22:35.*

Connected with the use of means. *1 Kings 21:19 with 1 Kings 22:37-38; Mic. 5:2 with Lk. 2:1-4; Acts 27:22, 31-32.*

The danger of denying. *Is. 10:13-17; Ezek. 28:2-10. Dan. 4:29-31; Hos. 2:8-9.*

PRUDENCE

Is shown in the manifestation of God's grace. *Eph. 1:8.*

The supreme example is Christ. *Is. 52:13; Mat. 21:24-27, 22:15-21.*

Is intimately connected with wisdom. *Prov. 8:12.*

The wise are celebrated for their. *Prov. 16:21.*

Those who have,

Get knowledge. *Prov. 18:15.*

Deal with knowledge. *Prov. 13:16.*

Look well to their goings. *Prov. 14:15.*

Understand the ways of God. *Hos. 14:9.*

Understand their own ways. *Prov. 14:8.*

Are crowned with knowledge. *Prov. 14:18*

Are humble in their knowledge. *Prov. 12:23.*

Foresee and avoid evil. *Prov. 22:3.*

Are preserved by it. *Prov. 2:11.*

Are able to suppress angry feelings, etc. *Prov. 12:16, 19:11.*

Listen carefully to reproof. *Prov. 15:5.*

Keep silent in evil times. *Amos 5:13.*

The saints act with. *Ps. 112:5.*

The saints should especially exercise, in their dealings with unbelievers. *Col. 4:6.*

Virtuous wives act with. *Prov 31:16, 26.*

The young should cultivate. *Prov. 3:21.*

Of the wicked, their lack of prudence

Will fail them in times of perplexity. *Jer. 49:7.*

Keeps them from the knowledge of the gospel. *Mat. 11:25.*

Is denounced by God. *Is. 5:21, 29:15.*

Causes them to be defeated by God. *Is. 29:14; 1 Cor. 1:19.*

The necessity for, is illustrated. *Lk. 14:28-32.*

Some examples. **Jacob**: *Gen. 32:3-23.* **Joseph**: *Gen. 41:39.* **Jethro**: *Ex. 18:19, etc.* **Gideon**: *Judg. 8:1-3.* **David**: *1 Sam. 16:8.* **The elderly counsellors of Rehoboam**: *1 Kings 12:7.* **Solomon**: *2 Chron. 2:12.* **Nehemiah**: *Neh. 2:12-16, 4:13-18.*

Gamaliel: *Acts 5:34-39.* **Sergius Paulus**: *Acts 13:7.* **Paul**: *Acts 23:6.*

PUNISHMENT OF THE WICKED, THE

Is from God. *Lev. 26:18; Is. 13:11.*
On account of their
Sin. *Lam. 3:39.*
Iniquity. *Jer. 36:31; Amos 3:2.*
Idolatry. *Lev. 26:30; Is. 10:10-11.*
Rejection of the Law of God.
Hos. 4:6-9.
Ignorance of God. *2 Thess. 1:8.*
Evil ways and doings. *Jer. 21:14;*
Hos.4:9, 12:2.
Pride. *Is. 10:12, 24:21.*
Unbelief. *Rom. 11:20; Heb. 3:18-19.*
Covetousness. *Is. 57:17; Jer. 51:13.*
Oppression. *Is. 49:26; Jer. 30:16, 20.*
Persecution. *Jer. 11:21-22; Mat. 23:34-36.*
Disobedience to God. *Neh. 9:26-27; Eph. 5:6.*
Disobeying the gospel. *2 Thess. 1:8.*
Is the fruit of their sin. *Job 4:8;*
Prov. 22:8; Rom. 6:21; Gal. 6:8.
Is the reward of their sin. *Ps. 91:8;*
Is. 3:11; Jer. 16:18; Rom. 6:23; Heb. 2:2.
Is often brought about by their
evil plans. *Esth. 7:10; Ps. 37:15, 57:6.*
Often commences in this life.
Prov. 1:31.
Comes in this life through
Sickness. *Lev. 26:16; Ps. 78:50.*
Famine. *Lev. 26:19-20, 26, 29; Ps. 107:34.*
Wild beasts. *Lev. 26:22.*
War. *Lev. 26:25, 32-33. Jer. 6:4.*
Being delivered up to their
enemies. *Neh. 9:27.*
Fear. *Lev. 26:36-37; Job 18:11.*
Trouble and distress. *Is. 8:22;*
Zeph. 1:15.
Being cut off. *Ps. 94:23.*
A bringing down of their pride.
Is. 13:11.
Future punishments will be
decided by Christ. *Mat. 16:27, 25:31, 41.*

Their future is described as
Hell. *Mat. 5:29; Lk. 12:5.*
Outer darkness. *Mat. 8:12; 2 Pet. 2:17.*
The resurrection of
condemnation. *Jn. 5:29.*
Rising to shame and everlasting
contempt. *Dan. 12:2.*
Everlasting destruction. *Ps. 52:5,*
92:7; 2 Thess. 1:9.
Everlasting fire. *Mat. 25:41;*
Jude verse 7.
Eternal death. *Rom. 6:23; Rev. 21:8.*
The condemnation of hell.
Mat. 23:33.
Eternal condemnation. *Mk. 3:29.*
The blackness of darkness.
2 Pet. 2:17; Jude verse 13.
Everlasting burnings. *Is. 33:14.*
The wine of the wrath of God.
Rev. 14:10.
Torment with fire. *Rev. 14:10.*
Torment forever and ever. *Rev. 14:11.*
The righteousness of God
requires. *2 Thess. 1:6.*
It is often sudden and
unexpected. *Ps. 35:8, 64:7; Prov. 29:1;*
1 Thess. 5:3.
Will be
According to their deeds.
Mat. 16:27; Rom. 2:6, 9; 2 Cor. 5:10.
According to the knowledge
possessed by them. *Lk. 12:47-48.*
Increased by their neglect of
privileges. *Mat. 11:21-24; Lk. 10:13-15.*
Without mitigation. *Lk. 16:23-26.*
Accompanied by lack of
remorse. *Is. 66:24 with Mk. 9:44.*
Joining forces will not keep them
from punishment. *Prov. 11:21.*
Deferred, tends to embolden
them in their stupidty. *Eccl. 8:11.*
Should be a warning to others.
Num. 26:10; Jude verse 7.
Will be consummated on the Day
of Judgement. *Mat. 25:31, 46; Rom. 2:5,*
16; 2 Pet. 2:9.

R

REBELLION AGAINST GOD

Is forbidden. *Num. 14:9; Josh. 22:19.*
Provokes God. *Num. 16:30; Neh. 9:26.*
Provokes Christ. *Ex. 23:20-21 with 1 Cor. 10:9.*
Grieves the Holy Spirit. *Is. 63:10.*

Is shown in

Unbelief. *Deut. 9:23; Ps. 106:24-25.*
The rejection of his govern-ment. *1 Sam. 8:7.*
Revolting against him. *Is. 1:5, 31:6.*
Despising his Law. *Neh. 9:26.*
Despising his counsels. *Ps. 107:11.*
Distrusting his power. *Ezek. 17:15.*
Murmuring against him. *Num. 20:3, 10.*
Their refusal to listen to him. *Deut. 9:23; Ezek. 20:8; Zech. 7:11.*
Departing from him. *Is. 59:13.*
Rebelling against governors appointed by him. *Josh. 1:18.*
Departing from his precepts. *Dan. 9:5.*
Departing from his instituted worship. *Ex. 32:8-9; Josh. 22:16-19.*
Sinning against the light. *Job 24:13.*
Walking after our own thoughts. *Is. 65:2.*

Connected with

Stubbornness. *Deut. 31:27.*
Injustice and corruption. *Is. 1:23.*
A contempt of God. *Ps. 107:11.*
Man is prone to. *Deut. 31:27.*
The heart is the seat of. *Jer. 5:23; Heb. 3:12.*

Those who are guilty of,

Aggravate their sin by. *Job 34:37.*
Practise hypocrisy to hide. *Hos. 7:14.*
Persevere in. *Deut. 9:7, 24.*
Increase in, even though chastised. *Is. 1:5.*
Are warned not to exalt themselves. *Ps. 66:7.*
Are denounced. *Is. 30:1.*
Have God as their enemy. *Is. 63:10.*
Have God's hand against them. *1 Sam. 12:15 with Ps. 106:26-27.*
Are impoverished for. *Ps. 68:6.*
Are brought low for. *Ps. 107:11-12.*
Are delivered into the hands of their enemies on account of. *Neh. 9:26-27.*
Are cast out in their sins for. *Ps. 5:10.*
Are cast out of the Church for. *Ezek. 20:38.*
Can be restored through Christ alone. *Ps. 68:18.*
The heinousness of. *1 Sam. 15:23.*

The guilt of,

Is aggravated by God's fatherly care. *Is. 1:2.*
Is aggravated by God's unceas-ing invitations to return to him. *Is. 65:2.*
Must be deprecated. *Josh. 22:29.*
Must be confessed. *Lam. 1:18, 20; Dan. 9:5.*
God alone can forgive. *Dan. 9:9.*
God is ready to forgive. *Neh. 9:17.*
Religious instruction is designed to prevent. *Ps. 78:5, 8.*
Promises to those who avoid. *Deut. 28:1-13. 1 Sam. 12:14.*
Is forgiven after repentance. *Neh. 9:26-27.*

Ministers

Are warned against. *Ezek. 2:8.*
Are sent to those guilty of. *Ezek. 2:3-7, 3:4-9; Mk. 12:4-8.*
Should warn against. *Num. 14:9.*
Should testify against. *Is. 30:8-9; Ezek. 17:12, 44:6.*
Should remind their people of the past. *Deut. 9:7, 31:27.*
The punishment for. *Lev. 26:14-39; 1 Sam. 12:15; Is. 1:20; Jer. 4:16-18; Ezek. 20:8, 38.*
The punishment for teaching. *Jer. 28:16.*
Their ingratitude is illustrated. *Is. 1:2-3.*

Some examples. **Pharaoh**: *Ex. 5:1-2.*
Korah, etc: *Num. 16:11.* **Moses and
Aaron**: *Num. 20:12, 24.* **The Israelites:**
Deut. 9:23-24. **Saul**: *1 Sam. 15:9, 23.*
Jeroboam: *1 Kings 12:28-33.*
Zedekiah: *2 Chron. 36:13.* **The
Kingdom of Israel**: *Hos. 7:14, 13:16.*

RECONCILIATION WITH GOD

Was predicted. *Dan. 9:24 with Is. 53:5.*
Was proclaimed by angels at the
birth of Christ. *Lk. 2:14.*
Was a necessary blotting out of
the hand-writing of ordinances.
Eph. 2:16; Col. 2:14.
Was effected for us
By God in Christ. *2 Cor. 5:19.*
By Christ as High Priest. *Heb. 2:17.*
By the death of Christ. *Rom. 5:10;
Eph. 2:16; Col. 1:21-22.*
By the blood of Christ. *Eph. 2:13;
Col. 1:20.*
While we were still alienated
from God. *Col. 1:21.*
While we were still enemies of
God. *Rom. 5:10.*
The ministry of, is committed to
us all, and, in particular, ministers.
2 Cor. 5:18-19.
In Christ's stead, we should beg
men to seek. *2 Cor. 5:20.*
The effects of;
Peace with God. *Eph. 2:16-17.*
Access to God. *Eph. 2:18.*
The union of Jews and Gentiles.
Eph. 2:14.
The union of things in heaven
and earth. *Col. 1:20 with Eph. 1:10.*
A pledge of full salvation. *Rom. 5:10.*
The necessity for, is illustrated.
Mat. 5:24-26.
Typified. *Lev. 8:15, 16:20.*

REDEMPTION

Is defined. *1 Cor. 7:23.*
Is of God. *Is. 44:21-23 with Lk. 1:68.*
Is by Christ. *Mat. 20:28; Gal. 3:13.*
Is by the blood of Christ. *Acts 20:28;
Heb. 9:12; 1 Pet. 1:19; Rev. 5:9.*

Christ was sent to effect. *Gal. 4:4-5.*
Christ is made, to us. *1 Cor. 1:30.*
Is from
The bondage of the Law. *Gal. 4:5.*
The curse of the Law. *Gal. 3:13.*
The power of sin. *Rom. 6:18, 22.*
The power of the grave. *Ps. 49:15.*
All troubles. *Ps. 25:22.*
All iniquity. *Ps. 130:8; Titus 2:14.*
All evil. *Gen. 48:16.*
This present evil world. *Gal. 1:4.*
Aimless conduct. *1 Pet. 1:18.*
Enemies. *Ps. 106:10-11; Jer. 15:21.*
Death. *Hos. 13:14.*
Destruction. *Ps. 103:4.*
Man cannot effect. *Ps. 49:7.*
Corruptible things cannot
purchase. *1 Pet. 1:18.*
Procures for us
Justification. *Rom. 3:24.*
The forgiveness of sin. *Eph. 1:7;
Col. 1:14.*
Adoption. *Gal. 4:4-5.*
Purification. *Titus 2:14.*
The present life is the only time
for. *Job 36:18-19.*
Is described as
Precious. *Ps. 49:8.*
Plentiful. *Ps. 130:7.*
Eternal. *Heb. 9:12.*
The subject of, is
The soul. *Ps. 49:15, 71:2-3.*
The body. *Rom. 8:23.*
The life. *Ps. 103:4; Lam. 3:58.*
The inheritance. *Eph. 1:14.*
Manifests
The power of God. *Is. 50:2.*
The grace of God. *Is. 52:3.*
The love and pity of God. *Is. 63:9.*
Is a subject for praise. *Is. 44:22-23, 51:11.*
The Old Testament saints were
also partakers of. *Heb. 9:15.*
Those who partake of,
Are the property of God. *Is. 43:1;
1 Cor. 6:20.*
Are the first-fruits to God. *Rev. 14:4.*
Are a special people. *2 Sam. 7:23;
Titus 2:14 with 1 Pet. 2:9.*
Are assured of. *Job 19:25; Ps. 31:5.*

Are sealed to the day of. *Eph. 4:30.*
Are zealous of good works.
Titus 2:14.
Walk safely in holiness. *Is. 35:8-9.*
Will return to Zion with joy.
Is. 35:10.
Alone, can learn the songs of heaven. *Rev. 14:3-4.*
Commit themselves to God.
Ps. 31:5.
Have a pledge of the completion of. *Eph. 1:14 with 2 Cor. 1:22.*
Wait for the completion of.
Rom. 8:23.
Pray for the completion of.
Ps. 26:11, 44:26.
Praise God for. *Ps. 71:23; Rev. 5:9.*
Should glorify God for. *1 Cor. 6:20.*
Should be without fear. *Is. 43:1.*

Typified. **Israel:** *Ex. 6:6.* **The firstborn:** *13:11-15; Num. 18:15.*
Atonement-money: *Ex. 30:12-15.* **The bondservant:** *Lev. 25:47-54.*

REPENTANCE
Commanded to all by God.
Acts 17:30.
Commanded by Christ. *Rev. 2:5, 16; Rev. 3:3.*
Given by God. *Acts 11:18; 2 Tim. 2:25.*
Christ came to call sinners to.
Mat. 9:13.
Christ is exalted to give. *Acts 5:31.*
Is by the operation of the Holy Spirit. *Zech. 12:10.*
Is called repentance to life.
Acts 11:18.
Is called repentance to salvation.
2 Cor. 7:10.
We should be led to, because of
The longsuffering of God.
Gen. 6:3 with 1 Pet. 3:20; 2 Pet. 3:9.
The goodness of God. *Rom. 2:4.*
The chastisements of God.
1 Kings 8:47; Rev. 3:19.
Godly sorrow works. *2 Cor. 7:10.*
Is necessary for the pardon of sin. *Acts 2:38, 3:19, 8:22.*

Conviction of sin is necessary for.
1 Kings 8:38; Acts 2:37-38.
Preached
By Christ. *Mat. 4:17; Mk. 1:15.*
By John the Baptist. *Mat. 3:2.*
By the Apostles. *Mk. 6:12; Acts 20:21.*
In the name of Christ. *Lk. 24:47.*
Sorrow of the world is to be repented of. *2 Cor. 7:10.*
Now is the time for. *Ps. 95:7-8 with Heb. 3:7-8, 4:7.*
There is joy in heaven over one sinner that. *Lk. 15:7, 10.*
Ministers should rejoice over their people when they repent.
2 Cor. 7:9.
Should be proved by their fruits.
Dan. 4:27; Mat. 3:8; Acts 26:20.
Should be accompanied by
Humility. *2 Chron. 7:14; Jas. 4:9-10.*
Shame and confusion. *Ezra 9:6-15; Jer. 31:19; Ezek. 16:61, 63; Dan. 9:7-8.*
Self-abhorrence. *Job 42:6.*
Confession. *Lev. 26:40; Job 33:27.*
Faith. *Mat. 21:32; Mk. 1:15; Acts 20:21.*
Prayer. *1 Kings 8:33; Acts 8:22.*
Conversion. *Acts 3:19, 26:20.*
Turning from sin. *2 Chron. 6:26.*
Turning from idolatry. *Ezek. 14:6; 1 Thess. 1:9.*
Greater zeal in the way of duty.
2 Cor. 7:11.
Exhortations to. *Ezek. 14:6, 18:30; Acts 2:38, 3:19.*
The wicked
Are averse to. *Jer. 8:6; Mat. 21:32.*
Are not led to, by the judgements of God. *Rev. 9:20- 21, 16:9.*
Are led to, by acts of grace.
Lk. 16:30-31.
Neglect the time given for. *Rev. 2:21.*
Are condemned for neglecting.
Mat. 11:20.
The danger of neglecting.
Mat. 11:20-24; Lk. 13:3, 5. Rev. 2:22.
Neglect of, is followed by swift judgement. *Rev. 2:5, 16.*
Is denied to apostates. *Heb. 6:4-6.*
Is illustrated. *Lk. 15:18-21, 18:13.*

Examples of true repentance. **The Israelites**: *Judg. 10:15-16.* **David**: *2 Sam. 12:13.* **Manasseh**: *2 Chron. 33:12-13.* **Job**: *Job 42:6.* **Nineveh**: *Jonah 3:5-8. Mat. 12:41.* **Peter**: *Mat. 26:75.* **Zaccheus**: *Lk. 19:8.* **The thief on the cross**: *Lk. 23:40-41.* **The Corinthians**: *2 Cor. 7:9.*

Examples of false repentance. **Saul**: *1 Sam. 15:24-30.* **Ahab**: *1 Kings 21:27-29.* **Judas Iscariot**: *Mat. 27:3-5.*

REPROOF

God gives, to the wicked. *Ps. 50:21; Is. 51:20.*
Christ sent to give. *Is. 2:4, 11:3.*
The Holy Spirit gives. *Jn. 16:7-8.*
Christ gives, in love. *Rev. 3:19.*
On account of
Impenitence. *Mat. 11:20-24.*
Not understanding. *Mat. 16:9, 11; Mk. 7:18; Jn. 8:43.*
Hardness of heart. *Mk. 8:17, 16:14.*
Fearfulness. *Mk. 4:40; Lk. 24:37-38.*
Unbelief. *Mat. 17:17, 20; Mk. 16:14.*
Hypocrisy. *Mat. 15:7, 23:13,*
Reviling Christ. *Lk. 23:40.*
Unruly conduct. *1 Thess. 5:14.*
Oppressing our brothers. *Neh. 5:7.*
Sinful practices. *Lk. 3:19.*
The Scriptures are profitable for. *Eph. 5:13; 2 Tim. 3:16.*
When, is from God,
It is for correction. *Ps. 39:11.*
It is despised by the wicked. *Prov. 1:30.*
It should not discourage the saints. *Heb. 12:5.*
Pray that it may not be in anger. *Ps. 6:1.*
It should be accompanied by an exhortation to repentance. *1 Sam. 12:20-25.*
It is declared to be
Better than secret love. *Prov. 27:5.*
Better than the praise of fools. *Eccl. 7:5.*

An excellent oil. *Ps. 141:5.*
More profitable to the saints, than stripes to a fool. *Prov. 17:10.*
A proof of faithful friendship. *Prov. 27:6.*
It leads to
Understanding. *Prov. 15:32.*
Knowledge. *Prov. 19:25.*
Wisdom. *Prov. 15:31, 29:15.*
. Honour. *Prov. 13:18.*
Happiness. *Prov. 6:23.*
Eventually, it brings more respect than flattery. *Prov. 28:23.*
Of those who offend, it is a warning to others. *1 Tim. 5:20.*
Hypocrites are not qualified to give. *Mat. 7:5.*
Ministers are sent to give. *Jer. 44:4.*
Ministers are empowered to give. *Mic. 3:8.*
Ministers should give,
Openly. *1 Tim. 5:20.*
Fearlessly. *Ezek. 2:3-7.*
With all authority. *Titus 2:15.*
With longsuffering, etc. *2 Tim. 4:2.*
Unreservedly. *Is. 58:1.*
Sharply, if necessary. *Titus 1:13.*
With Christian love. *2 Thess. 3:15.*
Those who give, are hated by scorners. *Prov. 9:8, 15:12.*
Hatred of, is a proof of low life. *Prov. 12:1.*
Hatred of, leads to destruction. *Prov. 15:10, 29:1.*
Contempt of, leads to remorse. *Prov. 5:17.*
Rejection of, leads to error. *Prov. 10:17.*
The saints should
Give. *Lev. 19:17; Eph. 5:11.*
Give no occasion for. *Phil. 2:15.*
Receive, kindly. *Ps. 141:5.*
Love those who give. *Prov. 9:8.*
Delight in those who give. *Prov. 24:25.*
Attention to, is a proof of prudence. *Prov. 15:5.*

Some examples. **Samuel**: *1 Sam. 13:13.* **Nathan**: *2 Sam. 12:7-9.* **Ahijah**: *1*

Kings 14:7-11. **Elijah**: 1 Kings 21:20.
Elisha: 2 Kings 5:26. **Joab**: 1 Chron. 21:3.
Shemaiah: 2 Chron. 12:5. **Hanani**: 2
Chron. 16:7. **Zechariah**: 2 Chron. 24:20.
Daniel: Dan. 5:22-23. **John the**
Baptist: Mat. 3:7; Lk. 3:19. **Stephen**:
Acts 7:51. **Peter**: Acts 8:20. **Paul**: Gal. 2:11.

RESIGNATION

Christ set an example of. Mat. 26:39,
42; Jn. 12:27, 18:11.
Commanded. Ps. 37:7, 46:10.
Should be shown in
  Submission to the will of God.
  2 Sam. 15:26; Mat.6:10.
  Submission to the sovereignty
  of God in his purposes.
  Rom. 9:20-21.
  The prospect of death. Acts 21:13.
  Loss of goods. Job 1:15-16, 21.
  Loss of children. Job 1:18-19, 21.
  Chastisements. Heb. 12:9.
  Bodily suffering. Job 2:8-10.
The wicked are devoid of. Prov. 19:3.
Motives for:
  God's greatness. Ps. 46:10.
  God's love. Heb. 12:6.
  God's justice. Neh. 9:33.
  God's wisdom. Rom. 11:32-33.
  God's faithfulness. 1 Pet. 4:19.
  Our own sinfulness. Lam. 3:39;
  Mic. 7:9.

Some examples. **Jacob**: Gen. 43:14.
Aaron: Lev. 10:3. **Israel**: Judg. 10:15. **Eli**:
1 Sam. 3:18. **David**: 2 Sam. 12:23.
Hezekiah: 2 Kings 20:19. **Job**: Job 2:10.
Stephen: Acts 7:59. **Paul**: Acts 21:13.
Disciples: Acts 21:14. **Peter**: 2 Pet. 1:14.

RESURRECTION, THE

A teaching found in the Old
Testament. Gen. 22:5; Job 19:26;
Ps. 49:15; Is. 26:19; Dan. 12:2; Heb. 11:19.
A first principle of the gospel.
Heb. 6:1-2.
Expected by the Jews. Jn. 11:24;
Heb. 11:35.
Denied by the Sadducees. Mat. 22:23;
Lk. 20:27; Acts 23:8.
Explained away by false teachers.
2 Tim. 2:18.
Called in question by some in the
early Church. 1 Cor. 15:12.
Is not unbelievable. Mk. 12:24;
Acts 26:8.
Is not contrary to reason. Jn. 12:24;
1 Cor. 15:35-44.
Assumed and proved by our
Lord. Mat. 22:29-32; Lk. 14:14; Jn. 5:28-29.
Preached by the Apostles. Acts 4:2,
17:18, 24:15.
The credibility of, is shown in the
resurrection of individuals.
Mat. 9:25, 27:53; Lk. 7:14; Jn. 11:44;
Heb. 11:35.
The certainty of, is proved by the
resurrection of Christ. 1 Cor. 15:12-20.
Is effected by the power of
  God. Mat. 22:29.
  Christ. Jn. 6:28-29, 6:39-40, 44.
  The Holy Spirit. Rom. 8:11.
Will not, at first, be of all the
dead. Jn. 5:28; Acts 24:15; Rev. 20:13.
The saints in, will
  Rise in Christ. Jn. 11:25; Acts 4:2;
  1 Cor. 15:21-22.
  Rise first. 1 Cor. 16:23; 1 Thess. 4:16.
  Rise to eternal life. Dan. 12:2;
  Jn. 5:29.
  Be glorified with Christ. Col. 3:4.
  Be as the angels. Mat. 22:30.
  Have imperishable bodies.
  1 Cor. 15:42.
  Have glorious bodies. 1 Cor. 15:43.
  Have powerful bodies. 1 Cor. 15:43.
  Have spiritual bodies. 1 Cor. 15:44.
  Have bodies like Christ's.
  Phil. 3:21.
  Be recompensed. Lk. 14:14.
The saints should look forward
to. Dan. 12:13; Phil. 3:11.
Of the saints will be followed by
a change in those still alive.
1 Cor. 15:51 with 1 Thess. 4:17.
The preaching of the, brought
  Mocking. Acts 17:32.
  Persecution. Acts 23:6, 24:11-15.

The blessedness of those who have a part in the first. *Rev. 20:6.*
Of the wicked, will be to
Shame and everlasting contempt. *Dan. 12:2.*
Condemnation. *Jn. 5:29.*
Is an illustration of the new birth. *Jn. 5:25.*
Is illustrated further. *Ezek. 37:1-10. 1 Cor. 15:36-37.*
Is associated with the Feast of Tabernacles. *Lev. chapter 23; Is. 25:6-9; 1 Cor. 15:54.*

RESURRECTION OF CHRIST, THE

Was foretold by the prophets. *Ps. 16:10 with Acts 13:34-35; Is. 26:19.*
Was foretold by himself. *Mat. 20:19; Mk. 9:9, 14:28; Jn. 2:19-22.*
Was necessary for
The fulfilment of Scripture. *Lk. 24:45-46.*
The forgiveness of sins. *1 Cor. 15:17.*
Justification. *Rom. 4:25, 8:34.*
Hope. *1 Cor. 15:19.*
The effectiveness of preaching. *1 Cor. 15:14.*
The effectiveness of faith. *1 Cor. 15:14, 17.*
A proof of his being the Son of God. *Ps. 2:7 with Acts 13:33; Rom. 1:4.*
Effected by
The power of God. *Acts 2:24, 3:15; Rom. 8:11; Eph. 1:20; Col. 2:12.*
His own power. *Jn. 2:19, 30:18.*
The power of the Holy Spirit. *1 Pet. 3:18.*
Came on the first day of the week. *Mk. 16:9*
Came on the third day after his death. *Gen. 1:11-13, 22:4-5, 40:20, 42:18; Ex. 3:18, 15:1; Lev. 23:11; Num. 19:12; Esth. 4:16, 6:1-2; Lk. 24:46; Acts 10:40; 1 Cor. 15:4.*
The Apostles
At first, did not understand the prophecies concerning. *Mk. 9:10; Jn. 20:9.*
Were very slow to believe.
Mk. 16:13; Lk. 24:9, 11, 37-38.
Were reproved for their unbelief concerning. *Mk. 16:14.*
He appeared after, to
Mary Magdalene. *Mk. 16:9; Jn. 20:18.*
The women. *Mat. 28:9.*
Simon Peter. *Lk. 24:34.*
Two disciples. *Lk. 24:13-31.*
All the Apostles except Thomas. *Jn. 20:19, 24.*
The Apostles, when Thomas was present. *Jn. 20:26.*
The Apostles at the sea of Tiberias. *Jn. 21:1.*
The Apostles in Galilee. *Mat. 28:16-17.*
More than five-hundred brothers. *1 Cor. 15:6.*
James. *1 Cor. 15:7.*
All the Apostles. *Lk. 24:51; Acts 1:9; 1 Cor. 15:7.*
Paul. *1 Cor. 15:8.*
Fraud was impossible concerning. *Mat. 27:63-66.*
He gave many infallible proofs of. *Lk. 24:35, 39, 43; Jn. 20:20, 27; Acts 1:3.*
It was attested to by
Angels. *Mat. 25:6-7; Lk. 24:4-7, 23.*
Apostles. *Acts 1:22, 2:32, 3:15, 4:33.*
His enemies. *Mat. 28:11-15.*
Asserted and preached by the Apostles. *Acts 25:19, 26:23.*
The saints
Are born again to a living hope by. *1 Pet. 1:3, 21.*
Desire to know the power of. *Phil. 3:10.*
Should keep, in remembrance. *2 Tim. 2:8.*
Will rise in the likeness of. *Rom. 6:5; 1 Cor. 15:49 with Phil. 3:21.*
Is an emblem of the new birth. *Rom. 6:4; Col. 2:12.*
The first-fruits of our resurrection. *Acts 26:23; 1 Cor. 15:20, 23.*
The truth of the gospel is involved in. *1 Cor. 15:14-15.*
Was followed by his exaltation. *Acts 4:10-11; Rom. 8:34; Eph. 1:20; Rev. 1:18.*

Is an assurance of the judgement. *Acts 17:31*

Typified by **Isaac**: *Gen. 22:13 with Heb. 11:19.* **Jonah**: *Jonah 2:10 with Mat. 12:40.*

REVENGE

Is forbidden. *Lev. 19:18; Prov. 24:29; Rom. 12:17, 19; 1 Thess. 5:15; 1 Pet. 3:9.*
Christ is the supreme example of forbearance. *1 Pet. 2:23.*
Was rebuked by Christ. *Lk. 9:54-55.*
Is inconsistent with the Christian spirit. *Lk. 9:55.*
Proceeds from a spiteful heart. *Ezek. 25:15.*

Instead of taking, we should
Trust in God. *Prov. 20:22; Rom. 12:19.*
Show love. *Lev. 19:18; Lk. 6:35.*
Give no place for wrath. *Rom. 12:19.*
Exercise forbearance. *Mat. 5:38-41.*
Bless, and not curse. *Rom. 12:14.*
Disarm others with kindness. *Prov. 25:21 with Rom. 12:20.*
Keep others from taking. *1 Sam. 24:7, 25:24-31, 26:9.*
Be thankful for being kept from taking. *1 Sam. 25:32-33.*
The wicked are earnest in taking. *Jer. 20:10.*
The punishment for. *Ezek. 25:15-17; Amos 1:11-12.*

Some examples. **Simeon and Levi**: *Gen. 34:25.* **Samson**: *Judg. 15:7-8, 16:28-30.* **Joab**: *2 Sam. 3:27.* **Absolom**: *2 Sam. 13:23-29.* **Jezebel**: *1 Kings 19:2.* **Ahab**: *1 Kings 22:26.* **Haman**: *Esth. 3:8-15.* **The Edomites**: *Ezek. 25:12.* **The Philistines**: *Ezek. 25:15.* **Herodias**: *Mk. 6:19-24.* **James and John**: *Lk. 9:54.* **The Chief Priests**: *Acts 5:33.* **The Jews**: *Acts 7:54, 59, 23:12.*

REVILING AND REPROACHING

Is forbidden. *1 Pet. 3:9.*
Of rulers, is specifically forbidden. *Ex. 22:28 with Acts 23:4-5.*

The wicked utter, against
God. *Ps. 74:22, 79:12.*
Christ. *Mat. 27:39; Lk. 7:34.*
The saints. *Ps. 102:8; Zeph. 2:8.*
Rulers. *2 Pet. 2:10-11; Jude verses 8-9.*
Of Christ, was predicted. *Ps. 69:9 with Rom. 15:3; Ps. 89:51.*
The conduct of Christ under. *1 Pet. 2:23.*

The saints
Endure. *1 Tim. 4:10; Heb. 10:33.*
Endure for God's sake. *Ps. 69:7.*
Endure for Christ's sake. *Lk. 6:22.*
Should expect. *Mat. 10:25.*
Should not fear. *Is. 51:7.*
Are sometimes depressed by. *Ps. 42:10-11, 44:16, 69:20.*
May take pleasure in. *2 Cor. 12:10.*
Are supported during. *2 Cor. 12:10.*
Trust in God under. *Ps. 57:3, 119:42.*
Pray under. *2 Kings 19:4, 16; Ps. 89:50.*
Return blessings for. *1 Cor. 4:12; 1 Pet. 3:9.*
Ministers should not fear. *Ezek. 2:6.*
The happiness of enduring, for Christ's sake. *1 Pet. 4:14.*
The blessedness of enduring for Christ's sake. *Mat. 5:11; Lk. 6:2.*
Excludes from heaven. *1 Cor. 6:10.*
The punishment for. *Zeph. 2:8-9; Mat. 5:22.*

Some examples. **Joseph's brothers**: *Gen 37:19.* **Goliath**: *1 Sam. 17:43.* **Michal**: *2 Sam. 6:20.* **Shimei**: *2 Sam. 16:7-8:* **Sennacharib**: *Is. 37:17, 23-24.* **The Moabites and Ammonites**: *Zeph. 2:8.* **Pharisees**: *Mat. 12:24.* **Jews**: *Mat. 27: 39-40; Jn. 8:48.* **One of the thieves**: *Lk. 23:39.* **The Athenian philosophers**: *Acts 17:18.*

REWARD OF THE SAINTS, THE

Is from God. *Col. 3:24; Heb. 11:6.*
Is of grace, through faith alone. *Rom. 4-5, 16, 11:6.*
Is of God's good pleasure. *Lk. 12:32.*
Is prepared by God. *Heb. 11:16.*
Is prepared by Christ. *Jn. 14:2.*

As servants of Christ. *Col. 3:24.*
Is not on account of their merits.
Rom. 4:5.

Is described as
Being with Christ. *Jn. 12:26, 14:3; Phil. 1:23; 1 Thess. 4:17.*
Beholding the face of God.
Ps. 17:15; Mat. 5:8; Rev. 22:4.
Beholding the glory of Christ.
Jn. 17:24.
Being glorified with Christ.
Rom. 8:7-18; Col. 3:4.
Sitting in judgement with
Christ. *Lk. 22:30 with 1 Cor. 6:2.*
Reigning with Christ. *2 Tim. 2:12; Rev. 5:10; Rev. 20:4.*
Reigning forever and ever.
Rev. 22:5.
A crown of righteousness.
2 Tim. 4:8.
A crown of glory. *1 Pet. 5:4.*
A crown of life. *Jas. 1:12; Rev. 2:10.*
An incorruptible crown.
1 Cor. 9:25.
Being joint-heirs of Christ.
Rom. 8:17.
The inheritance of all things.
Rev. 21:7.
An inheritance with the saints
in light. *Acts 20:32, 26:18; Col. 1:12.*
An eternal inheritance. *Heb. 9:15.*
An incorruptible inheritance,
etc. *1 Pet. 1:4.*
A kingdom. *Mat. 25:34; Lk. 22:29.*
An immovable kingdom.
Heb. 12:28.
Shining as the stars. *Dan. 12:3.*
Everlasting light. *Is. 60:19.*
Everlasting life. *Lk. 18:30; Rom. 6:23.*
An enduring substance.
Heb. 10:34.
A house, eternal in the heavens.
2 Cor. 5:1.
A city that has foundations.
Heb. 11:10.
Entering into the joy of the
Lord. *Mat. 25:21 with Heb. 12:2.*
Rest. *Heb. 4:9; Rev. 14:13.*
Fullness of joy. *Ps. 16:11.*

The prize of the high calling of
God in Christ. *Phil. 3:14.*
Treasure in heaven. *Mat. 19:21; Lk. 12:33.*
An eternal weight of glory.
2 Cor. 4:17.
Is great. *Mat. 5:12; Lk. 6:35; Heb. 10:35.*
Is full. *2 Jn. verse 8.*
Is sure. *Prov. 11:18.*
Is satisfying. *Ps. 17:15.*
Is inestimable. *Is. 64:4 with 1 Cor. 2:9.*
The saints may feel confident of.
Ps. 73:24; 2 Cor. 5:1; 2 Tim. 4:8.
The hope of, a cause of rejoicing.
Rom. 5:2.
Be careful not to lose. *2 Jn. verse 8.*

The prospect of, should lead to
Diligence. *2 Jn. verse 8.*
Pressing forward. *Phil. 3:14.*
Enduring suffering for Christ.
2 Cor. 4:16-18; Heb. 11:26.
Faithfulness to death. *Rev. 2:10.*
Present afflictions are not to be
compared with. *Rom. 8:18.*
Will be given at the Second
Coming of Christ. *Mat. 16:27; Rev. 22:12; 2 Tim. 4:1, 8.*

RICHES
God gives. *1 Sam. 2:7; Eccl. 5:19.*
God gives the power to obtain.
Deut. 8:18.
The blessing of the Lord brings.
Prov. 10:22.
Give worldly power. *Prov. 22:7.*
Are described as
Temporary. *Prov. 27:24.*
Uncertain. *1 Tim. 6:17.*
Unsatisfying. *Eccl. 4:8, 5:10.*
Corruptible. *Jas. 5:2; 1 Pet. 1:18.*
Fleeting. *Prov. 23:5; Rev. 18:16-17.*
Deceitful. *Mat. 13:22.*
Liable to be stolen. *Mat. 6:19.*
Perishable. *Jer. 48:36.*
Thick clay. *Hab. 2:6.*
Often act as an obstruction to
the reception of the gospel.
Mk. 10:23-25.
The deceitfulness of, chokes the

Word. *Mat. 13:22.*
A love of, is the root of all evil.
1 Tim. 6:10.

Often lead to
Pride. *Ezek. 28:5; Hos. 12:8.*
Forgetting God. *Deut. 8:13-14.*
Denying God. *Prov. 30:8-9.*
Forsaking God. *Deut. 32:15.*
Rebelling against God. *Neh. 9:25-26.*
Rejecting Christ. *Mat. 19:22;*
Mk. 10:22.
Self-sufficiency. *Prov. 28:11.*
Anxiety. *Eccl. 5:12.*
An overbearing spirit. *Prov. 18:23.*
Violence. *Mic. 6:12.*
Oppression. *Jas. 2:6.*
Fraud. *Jas. 5:4.*
The indulgence of the senses.
Jas. 5:5.
Life does not consist of the
abundance of. *Lk. 12:15.*
Do not be over-anxious for.
Prov. 30:8.
Do not live and work for. *Prov. 23:4.*

Those who covet,
Fall into temptation and a
snare. *1 Tim. 6:9.*
Fall into harmful lusts. *1 Tim. 6:9.*
Err from the faith. *1 Tim. 6:10.*
Use illegal means to acquire.
Prov. 28:20.
Bring trouble on themselves.
1 Tim. 6:10.
Bring trouble on their families.
Prov. 15:27.
Will not profit in the day of
wrath. *Prov. 11:4.*
Cannot secure prosperity. *Jas. 1:11.*
Cannot redeem the soul. *Ps. 49:6-9;*
1 Pet. 1:18.
Cannot be delivered in the day of
God's wrath. *Zeph. 1:18; Rev. 6:15-17.*

Those who possess, should
Ascribe them to God.
1 Chron. 29:12.
Not trust in them. *Job 31:24;*
1 Tim. 6:17.
Not set their hearts on them.
Ps. 62:10.

Not boast of obtaining them.
Deut. 8:17.
Not glory in them. *Jer. 9:23.*
Not hoard them up. *Mat. 6:19.*
Dedicate them to God's service.
1 Chron. 29:3.
Give some of them to the poor.
Mat. 19:21; 1 Jn. 3:17.
Use them in promoting the
salvation of others. *Lk. 16:9.*
Be generous in all things.
1 Tim. 6:18.
Esteem it a privilege to be
allowed to give. *1 Chron. 29:14.*
Not be high-minded. *1 Tim. 6:17.*
When converted, rejoice in
being humbled. *Jas. 1:9-10.*
Heavenly treasures are the best.
Mat. 6:19-20.
Will be taken from the wicked
and given to the just. *Prov. 13:22.*

The wicked
Often increase in. *Ps. 73:12.*
Often spend their days in.
Job 21:13.
Swallow up. *Job 20:15.*
Trust in the abundance of.
Ps. 52:7.
Heap up. *Job 27:16. Eccl. 2:26.*
Grasp hold of, to their harm.
Eccl. 5:13.
Boast of them. *Ps. 49:6.*
Do not profit by them. *Prov. 13:7;*
Eccl. 5:11.
Have trouble with. *Prov. 15:6.*
Must leave, to others. *Ps. 49:10.*
The vanity of heaping up. *Ps. 39:6;*
Eccl. 5:10-11.
The guilt of trusting in. *Job 31:24, 28.*
The guilt of rejoicing in. *Job 31:25, 28.*

Denunciations against those who
Get, by dishonesty. *Prov. 13:11.*
Get, illegally. *Jer. 17:11.*
Increase, by oppression.
Prov. 22:16; Hab. 2:6-8; Mic. 2:2-3.
Hoard. *Eccl. 5:13-14; Jas. 5:3.*
Trust in. *Prov. 11:28.*
Receive their consolation from.
Lk. 6:24.

Abuse. *Jas. 5:1, 5.*
Spend, on their appetites.
Job 20:15-17.
The folly and danger of trusting
in, is illustrated in *Lk. 12:16-21.*
The danger of misusing, is
illustrated in *Lk. 16:19-25.*

Some examples of saints
possessing. **Abra(ha)m**: *Gen. 13:2.*
Lot: *Gen. 13:5-6.* **Isaac**: *Gen. 26:13-14.*
Jacob: *Gen. 32:5, 10.* **Joseph**: *Gen. 45:8,
13.* **Boaz** *Ruth 2:1.* **Barzillai**: *2 Sam. 19:32.*
A Shunammite: *2 Kings 4:8.* **David**:
1 Chron. 29:28. **Jehoshaphat**:
2 Chron. 17:5. **Hezekiah**: *2 Chron. 32:27-
29.* **Job**: *Job 1:3.* **Joseph of
Arimathea**: *Mat. 27:57.* **Zaccheus**:
Lk. 19:2. **Dorcas**: *Acts 9:36.*

Some examples of wicked men
possessing riches. **Laban**: *Gen. 30:30.*
Esau: *Gen. 36:7.* **Nabal**: *1 Sam. 25:2.*
Haman: *Esther 5:11.* **The Ammo-
nites**: *Jer. 49:4.* **The Tyrians**: *Ezek. 28:5.*
A rich young man: *Mat. 19:22.*

RIGHTEOUSNESS
Is obedience to God's Law.
Deut. 6:25 with Rom. 10:5.
God loves. *Ps. 11:7.*
God looks for. *Is. 5:7.*
Christ
Is the Sun of. *Mal. 4:2.*
Loves. *Ps. 45:7 with Heb. 1:9.*
Has a belt of. *Is. 11:5.*
Put on, as a breastplate. *Is. 59:17.*
Was sustained by. *Is. 59:16.*
Preached. *Ps. 40:9.*
Fulfilled all. *Mat. 3:15.*
Is made, to his people. *1 Cor. 1:30.*
Is the end of the Law for.
Rom. 10:4.
Has brought in everlasting.
Dan. 9:24.
Will judge with. *Ps. 72:2. Is. 11:4;
Acts 17:31; Rev. 19:11.*
Will reign in. *Ps. 45:6; Is. 32:1; Heb. 1:8.*
Will execute. *Ps. 99:4; Jer. 23:5.*

No one, by nature, has. *Job 15:14;
Ps. 14:3 with Rom. 3:10.*
Cannot obtain, by the Law. *Gal. 2:21,
3:21.*
There is no justification by works
of. *Rom. 3:20, 9:31-32; Gal. 2:16.*
There is no salvation by works of.
Eph. 2:8-9; 2 Tim. 1:9; Titus 3:5.
Unregenerate men seeks justifi-
cation by works of. *Lk. 18:9;
Rom. 10:3.*
The blessing of God must not to
be attributed to our works of.
Deut. 9:5.
The saints
Have, in Christ. *Is. 45:24, 54:17;
2 Cor. 5:21.*
Have, imputed to them.
Rom. 4:11, 22.
Are covered with the robe of.
Is. 61:10.
Receive, from God. *Ps. 24:5.*
Are renewed in. *Eph. 4:24.*
Are led in the paths of. *Ps. 23:3.*
Are servants of. *Rom. 6:16, 18.*
Are characterised by. *Gen. 18:25;
Ps. 1:5-6.*
Know. *Is. 51:7.*
Do works of. *1 Jn. 2:29, 3:7.*
Work, by faith. *Heb. 11:33.*
Follow after. *Is. 51:1.*
Put on. *Job 29:14.*
Wait for the hope of. *Gal. 5:5.*
Pray for the spirit of. *Ps. 51:10.*
Hunger and thirst after. *Mat. 5:6.*
Walk before God in. *1 Kings 3:6.*
Offer the sacrifice of. *Ps. 4:5, 51:19.*
Put no trust in their own.
Phil. 3:6-8.
Count their own, as filthy rags.
Is. 64:6.
Should seek. *Zeph. 2:3.*
Should live in. *Titus 2:12; 1 Pet. 2:4.*
Should serve God in. *Lk. 1:75.*
Should yield their members as
instruments of. *Rom. 6:13.*
Should yield their bodily
members as servants to. *Rom. 6:19.*

Should wear the breastplate of. *Eph. 6:14.*

Will receive a crown of. *2 Tim. 4:8.*

Will see God's face in. *Ps. 17:15.*

Of the saints, endures forever. *Ps. 112:39 with 2 Cor. 9:9.*

An evidence of the new birth. *1 Jn. 2:29.*

The kingdom of God is. *Rom. 14:17.*

The fruit of the Spirit is in all. *Eph. 5:9.*

The Scriptures instruct in. *2 Tim. 3:16.*

Judgements are designed to lead to. *Is. 26:9.*

Chastisements yield the fruit of. *Heb. 12:11.*

Have no fellowship with workers of unrighteousness. *2 Cor. 6:14.*

Ministers should

Be preachers of. *2 Pet. 2:5.*

Reason for. *Acts 24:25.*

Follow after. *1 Tim. 6:11; 2 Tim. 2:22.*

Be clothed with. *Ps. 132:9.*

Be armed with. *2 Cor. 6:7.*

Pray for fruit of, in their people. *2 Cor 9:10; Phil. 1:11.*

Keeps the saints in the right way. *Prov. 11:5, 13:6.*

Judgement should be executed in. *Lev 19:15.*

Those who walk in, and follow after,

Are righteous. *1 Jn. 3:7.*

Are the excellent of the earth. *Ps. 16:3 with Prov. 12:26.*

Are accepted by God. *Acts 10:35.*

Are loved by God. *Ps. 146:8; Prov 15:9.*

Are blessed by God. *Ps. 5:12.*

Are objects of God's watchful care. *Job 36:7; Ps. 34:15; 1 Pet. 3:12.*

Are tried by God. *Ps. 11:5.*

Are exalted by God. *Job 36:7.*

Dwell in security. *Is. 33:15-16.*

Are as bold as a lion. *Prov. 28:1.*

Are delivered out of all troubles. *Ps. 34:19; Prov. 11:8.*

Are never forsaken by God. *Ps. 37:25.*

Are abundantly provided for. *Prov. 13:25.*

Are enriched. *Ps. 112:3; Prov. 15:6.*

Think and desire good. *Prov. 11:23, 12:5.*

Know the secret of the Lord. *Prov. 3:32.*

Have their prayers heard. *Ps. 34:17; Prov. 15:29; 1 Pet. 3:12.*

Have their desires granted. *Prov. 10:24.*

Find it with life and honour. *Prov. 21:21.*

Will hold to their way. *Job 17:9.*

Will never be moved. *Ps. 15:2, 6, 55:22; Prov. 10:30, 12:3.*

Will be ever remembered. *Ps. 112:6.*

Will flourish as a branch. *Prov. 11:28.*

Will be glad in the Lord. *Ps. 64:10.*

It brings its own reward. *Prov. 11:8; Is. 3:10.*

It tends to life. *Prov. 11:19, 12:28.*

The work of, will be peace. *Is. 32:17.*

The effect of, will be quietness and assurance forever. *Is. 32:17.*

Is a crown of glory to the elderly. *Prov. 16:31.*

The wicked

Are far from. *Ps. 119:160; Is. 46:12.*

Are free from. *Rom. 6:20.*

Are enemies of. *Acts 13:10.*

Leave off. *Amos 5:7 with Ps. 36:3.*

Do not follow after. *Rom. 9:30.*

Do not practice. *1 Jn. 3:10.*

Do not obey. *Rom. 2:8 with 2 Thess. 2:12.*

Love lying rather than. *Ps. 52:3.*

Make mention of God, but not in. *Is. 48:1.*

Though favoured, they will not learn. *Is. 26:10 with Ps. 106:43.*

Speak contemptuously against those who follow after. *Ps. 31:18.*

Hate those who follow. *Ps. 34:21.*

Slay those who follow. *Ps. 37:32; 1 Jn. 3:12 with Mat. 23:35.*

Should break off their sins by. *Dan. 4:27.*

Should awake to. *1 Cor. 15:34.*

Should sow to themselves in. *Hos. 10:12.*

Vainly wish to die as those who follow. *Num. 23:10.*

The throne of kings is established by. *Prov. 16:12; 25:5.*

Nations are exalted by. *Prov. 14:34.*

The blessedness of

Having, imputed without works. *Rom. 4:6.*

Doing. *Ps. 106:3.*

Hungering and thirsting after. *Mat. 5:6.*

Suffering for. *1 Pet. 3:14.*

Being persecuted for. *Mat. 5:10.*

Turning others to. *Dan. 12:3.*

Is promised to the Church. *Is. 32:16, 45:8, 61:11, 62:1.*

Is promised to the saints. *Is. 60:21, 61:3.*

Some examples. **Jacob**: *Gen. 30:33.* **David**: *2 Sam. 22:21.* **Zacharias**, etc: *Lk. 1:6.* **Abel**: *Heb. 11:4.* **Lot**: *2 Pet. 2:8.*

RIGHTEOUSNESS OF GOD, THE

Is part of his character. *Ps. 7:9, 116:5, 119:137.*

Is described as

Very high. *Ps. 71:19.*

Abundant. *Ps. 48:10.*

Beyond computation. *Ps. 71:15.*

Everlasting. *Ps. 119:142.*

Enduring forever. *Ps. 111:3.*

The habitation of his throne. *Ps. 97:2.*

Christ acknowledged. *Jn. 17:25.*

Christ committed his cause to. *1 Pet. 2:23.*

Angels acknowledge. *Rev. 16:5.*

Is shown in

His testimonies. *Ps. 119:138, 144.*

His commandments. *Deut. 4:8; Ps. 119:172.*

His judgements. *Ps. 19:9, 119:7, 62.*

His Word. *Ps. 119:123.*

His ways. *Ps. 145:17.*

His acts. *Judg. 5:11. 1 Sam. 12:7.*

His government. *Ps. 96:13, 98:9.*

The gospel. *Ps. 85:10 with Rom. 3:25-26.*

The final judgement. *Acts 17:31.*

The punishment of the wicked. *Rom. 2:5; 2 Thess. 1:6; Rev. 16:7, 10:2.*

Shown to the posterity of the saints. *Ps. 103:17.*

Shown openly before the nations. *Ps. 98:2.*

God delights in the exercise of. *Jer. 9:24.*

The heavens will declare. *Ps. 50:6, 97:6.*

The saints

Ascribe, to him. *Job 36:3; Dan. 9:7.*

Acknowledge, in his dealings. *Ezra 9:15*

Acknowledge, although the wicked prosper. *Jer. 12:1 with Ps. 73:12-17.*

Recognise, in the fulfilment of his promises. *Neh. 9:8.*

Are confident of beholding. *Mic. 7:9.*

Are upheld by. *Is. 41:10.*

Do not conceal. *Ps. 40:10.*

Mention, only. *Ps. 71:16.*

Talk of. *Ps. 35:28, 71:15, 24.*

Declare, to others. *Ps. 22:31.*

Magnify. *Ps. 7:17, 51:14, 145:7.*

Plead for, in prayer. *Ps. 143:11; Dan. 9:19.*

Leads them to love righteousness. *Ps. 11:7.*

We should pray

To be led in. *Ps. 5:8.*

To be made alive in. *Ps. 119:40.*

To be delivered in. *Ps. 31:1, 71:2.*

To be answered in. *Ps. 143:1.*

To be judged according to. *Ps. 35:24.*

For its continued manifestation. *Ps. 36:10.*

His care and defence of his people is designed to teach. *Mic. 6:4-5.*

The wicked have no interest in.

Ps. 69:27.

Illustrated in Ps. 36:6.

RIGHTEOUSNESS, IMPUTED

Was prophesied. Is. 46:13, 51:5, 56:1.

Is revealed in the gospel. Rom. 1:17.

Is of the Lord. Is. 54:17.

Is described as

The righteousness of faith.
Rom. 4:13, 9:30, 10:6.

The righteousness of God,
without the Law. Rom. 3:21.

The righteousness of God by
faith in Christ. Rom. 3:22.

Christ being made righteousness to us. 1 Cor. 1:30.

Our being made the righteousness of God in Christ. 2 Cor. 5:21.

Christ is the end of the Law for.
Rom. 10:4.

Christ is called 'The Lord our
Righteousness' because of. Jer. 23:6.

Is an everlasting righteousness.
Dan. 9:24.

Is a free gift. Rom. 5:17.

Never to be abolished. Is. 51:6.

The promises made through.
Rom. 4:13, 16.

The saints

Have, on believing. Rom. 4:5, 11, 24.

Are clothed with. Is. 61:10.

Are made righteous by. Rom. 5:19.

Are justified by. Rom. 3:26.

Are exalted in. Ps. 89:16.

Desire to be found in. Phil. 3:9.

Glory in having. Is. 45:24-25.

An exhortation to seek. Mat. 6:33.

The Gentiles have attained to.
Rom. 9:30.

The blessedness of those who
have. Rom. 4:6.

The wicked

Are ignorant of. Rom. 10:3.

Stumble at. Rom. 9:32.

Will not submit to. Rom. 10:3.

Are excluded from. Ps. 69:27.

Two examples. **Abraham**: Rom. 4:9,
22; Gal. 3:6. **Paul**: Phil. 3:7-9.

S

SABBATH, THE

Was instituted by God. Gen. 2:3.

The grounds for its institution.
Gen. 2:2-3; Ex. 20:11.

The seventh day was observed as.
Ex. 20:9-10.

Was made for man. Mk. 2:27.

God

Blessed it. Gen. 2:3. Ex. 20:11.

Sanctified it. Gen. 2:3; Ex. 31:15.

Hallowed it. Ex. 20:11.

Commanded it to be kept.
Lev. 19:3, 30.

Commanded it to be sanctified.
Ex. 20:8.

Has his goodness commemo-
rated in its observance. Deut. 5:15.

Shows favour in appointing.
Neh. 9:14.

Shows considerate kindness in
appointing. Ex. 23:12.

A sign of the covenant. Ex. 31:13, 17.

A type of the heavenly rest.
Heb. 4:4, 9.

Christ

Is Lord of. Mk. 2:28.

Was accustomed to observe.
Lk. 4:16.

Taught on. Lk. 4:31, 6:6.

Servants and cattle should be
allowed to rest on. Ex. 20:10;
Deut. 5:14.

No kind of work should be done
on. Ex. 20:10; Lev. 23:3.

No purchases should be made
on. Neh. 10:31, 13:15-17.

No burdens should be carried
on. Neh. 13:19; Jer. 17:21.

Divine worship should be
celebrated on. Ezek. 46:3; Acts 16:13.

The Scriptures should be read on.
Acts 13:27, 15:21.

The Word of God should be preached on. *Acts 13:14-15, 44, 17:2, 18:4.*

Works connected with religious service were lawful on. *Num. 28:9; Mat. 12:5; Jn. 7:23.*

Works of mercy are lawful on. *Mat. 12:12; Lk. 13:16; Jn. 9:14.*

Urgent needs may be attended to on. *Mat. 12:1; Lk. 13:5, 14:1.*

Is called

The Sabbath of the Lord. *Ex. 20:10; Lev. 23:3; Deut. 5:14.*

The Sabbath of rest. *Ex. 31:15.*

The rest of the holy Sabbath. *Ex. 16:23.*

God's holy day. *Is. 58:13.*

Is now the Lord's Day. *Rev. 1:10.*

The first day of the week was kept as, by the early Church. *Jn. 20:26; Acts 20:7; 1 Cor. 16:2.*

The saints

Observe. *Neh. 13:22.*

Honour God in their observ-ance of. *Is. 58:13.*

Rejoice in. *Ps. 118:24. Is. 58:13.*

Testify against those who desecrate. *Neh. 13:15, 20-21.*

Observance of, to be perpetual. *Ex. 31:16-17 with Mat. 5:17-18.*

The blessedness of honouring. *Is. 58:13-14.*

The blessedness of keeping. *Is. 56:2, 6.*

Denunciations against those who break. *Neh. 13:18; Jer. 17:27.*

The punishment of those who break. *Ex. 31:14-15; Num. 15:32-36.*

The wicked

Mock at. *Lam. 1:7.*

Pollute. *Is. 56:2; Ezek. 20:13, 16.*

Break. *Neh.13:17; Ezek. 22:8.*

Are wearied by. *Amos 8:5.*

Hide their eyes from. *Ezek. 22:26.*

Pursue their own pleasure on. *Is. 58:13.*

Carry burdens on. *Neh. 13:15.*

Work on. *Neh. 13:15.*

Trade on. *Neh. 10:31, 13:15-16.*

Sometimes pretend to be zealous for. *Lk. 13:14; Jn. 9:16.*

May be judicially deprived of. *Lam. 2:6; Hos. 2:11.*

Examples of honouring the Sabbath. **Moses**, etc: *Num. 15:32-34.* **Nehemiah**: *Neh. 13:15, 21.* **Women**: *Lk. 23:56.* **Paul**: *Acts chapters 13-14.* **Disciples**: *Acts 16:13.* **John**: *Rev. 1:10.*

Examples of dishonouring the Sabbath. **Gatherers of manna**: *Ex. 16:27.* **Gatherers of sticks**: *Num. 15:32.* **Men of Tyre**: *Neh. 13:16.* **The inhabitants of Jerusalem**: *Jer. 17:21-23.*

SAINTS ARE COMPARED WITH, THE

The sun. *Judg 5:31; Mat. 13:43.*

Stars. *Dan. 12:3.*

Lights. *Mat.5:14; Phil. 2:15.*

Mount Zion. *Ps. 125:1-2.*

Lebanon. *Hos. 14:5-7.*

Treasure. *Ex. 19:5; Ps. 135:4.*

Jewels. *Mal. 3:17.*

Gold. *Job 23:10. Lam. 4:2.*

Vessels of gold and silver. *2 Tim. 2:20.*

Stones of a crown. *Zech. 9:16.*

Living stones. *1 Pet. 2:5.*

Babies. *Mat. 11:25; 1 Pet. 2:2.*

Little children. *Mat. 18:3; 1 Cor. 14:20.*

Obedient children. *1 Pet. 1:14.*

Members of the body. *1 Cor. 12:20, 27.*

Soldiers. *2 Tim. 2:3-4.*

Runners in a race. *1 Cor. 9:24; Heb. 12:1.*

Wrestlers. *2 Tim. 2:5.*

Good servants. *Mat. 25:21.*

Strangers and pilgrims. *1 Pet. 2:11.*

Sheep. *Ps. 44:22 with Rom. 8:36-37; Ps. 78:52; Mat. 25:33; Jn. 10:4.*

Lambs. *Is. 40:11; Jn. 21:15.*

Calves of the stall. *Mal. 4:2.*

Lions. *Prov. 28:1. Mic. 5:8.*

Eagles. *Ps. 103:5. Is. 40:31.*

Doves. *Ps. 68:13. Is. 60:8.*
Thirsty deer. *Ps. 42:1.*
Good fish. *Mat. 13:48.*
Dew and showers. *Mic. 5:7.*
Watered gardens. *Is. 5 8:11.*
Unfailing springs. *Is. 58:11.*
Vines. *Song 6:11. Hos. 14:7.*
Branches of a vine. *Jn. 16:2, 4-5.*
Pomegranates. *Song 4:13.*
Good figs. *Jer. 24:2-7.*
Lilies. *Song 2:2; Hos. 14:5.*
Willows by the water courses.
Is. 44:4.
Trees planted beside rivers.
Ps. 1:3.
Cedars of Lebanon. *Ps. 92:12.*
Palm trees. *Ps. 92:12.*
Green olive trees. *Ps. 52:8; Hos. 14:6.*
Fruitful trees. *Ps. 1:3. Jer. 17:8.*
Corn. *Hos. 14:7.*
Wheat. *Mat. 3:12, 13:29-30.*
Salt. *Mat. 5:13.*

SALVATION

Is of God. *Ps. 3:8, 37:39; Jer. 3:23.*
Is in the purposes of God.
2 Tim. 1:9.
Is of the appointment of God.
1 Thess. 5:9.
God is willing to give. *1 Tim. 2:4.*
Is by Christ. *Is. 63:9; Eph. 5:23.*
Is by Christ alone. *Is. 45:21, 23, 59:16;*
Acts 4:12.
Announced after the Fall. *Gen. 3:15.*
Of Israel, was prophesied. *Is. 35:4,*
45:17; Zech. 9:16; Rom. 11:26.
Of the Gentiles, was prophesied.
Is. 45:22, 49:6, 52:10.
Is revealed in the gospel. *Eph. 1:13;*
2 Tim. 1:10.
Came to the Gentiles through the
cutting off of the Jews. *Rom. 11:11.*
Christ
Is the Captain of. *Heb. 2:10.*
Is the Author of. *Heb. 5:9.*
Was appointed for. *Is. 49:6.*
Was raised up for. *Lk. 1:69.*
Possesses. *Zech. 9:9.*
Brings, with him. *Is. 62:11; Lk. 19:9.*

Is mighty to effect. *Is. 63:1;*
Heb. 7:25.
Came to effect. *Mat. 18:11;*
1 Tim. 1:15.
Died to effect. *Jn. 3:14-15; Gal. 1:4.*
Was exalted to give. *Acts 5:31.*
Is not by works. *Rom. 11:6. Eph. 2:9; 2*
Tim. 1:9; Titus 3:5.
Is of grace. *Eph. 2:5, 8; 2 Tim. 1:9;*
Titus 2:11.
Is of love. *Rom. 5:8; 1 Jn. 4:9-10.*
Is of mercy. *Ps. 6:4; Titus 3:5.*
Is of the longsuffering of God.
2 Pet. 3:15.
Is through faith in Christ. *Mk. 16:16;*
Acts 16:31; Rom. 10:9; Eph. 2:8; 1 Pet. 1:5.
Reconciliation to God is a pledge
of. *Rom. 5:10.*
Is deliverance from
Sin. *Mat. 1:21 with 1 Jn. 3:5.*
Uncleanness. *Ezek. 36:29.*
The devil. *Col. 2:15; Heb. 2:14-15.*
Wrath. *Rom. 5:9; 1 Thess. 1:10.*
This present evil world. *Gal. 1:4.*
Enemies. *Lk. 1:71, 74.*
Perishing. *Jn. 3:16-17.*
Confession of Christ is necessary
for. *Rom. 10:10.*
Regeneration is necessary for.
1 Pet. 3:21.
Final perseverance is necessary
for. *Mat. 10:22.*
Is described as
Great. *Heb. 2:3.*
Glorious. *2 Tim. 2:10.*
Common. *Jude verse 3.*
From generation to generation.
Is. 51:8.
To the uttermost. *Heb. 7:25.*
Eternal. *Is. 45:17, 51:6; Heb. 5:9.*
Was searched into and preached
by the prophets. *1 Pet. l:10.*
The gospel is the power of God
unto. *Rom. 1:16; 1 Cor. 1:18.*
Preaching the Word is the
appointed means of. *1 Cor. 1:21.*
The Scriptures are able to make
us wise unto. *2 Tim. 3:15; Jas. 1:21.*
Now is the day of. *Is. 49:8; 2 Cor. 6:2.*

From sin, and is worked out with fear and trembling. *Phil. 2:12.*
The saints
Are chosen to. *2 Thess. 2:13; 2 Tim. 1:9.*
Are appointed to obtain. *1 Thess. 5:9.*
Are heirs of. *Heb. 1:14.*
Have, through grace. *Acts 15:11.*
Have a token of, in their patient suffering for Christ. *Phil. 1:28-29.*
Are kept by the power of God unto. *1 Pet. 1:5.*
Are beautified with. *Ps. 149:4.*
Are clothed with. *Is. 61:10.*
Satisfied by. *Lk. 2:30.*
Love. *Ps. 40:16.*
Hope for. *Lam. 3:26; Rom. 8:24.*
Wait for. *Gen. 49:18; Lam. 3:26.*
Long for. *Ps. 119:81, 174.*
Earnestly look for. *Ps. 119:123.*
Daily approach nearer to. *Rom. 13:11.*
Receive, as the end of their faith. *1 Pet. 1:9.*
Welcome the news of. *Is. 52:7 with Rom. 10:15.*
Pray to be visited with. *Ps. 85:7, 108:4, 119:41.*
Pray for assurance of. *Ps. 35:3.*
Pray for a joyful sense of. *Ps. 51:12.*
Give evidence by works. *Heb. 6:9-10.*
Ascribe, to God. *Ps. 25:5; Is. 12:2.*
Praise God for. *1 Chron. 16:23; Ps. 96:2.*
Remember, with thanks. *Ps. 116:13.*
Rejoice in. *Ps. 9:14, 21:1; Is. 25:9.*
Glory in. *Ps. 21:5.*
Declare. *Ps. 40:10, 71:15.*
Godly sorrow works repentance to. *2 Cor. 7:10.*
All the earth will see. *Is. 52:10; Lk. 3:6.*
Ministers
Give the knowledge of. *Lk. 1:77.*
Show the way of. *Acts 16:17.*
Should exhort to. *Ezek. 3:18; Acts 2:40.*
Should labour to lead others to. *Rom. 11:14.*
Should be clothed with. *2 Chron. 6:41; Ps. 132:16.*
Should use self-denial to lead others to. *1 Cor. 9:22.*
Should endure suffering that the elect might obtain. *2 Tim. 2:10.*
Are a sweet savour of Christ, to God, in those who obtain. *2 Cor. 2:15.*
The heavenly host ascribe, to God. *Rev. 7:10, 19:1.*
Is sought in vain from
Idols. *Is. 45:20; Jer. 2:28.*
Earthly power. *Jer. 3:23.*
There is no escape for those who neglect. *Heb. 2:3.*
Is far off from the wicked. *Ps. 119:155; Is. 59:11.*
Is illustrated by
A rock. *Deut. 32:15; Ps. 95:1.*
A horn. *Ps. 18:2; Lk. 1:69.*
A tower. *2 Sam. 22:51.*
A helmet. *Is. 59:17; Eph. 6:17.*
A shield. *2 Sam. 22:36.*
A lamp. *Is. 62:1.*
A cup. *Ps. 116:13.*
Clothing. *2 Chron. 6:41; Ps. 132:16, 149:4; Is. 61:10.*
Wells. *Is. 12:3.*
Walls and bulwarks. *Is. 26:1, 60:18.*
Chariots. *Hab. 3:8.*
A victory. *1 Cor. 15:57.*
Typified. *Num. 21:4-9 with Jn. 3:14-15.*

SANCTIFICATION
Is separation from whatever is sinful. *Is. 52:11, Ezek. 20:34, 41 with 2 Cor. 6:12-18.*
Is separation for the service of God. *Ps. 4:3; 2 Cor. 6:17.*
Is effected by
God. *Ezek. 37:28; 1 Thess. 5:23; Jude verse 1.*
Christ. *Heb. 2:11, 13:12.*
The Holy Spirit. *Rom. 15:16; 1 Cor. 6:11.*
Is in Christ. *1 Cor. 1:2, 30.*

Is through the atonement of Christ. *Heb. 10:10, 13:12.*

Is through the Word of God. *Jn. 17:17, 19; Eph. 5:26.*

Christ is made, of God, to us. *1 Cor. 1:30.*

The saints are elected to salvation through. *2 Thess. 2:13; 1 Pet. 1:2.*

All the saints are in a state of. *Acts 20:32, 26:18; 1 Cor. 6:11.*

The Church is made glorious by. *Eph. 5:26-27.*

Should lead to

Mortification of sin. *1 Thess. 4:3-4.*

Holiness. *Rom. 6:22; Eph. 5:7-9.*

The offering up of the saints is acceptable through. *Rom. 15:16.*

The saints are made fit for the service of God by. *2 Tim. 2:21.*

God wills all the saints to have. *1 Thess. 4:3.*

Ministers

Are set apart for God's service by. *Jer. 1:5.*

Should pray that their people may enjoy complete. *1 Thess. 5:23.*

Should exhort their people to walk in. *1 Thess. 4:1, 3.*

None can inherit the kingdom of God without. *1 Cor. 6:9-11.*

Typified. *Gen. 2:3; Ex. 13:2, 19:14, 40:9-15; Lev. 27:14-16.*

SCORNING AND MOCKING

The sufferings of Christ by, were prophesied. *Ps. 22:6-8; Is. 53:3; Lk. 18:32.*

Christ endured. *Mat. 9:24, 27:29.*

The saints endure, on account of

Being the children of God. *Gen. 21:9 with Gal. 4:29.*

Their uprightness. *Job 12:4.*

Their faith. *Heb. 11:36.*

Their faithfulness in declaring the Word of God. *Jer. 30:7-8.*

Their zeal for God's house. *Neh. 2:19.*

The wicked indulge in, against

The Second Coming of Christ. *2 Pet. 3:3-4.*

The gifts of the Spirit. *Acts 2:13.*

God's threatenings. *Is. 5:19; Jer. 17:15.*

God's ministers. *2 Chron. 36:16.*

God's ordinances. *Lam. 1:7.*

The saints. *Ps. 123:4; Lam. 3:14, 63.*

The resurrection of the dead. *Acts 17:32.*

All solemn admonitions. *2 Chron. 30:6-10.*

Idolaters are addicted to. *Is. 57:3-6.*

Drunkards are addicted to. *Ps. 69:12; Hos. 7:5.*

Those who are addicted to,

Delight in. *Prov. 1:22.*

Are argumentative. *Prov. 22:10.*

Are scorned by God. *Prov. 3:34.*

Are hated by others. *Prov. 24:9.*

Are avoided by the saints. *Ps. 1:1; Jer. 15:17.*

Walk after their own lusts. *2 Pet. 3:3.*

Are proud and haughty. *Prov. 21:24.*

Will not listen to rebuke. *Prov. 13:1.*

Do not like those who reprove. *Prov. 15:12.*

Hate those who reprove. *Prov. 9:8.*

Do not go to the wise. *Prov. 15:12.*

Bring others into danger. *Prov. 29:8.*

Will not themselves endure. *Ezek. 23:32.*

Are characteristic of the latter days. *2 Pet. 3:3; Jude verse 18.*

A woe is denounced against. *Is. 5:18-19.*

Punishment for. *2 Chron. 36:17; Prov. 19:29; Is. 29:20; Lam. 3:64-66.*

Some examples. **Ishmael**: *Gen. 21:9.* **The youths of Bethel**: *2 Kings 2:23.* **Ephraim and Manasseh**: *2 Chron. 30:10.* **The chiefs of Judah**: *2 Chron. 36:16.* **Sanballat**: *Neh. 4:1.* **Enemies of Job**: *Job 30:1, 9.* **Enemies of David**: *Ps. 35:15-16.*

Rulers of Israel: *Is. 28:14.* **Ammonites**: *Ezek. 25:3.* **Tyrians**: *Ezek. 26:2.* **The nations**: *Ezek. 36:2-3.* **Soldiers**: *Mat. 27:28-30; Lk. 23:36.* **Chief priests**, etc: *Mat. 27:41.* **Pharisees**: *Lk. 16:14.* **The men who held Jesus**: *Lk. 22:63-64.* **Herod**, etc: *Lk. 23:11.* **People and rulers**: *Lk. 23:35.* **Some of the multitude**: *Acts 2:13.* **The Athenians**: *Acts 17:32.*

SCRIPTURES, THE

Were given by inspiration of God. *2 Tim. 3:16.*

Were given by inspiration of the Holy Spirit. *Acts 1:16; Heb. 3:7; 2 Pet. 1:21.*

Christ explained, by appealing to them. *Mat. 4:4; Mk. 12:10; Jn. 7:42.*

Christ taught out of. *Lk. 24:27.*

Are called the

    Word. *Jas. 1:21-23; 1 Pet. 2:2.*

    Word of God. *Lk. 11:28; Heb. 4:12.*

    Word of Christ. *Col. 3:16.*

    Word of truth. *Jn. 17:17; Jas. 1:18.*

    Holy Scriptures. *Rom. 1:2; 2 Tim. 3:15.*

    Scripture of truth. *Dan. 10:21.*

    Book. *Ps. 40:7; Rev. 22:19.*

    Book of the Lord. *Is. 34:16.*

    Book of the Law. *Neh. 8:3; Gal. 3:10.*

    Law of the Lord. *Ps. 1:2; Is. 30:9.*

    Sword of the Spirit. *Eph. 6:17.*

    Oracles of God. *Rom. 3:2. 1 Pet. 4:11.*

Contain the promises of the gospel. *Rom. 1:2.*

Reveal the laws, statutes, and judgements of God. *Deut. 4:5, 14 with Ex. 24:3-4.*

Record divine prophecies. *2 Pet. 1:19-21.*

Testify of Christ. *Jn. 5:39; Acts 10:43, 18:28; 1 Cor. 15:3.*

Are full and sufficient. *Lk. 16:29, 31.*

Are an unerring guide. *Prov. 6:23; 2 Pet. 1:19.*

Are able to make one wise to salvation through faith in Christ Jesus. *2 Tim. 3:15.*

Are profitable both for doctrine and practice. *2 Tim. 3:16-17.*

Are described as

    Pure. *Ps. 12:6, 119:140; Prov. 30:5.*

    True. *Ps. 119:169; Jn. 17:17.*

    Perfect. *Ps. 19:7.*

    Precious. *Ps. 19:10.*

    Living and powerful. *Heb. 4:12.*

Are written for our instruction. *Rom. 15:4.*

Are intended for the use of all men. *Rom. 16:26.*

Nothing should be taken from, or added to. *Deut. 4:2, 12:32; Prov. 30:5-6; Rev. 22:18-19.*

One part of, should be compared with another. *1 Cor. 2:13.*

Are designed for

    Regenerating. *Jas. 1:18; 1 Pet. 1:23.*

    Enlivening. *Ps. 119:50, 93.*

    Illuminating. *Ps. 119:130.*

    Converting the soul. *Ps. 19:7.*

    Making wise the simple. *Ps. 19:7.*

    Sanctifying. *Jn. 17:17; Eph. 5:26.*

    Producing faith. *Jn. 20:31.*

    Producing hope. *Ps. 119:49; Rom. 15:4.*

    Producing obedience. *Deut. 17:19-20.*

    Cleansing the heart. *Jn. 15:3; Eph. 5:26.*

    Cleansing the ways. *Ps. 119:9.*

    Keeping from destructive paths. *Ps. 17:4.*

    Supporting life. *Deut. 8:3 with Mat. 4:4.*

    Promoting growth in grace. *1 Pet. 2:2.*

    Building up in the faith. *Acts 20:32.*

    Admonishing. *Ps. 19:14; 1 Cor. 10:11.*

    Comforting. *Ps. 119:82; Rom. 15:4.*

    Rejoicing the heart. *Ps. 19:8, 119 111.*

Work effectively in those who believe. *1 Thess. 2:13.*

The letter of, without the spirit, kills. *Jn. 6:63 with 2 Cor. 3:6.*

Ignorance of, is a source of error. *Mat. 22:29; Acts 13:27.*

Christ enables us to understand. *Lk. 24:45.*

The Holy Spirit enables us to understand. *Jn. 16:13; 1 Cor. 2:10-14.*

No prophecy of, is of any private interpretation. *2 Pet. 1:20.*

Everything should be tested by. *Is. 8:20; Acts 17:11.*

Should be

The standard for teaching. *1 Pet. 4:11.*

Believed. *Jn. 2:22.*

Appealed to. *1 Cor. 1:31; 1 Pet. 1:16.*

Read. *Deut. 17:19; Is. 34:16.*

Read publicly to all. *Deut. 31:11-13; Neh. 8:3; Jer. 36:6; Acts 13:15.*

Made known. *2 Tim. 3:15.*

Received, not as the word of men, but as the Word of God. *1 Thess. 2:13.*

Received with meekness. *Jas. 1:21.*

Searched. *Jn. 5:39, 7:52.*

Searched daily. *Acts 17:11.*

Laid up in the heart. *Deut. 6:6, 11:18.*

Taught to children. *Deut. 6:7, 11:19; 2 Tim. 3:15.*

Taught to all. *2 Chron. 17:7-9; Neh. 8:7-8.*

Talked of continually. *Deut. 6:7.*

Not handled deceitfully. *2 Cor. 4:2.*

Not only heard, but obeyed. *Mat. 7:24 with Lk. 11:28; Jas. 1:22.*

Used, against spiritual enemies. *Mat. 4:4, 7, 10 with Eph. 6:11, 17.*

All should desire to hear. *Neh. 8:1.*

Mere hearers of, deceive themselves. *Jas. 1:22.*

Advantage of possessing. *Rom. 3:2.*

The saints

Love exceedingly. *Ps. 119:97, 113, 159, 167.*

Delight in. *Ps. 1:2.*

Regard, as sweet. *Ps. 119:103.*

Esteem, above all things. *Job 23:12.*

Long after. *Ps. 119:82.*

Stand in awe of. *Ps. 119:161; Is. 66:2.*

Keep, in remembrance. *Ps. 119:16.*

Grieve when men disobey. *Ps. 119:158.*

Hide, in their heart. *Ps. 119:11.*

Hope in. *Ps. 119:74, 81, 147.*

Meditate in. *Ps. 1:2, 119:99, 148.*

Rejoice in. *Ps. 119:162; Jer. 15:16.*

Trust in. *Ps. 119:42.*

Obey. *Ps. 119:67; Lk. 8:21; Jn. 17:6.*

Speak of. *Ps. 119:172.*

Esteem, as a light and a lamp. *Ps. 119:105.*

Pray to be taught. *Ps. 119:12, 18, 33, 66.*

Pray to be conformed to. *Ps. 119:133.*

Plead the promises of, in prayer. *Ps. 119:25, 28, 41, 76, 169.*

Those who search, are truly noble. *Acts 17:11.*

The blessedness of hearing and obeying. *Lk. 11:28. Jas. 1:25.*

Let them dwell richly in you. *Col. 3:16.*

The wicked

Corrupt. *2 Cor. 2:17.*

Make ineffective, through their traditions. *Mk. 7:9-13.*

Reject. *Jer. 8:9.*

Stumble at. *1 Pet. 2:8.*

Do not obey. *Ps. 119:158.*

Frequently twist, to their own destruction. *2 Pet. 3:16.*

Denunciations against those who add to, or take away from. *Rev. 22:18-19.*

Destruction comes to, with punishment. *Jer. 36:29-31.*

SEALING OF THE HOLY SPIRIT, THE

Christ received. *Jn. 6:27.*

The saints receive. *2 Cor. 1:22; Eph. 1:13.*

Is to the day of redemption. *Eph. 4:30*

The wicked do not receive. *Rev. 9:4.*

Judgement is suspended until all the saints receive. *Rev. 7:3.*

Typified. *Rom. 4:11.*

SECOND COMING OF CHRIST, THE

The time of, is unknown. *Mat. 24:36; Mk. 13:32.*

Called the

Times of refreshing from the presence of the Lord. *Acts 3:19.*

Times of the restitution of all things. *Acts 3:21 with Rom. 8:21.*

Last time. *1 Pet. 1:5.*

Appearing of Jesus Christ. *1 Pet. 1:7.*

Revelation of Jesus Christ. *1 Pet. 1:13; 1 Cor. 1:7.*

Glorious appearing of the great God and our Saviour. *Titus 2:13.*

Coming of the day of God. *2 Pet. 3:12.*

Day of our Lord Jesus Christ. *1 Cor. 1:8.*

Foretold by

The prophets. *Dan. 7:13; Jude verse 14.*

Christ himself. *Mat. 25:31; Jn. 14:3.*

The apostles. *Acts 3:20; 1 Tim. 6:14.*

Angels. *Acts 1:10-11.*

Signs preceding. *Mat. 24:3, etc.*

The manner of;

In the clouds. *Mat. 24:30, 26:24; Rev. 1:7.*

In the glory of his Father. *Mat. 16:17.*

In his own glory. *Mat. 25:31.*

In flaming fire. *2 Thess. 1:8.*

With power and great glory. *Mat. 24:30.*

As he ascended. *Acts 1:9, 11.*

With a shout and the voice of the Archangel, etc. *1 Thess. 4:16.*

Accompanied by angels. *Mat. 16:27, 25:31; Mk. 8:38; 2 Thess. 1:7.*

With his saints. *1 Thess. 3:13; Jude verse 14.*

Suddenly. *Mk. 13:36.*

Unexpectedly. *Mat. 24:44; Lk. 12:40.*

Like a thief in the night. *1 Thess. 5:2; 2 Pet. 3:10; Rev. 16:15.*

Like the lightning. *Mat. 24:27.*

The heavens and earth will be dissolved, etc. *2 Pet. 3:10, 12.*

Those who die in Christ will rise first at. *1 Thess. 4:16.*

The saints alive at, will be caught up to meet him. *1 Thess. 4:17.*

Is not to make atonement. *Heb. 9:28 with Rom. 6:9-10 and Heb. 10:14.*

The purpose of, is to

Complete the salvation of the saints. *Heb. 9:28; 1 Pet. 1:5.*

Be glorified in his saints. *2 Thess. 1:10.*

Be admired in those who believe. *2 Thess. 1:10.*

Bring to light the hidden things of darkness, etc. *1 Cor. 4:5.*

Judge. *Ps. 50:3-4 with Jn. 5:22; 2 Tim. 4:1; Jude verse 15; Rev. 20:11-13.*

Reign. *Is. 24:23; Dan. 7:14; Rev. 11:15.*

Destroy death. *1 Cor. 15:23, 26.*

Every eye will see him at. *Rev. 1:7.*

Should be always considered as at hand. *Rom. 13:12; Phil. 4:5; 1 Pet. 4:7.*

The blessedness of being prepared for. *Mt. 24:46; Lk. 12:37-38.*

The saints

Are assured of. *Job 19:25-26.*

Love. *2 Tim. 4:8.*

Look for. *Phil. 3:20; Titus 3:13.*

Wait for. *1 Cor. 1:7; 1 Thess. 1:10.*

Haste to. *2 Peter 3:12.*

Pray for. *Rev. 22:20.*

Should be ready for. *Mat. 24:44; Lk. 12:40.*

Should watch out for. *Mat. 24:42; Mk. 13:35-37; Lk. 21:36.*

Should be patient until. *2 Thess. 3:5; Jas. 5:7-8.*

Will be preserved unto. *Phil. 1:6; 2 Tim. 4:18; 1 Pet. 1:5; Jude verse 24.*

Will not be ashamed at. *1 Jn. 2:28.*

Will be blameless at. *1 Cor. 1:8; 1 Thess. 3:13; 1 Thess. 5:23; Jude verse 24.*

Will be like him at. *Phil. 3:21; 1 Jn. 3:2.*

Will see him as he is, at. *1 Jn. 3:2.*

Will appear with him in glory at. *Col. 3:4.*

Will receive a crown of glory at. *2 Tim. 4:8; 1 Pet. 5:4.*

Will reign with him at. *Dan. 7:27; 2 Tim. 2:12; Rev. 5:10, 20:6, 22:5.*

Faith of, will be found to praise, honour and glory at. *1 Pet. 1:7.*

The wicked

Scoff at. *2 Pet. 3:3-4.*

Presume upon the delay of. *Mat. 24:48.*

Will be surprised at. *Mat. 24:37-39; 1 Thess. 5:3; 2 Pet. 3:10.*

Will be punished at. *2 Thess. 1:8-9.*

The lawless one will be destroyed at. *2 Thess. 2:8.*

Illustrated. *Mat. 25:6; Lk. 12:36, 39; Lk. 19:12, 15.*

SEEKING GOD

Commanded. *Is. 55:6; Mat. 7:7.*

Involves seeking

His name. *Ps. 83:16.*

His Word. *Amos 8:12.*

His face. *Ps. 27 8, 105:4.*

His strength. *1 Chron. 16:11; Ps. 105:4.*

His commandments. *1 Chron. 28:8.*

His precepts. *Ps. 119:45, 94.*

His kingdom. *Mat. 6:33.*

Christ. *Mal. 3:1; Lk. 2:15-16.*

The honour that alone comes from him. *Jn. 5:44.*

By prayer. *Job 8:5; Dan. 9:3.*

In his house. *Deut. 12:5; Ps. 27:4.*

Should be

Immediate. *Hos.10:12.*

Evermore. *Ps. 105:4.*

While he may be found. *Is. 55:6.*

With diligence. *Heb. 11:6.*

With the heart. *Deut. 4:29; 1 Chron. 22:19.*

In the day of trouble. *Ps. 77:2.*

Ensures

His being found. *Deut. 4:29; 1 Chron. 28:9; Prov. 8:17; Jer. 29:13.*

His favour. *Lam. 3:25.*

His protection. *Ezra 8:22.*

His not forsaking us. *Ps. 9:10.*

Life. *Ps. 69:32; Amos 5:4, 6.*

Prosperity. *Job 8:5-6; Ps. 34:10.*

Being heard by him. *Ps 34:4.*

Understanding all things. *Prov. 28:5.*

Gifts of righteousness. *Hos. 10:12.*

Is imperative for all. *Is. 8:19.*

Afflictions designed to lead to. *Ps. 78:33-34; Hos. 5:15.*

None, by nature, are found to be engaged in. *Ps. 14:2 with Rom. 3:11.*

The saints

Are specially exhorted to. *Zeph. 2:3.*

Desire. *Job 5:8.*

Purpose in their heart. *Ps. 27:8.*

Prepare their hearts for. *2 Chron. 30:19.*

Set their hearts on. *2 Chron. 11:16.*

Engage in, with the whole heart. *2 Chron. 15:12; Ps. 119:10.*

Are early in. *Job 8:5; Ps. 63:1; Is. 26:9.*

Are earnest in. *Song 3:2.*

Are characterised by. *Ps. 24:6.*

Is never in vain. *Is. 45:19.*

The blessedness of. *Ps. 119:2.*

Leads to joy. *Ps. 70:4, 105:3.*

Ends in praise. *Ps. 22:26.*

A promise connected with. *Ps. 69:32.*

Will be rewarded. *Heb. 11:6.*

The wicked

Have gone out of the way of. *Ps. 14:2-3 with Rom. 3:11-12.*

Do not prepare their hearts for. *2 Chron. 12:14.*

Refuse, through pride. *Ps. 10:4.*

Are not led to, by affliction. *Is. 9:13; Rev. 9:20-21, 16:8-11.*

Sometimes pretend to be. *Ezra 4:2; Is. 58:2.*

Rejected, when too late in. *Prov. 1:28.*

Those who neglect, are denounced. *Is. 31:1.*

The punishment of those who neglect. *Zeph. 1:4-6.*

Some examples. **Asa**: *2 Chron. 14:7.* **Jehoshaphat**: *2 Chron. 17:3-4.* **Uzziah**: *2 Chron. 26:5.* **Hezekiah**: *2 Chron. 31:21.* **Josiah**: *2 Chron. 34:3.* **Ezra**: *Ezra 7:10.* **David**: *Ps. 34:4.* **Daniel**: *Dan. 9:3-4.*

SELF-DELUSION

Is a characteristic of the wicked.
Ps. 49:18.

Prosperity frequently leads to.
Ps. 30:6; Hos. 12:8; Lk. 12:17-19.

Obstinate sinners often give
themselves up to. Ps. 81:11-12;
Hos. 4:17; 2 Thess. 2:10-11.

Is shown in thinking that

Our own ways are right.
Prov. 14:12.

We should stick to our wicked
practices. Jer. 44:17.

We are pure. Prov. 30:12.

We are better than others.
Lk. 18:11.

We are rich in spiritual things.
Rev. 3:17.

We have peace while remaining
in sin. Deut. 29:19.

We are above adversity. Ps. 10:6.

Gifts entitles us to heaven.
Mat. 7:21-22.

Privilege entitle us to heaven.
Mat. 3:9; Lk. 13:25-26.

God will not punish our sins.
Jer. 5:12.

Christ will not come to judge
us. 2 Pet. 3:4.

Our lives will be prolonged.
Is. 56:12; Lk. 12:19; Jas. 4:13.

Is frequently persevered in to the
last. Mat. 7:22, 25:11-12; Lk. 13:24-25.

The fatal consequences of.
Mat. 7:23, 24:48-51; Lk. 12:20; 1 Thess. 5:3.

Some examples. **Ahab**: 1 Kings 20:27,
34. **Israelites**: Hos. 12:8. **Jews**:
Jn. 8:33, 41. **The Church of Laodicea**:
Rev. 3:17.

SELF-DENIAL

Christ set an example of. Mat. 4:8-10,
8:20; Rom. 15:3; Phil. 2:6-8.

A test of devotion to Christ.
Mat. 10:37-38; Lk. 14:27, 33.

Is necessary

In following Christ. Lk. 9:23-24.

In the warfare of the saints.

2 Tim. 2:4.

For the triumph of the saints.
1 Cor. 9:25.

Ministers are especially called to
exercise. 2 Cor. 6:4-5.

Should be practised by

Denying ungodliness and
worldly lusts. Rom. 6:12; Titus 2:12.

Controlling the appetite.
Prov. 23:2.

Abstaining from fleshly lusts.
1 Pet. 2:11.

No longer living for lusts.
1 Pet. 4:2.

Mortifying sinful lusts. Mk. 9:43;
Col. 3:5.

Mortifying the deeds of the
body. Rom.8:13.

Not pleasing ourselves. Rom. 15:1-3.

Not seeking our own profit.
1 Cor. 10:24, 33, 13:5; Phil. 2:4.

Preferring the well-being of
others. Rom. 14:20-21; 1 Cor. 10:24, 33.

Helping others. Lk. 3:11.

Even inlawful things. 1 Cor. 10:23.

Forsaking all. Lk. 14:33.

Taking up the cross and
following Christ. Mat. 10:38, 16:24.

Crucifying the flesh. Gal. 5:24.

Being crucified with Christ.
Rom. 6:6.

Being crucified to the world.
Gal. 6:14.

Putting off the old man, which
is corrupt. Eph. 4:22; Col. 3:9.

Preferring Christ to all family
ties. Mat. 8:21-22; Lk. 14:26.

Becoming strangers and pilgrims.
Heb. 11:13-18; 1 Pet. 2:11.

The danger of neglecting.
Mat. 16:25-26; 1 Cor. 9:27.

The reward of. Mat. 19:28-29; Rom. 8:13.

The happy result of. 2 Pet. 1:4.

Some examples. **Abraham**:
Gen. 13:9; Heb. 11:8-9. **Moses**: Heb. 11:24-25.
The widow of Zarephath:
1 Kings 17:12-15. **Esther**: Esther 4:16. **The
Rechabites**: Jer. 35:6-7. **Daniel**:

Dan. 5:16-17. **The apostles**: *19:27.*
Simon, Andrew, James and John:
Mk. 1:16-20. **A poor widow**: *Lk. 21:4.*
Early Christians: *Acts 2:45, 4:34.*
Barnabas: *Acts 4:36-37.* **Paul**: *Acts 20:24.*
1 Cor. 9:19, 27.

SELF-EXAMINATION

Is recommended. *2 Cor. 13:5.*
Is necessary before partaking in
the Communion. *1 Cor. 11:28.*
Causes of difficulty in. *Jer. 17:9.*
Should be engaged in
    With holy awe. *Ps. 4:4.*
    With a diligent search. *Ps. 77:6;*
    Lam. 3:40.
    With prayer for divine search-
    ing. *Ps. 26:2, 139:23-24.*
    With the purpose of amend-
    ment. *Ps. 119:59; Lam. 3:40.*
The advantages of. *1 Cor. 11:31;*
Gal. 6:4.

SELFISHNESS

Is contrary to the Law of God.
Jas. 2:8.
The example of Christ condemns.
Jn. 4:34; Rom. 15:3; 2 Cor. 8:9.
God hates. *Mal. 1:10.*
Shown in
    Being lovers of ourselves.
    2 Tim. 3:2.
    Pleasing ourselves. *Rom. 15:1.*
    Seeking our own way. *1 Cor. 10:33;*
    Phil. 2:21.
    Seeking selfish gain. *Is. 56:11.*
    Seeking undue regard. *Mat. 20:21.*
    Living for ourselves. *2 Cor. 5:15.*
    Our neglect of the poor. *1 Jn. 3:17.*
    Serving God for reward. *Mal. 1:10.*
    Performing duty for reward.
    Mic. 3:11.
It is inconsistent with Christian
love. *1 Cor. 13:5.*
It is inconsistent with Christian
fellowship. *Rom. 12:4-5 with*
1 Cor. 12:12-47.
Is especially forbidden to the
saints. *1 Cor. 10:24; Phil. 2:4.*

The love of Christ should
constrain us to avoid. *2 Cor. 5:14-15.*
Ministers should be devoid of.
1 Cor. 9:19-23, 10:33.
All are addicted to. *Phil. 2:21.*
The saints are falsely accused of.
Job 1:9-11.
Characteristic of the last days.
2 Tim. 3:1-2.

Some examples. **Cain**: *Gen. 4:9.*
Nabal: *1 Sam. 25:3, 11.* **Haman**:
Esth. 6:6. **Some priests**: *Is. 56:11.* **Jews**:
Zech. 7:6. **James and John**: *Mk. 10:37.*
The multitude: *Jn. 6:26.*

SELF-RIGHTEOUSNESS

All are prone to. *Prov. 20:6; Prov. 30:12.*
Is hateful to God. *Lk. 16:15.*
**Is useless, because our righteous-
ness is**
    Only outward. *Mat. 23:25-28;*
    Lk. 11:39-44.
    Only partial. *Mat. 23:25; Lk. 11:42.*
    Is no better than filthy rags.
    Is. 64:6.
    Is ineffective for salvation.
    Mat. 5:20 with Rom. 3:20.
    Is unprofitable. *Is. 57:12.*
Is boastful. *Mat. 23:30.*
Those who are given over to,
    Audaciously approach God.
    Lk. 18:11.
    Seek to justify themselves.
    Lk. 10:29.
    Seek to justify themselves
    before others. *Lk. 16:15.*
    Reject the righteousness of
    God. *Rom. 1:3.*
    Condemn others. *Mat. 9:11-13;*
    Lk. 7:39.
    Consider their own way right.
    Prov. 21:2.
    Despise others. *Is. 65:5. Lk. 18:9.*
    Proclaim their own goodness.
    Prov. 20:6.
    Are pure in their own eyes.
    Prov. 30:12.

Are abominable before God. *Is. 65:5.*
The folly of. *Job 9:20.*
The saints renounce. *Phil. 3:7-10.*
A warning against. *Deut. 9:4.*
Denunciation of. *Mat. 23:27-28.*
Illustrated. *Lk. 18:10-12.*

Some examples. **Saul**: *1 Sam. 15:13.*
A young man: *Mat. 19:20.* **A lawyer**:
Lk. 10:25, 29. **The Pharisees**: *Lk. 11:39;*
Jn. 8:33, 9:28. **Israel**: *Rom. 10:3.* **The**
Church at Laodicea: *Rev. 3:17.*

SELF-WILL AND STUBBORNNESS
Are forbidden. *2 Chron. 30:8. Ps. 75:5.*
Proceed from
  Unbelief. *2 Kings 17:14.*
  Pride. *Neh. 9:16, 29.*
  An evil heart. *Jer. 7:24.*
God knows. *Is. 48:4.*
Are shown in
  Refusing to listen to God.
  Prov. 1:24.
  Refusing to receive the messen-
  gers of God. *1 Sam. 8:19; Jer. 44:16;*
  Zech. 7:11.
  Refusing to walk in the ways of
  God. *Neh. 9:17; Ps. 78:10; Is. 42:24.*
  Refusing to listen to parents.
  Deut. 21:18-19.
  Refusing to receive correction.
  Deut. 21:18; Jer. 5:3, 7:28.
  Rebelling against God. *Deut. 31:27;*
  Ps. 78:8.
  Resisting the Holy Spirit. *Acts 7:51.*
  Walking in the counsels of an
  evil heart. *Jer. 7:24 with Jer. 23:17.*
  Hardening the neck. *Neh. 9:16.*
  Hardening the heart.
  2 Chron. 36:13.
  Going backward and not
  forward. *Jer. 7:24.*
The heinousness of. *1 Sam. 15:23.*
Ministers should
  Be without. *Titus 1:7.*
  Warn their people against.
  Heb. 3:7-12.
  Pray that their people may be

forgiven their. *Ex. 34:9; Deut. 9:27.*
A characteristic of the wicked.
Prov. 7:11; 2 Pet. 2:10.
The wicked do not cease from.
Judg. 2:10.
The punishment for. *Deut. 21:21;*
Prov. 29:1.
Illustrated. *Ps. 32:9. Jer. 31:18.*

Some examples. **Simeon and**
Levi: *Gen. 49:6.* **The Israelites**: *Ex. 32:9;*
Deut. 9:6, 13. **Saul**: *1 Sam. 15:19-23.*
David: *2 Sam. 24:4.* **Josiah**:
2 Chron. 35:22. **Zedekiah**: *2 Chron. 36:13.*

SERIOUSNESS
Is commanded. *1 Pet. 1:13, 5:8.*
The gospel is designed to teach.
Titus 2:11,
With watchfulness. *1 Thess. 5:6.*
With prayer. *1 Pet. 4:7.*
Required in
Ministers. *1 Tim. 3:2-3; Titus 1:8.*
Ministers' wives. *1 Tim. 8:11.*
Elderly men. *Titus 2:2.*
Young men. *Titus 2:6.*
Young women. *Titus 2:4.*
All young children. *1 Thess. 5:6, 8.*
Women should show, in their
dress. *1 Tim. 2:9.*
We should estimate our character
and talents with. *Rom. 12:3.*
We should live with. *Titus 2:12.*
Motives for. *1 Pet. 4:7, 5:8.*

SERVANTS
Christ condescended to the
status of. *Lk. 22:27; Jn. 13:5; Phil. 2:7.*
Are inferior to their masters.
Lk. 22:27.
Should follow Christ's example.
1 Pet. 2:21.
Duties of, to masters;
  To pray for them. *Gen. 24:12.*
  To honour them. *Mal. 1:8; 1 Tim. 6:1.*
  To respect them the more,
  particularly when they are
  fellow-believers. *1 Tim. 6:2.*
  To be subject to them. *1 Pet. 2:18.*

To obey them. *Eph. 6:5; Titus 2:9.*
To respond to their call. *Ps. 123:2.*
To please them well in all
things. *Titus 2:9.*
To sympathise with them.
2 Sam. 12:18.
To prefer their business to their
own necessary food. *Gen. 24:33.*
To bless God for mercies
shown to them. *Gen. 24:27, 48.*
To be faithful to them. *Lk. 16:10-
12; 1 Cor. 4:2; Titus 2:10.*
To be profitable to them.
Lk. 19:15, 16, 18; Philem. verse 11.
To be anxious for their welfare.
1 Sam. 25:14-17; 2 Kings 5:2-3.
To be earnest in transacting
their business. *Gen. 24:54-56.*
To be prudent in the manage-
ment of their affairs. *Gen. 24:34-49.*
To be industrious in labouring
for them. *Neh. 4:16, 23.*
To be kind and attentive to
guests. *Gen. 43:23-24.*
To be submissive, even when
the master is difficult. *Gen. 16:6,
9;1 Pet. 2:18.*
Not to answer rudely. *Titus 2:9.*
Not to serve with eye-service,
as men-pleasers. *Eph. 6:6; Col 3:22.*
Not to defraud them. *Titus 2:10.*
Should be content with their
situation. *1 Cor. 7:20-21.*
Should be compassionate to
their fellows. *Mat. 18:33.*
Should serve
In good conscience towards
God. *1 Pet. 2:19.*
In the fear of God. *Eph. 6:5; Col. 3:22.*
As servants of Christ. *Eph. 6:5-6.*
Heartily, as to the Lord, and not
to men. *Eph. 6:7; Col. 3:23.*
As doing the will of God from
the heart. *Eph. 6:6.*
In singleness of heart. *Eph. 6:5;
Col. 3:22.*
With good will. *Eph. 6:7.*
Patience under injury is accept-
able to God. *1 Pet. 2:19-20.*

When good
Are truly servants of Christ.
Col. 3:24.
Are brothers beloved in the
Lord. *Philem. verse 16.*
Are the Lord's freemen.
1 Cor. 7:22.
Are partakers of gospel
privileges. *1 Cor. 12:13; Gal 3:28;
Eph. 6:8; Col. 3:11.*
Deserve the confidence of their
masters. *Gen. 24:2,4, 10, 39:4.*
Are often exalted. *Gen. 41:40;
Prov. 17:2.*
Are often advanced by their
masters. *Gen. 39:4-5.*
Are to be honoured. *Gen. 24:31;
Prov. 27:18.*
Bring God's blessing upon their
masters. *Gen. 30:27, 30, 39:3.*
Adorn the doctrine of God
their Saviour in all things.
Titus 2:10.
Have God with them. *Gen. 31:42,
39:21; Acts 7:9-10.*
Are prospered by God. *Gen. 39:3.*
Are protected by God. *Gen 31:7.*
Are guided by God. *Gen. 24:7, 27.*
Are blessed by God. *Mat. 24:46.*
Are mourned over after their
death. *Gen. 35:8.* (See marginal
note)
Will be rewarded. *Eph. 6:8;
Col. 3:24.*
The property of masters is
increased by faithful. *Gen. 30:29-30.*
When wicked,
Are eye-servants only. *Eph. 6:6;
Col. 3:22.*
Are men-pleasers. *Eph. 6:6;
Col. 3:22.*
Are deceitful. *2 Sam. 19:26; Ps. 101:6-7.*
Are quarrelsome. *Gen.13:7, 26:20.*
Are covetous. *2 Kings 5:20.*
Are liars. *2 Kings 5:22, 25.*
Are thieves. *Titus 2:10.*
Are gluttonous and drunken.
Mat. 24:49.
Are unmerciful to their fellows.

Mat. 18:30.
Will not submit to correction.
Prov. 29:19.
Are not fit to be advanced.
Prov. 30:21-22 with Is. 3:5.
Will be punished. Mat. 24:50.

Some examples of good servants. **Eliezer**: Gen. chapter 24.
Deborah: Gen. 24:59 with Gen. 35:8.
Jacob: Gen. 31:36-40. **Joseph**: Gen.
39:3; Acts 7:10. **The servant of Boaz**:
Ruth 2:4. **Jonathan's armour
bearer**: 1 Sam. 14:6-7. **David's
servants**:
2 Sam. 12:18. **A captive maid**: 2 Kings
5:2-4. **The servants of Naaman**:
2 Kings 5:13. **A centurion's servant**:
Mat.8:9. **Cornelius' servants**: Acts
10:7. **Converted Onesimus**: Philem.
Verse 11.

Some examples of bad servants.
Servants of Abraham and Lot:
Gen. 13:7. **Servants of Abimelech**:
Gen. 21:25. **Absolom's servants**:
2 Sam. 13:28-29, 14:30. **Ziba**: 2 Sam. 16:1-4.
Servants of Shimei: 1 Kings 2:39.
Jeroboam: 1 Kings 11:26. **Zimri**:
1 Kings 16:9. **Gehazi**: 2 Kings 5:20.
Servants of Amon: 2 Kings 21:23.
Job's servants: Job 19:16. **Servants
of the High Priest**: Mk. 14:65.
Unconverted Onesimus:
Philem. verse 11.

SICKNESS

Is sent by God. Deut. 32:39;
2 Sam. 12:15; Acts 12:23.
The devil is sometimes permit-
ted to inflict. Job 2:6-7; Lk. 9:39, 13:16.
Often brought on by intemper-
ance. Hos. 7:5.
Often sent as a punishment for
sin. Lev. 26:14-16; 2 Chron. 21:12-15;
1 Cor. 11:30.
God
  Promises to heal. Ex. 23:25.
  2 Kings 20:5.

Heals: Deut. 32:39; Ps. 103:3; Is. 38:5, 9.
Shows his mercy in healing.
Phil. 2:27.
Shows his power in healing.
Lk. 5:17.
Shows his love in healing.
Is. 38:17.
Often shows saving grace in
sinners during. Job 33:19-24.
Permits the saints to be tested
by. Job 2:5-6.
Strengthens the saints in. Ps. 41:3.
Comforts the saints in. Ps. 41:3.
Hear the prayers of those in.
Ps. 30:2, 107:18-20.
Preserves the saints in times of.
Ps. 91:3-7.
Abandons the wicked to.
Jer. 34:17.
Persecutes the wicked by.
Jer. 29:18.
The healing of, is lawful on the
Sabbath. Lk. 13:14-16.
Christ had compassion on those
in. Is. 53:4 with Mat. 8:16-17.
Christ healed,
When he was present. Mk. 1:31;
Mat. 4:2-3.
When he was not present.
Mat. 8:13.
With the laying on of hands.
Mk. 6:5; Lk. 13:13.
With a touch. Mat. 8:3.
Through touching his garment.
Mat. 14:35-36; Mk. 5:27-34.
With a word. Mat. 8:8, 13.
Faith was required in some
healed by Christ. Mat. 9:28-29;
Mk. 5:34, 10:52.
Often incurable by human
means. Deut. 28:27; 2 Chron. 21:18.
The Apostles were endued with
power to heal. Mat. 10:1; Mk. 16:18, 20.
The saints
  Acknowledge that, comes from
  God. Ps. 38:1-8; Is. 38:12, 15.
  Are resigned in times of. Job 2:10.
  Mourn under, with prayer.
  Is. 38:14.

Pray for recovery from. *Is. 38:2-3.*
Ascribe recovery from, as from God. *Is. 38:20.*
Praise God for recovery from. *Ps. 103:1-3; Is. 38:19; Lk. 17:15.*
Thank God publicly for recovery from. *Is. 38:20; Acts 3:8.*
Feel for others in. *Ps. 35:13.*
Visit those in. *Mat. 25:36.*
Visiting those in, an evidence of belonging to Christ. *Mat. 25:34, 36, 40.*
Pray for those afflicted with. *Acts 28:8. Jas. 5:14-15.*

The wicked
Experience great sorrow, etc., with. *Eccl. 5:17.*
Do not look to God for help in. *2 Chron. 16:12.*
Forsake those in. *1 Sam. 30:13.*
Do not visit those in. *Mat. 25:43.*
Not visiting the sick is an evidence of not belonging to Christ. *Mat. 25:43, 45.*
Is illustrative of sin. *Is. 1:5; Jer. 8:22; Mat. 9:12.*

SIMPLICITY
Is opposed to worldly wisdom. *2 Cor. 1:12.*
The necessity for. *Mat. 18:2-3.*

Should be shown
In the preaching of the gospel. *1 Thess. 2: 3-7.*
In acts of generosity. *Rom. 12:8.*
In all our conduct. *2 Cor. 1:12.*
Concerning our own wisdom. *1 Cor. 3:18.*
Concerning evil. *Rom. 16:19.*
Concerning malice. *1 Cor. 14:20.*
Exhortation to. *Rom. 16:19; 1 Pet. 2:2.*

Those who have the grace of,
Are made wise by God. *Mt. 11:25.*
Are made wise by the Word of God. *Ps. 19:7, 119:130.*
Are preserved by God. *Ps. 116:6.*
Are made prudent by instruction. *Prov. 1:4.*
Benefit by the correction of others. *Prov. 19:25, 21:11.*

Beware of being corrupted from that which comes from being in Christ. *2 Cor. 11:3.*
Illustrated. *Mat. 6:22.*

Some examples. **David**: *Ps. 131:1-2.*
Jeremiah: *Jer. 1:6.* **The early Christians**: *Acts 2:46, 4:32.* **Paul**: *2 Cor. 1:12.*

SIN
Is the transgression of the Law. *1 Jn. 3:4.*
Is of the devil. *1 Jn. 3:8 with Jn. 8:44.*
Is all unrighteousness. *Is. 1 Jn. 5:17.*
Is the omission of what we know to be good. *Jas. 4:17.*
Whatever is not of the faith is. *Rom. 14:23.*
The thought of foolishness is. *Prov. 24:9.*
All the imaginations of the unregenerate heart are. *Gen. 6:5, 8:21.*

Is described as
Coming from the heart. *Mat. 15:19.*
The fruit of lust. *Jas. 1:15.*
The sting of death. *1 Cor. 15:56.*
Rebellion against God. *Deut. 9:7; Josh. 1:18.*
The works of darkness. *Eph. 5:11.*
Dead works. *Heb. 6:1, 9:14.*
The abominable thing that God hates. *Prov. 15:9; Jer. 44:4, 11.*
Defiling. *Prov. 30:12. Is. 59:3.*
Deceitful. *Heb. 3:13.*
Disgraceful. *Prov. 14:34.*
Often very great. *Ex. 32:30. 1 Sam. 2:17.*
Often mighty. *Amos 5:12.*
Often manifold. *Amos 5:12.*
Often presumptuous. *Ps. 19:13.*
Sometimes open and manifest. *1 Tim. 5:24.*
Sometimes secret. *Ps. 90:8; 1 Tim. 5:24.*
Ensnaring. *Heb. 12:1.*
Like scarlet and crimson. *Is. 1:18.*
Reaches up to heaven. *Rev. 48:5.*
Came into the world through

Adam and Eve. *Gen. 3:6-7 with Rom. 5:12.*

All men are conceived and born in. *Gen. 5:3; Job 15:14, 25:4; Ps. 51:5.*

All men are shaped in. *Ps. 51:5.*

Scripture concludes all under. *Gal. 3:22.*

No man is without. *1 Kings 8:46; Eccl. 7:20.*

Christ alone was without. *2 Cor. 5:21; Heb. 4:15, 7:26; 1 Jn. 3:6.*

God

Abominates. *Deut.25:16; Prov. 6:16-19.*

Marks. *Job 10:14.*

Remembers. *Rev. 18:5.*

Is provoked to jealousy by. *1 Kings 14:22.*

Is provoked to anger by. *1 Kings 16:2.*

Alone can forgive. *Ex. 34:7; Dan. 9:9; Mic. 7:18; Mk. 2:7.*

Recompenses. *Jer. 16:18; Rev. 18:6.*

Punishes. *Is. 13:11; Amos 3:2.*

The Law

Is transgressed by everyone. *Jas. 2:10-11 with 1 Jn. 3:4.*

Gives a knowledge of. *Rom. 3:20, 7:7.*

Shows the exceeding sinfulness of. *Rom. 7:13.*

Was designed to restrain. *1 Tim. 1:9-10.*

By its strictness, it stirs up. *Rom. 7:5, 8, 11.*

Is the strength of. *1 Cor. 15:56.*

Curses those guilty of. *Gal. 3:10.*

No one can cleanse himself from. *Job 9:30-31; Prov. 20:9; Jer. 2:22.*

No one can atone for. *Mic. 6:7.*

God has opened a fountain for. *Zech. 13:1.*

Christ was manifested to take away. *Jn. 1:29; 1 Jn. 3:5.*

Christ's blood redeems from. *Eph. 1:7.*

Christ's blood cleanses from. *1 Jn. 1:7.*

The saints

Are set free from. *Rom. 6:18.*

Are dead to. *Rom. 6:2, 11; 1 Pet. 2:24.*

Profess to have ceased from. *1 Pet. 4:1.*

Cannot live in. *1 Jn. 3:9, 5:18.*

Resolve against. *Job 34:32.*

Are ashamed of having committed. *Rom. 6:21.*

Abhor themselves on account of. *Job 42:6; Ezek. 20:43.*

Have yet the remains of, in them. *Rom. 7:17, 23 with Gal. 5:17.*

The fear of God restrains. *Ex. 20:20; Ps. 4:4; Prov. 16:6.*

The Word of God keeps us from. *Ps. 119:11.*

The Holy Spirit convincts us of. *Jn. 16:8-9.*

If we say that we have no, we deceive ourselves, and the truth is not in us. *1 Jn. 1:8.*

If we say that we have no, we make God a liar. *1 Jn. 1:10.*

Confusion of face belongs to those guilty of. *Dan. 9:7-8.*

Should be

Confessed. *Job 33:27; Prov. 28:13.*

Mourned over. *Ps. 38:18; Jer. 3:21.*

Hated. *Ps. 97:10; Prov. 8:13; Amos 5:15.*

Abhorred. *Rom. 12:9.*

Put away. *Job 11:14.*

Departed from. *Ps. 34:14; 2 Tim. 2:19.*

Avoided, even in appearance. *1 Thess. 5:22.*

Guarded against. *Ps. 4:4, 39:1.*

Striven against. *Heb. 12:4.*

Mortified. *Rom. 8:13; Col.3:5.*

Completely destroyed. *Rom. 6:6.*

Specially strive against ensnaring. *Heb. 12:1.*

Aggravated by neglected advantages. *Lk. 12:47; Jn. 15:22.*

The guilt of concealing. *Job 31:33; Prov. 28:13.*

We should pray to God

To search for, in our hearts. *Ps. 139:23-24.*

To make us know our. *Job 13:23.*

To forgive our. *Ex. 34:9; Lk. 11:4.*

To keep us from. *Ps. 19:13.*

To deliver us from. *Mat. 6:13.*

To cleanse us from. *Ps. 51:2.*
Prayer is hindered by. *Ps. 66:18; Is. 59:2.*
Blessings are withheld on account of. *Jer. 5:25.*

The wicked
Are servants of. *Jn. 8:34; Rom. 6:16.*
Are dead in. *Eph. 2:1.*
Are guilty of, in everything they do. *Prov. 21:4; Ezek. 21:24.*
Plead the necessity of. *1 Sam. 13:11-12.*
Excuse. *Gen. 3:12-13; 1 Sam. 15:13-15.*
Encourage themselves in. *Ps. 64:5.*
Defy God in committing. *Is. 5:18-19.*
Boast of. *Is. 3:9.*
Are fools for mocking. *Prov. 14:9.*
Expect impunity from. *Ps. 50:21, 94:7.*
Cannot cease from. *2 Pet. 2:14.*
Heap up. *Ps. 78:17; Is. 30:1.*
Are encouraged in, by their prosperity. *Prov. 10:16.*
Are led by despair to continue in. *Jer. 18:12.*
Try to conceal, from God. *Gen. 3:8, 10 with Job 31:33.*
Throw the blame for, on God. *Gen. 3:12; Jer. 7:10.*
Throw the blame for, on others. *Gen. 3:12-13; Ex. 32:22-24.*
Tempt others to. *Gen. 3:6. 1 Kings 16:2.*
Delight in those who commit. *Rom. 1:32.*
Will bear the shame of. *Ezek. 16:52.*
Will find out the wicked. *Num. 32:23.*
Ministers should warn the wicked to forsake. *Ezek. 33:9; Dan.4:27.*

Leads to
Shame. *Rom. 6:21.*
Disquiet. *Ps. 38:3-8.*
Disease. *Job 20:11.*
Physical and spiritual death. *Rom. 6:23; Eph. 2:1.*

The ground was cursed on account of. *Gen. 3:17-18.*
Toil and sorrow originated with. *Gen. 3:16-17, 19 with Job 14:1.*
Excludes from heaven. *Gal. 5:19-21; Eph. 5:5; Rev. 21:27.*
When finished, it brings forth death. *Jas. 1:15.*
Death is the wages of. *Rom. 6:23.*
Death is the punishment for. *Gen. 2:17. Ezek. 18:4.*

SINS, NATIONAL
Often pervade all ranks. *Is. 1:5; Jer. 5:1-5, 6:13.*
Are often caused and encouraged by leaders and rulers. *1 Kings 12:26-33; 2 Chron. 21:11-13.*
Are often caused by prosperity. *Deut. 32:15; Ezek. 28:5.*

Pollute
The land. *Lev. 18:25; Is. 24:5.*
The people. *Lev. 18:24; Ezek. 14:11.*
National worship. *Hag. 2:14.*
Are aggravated by privileges. *Is. 5:4-7; Ezek. 20:11-13; Mat. 11:21-24.*
Lead the nations to blaspheme. *Rom. 2:24.*
Are a reproach to any people. *Prov. 14:34.*

Should be
Repented of. *Jer. 18:8; Jn. 3:5.*
Mourned over. *Joel 2:12.*
Confessed. *Judg. 10:10; 1 Jn. 1:9.*
Turned from. *Is. 1:16; Jonah 3:10.*
The saints especially mourn over. *Ps. 119:136; Ezek. 9:4.*

Ministers should
Mourn over. *Ezra 10:6; Ezek. 6:11; Joel 2:17.*
Testify against. *Is. 30:8-9; Ezek. 2:3-5, 22:2; Jonah 1:2.*
Try to turn the people from. *Jer. 23:22.*
Pray for the forgiveness of. *Ex. 32:31-32; Joel 2:17.*
National prayer is rejected on account of. *Is. 1:15, 59:2.*
National worship is rejected on

account of. *Is. 1:10-14; Jer. 6:19-20.*
Cause the withdrawal of privileges. *Lam. 2:9; Amos 8:11.*
Bring down national judgements. *Mat. 23:35-36, 27:25.*
Denunciations against. *Is. 1:24, 30:1; Jer. 5:9, 42:17.*
The punishment for. *Is. 3:8; Jer. 12:17, 25:12; Ezek.28:7-10.*
Punishment for, is averted after repentance. *Judg. 10:15-16; 2 Chron. 12:6-7; Jonah 3:10.*
Some examples. **Sodom and Gomorrah**: *Gen. 18:20; 2 Pet. 2:6.* **The children of Israel**: *Ex. 16:8, 32:31.* **The nations of Canaan**: *Deut. 9:4.* **The kingdom of Israel**: *2 Kings 17:8-12; Hos. 4:1-2.* **The kingdom of Judah**: *2 Kings 17:19; Is. 1:2-7.* **Moab**: *Jer. 48:29-30.* **Babylon**: *Jer. 51:6, 12-13, 52-53.* **Tyre**: *Ezek. 28:2.* **Nineveh**: *Nahum 3:1.*

SINCERITY

Christ is an example of. *1 Pet. 2:22.*
Ministers should be examples of. *Titus 2:7.*
Is opposed to worldly wisdom. *2 Cor. 1:12.*
Should characterise
　Our love for God. *2 Cor. 8:8, 24.*
　Our love for Christ. *Eph. 6:24.*
　Our service to God. *Josh. 24:14.*
　Our faith. *1 Tim. 1:5.*
　Our love for one another. *Rom. 12:9; 1 Pet. 1:22; 1 Jn. 3:18.*
　Our whole conduct. *2 Cor. 1:12.*
　The preaching of the gospel. *2 Cor. 2:17. 1 Thess. 2:3-5.*
Is a characteristic of the doctrines of the gospel. *1 Pet. 2:2.*
The gospel is sometimes preached without. *Phil. 1:16.*
The wicked are devoid of. *Ps. 5:9, 55:21.*
Exhortation to. *1 Cor. 5:8; 1 Pet. 2:1.*
Pray for, on behalf of others. *Phil. 1:10.*
The blessedness of. *Ps. 32:2.*

Some examples. **The men of Zebulun**: *1 Chron. 12:33.* **Hezekiah**: *Is. 38:3.* **Nathanael**: *Jn. 1:47.* **Paul**: *2 Cor. 1:12.* **Timothy**: *2 Tim. 1:5.* **Lois and Eunice**: *2 Tim. 1:5.* **The Lord Jesus Christ**: *Is. 53:9.*

SLANDER

Is an abomination to God. *Prov. 6:16, 19.*
Is forbidden. *Ex. 23:1; Jas. 4:11.*
Involves
　Whispering. *Rom. 1:29; 2 Cor. 12-20.*
　Backbiting. *Rom. 1:30; 2 Cor. 12:20.*
　Evil conclusions. *1 Tim. 6:4.*
　Tale-bearing. *Lev. 19:16.*
　Babbling. *Eccl. 10:11.*
　Tattling. *1 Tim. 5:13.*
　Evil speaking. *Ps. 41:5, 109:20.*
　Defaming. *Jer. 20:10; 1 Cor. 4:13.*
　Bearing false witness. *Ex. 20:16; Deut. 5:20; Lk. 3:14.*
　Judging uncharitably. *Jas. 4:11-12.*
　Raising false reports. *Ex. 23:1.*
　Repeating matters. *Prov. 17:9.*
Is a deceitful work. *Ps. 52:2.*
Comes from an evil heart. *Lk. 6:45.*
Often arises out of hatred. *Ps. 41:7, 109:3.*
Idleness leads to. *1 Tim. 5:13.*
The wicked are addicted to. *Ps. 50:20; Jer. 6:28, 9:4.*
Hypocrites are addicted to. *Prov. 11:9.*
A characteristic of the devil. *Rev. 12:10.*
The wicked love. *Ps. 52:4.*
Those who indulge in, are fools. *Prov. 10:18.*
Those who indulge in, are not to be trusted. *Jer. 9:4.*
Women are warned against. *Titus 2:3.*
Ministers' wives should avoid. *1 Tim. 3:11.*
Christ was exposed to. *Ps. 35:11. Mat. 26:60.*
Rulers are exposed to. *2 Pet. 2:10; Jude verse 8.*

Ministers are exposed to. *Rom. 3:8; 2 Cor. 6:8.*

Our nearest relatives are exposed to. *Ps. 50:20.*

The saints are exposed to. *Ps. 38:12, 109:2; 1 Pet. 4:4.*

The saints

Should keep their tongue from. *Ps. 34:13 with 1 Pet. 3:10.*

Should lay aside. *Eph. 4:31; 1 Pet. 2:1.*

Should be warned against. *Titus 3:1-2.*

Should give no occasion for. *1 Pet. 2:12, 3:16.*

Should return good for. *1 Cor. 4:13.*

Are blessed in enduring. *Mat. 5:11.*

Are characterised as avoiding. *Ps. 15:1, 3.*

Should not be listened to. *1 Sam. 24:9.*

Should be renounced with anger. *Prov. 25:23.*

The effect of;

Separates friends. *Prov. 16:28, 17:9.*

Makes deadly wounds. *Prov. 18:8, 26:22.*

Strife. *Prov. 26:29.*

Discord among the brothers. *Prov. 6:19.*

Murder. *Ps. 31:13; Ezek. 22:9.*

The tongue of, is a scourge. *Job. 5:21.*

Is venomous. *Ps. 140:8; Eccl. 10:11.*

Is destructive. *Prov. 11:9.*

The end of, is mischievous madness. *Eccl. 10:13.*

Men must give an account for. *Mat. 12:36.*

The punishment for. *Deut. 19:16-21; Ps. 101:5.*

Is illustrated. *Prov. 12:18, 25:18.*

Some examples. **Laban's sons**: *Gen. 31:1.* **Doeg**: *1 Sam. 22:9-11.* **Princes of Ammon**: *2 Sam. 10:3.* **Ziba**: *2 Sam. 16:3.* **Children of Belial**: *1 Kings 21:13.* **Enemies of the Jews**: *Ezra 4:7-16.* **Gashmu**: *Neh. 6:6.* **Haman**: *Esther 3:8.*

David's enemies: *Ps. 31:13.* **Jeremiah's enemies**: *Jer. 38:4.* **The Chaldeans**: *Dan. 3:8.* **Daniel's accusers**: *Dan. 6:13.* **The Jews**: *Mat. 11:18-19.* **Witnesses against Christ**: *Mat. 26:59-61.* **Priests**: *Mk. 15:3.* **Enemies of Stephen**: *Acts 6:11.* **Enemies of Paul**, etc: *Acts 17:7.* **Tertullus**: *Acts 24:2, 5.*

STEADFASTNESS

Is shown by God in all his purposes and ways. *Dan. 6:26.*

Is commanded. *Phil. 4:1; 2 Thess. 2:15.*

Godliness is necessary for. *Job 11:13-15.*

Is secured by

The power of God. *Ps. 55:22, 62:2.*

The presence of God. *Ps. 16:8.*

Trust in God. *Ps. 26:1.*

The intercession of Christ. *Lk. 22:31-32.*

Is a characteristic of the saints. *Job 17:9; Jn. 8:31.*

Should be shown

In continuing with God. *Deut. 10:20; Acts 11:23.*

In the work of the Lord. *1 Cor. 15:58.*

In continuing in the Apostles' doctrine and fellowship. *Acts 2:42.*

In holding fast our profession. *Heb. 4:14, 10:23.*

In holding fast the confidence and rejoicing of the hope. *Heb. 3:6, 14.*

In keeping the faith. *Col. 2:5. 1 Pet. 5:9.*

In standing fast in the faith. *1 Cor. 16:13.*

In holding fast what is good. *1 Thess. 5:21.*

In maintaining Christian liberty. *Gal. 5:1.*

In striving for the faith of the gospel. *Phil. 1:27 with Jude verse 3.*

Even under affliction. *Ps. 44:17-19; 1 Thess. 3:3.*

The saints pray for. *Ps. 17:5.*

The saints praise God for. *Ps. 116:8.*

Ministers

Are exhorted to. *2 Tim. 1:13-14; Titus 1:9.*

Should exhort others to. *Acts 13:43, 14:22.*

Should pray for, in their people. *1 Thess. 3:13; 2 Thess. 2:17.*

Are encouraged by the, of their people. *1 Thess. 3:8.*

Rejoice in the, of their people. *Col. 2:5.*

The wicked are devoid of. *Ps. 78:8, 37.*

The principle of, is illustrated. *Mat. 7:24-25.*

The lack of, is illustrated. *Lk. 8:6, 13; 2 Pet. 2:17; Jude verse 12.*

Some examples. **Caleb**: *Num. 14:24.* **Joshua**: *Josh. 24:15.* **Josiah**: *2 Kings 22:2.* **Job**: *Job 2:3.* **David**: *Ps. 18:21-22.* **Shadrach**, etc: *Dan. 3:18.* **Daniel**: *Dan. 6:10.* **Early Christians**: *Acts 2:42.* **The Corinthians**: *1 Cor. 15:1.* **The Colossians**: *Col. 2:5.*

STRIFE

Christ is an example of avoiding. *Is. 42:2 with Mat. 12:15-19.*

Is forbidden. *Prov. 3:30, 25:8.*

Is a work of the flesh. *Gal. 5:20.*

Is an evidence of a worldly spirit. *1 Cor. 3:3.*

Existed in the early Church. *1 Cor. 1:11.*

Is excited by

Hatred. *Prov. 10:12.*

Pride. *Prov. 13:10, 28:25.*

Wrath. *Prov. 15:18, 30:33.*

Perversity. *Prov. 16:28.*

An argumentative disposition. *Prov. 26:21.*

Tale-bearing. *Prov. 26:20.*

Drunkenness. *Prov. 23:29-30.*

Lusts. *Jas.4:1.*

Strange questions. *1 Tim. 6:4; 2 Tim. 2:23.*

Scorning. *Prov. 22:10.*

The difficulty of stopping, is a reason for avoiding. *Prov. 17:14.*

Is shameful in the saints. *2 Cor. 12:20; Jas. 3:14.*

The saints should

Avoid. *Gen. 13:8.*

Avoid questions that lead to. *2 Tim. 2:14.*

Not walk in. *Rom. 13:13.*

Not act out of. *Phil. 2:3.*

Do all things without. *Phil. 2:14.*

Submit to wrong rather than engage in. *Mat. 5:39-40; 1 Cor. 6:7.*

Seek God's protection from. *Ps. 35:1; Jer. 18:19.*

Praise God for protection from. *. 2 Sam. 22:44; Ps. 18:43.*

The saints are kept from the tongues of. *Ps. 31:20.*

Ministers should

Avoid. *1 Tim. 3:3; 2 Tim. 2:24.*

Avoid questions that lead to. *2 Tim. 2:23; Titus 3:9.*

Not preach through. *Phil. 1:15-16.*

Warn against. *1 Cor. 1:10; 2 Tim. 2:14.*

Reprove. *1 Cor. 1:11-12, 3:3, 11:17-18.*

Appease with a slowness to anger. *Prov. 15:18.*

It is honourable to cease from. *Prov. 20:3.*

Hypocrites make religion a pretence for. *Is. 58:4.*

Fools engage in. *Prov. 18:6.*

Is evidence of a love of transgression. *Prov. 17:19.*

Leads to

Blasphemy. *Lev. 24:10-11.*

Injustice. *Hab. 1:3-4.*

Confusion and every evil work. *Jas. 3:16.*

Violence. *Ex. 21:18, 22.*

Mutual destruction. *Gal. 5:15.*

Temporal blessings are embittered by. *Prov. 17:1.*

Excludes from heaven. *Gal. 5:20-21.*

Promoters of, should be expelled. *Prov. 22:10.*

Punishment for. *Ps. 55:9.*

Strength and violence of, is illustrated. *Prov. 17:14, 18:19.*

The danger of joining in, is illustrated. *Prov 26:17.*

Some examples. **Herdsmen of Abra(ha)m and Lot**: *Gen. 13:7.* **Herdsmen of Gerar and of Isaac**: *Gen. 26:20.* **Laban and Jacob**: *Gen. 31:36.* **Two Hebrews**: *Ex. 2:1.* **Israelites**: *Deut. 1:12.* **Jephthah and the Ammonites**: *Judg. 12:2.* **Judah and Israel**: *2 Sam. 19:41-43.* **The disciples**: *Lk. 22:24.* **Jews**: *Jn. 8:52, 10:19.* **Judaising teachers**: *Acts 15:2.* **Paul and Barnabas**: *Acts 15:39.* **Pharisees and Sadducees**: *Acts 23:7.* **The Corinthians**: *1 Cor. 1:11, 6:6.*

SWEARING FALSELY
Is forbidden. *Lev. 19:12; Num. 30:2; Mat. 5:33.*
Hateful to God. *Zech. 8:17.*
We should not love. *Zech. 8:17.*
Fraud often leads to. *Lev. 6:2-3.*
The saints must abstain from. *Josh. 9:20; Ps. 15:4.*
The blessedness of abstaining from. *Ps. 24:4-5.*
The wicked
Are addicted to. *Jer. 5:2; Hos. 10:4.*
Plead excuses for. *Jer. 7:9-10.*
Will be judged on account of. *Mal. 3:5.*
Will be cut off for. *Zech. 5:3.*
Will have a curse on their houses for. *Zech. 5:4.*

False witnesses are guilty of. *Deut. 19:16, 18.*

Some examples. **Saul**: *1 Sam. 19:6, 10.* **Shimei**: *1 Kings 2:41-43.* **Jews**: *Ezek.16:59.* **Zedekiah**: *Ezek. 17:13-19.* **Peter**: *Mat. 26:72, 74.*

SWEARING PROFANELY
Of all kinds, is a desecration of God's name. *Mat. 5:34-35, 23:21-22.*
Is forbidden. *Ex. 20:7; Mat. 5:34-36; Jas. 5:12.*
The saints must pray to be kept from. *Prov 30:9.*
The wicked
Are addicted to. *Ps. 10:7; Rom. 3:14.*
Love. *Ps. 109:17.*
Clothe themselves with. *Ps. 109:18.*
The guilt of. *Ex. 20:7; Deut. 5:11.*
Woe denounced against. *Mat. 23:16.*
Nations are visited for. *Jer. 23:10; Hos. 4:1-3.*
The punishment for. *Lev. 24:16, 23; Ps. 59:12, 109:17-18.*

Some examples. **Joseph**: *Gen. 42:15-16.* **The son of an Israelite woman**: *Lev. 24:11.* **Saul**: *1 Sam. 28:10.* **Gehazi**: *2 Kings 5:20.* **Jehoram**: *2 Kings 6:31.* **Peter**: *Mat. 26:74.* **Herod**: *Mk. 6:23, 26.* **Enemies of Paul**: *Acts 23:21.*

T

TEMPTATION
God cannot be the subject of. *Jas. 1:13.*
Does not come from God. *Jas. 1:13.*
Comes from
Men's lusts. *Jas.1:14.*
Covetousness. *Prov. 28:20; 1 Tim. 6:9.*
The devil is the author of. *1 Chron. 21:1; Mat. 4:1; 1 Thess. 3:5.*
Evil associates are often the

instruments of. *Prov. 1:10, 16:29.*
Often arises through
Poverty. *Prov. 30:9; Mat. 4:2-3.*
Prosperity. *Prov. 30:9; Mat. 4:8.*
Worldly glory. *Num. 22:17; Mat. 4:8.*
Is to distrust God's providence. *Mat. 4:3.*
Leads to presumption. *Mat. 4:6.*
Often means worshipping the god of this world. *Mat. 4:9.*
Is often strengthened by the

perversion of God's Word. *Mat. 4:6.*

Is permitted, as a testing of
> Faith. *1 Pet. 1:7.*
> Questionable faith. *Job 1:9-12.*

Is always conformable to the nature of man. *1 Cor. 10:13.*

Often ends in sin and perdition. *1 Tim. 6:9; Jas. 1:15.*

Christ
> Endured, from the devil. *Mk. 1:13.*
> Endured, from the wicked. *Mat. 16:1, 22:18; Lk. 10:25.*
> Endured the same kind of, as man. *Heb. 4:15.*
> Endured, yet without sin. *Heb. 4:15.*
> Resisted by the Word of God. *Mat. 4:4, 7, 10.*
> Overcame. *Mat. 4:11; Jn. 16:33.*
> Sympathises with those under. *Heb. 4:15.*
> Is able to succour those under. *Heb. 2:18.*
> Intercedes for his people under. *Lk. 22:31-32; Jn. 17:15.*

God will not allow his saints to be exposed to, beyond their power to bear. *1 Cor. 10:13.*

God will make a way for the saints to escape out of. *1 Cor. 10:13.*

God enables the saints to bear. *1 Cor. 10:13.*

God knows how to deliver the saints out of. *2 Pet. 2:9.*

Christ keeps faithful saints from the hour of. *Rev. 3:10.*

The saints may be in heaviness through. *1 Pet. 1:6.*

The saints should
> Resist, in faith. *Eph. 6:16; 1 Pet. 5:9.*
> Watch against. *Mat. 26:41; 1 Pet. 5:8.*
> Pray to be kept from. *Mat. 6:13, 26:41.*
> Not be the cause of, to others. *Rom. 14:13.*
> Restore those overcome by. *Gal. 6:1.*
> Avoid the way of. *Prov. 4:14-15.*

The devil will renew many. *Lk. 4:13.*

Gains strength through the weakness of the flesh. *Mat. 26:41.*

Hypocrites fall away in times of. *Lk. 8:13.*

The blessedness of those who meet and overcome. *Jas. 1:2-4, 12.*

Some examples. **Eve:** *Gen. 3:1, 4-5.* **Joseph:** *Gen. 39:7.* **Balaam:** *Num. 22:17.* **Achan:** *Josh. 7:21.* **David:** *2 Sam. 11:2.* **Jeroboam:** *1 Kings 15:30.* **Peter:** *Mk. 14:67-71.* **Paul:** *2 Cor. 12:7 with Gal. 4:14.*

THANKSGIVING

Christ set an example of. *Mat. 11:25, 26:27; Jn. 11:41.*

The heavenly host engage in. *Rev. 4:9, 7:11-12, 11:16-17.*

Commanded. *Ps. 50:14.*

Is a good thing. *Ps. 92:1.*

Should be offered
> To God. *Ps. 50:14.*
> To Christ. *1 Tim. 1:12.*
> Through Christ. *Rom. 1:8; Col. 3:17; Heb. 13:15.*
> In the name of Christ. *Eph. 5:20.*
> On behalf of ministers. *2 Cor. 1:11.*
> In private worship. *Dan. 6:10.*
> In public worship. *Ps. 5:18.*
> In everything. *1 Thess. 5:18.*
> At the completion of great undertakings. *Neh. 12:31, 40.*
> Before taking food. *Jn. 6:11; Acts 27:35.*
> Always. *Eph. 1:16, 5:20; 1 Thess. 1:2.*
> At the remembrance of God's holiness. *Ps. 30:4, 97:12.*
> For the goodness and mercy of God. *Ps. 106:1, 107:1, 136:1-3.*
> For the gift of Christ. *2 Cor. 9:15.*
> For Christ's power and reign. *Rev. 11:17.*
> For the reception and effective working of the Word of God in others. *1 Thess. 2:13.*
> For deliverance through Christ, from indwelling sin. *Rom. 7:23-25.*
> For victory over death and the

grave. *1 Cor. 15:47.*

For wisdom and might. *Dan. 2:23.*

For the triumph of the gospel.
2 Cor. 2:14.

For the conversion of others.
Rom. 6:17.

Faith is shown by others. *Rom 1:8;*
2 Thess. 1:3.

For love shown by others.
2 Thess. 1:3.

For the grace bestowed on
others. *1 Cor. 1:4; Phil 1:3-5; Col. 1:3-6.*

For the zeal shown by others.
2 Cor. 8:16.

For the nearness of God's
presence. *Ps. 75:1.*

For appointment to the
ministry. *1 Tim. 1:12.*

For willingness to offer our
property for God's service.
2 Chron. 29:6-14.

For the supply of our bodily
needs. *Rom. 14:6-7; 1 Tim. 4:3-4.*

For all men. *1 Tim. 2:1.*

For all things. *1 Cor. 9:11; Eph. 5:20.*

Should be accompanied by
intercession for others. *1 Tim. 2:1;*
2 Tim. 1:3; Philem. verse 4.

Should always accompany prayer.
Neh. 11:17; Phil. 4:6; Col. 4:2.

Should always accompany praise.
Ps. 92:1; Heb. 13:15.

Expressed in psalms. *1 Chron. 16:7.*

Ministers appointed to offer, in
public. *1 Chron. 16:4, 7, 23:30;*
2 Chron. 31:2.

The saints

Are exhorted to. *Ps. 105:1; Col. 3:15.*

Resolve to offer. *Ps. 18:49; Ps. 30:12.*

Habitually offer. *Dan. 6:10.*

Offer sacrifices of. *Ps. 116:17.*

Abound in the faith with. *Col. 2:7.*

Magnify God by. *Ps. 69:30.*

Come before God with. *Ps. 95:2.*

Should enter God's gates with
praise. *Ps. 104:4.*

Of hypocrites, full of boasting.
Lk. 18:11.

The wicked are averse to. *Rom. 1:21.*

Some examples. **David:** *1 Chron.*
29:13. **Levites:** *2 Chron. 5:12-13.* **Daniel:**
Dan. 2:23. **Jonah:** *Jonah 2:9.* **Simeon:**
Lk. 2:28. **Anna:** *Lk. 2:38.* **Paul:** *Acts 28:15.*

THEFT

Is an abomination. *Jer. 7:9-10.*

Is forbidden. *Ex. 20:15 with Mk. 10:19;*
Rom. 13:9; 1 Thess. 4:6.

From the poor is especially
forbidden. *Prov 22:22.*

Includes fraud in general. *Lev 19:13.*

Includes fraud concerning wages.
Lev 19:13; Mal. 3:5; Jas. 5:4.

Proceeds from the heart. *Mat. 15:19.*

Defiles a man. *Mat. 15:20.*

The wicked

Are addicted to. *Ps. 119:61; Jer. 7:9.*

Store up the fruits of. *Amos 3:10.*

Lie in wait to commit. *Hos. 6:9.*

Commit, under shelter of the
night. *Job 24:14; Obad. verse 5.*

Consent to those who commit.
Ps. 50:18.

Associate with those who
commit. *Is. 1:23.*

May, for a time, prosper in their.
Job. 12:6.

Plead excuses for. *Jer. 7:9-10.*

Do not repent of their. *Rev. 9:21.*

Destroy themselves with.
Prov. 21:7.

Connected with murder. *Jer. 7:9;*
Hos. 4:2.

Shame follows the detection of.
Jer. 2:26.

Brings a curse on those who
commit. *Zech.5:3; Mal. 3:5.*

Brings a curse on the family of
those who commit. *Zech. 5:4.*

Brings the wrath of God on those
who commit. *Ezek. 22:29, 31.*

Brings down judgement on the
land. *Hos. 4:2-3.*

Excludes from heaven. *1 Cor. 6:10.*

Those who connive at,

Hate their own souls. *Prov 29:24.*

Will be reproved by God.
Ps. 50:18, 21.

The Law of Moses concerning.
Ex. 22:1-8.

The saints

Are warned against. *Eph. 4:28;*
1 Pet. 4:15.

Pray to be kept from. *Prov. 30:7-9.*

Repudiate the charge of.
Gen. 31:37.

All earthly treasure is subject to.
Job 5:5; Mt. 6:19.

Heavenly treasure is secure from.
Mat. 6:20; Lk. 12:33.

Woe is denounced against. *Is. 10:2;*
Nahum 3:1.

Illustrates the guilt of false
teachers. *Jer. 23:30; Jn. 10:1, 8 10.*

Some examples. **Rachel**: *Gen. 31:19.*
Achan: *Josh. 7:21.* **The Shechemites**:
Judg. 9:25. **Micah**: *Judg. 17:2.* **Gehazi**:
2 Kings 5:20-24. **Two thieves**: *Mat. 27:38.*
Judas: *Jn. 12:6.* **Barabbas**: *Jn. 18:40.*

TITHE, TITHING

A tenth of anything. *1 Sam. 8:15, 17.*

Antiquity of the custom of giving
to God's ministers. *Gen. 14:20;*
Heb.7:6.

Was considered a fair return to
God for all his blessings. *Gen. 28:22.*

Under the Law, a tenth belonged
to God. *Lev. 27:30.*

Consisted of a tenth

Of all the produce of the land.
Lev. 27:30.

Of all cattle. *Lev. 27:32.*

Of holy things dedicated.
2 Chron. 31:6.

Given by God to the Levites for
their services. *Num. 18:21, 24;*
Neh. 10:37.

The tenth of, offered by the
Levites as a heave-offering to
God. *Num. 18:26-27.*

The tenth part was given by the
Levites to the priests as their
portion. *Num. 18:26, 28; Neh. 10:38.*

The reasonableness of appoint-
ing, for the Levites. *Num. 18:20, 23-24;*
Josh. 13:33.

When redeemed, to have a fifth
part of the value added. *Lev. 27:31.*

The punishment for changing.
Lev. 27:33.

The Jews were slow in giving.
Neh. 13:10.

The Jews were reproved for
withholding. *Mal. 3:8.*

The pious governors of Israel
caused the payment to be made
of. *2 Chron. 31:5; Neh. 13:11-12.*

Rulers were appointed for
distributing. *2 Chron. 31:12; Neh. 13:13.*

The Pharisees were scrupulous in
paying. *Lk. 11:42; Lk. 18:12.*

A second tithe

Or its value, was brought yearly
to the tabernacle, and eaten
before the Lord. *Deut. 12:6-7, 17-19,*
14:22-27.

Was to be consumed at home
every third year to promote
hospitality and charity. *Deut. 14:28-*
29, 26:12-15.

TITLES AND NAMES OF CHRIST, THE

Almighty. *Rev. 1:8.*

Amen. *Rev. 8:14.*

Alpha and Omega. *Rev. 1:8, 22:13.*

Advocate. *1 Jn. 2:1.*

Angel of God's presence. *Is. 63:9.*

Apostle. *Heb. 3:1.*

Arm of the Lord. *Is. 51:9, 53:1.*

Author and Finisher of our faith.
Heb. 12:2.

Blessed and only Potentate.
1 Tim. 6:15.

Beginning of the creation of God.
Is. 4:2; Rev. 3:14.

Branch of righteousness. *Jer. 23:5;*
Zech. 3:8, 6:12.

Bread of life. *Jn. 6:35, 48.*

Breaker. *Mic. 2:13.*

Captain of the Lord's host.
Josh. 5:14-15.

Captain of salvation. *Heb. 2:10.*

Chief Shepherd. *1 Pet. 5:4.*

Christ of God. *Lk. 9:20.*

Consolation of Israel. *Lk. 2:25.*

Chief Cornerstone. *Eph. 2:20; 1 Pet. 2:6.*

Commander. *Is. 55:4.*

Counsellor. *Is. 9:6.*

David. *Jer. 30:9; Ezek. 34:23.*

Dayspring. *Lk. 1:78.*

Deliverer. *Rom. 11:26.*

Desire of all nations. *Hag. 2:7.*

Door. *Jn. 10:7.*

Elect of God. *Is. 42:1.*

Emmanuel. *Is. 7:14 with Mat. 1:23.*

Eternal life. *1 Jn. 1:2, 5:20.*

Everlasting Father. *Is. 9:6.*

Faithful witness. *Rev. 1:5, 3:14.*

First and the last. *Rev. 1:17, 2:8.*

Firstborn from the dead. *Rev. 1:5.*

Forerunner. *Heb. 6:20.*

God. *Ps. 45:6; Is. 40:9; Jn. 20:28; Heb. 1:8.*

God blessed forever. *Rom. 9:5.*

God's Fellow. *Zech. 13:7.*

Glory of the Lord. *Is. 40:5.*

Good Shepherd. *Jn. 10:14.*

Great High Priest. *Heb. 4:14.*

Governor. *Mat. 2:6.*

Head of the Church. *Eph. 5:23; Col. 1:18.*

Heir of all things. *Heb. 1:2.*

Holy Child Jesus. *Acts 4:30.*

Holy One. *Ps. 16:10 with Acts 2:27, 31.*

Holy One of God. *Mk. 1:24.*

Holy One of Israel. *Is. 41:14.*

Horn of salvation. *Lk. 1:69.*

I AM. *Ex. 3:14 with Jn. 8:58.*

JEHOVAH. *Is. 26:4, 40:3.*

Jesus. *Mat. 1:21; 1 Thess. 1:10.*

Judge of Israel. *Mic. 5:1.*

Just One. *Acts 7:52.*

King. *Zech. 9:9 with Mat. 21:5.*

King of Israel. *Mat. 27:42; Jn. 1:49.*

King of the Jews. *Mat. 2:2, 27:37.*

King of the saints. *Rev. 15:3.*

King of kings. *1 Tim. 6:15; Rev. 17:14.*

Lamb. *Rev. 13:8.*

Lamb of God. *Jn. 1:29, 36.*

Last Adam. *1 Cor. 15:45.*

Law-giver. *Is. 33:22; Jas. 4:12.*

Leader. *Is. 55:4.*

Life. *Jn. 14:6; Col. 3:4; 1 Jn. 1:2.*

Light of the world. *Jn. 8:12.*

Lion of the tribe of Judah. *Rev. 5:5.*

Lord of glory. *1 Cor. 2:8.*

Lord of all. *Acts 10:36; Rom. 10:12.*

Lord of lords. *Rev. 17:14.*

LORD OUR RIGHTEOUSNESS. *Jer. 23:6.*

Lord God of the holy prophets. *Rev. 22:6,*

Lord God Almighty. *Rev. 15:3.*

Mediator. *1 Tim. 2:5.*

Messenger of the covenant. *Mal. 3:1.*

Messiah (Christ). *Dan. 9:25; Jn. 1:41.*

Mighty God. *Is. 9:6.*

Mighty One of Jacob. *Is. 60:16.*

Morning star. *Rev. 22:16.*

Nazarene. *Mat. 2:23.*

Offspring of David. *Rev. 22:16.*

Only-begotten. *Jn. 1:14.*

Our Passover. *1 Cor. 5:7.*

Plant of renown. *Ezek. 34:29.*

Prince of life. *Acts 3:15.*

Prince of peace. *Is. 9:6.*

Prince of the kings of the earth. *Rev. 1:5.*

Prophet. *Lk. 24:19; Jn. 7:40.*

Ransom. *1 Tim. 2:6.*

Redeemer. *Job 19:25; Is. 59:20, 60:16.*

Resurrection and life. *Jn. 11:25.*

Rock. *1 Cor. 10:4.*

Root of David. *Rev. 22:16.*

Root of Jesse. *Is. 11:10.*

Rose of Sharon. *Song 2:1.*

Ruler in Israel. *Mic. 5:2.*

Saviour. *2 Pet. 2:20, 3:18.*

Sceptre. *Num. 25:17.*

Servant. *Is. 42:1.*

Shepherd and Bishop of souls. *1 Pet. 2:25.*

Shiloh. *Gen. 49:10.*

Son of the Blessed. *Mk. 14:61.*

Son of God. *Lk. 1:35; Jn. 1:49.*

Son of the Highest. *Lk. 1:32.*

Son of David. *Mal. 9:27; Mat. 9:27, 15:22, etc.*

Son of Man. *Jn. 5:27, 6:27.*

Star. *Num. 24:17.*

Sun of righteousness. *Mal. 4:2.*
Surety. *Heb. 7:22.*
True God. *1 Jn. 5:20.*
True Light. *Jn. 1:9.*
True Vine. *Jn. 15:1.*
Truth. *Jn. 14:6.*
Way. *Jn. 14:6.*
Wisdom. *Prov. 8:12.*
Witness. *Is. 55:4; Rev. 1:5.*
Wonderful. *Is. 9:6.*
Word. *Jn. 1:1; 1 Jn. 5:7.*
Word of God. *Rev. 19:13.*
Word of life. *1 Jn. 1:1.*

TITLES AND NAMES OF THE HOLY SPIRIT, THE

Breath of the Almighty. *Job 33:4; Ezek. 37:9.*
Comforter. *Jn. 14:16, 26, 15:26.*
Eternal Spirit. *Heb. 9:14.*
Free Spirit. *Ps. 51:12.*
God. *Acts 5:3-4.*
Good Spirit. *Neh. 9:20; Ps. 143:10.*
Holy Spirit. *Ps. 51:11; Lk. 11:13.*
Holy Spirit of God. *Eph. 4:30.*
Holy Spirit of promise. *Eph. 1:13.*
Lord, The. *2 Thess. 3:5.*
Power of the Highest. *Lk. 1:35.*
Spirit, The. *Mat. 4:1; Jn. 3:6; 1 Tim. 4:1.*
Spirit of the Lord God. *Is. 61:1.*
Spirit of the Lord. *Is. 11:2; Acts 5:9.*
Spirit of God. *Gen. 1:2; 1 Cor. 2:11.*
Spirit of the Father. *Mat. 10:20.*
Spirit of Christ. *Rom. 8:9; 1 Pet. 1:11.*
Spirit of the Son. *Gal. 4:6.*
Spirit of adoption. *Rom. 8:15.*
Spirit of counsel. *Is. 11:2.*
Spirit of burning. *Is. 4:4.*
Spirit of glory. *1 Pet. 4:14.*
Spirit of grace. *Zech. 12:10; Heb. 10:29.*
Spirit of holiness. *Rom. 1:4.*
Spirit of judgement. *Is. 4:4, 28:6.*
Spirit of knowledge. *Is. 11:2.*
Spirit of life. *Rom. 8:2; Rev. 11:11.*
Spirit of might. *Is. 11:2.*
Spirit of prophecy. *Rev. 19:10.*
Spirit of truth. *Jn. 14:17, 15:26.*
Spirit of understanding. *Is. 11:2.*
Spirit of wisdom. *Is. 11:2; Eph. 1:17.*
Spirit of the fear of the Lord. *Is. 11:2.*
The seven Spirits of God. *Rev. 1:4.*
The voice of the Lord. *Is. 6:8.*

TITLES AND NAMES OF THE CHURCH, THE

Assembly of the saints. *Ps. 89:7.*
Assembly of the upright. *Ps. 111:1.*
Body of Christ. *Eph. 1:22-23; Col. 1:24.*
Branch of God's planting. *Is. 60:21.*
Bride of Christ. *Rev. 21:9.*
Church of God. *Acts 20:28.*
Church of the Living God. *1 Tim. 3:15.*
Church of the first-born. *Heb. 12:22.*
City of the Living God. *Heb. 12:22.*
Congregation of the saints. *Ps. 149:1.*
Congregation of the Lord's poor. *Ps. 74:19.*
Dove. *Song. 2:14, 5:2.*
Family in heaven and earth. *Eph. 3:15.*
Flock of God. *Ezek. 34:15; 1 Pet. 5:2.*
Fold of Christ. *Jn. 10:16.*
General assembly of the first-born. *Heb. 12:23.*
Golden lampstand. *Rev. 1:20.*
God's building. *1 Cor. 3:9.*
God's husbandry. *1 Cor. 3:9.*
God's heritage. *Joel 3:2; 1 Pet. 5:3.*
Habitation of God. *Eph. 2:22.*
Heavenly Jerusalem. *Gal. 4:26; Heb. 12:22.*
Holy city. *Rev. 21:2.*
Holy mountain. *Zech. 8:3.*
Holy hill. *Ps. 15:1.*
House of God. *1 Tim. 3:15; Heb. 10:21.*
House of the God of Jacob. *Is. 2:3.*
House of Christ. *Heb. 3:6.*
Household of God. *Eph. 2:19.*
Inheritance. *Ps. 28:9; Is. 19:25.*
Israel of God. *Gal. 6:16.*
King's daughter. *Ps. 45:13.*
Lamb's wife. *Rev. 19:7, 21:9.*
Mount Zion. *Ps. 2:6; Heb. 12:22.*
Mountain of the Lord of hosts. *Zech. 8:3.*

Mountain of the Lord's house. *Is. 2:2.*

New Jerusalem. *Rev. 21:2.*

Pillar and ground of the truth. *1 Tim. 3:15.*

Place of God's throne. *Ezek. 43:7.*

Pleasant portion. *Jer. 12:10.*

Portion of God's inheritance. *Deut. 32:9.*

Sanctuary of God. *Ps. 114:2.*

Sister of Christ. *Song. 4:12, 5:2.*

Spiritual house. *1 Pet. 2:5.*

Spouse of Christ. *Song. 4:12, 5:1.*

Strength and glory of God. *Ps. 78:81.*

Sought out, a city not forsaken. *Is. 62:12.*

Tabernacle. *Ps. 15:1.*

The Lord's portion. *Deut. 32:9.*

Temple of God. *1 Cor. 3:10, 17.*

Temple of the Living God. *2 Cor. 6:16.*

Vineyard. *Jer. 12:10. Mat. 21:41.*

TITLES AND NAMES OF MINISTERS, THE

Ambassadors for Christ. *2 Cor. 5:20.*

Angels of the Church. *Rev. 1:20, 2:1.*

Apostles. *Lk. 6:13; Rev. 18:20.*

Apostles of Jesus Christ. *Titus 1:1.*

Elders. *1 Tim. 5:17; 1 Pet. 5:1.*

Evangelists. *Eph. 4:11; 2 Tim. 4:5.*

Fishers of men. *Mat. 4:19; Mk. 1:17.*

Labourers. *Mat. 9:38 with Philem. verse 1.*

Labourers in the gospel of Christ. *1 Thess. 3:2.*

Lights. *Jn. 5:35.*

Men of God. *Deut. 33:1; 1 Tim. 6:11.*

Messengers of the Church. *2 Cor. 8:23.*

Messengers of the Lord of hosts. *Mal. 2:7.*

Ministers of God. *2 Cor. 6:4.*

Ministers of the Lord. *Joel 2:17.*

Ministers of Christ. *Rom. 15:16; 1 Cor. 4:1.*

Ministers of the sanctuary. *Ezek. 45:4.*

Ministers of the gospel. *Eph. 3:7; Col. 1:23.*

Ministers of the Word. *Lk. 1:2.*

Ministers of the New Testament. *2 Cor. 3:6.*

Ministers of the Church. *Col. 1:24-25.*

Ministers of righteousness. *2 Cor. 11:15.*

Overseers. *Acts 20:28.*

Pastors. *Jer. 3:15; Eph. 4:11.*

Preachers. *Rom. 10:14; 1 Tim. 2:7.*

Preachers of righteousness. *2 Pet. 2:5.*

Servants of God. *Titus 1:1; Jas. 1:1.*

Servants of the Lord. *2 Tim. 2:24.*

Servants of Jesus Christ. *Phil. 1:1; Jude verse 1.*

Servants of the Church. *2 Cor. 4:5.*

Shepherds. *Jer. 23:4.*

Soldiers of Christ. *Phil. 2:25; 2 Tim. 2:3-4.*

Stars. *Rev. 1:20, 2:1.*

Stewards of God. *Titus 1:7.*

Stewards of the grace of God. *1 Pet. 4:10.*

Stewards of the mysteries of God. *1 Cor. 4:1.*

Teachers. *Is. 30:20; Eph. 4:11.*

Watchmen. *Is. 62:6; Ezek. 33:7.*

Witnesses. *Acts 1:8, 5:32, 26:16.*

Workers together with God. *2 Cor. 6:1.*

TITLES AND NAMES OF THE SAINTS, THE

Believers. *Acts 5:14; 1 Tim. 4:12.*

Beloved of God. *Rom. 1:7.*

Beloved brothers. *1 Cor. 15:58; Jas. 2:5.*

Blessed of the Lord. *Gen. 24:31, 26:29.*

Blessed of the Father. *Mat. 25:34.*

Brothers. *Mat. 23:8; Acts 12:17.*

Brothers of Christ. *Lk. 8:21; Jn. 20:17.*

Called of Jesus Christ. *Rom. 1:6.*

Children of the Lord. *Deut. 14:1.*

Children of God. *Jn. 11:62; 1 Jn. 3:10.*

Children of the Living God. *Rom. 9:26.*

Children of the Father. *Mat. 5:45.*

Children of the Highest. *Lk. 6:35.*

Children of Abraham. *Gal. 3:7.*

Children of Jacob. *Ps. 105:6.*

Children of promise. *Rom. 9:8; Gal. 4:28.*

Children of the free woman. *Gal. 4:31.*

Children of the kingdom. *Mat. 13:38.*

Children of Zion. *Ps. 149:2; Joel 2:23.*

Children of the bride-chamber. *Mat. 9:15.*

Children of light. *Lk. 16:8; Eph. 5:8.*

Children of the day. *1 Thess. 6:5.*

Children of the resurrection. *Lk. 20:36.*

Chosen generation. *1 Pet. 2:9.*

Chosen ones. *1 Chron. 10:13.*

Chosen vessels. *Acts 9:15.*

Christians. *Acts 11:26, 26:28.*

Counsellors of peace. *Prov. 12:20.*

Dear children. *Eph. 5:1.*

Disciples of Christ. *Jn. 8:31, 15:8.*

Elect of God. *Col. 3:12; Titus 1:1.*

Epistles of Christ. *2 Cor. 3:3.*

Excellent, The. *Ps. 16:3.*

Faithful brothers in Christ. *Col. 1:2.*

Faithful, The. *Ps. 12:1.*

Faithful of the land, The. *Ps. 101:6.*

Fellow-citizens. *Eph. 9:19.*

Fellow-heirs. *Eph. 3:6.*

Fellow-servants. *Rev. 6:11.*

Friends of God. *2 Chron. 20:7; Jas. 2:23.*

Friends. *Song. 5:1; Jn. 15:15.*

Godly, The. *Ps. 4:3; 2 Pet. 2:9.*

Heirs of God. *Rom. 8:17; Gal. 4:7.*

Heirs of the grace of life. *1 Pet. 3:7.*

Heirs of the kingdom. *Jas. 2:5.*

Heirs of the promise. *Gal. 3:29; Heb. 6:17.*

Heirs of salvation. *Heb. 1:14.*

Hidden ones. *Ps. 83:3.*

Holy brothers. *1 Thess. 5:27; Heb. 3:1.*

Holy and mighty people. *Dan. 8:24.*

Holy nation. *Ex. 19:6; 1 Pet. 2:9.*

Holy people. *Deut. 26:19; Is. 62:12.*

Holy priesthood. *1 Pet. 2:5.*

Holy seed. *Is. 6:13.*

Joint-heirs with Christ. *Rom. 8:17.*

Just, The. *Prov. 20:7; Hab. 2:4.*

Kings and priests to God. *Rev. 1:6.*

Kingdom of priests. *Ex. 19:6.*

Lambs. *Is. 40. 11; Jn. 21:15.*

Lights of the world. *Mat. 5:14.*

Little children. *Jn. 13:33; 1 Jn. 2:1.*

Living stones. *1 Pet. 2:5.*

Members of Christ. *1 Cor. 6:15; Eph. 5:30.*

Men of God. *Deut. 33:1; 1 Tim. 6:11.*

Obedient children. *1 Pet. 1:14.*

People of God. *Heb. 4:9; 1 Pet. 2:10.*

People of God's pasture. *Ps. 95:7.*

People of the inheritance. *Deut. 4:20.*

People near to God. *Ps. 148:14.*

People prepared for the Lord. *Lk. 1:17.*

People saved by the Lord. *Deut. 33:29.*

Pillars in the temple of God. *Rev. 3:12.*

Ransomed of the Lord. *Is. 35:10.*

Redeemed of the Lord. *Is. 51:11.*

Righteous, The. *Ps. 1:6. Mal. 3:18.*

Royal priesthood. *1 Pet. 2:9.*

Salt of the earth. *Mat. 5:13.*

Seed of Abraham. *Ps. 105:6.*

Seed of the blessed of the Lord. *Is. 65:23.*

Servants of Christ. *1 Cor. 7:22. Eph. 6:6.*

Servants of the Lord. *Deut. 34:5; Is. 54:17.*

Servants of the Most High God. *Dan. 3:26.*

Servants of righteousness. *Rom. 6:18.*

Sheep of Christ. *Jn. 10:1-16, 21:16.*

Sheep of the flock. *Mat. 26:31.*

Sheep of God's hand. *Ps. 95:7.*

Sheep of God's pasture. *Ps. 79:13.*

Sojourners with God. *Lev. 25:23; Ps. 39:12.*

Sons of God. *Jn. 1:12; Phil. 2:15.*

Sons of the Living God. *Hab. 1:10.*

Special people. *Deut. 7:6, 14:2; Titus 2:14.*

Special treasure. *Ex. 19:5; Ps. 135:4.*

The Lord's freemen. *1 Cor. 7:22.*

The Lord's people. *1 Sam. 2:24; 2 Kings 11:17.*

Trees of righteousness. *Is. 61:3.*

Vessels to honour. *2 Tim. 2:21.*
Vessels of mercy. *Rom. 9:23.*
Witnesses for God. *Is. 43:10, 44:8.*

TITLES AND NAMES OF THE WICKED, THE

Adversaries of the Lord. *1 Sam. 2:10.*
Children of Belial. *Deut. 13:13; 2 Chron. 13:7.*
Children of the devil. *Acts 13:10; 1 Jn. 3:10.*
Children of the wicked one. *Mat. 13:38.*
Children of hell. *Mat. 23:15.*
Children of the bond-woman. *Gal. 4:31.*
Children of vile men. *Job 30:8.*
Children of fools. *Job 30:8.*
Children of strangers. *Is. 2:6.*
Children of transgression. *Is. 57:4.*
Children of disobedience. *Eph. 2:2; Col. 3:6.*
Children in whom is no faith. *Deut. 32:20.*
Children of the flesh. *Rom. 9:8.*
Children of iniquity. *Hos. 10:9.*
Children that will not hear the Law of the Lord. *Is. 30:9.*
Children of pride. *Job 41:34.*
Children of this world. *Lk. 16:8.*
Children of wickedness. *2 Sam. 7:10.*
Children of wrath. *Eph. 2:3.*
Children that are corrupters. *Is. 1:4.*
Cursed children. *2 Pet. 2:14.*
Enemies of God. *Ps. 37:20; Jas. 4:4.*
Enemies of the cross of Christ. *Phil. 3:18.*
Enemies of all righteousness. *Acts 13:10.*
Evildoers. *Ps. 37:1; 1 Pet. 2:14.*
Evil men. *Prov. 4:14; 2 Tim. 3:18.*
Evil generation. *Deut. 1:35.*
Evil and adulterous generation. *Mat. 12:39.*
Fools. *Prov. 1:7; Rom. 1:22.*
Generation of vipers. *Mat. 3:7, 12:34.*
Grievous rebels. *Jer. 6:28.*
Haters of God. *Ps. 81:15; Rom. 1:30.*
Impudent children. *Ezek. 2:4.*

Inventors of evil things. *Rom. 1:30.*
Lying children. *Is. 30:9.*
Men of the world. *Ps. 17:14.*
Obstinate generation. *Deut. 32:20.*
People laden with iniquity. *Is. 1:4.*
Perverse generation. *Acts 2:40.*
Perverse and crooked generation. *Deut. 32:5; Mat.17:17; Phil. 2:15.*
Rebellious children. *Is. 30:1.*
Rebellious people. *Is. 30:9, 65:2.*
Rebellious nation. *Ezek. 2:3.*
Rebellious house. *Ezek. 2:5, 8, 12:2.*
Reprobates. *2 Cor 13:5-7.*
Scornful, The. *Ps. 1:1.*
Seed of falsehood. *Is. 57:4.*
Seed of the wicked. *Ps. 37:28.*
Seed of evil doers. *Is. 1:4, 14:20.*
Serpents. *Mat. 23:33.*
Servants of corruption. *2 Pet. 2:19.*
Servants of sin. *Jn. 8:34; Rom. 6:20.*
Sinful generation. *Mk. 8:28.*
Sinners. *Ps. 26:9. Prov. 1:10.*
Sons of Belial. *1 Sam. 2:12; 1 Kings 21:10.*
Silly children. *Jer. 4:22.*
Strange children. *Ps. 144:7.*
Stubborn and rebellions generation. *Ps. 78:8.*
Transgressors. *Ps. 37:38, 51:13.*
Ungodly, The. *Ps. 1:1.*
Ungodly men. *Jude verse 4.*
Unprofitable servants. *Mat. 25:30.*
Vessels of wrath. *Rom. 9:22.*
Wicked of the earth. *Ps. 75:8.*
Wicked transgressors. *Ps. 59:5.*
Wicked servants. *Mat. 25:26.*
Wicked generation. *Mat. 12:45, 16:4.*
Wicked ones. *Jer. 2:33.*
Wicked doers. *Ps. 101:8; Prov. 17:4.*
Workers of iniquity. *Ps. 28:3, 36:12.*

TITLES AND NAMES OF THE DEVIL, THE

Abaddon (destroyer). *Rev. 9:11.*
Accuser of our brothers (see Devil). *Rev. 12:10.*
Adversary (see Satan). *1 Pet. 5:8.*
Angel of the bottomless pit. *Rev. 9:11.*

Apollyon (Greek form ofAbaddon). *Rev. 9:11.*

Beelzebub (Lord of the flies). *Mat.12:24.*

Belial(lit. death, perdition, see Ps. 18:4). *2 Cor. 6:15.*

Crooked serpent. *Is. 27:1.*

Devil (diabolos = accuser). *Mat. 4:1, 25:41; Jn. 8:44; Acts 10:38; Eph 6:11; 2 Tim 2:26; 1 Pet. 5:8; Jude verse 9; Rev 12:9, etc, etc.*

Dragon. *Is. 27:1; Rev. 20:2.*

Enemy. Mat. *13:39.*

Evil spirit. *1 Sam. 16:14.*

Father of lies. *Jn. 8:44.*

Great red dragon. *Rev. 12:3.*

Leviathan (Hebrew, meaning twisted, or sea monster, see *Job 3:8, 41:1-34; Ps.74:14, 114:26*). *Is. 27:1.*

Liar. *Jn. 8:44.*

Lying spirit. *1 Kings 22:22.*

Murderer. *Jn. 8:44.*

Old serpent. *Rev. 12:9, 20:2.*

Piercing serpent. *Is. 27:1.*

Power of darkness. *Col. 1:13.*

Prince of this world. *Jn. 14:30.*

Prince of the devils. *Mat. 12:24.*

Prince of the power of the air. *Eph. 2:2.*

Ruler of the darkness of this world. *Eph. 6:12.*

Satan (adversary). *1 Chron. 21:1; Job 1:8; Mat. 16:23.*

Serpent. *Gen. 3:4, 14; 2 Cor. 11:8.*

Spirit that works in the children of disobedience. *Eph. 2:2.*

Tempter. *Mat. 4:3; 1 Thess. 3:5.*

The god of this world. *2 Cor. 4:4.*

Unclean spirit. *Mat. 12:43.*

Wicked one. *Mat. 13:19, 38.*

TRINITY, THE HOLY

The doctrine of, is proved from Scripture. *Mat. 3:16-17; Rom. 8:9; 1 Cor. 12:3-6; Eph. 4:4-6; 1 Pet. 1:2; 1 Jn. 5:7; Jude verses 20-21.*

Divine titles are applied to all three Persons in. *Ex. 20:2 with Jn. 20:28 and Acts 5:3-4.*

Each Person is described as

Eternal. *Rom. 16:26 with Rev. 22:13 and Heb. 9:14.*

Holy. *Rev. 4:8, 15:4 with Acts 3:14 and 1 Jn. 2:20.*

True. *Jn. 7:28 with Rev. 3:7 and 1 Jn. 5:6.*

Omnipresent. *Jer. 23:24 with Ps. 139:7 and Eph. 1:23.*

Omnipotent. *Gen. 17:1 with Rev. 1:8 and Rom. 15:19; Jer. 32:17 with Lk. 1:35 and Heb. 1:3.*

Omniscient. *Jn. 22:17 with Acts 15:18 and 1 Cor. 2:10-11.*

Creator. Gen. *1:1 with Job 33:4 and Col. 1:16; Job 26:13 with Ps. 148:5 and Jn. 1:3.*

Sanctifier. *Heb. 2:11 with 1 Pet. 1:2 and Jude verse 1.*

Author of all spiritual operations. *Heb. 13:21 with Col. 1:29 and 1 Cor. 12:11.*

Source of eternal life. *Rom. 6:23 with Jn. 10:28 and Gal. 6:8.*

Teacher. *Is. 54:13 with Lk. 21:15 and Jn. 14:26; Is. 48:17 with Gal. 1:12 and 1 Jn. 2:20.*

Raising Christ from the dead. *1 Cor. 6:14 with Jn. 2:19 and 1 Pet. 3:18.*

Inspiring the prophets, etc. *Heb. 1:1 with 2 Cor. 13:3 and Mk. 13:11.*

Supplying ministers to the Church. *Jer. 3:15 with Eph. 4:11 and Acts 20:28; Jer. 26:5 with Mat. 10:5 and Acts 13:2.*

Salvation is the work of. *2 Thess. 2:13-14; Titus 3:4-6; 1 Pet. 1:2.*

Baptism is to be administered in the name of. *Mat. 28:19.*

The Benediction is to be given in the name of. *2 Cor. 13:14.*

The saints

Are the temple of. *2 Cor. 6:16 with Eph. 3:17 and 1 Cor. 3:16; Eph. 2:22 with Col. 1:27 and 1 Cor. 6:19.*

Have fellowship with. *1 Jn. 1:3 with Phil. 2:1.*

Sin is a tempting of. *Deut. 6:16 with 1 Cor. 10:9 and Acts 5:9.*

The Israelites in the wilderness tempted. *Ex. 17:7 with 1 Cor. 10:9 and Heb. 3:7-9.*

TRUST

God is the true object of. *Ps. 65:5.*
The fear of God leads to.
Prov. 14:26.

Encouragements to, in

The everlasting strength of God. *Is. 26:4.*
The goodness of God. *Nahum 1:7.*
The loving kindness of God.
Ps. 36:7.
The rich bounty of God.
1 Tim. 6:17.
The care of God for us. *1 Pet. 5:7.*
Former deliverances. *Ps. 9:10; 2 Cor. 1:10.*
Should be with the whole heart.
Prov. 3:5.
Should be from one's youth up.
Ps. 71:5.

Of the saints, is

Not in the flesh. *Phil. 3:3-4.*
Not in themselves. *2 Cor. 1:9.*
Not in using worldly weapons.
1 Sam. 17:38-39, 45; Ps. 44:6; 2 Cor. 10:4.
In God. *Ps. 11:1, 31:14; 2 Cor. 1:9.*
In the Word of God. *Ps. 110:42.*
In the mercy of God. *Ps. 13:5, 52:8.*
In Christ. *Eph. 3:12.*
Through Christ. *2 Cor. 3:4.*
Grounded on the covenant.
2 Sam. 23:5.
Strong at the prospect of death.
Ps. 23:4.
Fixed. *2 Sam. 22:3; Ps. 112:7.*
Unalterable. *Job 13:15.*
Despised by the wicked. *Is. 36, 4, 7.*
At all times. *Ps. 62:8.*
Forever. *Ps. 52:8; Is. 26:4.*
The saints plead, in prayer. *Ps. 25:20, 31:1, 141:8.*
The Lord knows those who have.
Nahum 1:7.
Exhortation to. *Ps. 4:5, 115:9-11.*

Leads to

Being compassed with mercy.
Ps. 32:10.
Enjoyment of perfect peace.
Is. 26:3.
Enjoyment of all temporal and spiritual blessings. *Is. 57:13.*
Enjoyment of happiness.
Prov. 16:20.
Rejoicing in God. *Ps. 5:11, 33:21.*
Fulfilment of all holy desires.
Ps. 37:5.
Deliverance from enemies.
Ps. 37:40.
Safety in times of danger.
Prov. 29:25.
Stability. *Ps. 125:1.*
Prosperity. *Prov. 28:25.*

Keeps from

Fear. *Ps. 56:11; Is. 12:2; Heb. 13:6.*
Slipping. *Ps. 26:1.*
Desolation. *Ps. 34:22.*
To be accompanied with doing good. *Ps. 37:3.*
The blessedness of placing, in God. *Ps. 2:12, 34:8, 40:4; Jer. 17:7.*

Of the wicked;

Is not in God. *Ps. 78:22; Zeph. 3:2.*
Is in idols. *Is. 42:17; Hab. 2:18.*
Is in man. *Judg. 9:26; Ps. 118:8-9.*
Is in their own heart. *Prov. 28:26.*
Is in their own righteousness.
Lk. 18:9, 12.
Is in their religious privileges.
Jer. 7:4, 8; Mic. 3:11; Jn. 8:33.
Is in oppression. *Ps. 62:10; Is. 30:12.*
Is in wickedness. *Is. 47:10.*
Is in vanity. *Job 15:31; Is. 59:4.*
Is in falsehood. *Is. 28:15; Jer. 13:25.*
Is in earthly alliances. *Is. 30:2; Ezek. 17:15.*
Is in fenced cities. *Jer. 5:17.*
Is in chariots and horses. *Ps. 20:7.*
Is in wealth. *Ps. 49:6, 52:7; Prov. 11:28; Jer. 48:7; Mk. 10:24.*
Is vain and delusive. *Is. 30:7; Jer. 2:37.*
Will make them ashamed.
Is. 20:5, 30:3, 5; Jer. 48:13.
Will be destroyed. *Job 18:14; Is. 28:18.*

The woe and curse of false. *Is. 30:1-2, 31:1-3; Jer. 17:5.*
Of the saints, is illustrated. *Ps. 91:12; Prov. 18:10.*
Of the wicked, is illustrated. *2 Kings 18:21; Job 8:14, 18:21.*

Examples in the saints. **David**: *1 Sam. 17:45, 30:6.* **Hezekiah**: *2 Kings 18:5.* **Jehoshaphat**: *2 Chron. 20:12.* **Shadrach**, etc: *Dan. 3:28.* **Paul**: *2 Tim. 1:12.*

Examples of the wicked. **Goliath**: *1 Sam. 17:43-45.* **Benhadad**: *1 Kings 20:10.* **Sennacherib**: *2 Chron. 32:8.* **Israelites**: *Is. 31:1.*

TRUTH

God is a God of. *Deut. 32:4; Ps. 31:5.*
Christ is. *Jn. 14:6 with Jn. 7:18.*
Christ was full of. *Jn. 1:14.*
Christ spoke. *Jn. 8:45.*
The Holy Spirit is the Spirit of. *Jn. 14:17.*
The Holy Spirit guides into all. *Jn. 16:13.*
The Word of God is. *Dan. 10:21; Jn. 17:17.*
God regards, with favour. *Jer. 5:3.*
The judgements of God are according to. *Ps. 96:13; Rom. 2:2.*
The saints should
  Worship God in. *Jn. 4:24 with Ps. 145:18.*
  Serve God in. *Josh. 24:14; 1 Sam. 12:24.*
  Walk before God in. *1 Kings 2:4; 2 Kings 20:3.*
  Keep religious feasts with. *1 Cor. 5:8.*
  Esteem, as inestimable. *Prov. 23:23.*
  Love. *Zech. 8:19.*
  Rejoice in. *1 Cor. 13:6.*
  Speak, to one another. *Zech. 8:16; Eph. 4 25.*
  Execute judgement with. *Zech. 8:16.*

Meditate upon. *Phil. 4:8.*
Bind, about the neck. *Prov. 3:3.*
Write, upon the tablets of the heart. *Prov. 3:3.*
God desires, in the heart. *Ps. 51:6.*
The fruit of the Spirit is in. *Eph. 5:9.*
Ministers should
  Speak. *2 Cor. 12:6; Gal. 4:16.*
  Teach in. *1 Tim. 2:7.*
  Approve themselves by. *2 Cor. 6:7-8.*
Magistrates should be men of. *Ex. 18:21*
Kings are preserved by. *Prov. 20:28.*
Those who speak,
Show truth and righteousness. *Prov. 12:17.*
Will be established. *Prov. 12:19.*
Are the delight of God. *Prov. 12:22.*
The wicked
  Are destitute of. *Hos. 4:1.*
  Do not speak. *Jer. 9:5.*
  Do not uphold. *Is. 59:14-15.*
  Do not plead for. *Is. 59:4.*
  Are not valiant for. *Jer. 9:3.*
  Are punished for lack of. *Jer. 9:5, 9; Hos. 4:1, 3.*
The gospel as,
  Came by Christ. *Jn. 1:17.*
  Christ bore witness to. *Jn. 18:37.*
  Is in Christ. *1 Tim. 2:7.*
  John bore witness to. *Jn. 5:33.*
  Is according to godliness. *Titus 1:1.*
  Is sanctifying. *Jn. 17:17, 19.*
  Is purifying. *1 Pet. 1:22.*
  Is part of the Christian armour. *Eph. 6:14.*
  Was revealed abundantly to the saints. *Jer. 33:6.*
  Abides continually with the saints. *2 Jn. verse 2.*
  Should be acknowledged. *2 Tim. 2:25.*
  Should be believed. *2 Thess. 2:12, 13; 1 Tim. 4:3.*
  Should be obeyed. *Rom. 2:8; Gal. 3:1.*
  Should be loved. *2 Thess. 2:10.*
  Should be manifested. *2 Cor. 4:2.*

Should be rightly divided. *2 Tim. 2:15.*

The wicked turn away from. *2 Tim. 4:4.*

The wicked resist. *2 Tim. 3:8.*

The wicked are destitute of. *1 Tim. 6:5.*

The Church is the pillar and ground of. *1 Tim. 3:15.*

The devil is devoid of. *Jn. 8:44.*

TRUTH OF GOD, THE

Is one of his attributes. *Deut. 32:4; Is. 65:16.*

Always goes before his face. *Ps. 89:14.*

He keeps, forever. *Ps. 146:6.*

Is described as

Great. *Ps. 57:10.*

Plentiful. *Ps. 86:15.*

Abundant. *Ex. 34:6.*

Inviolate. *Num. 23:19; Titus 1:1-2.*

Reaching up to the clouds. *Ps. 57:10.*

Enduring to all generations. *Ps. 100:5.*

Is united with mercy in redemption. *Ps. 85:10.*

Shown in his

His counsels of old. *Is. 25:1.*

His ways. *Rev. 15:3.*

His works. *Ps. 33:4. Ps. 111:7; Dan 4:37.*

His judicial statutes. *Ps. 19:9.*

His administration of justice. *Ps. 96:13.*

His Word. *Ps. 119:160. Jn. 17:17.*

·The fulfilment of his promises in Christ. *2 Cor. 1:20.*

The fulfilment of his covenant. *Mic. 7:20.*

His dealings with the saints. *Ps. 25:10.*

The deliverance of the saints. *Ps. 57:3.*

The punishment of the wicked. *Rev. 16:7.*

Remembered towards the saints. *Ps. 98:3.*

Is a shield and buckler to the saints. *Ps. 91:4.*

We should

Have confidence in. *Ps. 31:1, 5; Titus 1:2.*

Plead, in prayer. *Ps. 89:49.*

Pray for its revelation to ourselves. *2 Chron. 6:17.*

Pray for its revelation to others. *2 Sam. 2:6.*

Make known, to others. *Is. 38:19.*

Magnify. *Ps. 71:22, 138:2.*

Is denied by

The devil. *Gen. 3:4-5.*

The self-righteous. *1 Jn. 1:10.*

Unbelievers. *1 Jn. 5:10.*

Three examples. **Abraham**: *Gen. 24:27.* **Jacob**: *Gen. 32:10* **Israel**: *Ps. 98:3.*

TYPES OF CHRIST

Adam. *Rom. 5:14; 1 Cor. 15:45.*

Abel. *Gen. 4:8, 10 with Acts 2:23; Heb. 12:24.*

Abraham. *Gen. 17:5 with Eph. 3:15.*

Aaron. *Ex. 28:1 with Heb. 5:4-5; Lev. 16:15 with Heb. 9:7, 24.*

The ark. *Gen. 7:16 with 1 Pet. 3:20-21.*

The ark of the covenant. *Ex. 15:16 with Ps. 40:8; Is. 42:6.*

Atonement, sacrifices offered on the day of. *Lev 16:15-16 with Heb. 9:12, 24.*

Bronze serpent. *Num. 21:9 with Jn. 3:14-15.*

Bronze altar. *Ex. 27:1-2 with Heb. 13:10.*

Burnt-offering. *Lev. 1:2, 4 with Heb. 10:10.*

Cities of refuge. *Num. 35:6 with Heb. 6:18.*

David. *2 Sam. 8:15 with Ezek. 37:24; Ps. 89:19-20 with Phil. 2:9.*

Eliakim. *Is. 22:20-22 with Rev. 3:7.*

Firstfruits. *Ex. 22:29 with 1 Cor. 15:20.*

Golden lampstand. *Ex. 25:31 with Jn. 8:12.*

Golden altar. *Ex. 40:5, 26-27 with Rev. 8:3 and Heb. 13:15.*

Isaac. *Gen. 22:1-2 with Heb. 11:17-19.*

Jacob. *Gen. 32:28 with Jn. 11:42; Heb. 7:25.*

Jacob's ladder. *Gen. 28:12 with Jn. 1:51.*

Joseph. *Gen. 50:19-20 with Heb. 7:25.*

Joshua. *Josh. 1:5-6 with Heb. 4:8-9; Josh. 11:23 with Acts 20:32.*

Jonah. *Jonah 1:17 with Mat. 12:40.*

Laver of bronze. *Ex. 30:18-20 with Zech. 13:1; Eph. 5:26, 27.*

A leper's offering. *Lev. 14:4-7 with Rom. 4:25.*

Manna. *Ex.18:11-15 with Jn.'6:32, '35.*

Melchizedek. *Gen. 14:18-20 with Heb. 7:1-17.*

Mercy seat. *Ex. 26:17-22 with Rom. 3:25; Heb. 4:16.*

Morning and evening sacrifices. *Ex. 29:38-41 with Jn. 1:29-30.*

Moses. *Num. 12:7 with Heb. 3:2; Deut. 18:15 with Acts 3:20-22.*

Noah. *Gen. 5:29; 2 Cor. 1:6.*

Paschal lamb. *Ex. 12:3-6, 46 with Jn. 19:36; 1 Cor. 6:7.*

Peace-offering. *Lev. 3:1 with Eph. 2:14, 16.*

Red heifer. *Num. 10:2-6 with Heb. 9:13-14.*

Rock of Horeb. *Ex. 17:6 with 1 Cor. 10:4.*

Samson. *Judg. 16:30 with Col. 2:14-15.*

Scapegoat. *Lev. 16:20-22 with Is. 53:6, 12.*

Sin-offering. *Lev. 4:2-3, 12 with Heb. 13:11-12.*

Solomon. *2 Sam. 7:12-13 with Lk. 1:32-33; 1 Pet. 2:5.*

Tabernacle. *Ex. 40:2, 34 with Heb. 9:11; Col. 2:9.*

Table and show-bread. *Ex. 25:23-30 with Jn. 1:16, 6:48.*

Temple. *1 Kings 6:1, 38 with Jn. 2:19, 21.*

Tree of life. *Gen. 2:9 with Jn. 1:4; Rev. 22:2.*

Trespass-offering. *Lev. 6:1-7 with Is. 53:10.*

Veil of the tabernacle and temple. *Ex. 40:21; 2 Chron. 3:14 with Heb. 10:20.*

Zerubbabel. *Zech. 4:7-9 with Heb. 12:2-3.*

U

UNBELIEF

Is sin. *Jn. 16:9.*

Defilement is inseparable from. *Titus 1:15.*

All, by nature, are included in. *Rom. 11:32.*

Proceeds from

An evil heart. *Heb. 3:12.*

Slowness of heart. *Lk. 24:25.*

Hardness of heart. *Mk. 16:14; Acts 19:9.*

An aversion to the truth. *Jn. 8:45-46.*

Judicial blindness. *Jn. 12:39-40.*

Not being Christ's sheep. *Acts 10:26.*

The devil blinding the mind. *2 Cor. 4:4.*

The devil taking away the Word out of the heart. *Lk. 8:12.*

Seeking honour from men. *Jn. 5:44.*

Calls into question the truthfulness of God. *1 Jn. 5:10.*

Shown in

Rejecting Christ. *Jn. 16:9.*

Rejecting the Word of God. *Ps. 106:24.*

Rejecting the gospel. *Is. 53:1; Jn. 12:38.*

Rejecting the evidence of miracles. *Jn. 12:37.*

Departing from God. *Heb. 3:12.*

Questioning the power of God. *2 Kings 7:2; Ps. 78:19-20.*

Not believing the works of God. *Ps. 78:32.*

Staggering at the promises of God. *Rom. 4:20.*

Rebuked by Christ. *Mat. 17:17; Jn. 20:27.*

Was an impediment to the performance of miracles. *Mat. 17:20; Mk. 6:5.*

Miracles were designed to convince those in. *Jn. 10:37, 38; 1 Cor. 14:22.*

The Jews were rejected for their. *Rom. 11:20.*

Believers should have no fellowship with those who live in. *2 Cor. 6:14.*

Those who are guilty of,

Do not have the Word of God in them. *Jn. 5:38.*

Cannot please God. *Heb. 11:6.*

Malign the gospel. *Acts 19:9.*

Persecute the ministers of God. *Rom. 15:31.*

Turn others against the saints. *Acts 14:2.*

Persevere in it. *Jn. 12:37.*

Stiffen their necks. *2 Kings 17:14.*

Are condemned already. *Jn. 3:18.*

Have the wrath of God abiding on them. *Jn. 3:36.*

Will not be established. *Is. 7:9.*

Will die in their sins. *Jn. 8:24.*

Will not enter into rest. *Heb. 3:19, 4:11.*

Will be condemned. *Mk. 16:16; 2 Thess. 2:12.*

Will be destroyed. *Jude verse 5.*

Will be cast into the lake of fire. *Rev. 21:8.*

Warnings against. *Heb.3:12, 4:11.*

Pray for help against. *Mk. 9:24.*

The portion of, is awarded to all unfaithful servants. *Lk. 12:46.*

Some examples. **Eve:** *Gen. 3:4-6.* **Moses and Aaron:** *Num. 20:12.* **Israelites:** *Deut. 9:23.* **The people of Jericho:** *Heb. 11:31.* **Naaman:** *2 Kings 5:12.* **A Samaritan Lord:** *2 Kings 7:2.* **Disciples:** *Mat. 17:17. Lk. 24:11, 25.* **Zacharias:** *Lk. 1:20.* **Chief Priests:** *Lk. 22:67.* **The Jews:** *Jn. 5:38.* **The brothers of Christ:** *Jn. 7:5.* **Thomas:** *Jn. 20:25.* **Jews of Iconium:** *Acts 14:2.* **Thessalonian Jews:** *Acts 17:5.* **The Ephesians:** *Acts 19:9.* **Saul:** *Acts 9:1-2, 26:9-11; 1 Tim. 1:13.*

UNION WITH CHRIST

As Head of the Church. *Eph. 1:22-23, 4:15-16; Col. 1:18.*

Christ prayed that all the saints might experience. *Jn. 17:21, 23.*

Is described as

Christ being in us. *Eph. 3:17; Col. 1:27.*

Our being in Christ. *2 Cor. 12:2; 1 Jn. 5:20.*

Includes union with the Father. *Jn. 17:21; 1 Jn. 2:24.*

Is of God. *1 Cor. 1:30.*

Is maintained by

Faith. *Gal. 2:20; Eph. 3:17.*

Abiding in him. *Jn. 15:4, 7*

His Word abiding in us. *Jn. 15:7; 1 Jn. 2:24; 2 Jn. verse 9.*

Feeding on him. *Jn. 6:56.*

Obeying him. *1 Jn. 3:24.*

The Holy Spirit witnesses to. *1 Jn. 3:24.*

The gift of the Holy Spirit is an evidence of. *1 Jn. 4:13.*

The saints

Have, in mind. *1 Cor. 2:16; Phil. 2:5.*

Have, in spirit. *1 Cor. 6:17.*

Have, in love. *Song 2:16, 7:10.*

Have, in their suffering. *Phil. 3:10; 2 Tim. 2:12.*

Have, in his death. *Rom. 6:3-8; Gal. 2:20.*

Have assurance of. *Jn. 14:20.*

Enjoy, in the Lord's Supper. *1 Cor. 10:16-17.*

Are identified with Christ by. *Mat. 25:40, 45; Acts 9:4 with Acts 8:1.*

Are complete through. *Col. 2:10.*

Are exhorted to maintain. *Jn. 15:4; Acts 11:23; Col. 2:7.*

Necessary for growth in grace. *Eph. 4:15-16; Col. 2:19.*

Necessary for fruitfulness. *Jn. 15:4-5.*

The beneficial results of;

Righteousness imputed. *2 Cor. 5:21; Phil. 3:9.*

Freedom from condemnation. *Rom 8:1.*

Freedom from the dominion of sin. *1 Jn. 3:6.*

Being created anew. 2 Cor. 5:17.
The spirit is made alive to
righteousness. Rom. 8:10.
Confidence at his coming.
1 Jn. 2:28
Abundant fruitfulness. Jn. 15:5.
Answers to prayer. Jn. 15:7.
Those who have, ought to walk
as he walked. 1 Jn. 2:6.
False teachers do not have.
Col. 2:18-19.
Is indissoluble. Rom. 8:35.
The punishment of those who
do not have. Jn. 15:6.

Various illustrations. **The vine and
the branches**: Jn. 15, 1, 5. **The
foundation and building**: 1 Cor. 3:10-11;
Eph. 2:20-21; 1 Pet. 2:4-6. **The body and
its members**: 1 Cor. 12:12, 27;
Eph. 5:30. **The husband and wife**:
Eph. 5 25-32.

UNITY OF GOD, THE
A ground for obeying him
exclusively. Deut. 4:39-40.
A ground for loving him su-
premely. Deut. 6:4-5 with Mk. 12:29-30.
Asserted by
God himself. Is. 44:6, 8, 45:18, 21.
Christ. Mk. 12:29; Jn. 17:3.
Moses. Deut. 4:39, 6:4.
The Apostles. 1 Cor. 8:4, 6; Eph. 4:6;
1 Tim. 2:5.
Consistent with the deity of
Christ and of the Holy Spirit.
Jn. 10:30 with 1 Jn. 5:7; Jn. 14:9-11.
Shown in
His greatness and wonderful
works. 2 Sam. 7:22. Ps. 86:10.
His works of creation and
providence. Is. 44:24, 45:6-8.
His being alone possessed of
foreknowledge. Is. 46:9-11.
His exercise of absolute
sovereignty. Deut. 32:39.
His being the sole object of
worship in heaven and earth.
Neh. 9:6; Mat. 4:10.

His being alone good. Mat. 19:17.
His being the only Saviour.
Is. 45:21-22.
His being the only source of
pardon. Mic. 7:18 with Mk. 2:7.
His unparalleled election and
care of his people. Deut. 4:32-35.
Knowledge of, is necessary for
eternal life. Jn. 17:3.
All the saints acknowledge, in
worshipping him. 2 Sam. 7:22;
2 Kings 19:15; 1 Chron. 17:20.
All should know and acknowl-
edge. Deut. 4:35; Ps. 83:18.
May be acknowledged without
saving faith. Jas. 2:19-20.

UPRIGHTNESS
God is perfect in. Is. 26:7.
God has pleasure in. 1 Chron. 29:17.
God created man in. Eccl. 7:29.
Man has deviated from. Eccl. 7:29.
Should be in
The heart. 2 Chron. 29:34; Ps. 125:4.
Speech. Is. 33:15.
The walk. Prov. 14:2.
Judging. Ps. 58:1, 75:2.
Ruling. Ps. 78:72.
Being kept from presumptuous
sins is necessary for. Ps. 19:13.
With poverty, is better than sin
with riches. Prov. 28:6.
With poverty, is better than folly.
Prov. 19:1.
Those who walk in,
Fear God. Prov. 14:2.
Love Christ. Song. 1:4.
Behold God's face
Ps. 11:7.
Are delighted in by God.
Prov. 11:20.
Their prayers delight God.
Prov. 15:8.
Are prospered by God. Job 8:6.
Prov. 14:11.
Are defended by God. Prov. 2:7.
Are upheld in it by God. Ps. 41:12.
Are recompensed by God.
Ps. 18:23-24.

Find strength in God's way. *Prov. 10:29.*

Obtain good from God's Word. *Mic. 2:7.*

Obtain light in darkness. *Ps. 112:4.*

Are guided by integrity. *Prov. 11:3.*

Walk surely. *Prov. 10:9.*

Direct their way surely. *Prov. 21:29.*

Are kept by righteousness. *Prov. 13:6.*

Are scorned by the wicked. *Job 12:4.*

Are spoken against by the wicked. *Prov. 29:10; Amos 5:10.*

Are abominated by the wicked. *Prov. 29:27.*

Are persecuted by the wicked. *Ps. 37:14.*

Are a blessing to others. *Prov. 11:11.*

Praise is beautiful in. *Ps. 33:1.*

The truly wise walk in. *Prov. 15:21.*

The way of, is to depart from evil. *Prov. 16:17.*

Those who walk in, will

Possess good things. *Prov. 28:10.*

Have nothing good withheld. *Ps. 84:11.*

Dwell in the land. *Prov. 2:21.*

Dwell on high and be provided for. *Is. 33:16.*

Dwell with God. *Ps. 15:2, 140:13.*

Be blessed. *Ps. 112:2.*

Be delivered by righteousness. *Prov. 11:6.*

Be delivered by their wisdom. *Prov. 12:6*

Be saved. *Prov. 28:18.*

Enter into peace. *Ps. 37:37; Is. 57:2.*

Have dominion over the wicked. *Ps. 49:14.*

Have an inheritance forever. *Ps. 37:18.*

A characteristic of the saints. *Ps. 111:1; Is. 26:7.*

The saints should resolve to walk in. *Ps. 26:11.*

The wicked

Do not have, in their hearts. *Hab. 2:4.*

Leave the path of. *Prov. 2:13.*

Do not act with. *Mic. 7:2 4.*

Pray for those who walk in. *Ps. 125:4.*

Reprove those who deviate from. *Gal. 2:14.*

V

VANITY

A consequence of the Fall. *Rom. 8:20.*

Every man's life is. *Ps. 39:11.*

Every state of man is. *Ps. 62:9.*

Man at his best estate is. *Ps. 35:5.*

Man is like to. *Ps. 144:4.*

The thoughts of man are. *Ps. 94:11.*

The days of man are. *Job 7:16; Eccl. 6:12.*

Childhood and youth are. *Eccl. 11:10.*

The beauty of man is. *Ps. 39:11; Prov. 31:30.*

The help of man is. *Ps. 60:11; Lam. 4:17.*

Man's own righteousness is. *Is. 57:12.*

Worldly wisdom is. *Eccl. 2:15, 21; 1 Cor. 3:20.*

Worldly pleasure is. *Eccles. 2:1.*

Worldly anxiety is. *Ps. 39:8, 127:2.*

Worldly labour is. *Eccl. 2:11, 4:4.*

Worldly enjoyment is. *Eccl. 2:3, 10-11.*

Worldly possessions are. *Eccl. 2:4-11.*

Treasures of wickedness are. *Prov. 10:2.*

Heaping up riches is. *Eccl. 2:26, 4:8.*

Love of riches is. *Eccl. 5:10.*

Unblessed riches are. *Eccl. 6:2.*

Riches gained by falsehood are. *Prov. 21:6.*

All earthly things are. *Eccl. 1:2.*

Foolish questions, etc., are.

1 Tim. 1:6-7, 6:20; 2 Tim. 2:14, 16; Titus 3:9.
The conduct of the ungodly is.
1 Pet. 1:18.
The religion of hypocrites is.
Jas. 1:26.
The worship of the wicked is.
Is. 1:13; Mat. 6:7.
Lying words are. *Jer. 7:8.*
False teaching is only. *Jer. 23:32.*
Mere external religion is. *1 Tim. 4:8; Heb. 13:9.*
Charitable giving without love is.
1 Cor. 13:3.
Faith without works is. *Jas. 2:14.*
Idolatry is. 2 Kings 17:15; Ps. 31:6; Is. 44:9-10; Jer. 10:8, 18:15.
Wealth gained by, diminishes.
Prov. 13:11.

The saints
Hate the thoughts of. *Ps. 119:113.*
Pray to be kept from. *Ps. 110:37; Prov. 30:8.*
Avoid. *Ps. 24:4.*
Avoid those given to. *Ps. 26:4.*

The wicked
Are especially characterised by.
Job 11:11.
Though full of, they pretend to be wise. *Job 11:12.*
Love. *Ps. 4:2.*
Imagine. *Ps. 2:1. Acts 4:25; Rom. 1:21.*
Devise. *Ps. 36:4.* (See margin)
Speak. *Ps. 10:7, 12:2, 41:6.*
Count God's service as. *Job 21:15; Mal.3:14.*
Seduce others by words of.
2 Pet. 2:18.
Walk after. *Jer. 2:5.*
Walk in. *Ps. 39:6; Eph. 4:17.*
Inherit. *Jer. 16:19.*
Reap. *Prov. 22:8; Jer. 12:13.*
Are judicially given up to.
Ps. 78:33; Is. 57:13.
Fools follow those given to.
Prov. 12:11.
Following those given to, leads to poverty. *Prov. 28:19.*
Those who trust in, are rewarded with. *Job 15:31.*

VISIONS AND DREAMS
God often made known his will by. *Ps. 89:19.*
God especially made himself known to the prophets by.
Num. 12:6.
A sign of the coming of the Holy Spirit. *Joel 2:38 with Acts 2:17.*

Often accompanied by
A representative of the divine person and glory. *Is. 6:1.*
An audible voice from heaven.
Gen. 15:1; 1 Sam. 3:4-5.
An appearance of angels. *Lk. 1:22 with Lk. 24:23; Acts 10:3.*
An appearance of human beings. *Acts 9:12, 16:9.*
Frequently difficult and perplexing to those who received them. *Dan. 7:15, 8:15; Acts 10:17.*

Often communicated
At night. *Gen. 46:2; Dan. 2:19.*
In a trance. *Num. 24:16; Acts 11:5.*
Often recorded for the benefit of the people. *Hab. 2:2.*
Often multiplied for the benefit of the people. *Hos. 12:10.*

Those mentioned in Scripture;
To Abraham. *Gen. 15:1.*
To Eliphaz. *Job 4:13-16.*
To Jacob. *Gen. 46:2.*
To Pharaoh. *Gen. 41:1-7.*
To Moses. *Ex. 3:2-3; Acts 7:30-32.*
To a soldier, in the hearing of Gideon. *Judg. 7:13-15.*
To Samuel. *1 Sam. 3:2-15.*
To Nathan. *2 Sam. 7:4, 17.*
To Solomon. *1 Kings 3:4-15.*
To Isaiah. *Is. 6:1-8.*
To Ezekiel. *Ezek. 1:4-14, 8:2, 14, chapter 10, 11:24-25, 37:1-10, chapters 40-48.*
To Nebuchadnezzar. *Dan. 2:28, 4:5.*
To Daniel. *Dan. 2:19, chapters 7-8, chapter 10.*
To Amos. *Amos 7:1-9, 8:1-6, 9:1.*
To Zechariah. *Zech. 1:8, 3:1, 4:2, 5:2, 6:1.*
To the wisemen. *Mat. 2:12.*
To Joseph. *Mat. 2:13, 19-20.*

To Pilate's wife. *Mat. 27:19.*
To Paul. *Acts 9:3, 6, 12, 16:9, 18:9, 22:18, 27:23; 2 Cor. 12:1-4.*
To Ananias. *Acts 9:10-11.*
To Cornelius. *Acts 10:3.*
To Peter. *Acts 10:9-17.*
To John. *Rev. 1:12, etc, chapters 4-22.*
Sometimes withheld for a long time. *1 Sam. 3:1.*
Concerning the withholding of a great calamity. *Prov. 29:18; Lam. 2:9.*
False prophets pretended to have seen. *Jer. 14:14, 23:16.*
The prophets of God were skilled in interpreting. *2 Chron. 26:5; Dan. 1:17.*

VOWS

Solemn promises to God. *Ps. 76:11.*
Were made with reference to
Devoting the person to God.
Num. 6:2.
Dedicating children to *God.*
1 Sam. 1:11.
Devoting property to God.
Gen. 28:22.
Offering sacrifices. *Lev. 7:16, 22:18-22; Num. 15:3.*
Afflicting the soul. *Num. 30:13.*
Should be voluntary. *Deut. 23:21-22.*
Should be performed faithfully.
Num. 30:2.
Should be performed without delay. *Deut. 23:21, 23.*
The danger of rashly making.
Prov. 20:25.
Of children, were void without the consent of their parents.
Num. 30:3-5.

Of married women, were void without the consent of their husbands. *Num. 30:6-8, 10-13.*
Of widows, and women divorced from their husbands, were binding. *Num. 30:9.*
Of wives, could only be objected to at the time of making.
Num. 30:14-15.
Might be redeemed by paying a fair compensation. *Lev. 27:1-8, 11-23.*
Clean beasts were the objects of, and could not be redeemed.
Lev. 27. 9-10.
Recorded in Scripture;
Jacob. *Gen. 28:20-22, 31:13.*
The Israelites. *Num. 21:2.*
Jephthah. *Judg. 11:30-31.*
Hannah. *1 Sam. 1:11.*
Elkanah. *1 Sam. 1:24.*
David. *Ps. 132:2, 5.*
The sailors who cast Jonah overboard. *Jonah 1:16.*
Jonah. *Jonah 2:9.*
Lemuel's mother. *Prov. 31:1-2.*
Paul. *Acts 18:18.*
Certain Jews concerning Paul.
Acts 21:23-24, 26.
All things dedicated by, were to be brought to the tabernacle.
Deut. 12:6, 11, 17-18, 26.
Things corrupt or blemished were an insult to God. *Lev. 22:23; Mal. 1:14.*
The hire of a prostitute, or the price of a dog, could not be made a subject of. *Deut. 23:18.*

W

WAITING ON GOD
As the God of providence.
Jer. 14. 22.
As the God of salvation.
Ps. 25:5.
As the Giver of all temporal blessings. *Ps. 104:27-28, 145:15-16.*

For
Mercy. *Ps. 123:2.*
Pardon. *Ps. 39:7 8.*
The consolation of Israel.
Lk. 2:25.
Salvation. *Gen. 49:18; Ps. 62:1-2.*
Guidance and teaching.
Ps. 25:5.

Protection. *Ps. 33:20, 59:9-10.*
The fulfilment of his Word.
Hab. 2:3.
The fulfilment of his promises.
Acts 1:4.
The Hope of righteousness by
faith. *Gal. 5:5.*
The coming of Christ. *1 Cor. 1:7;*
1 Thess. 1:10.
Is good. *Ps. 52:9.*
God calls us to. *Zeph. 3:8.*
Exhortation and encouragement
to. *Ps. 27:14, 37:7; Hos. 12:6.*

Should be
With the soul. *Ps. 62:1, 5.*
With an earnest desire. *Ps. 130:6.*
With patience. *Ps. 37:7, 40:1.*
With resignation. *Lam. 3:26.*
With hope in his Word. *Ps. 130:5.*
With full confidence. *Mic. 7:7.*
Continually. *Hos. 12:6.*
All the day. *Ps. 25:5.*
Especially in adversity. *Ps. 59:1-9;*
Is. 8:17.
In the way of his judgements.
Is. 26:8.
The saints resolve on. *Ps. 52:9, 59:9.*
The saints have expectation from.
Ps. 62:5.
The saints plead while, in prayer.
Ps. 25:21; Is. 33:2.
The patience of the saints is often
tested while. *Ps. 69:3.*

Those who engage in,
Wait upon him only. *Ps. 62:5.*
Are heard. *Ps. 40:1.*
Are blessed. *Is. 30:18; Dan. 12:12.*
Experience his goodness.
Lam. 3:25.
Will not be ashamed. *Ps. 25:3;*
Is. 49:23.
Will renew their strength, etc.
Is. 40:31.
Will inherit the earth. *Ps. 37:9.*
Will be saved. *Prov. 20:22; Is. 25:9.*
Will rejoice in salvation. *Is. 25:9.*
Will receive the glorious things
prepared by God for them.
Is. 64:4.

Was prophesied of the Gentiles.
Is. 42:4, 60:9.
Illustrated. *Ps. 123:2; Lk. 12:36; Jas. 5:7.*

Some examples. **Jacob:** *Gen. 49:18.*
David: *Ps. 39:7.* **Isaiah:** *Is. 8:17.* **Micah:**
Mic. 7:7. **Joseph of Arimathea:**
Mk. 15:43.

WARFARE OF THE SAINTS, THE
Is not according to the flesh.
2 Cor. 10:3.
Is a good warfare. *1 Tim. 1:18-19.*
Is called the good fight of faith.
1 Tim. 6:12.

Is against
The devil. *Gen. 3:15; 2 Cor. 2:11;*
Eph 6:12; Jas. 4:7; 1 Pet. 5:8; Rev. 12:17.
The flesh. *Rom. 7:23; 1 Cor. 9:25-27;*
2 Cor. 12:7; Gal. 5:17; 1 Pet. 2:11.
Enemies. *Ps. 38:19, 56:2, 59:3.*
The world. *Jn. 10:33; 1 Jn. 5:4-5.*
Death. *1 Cor. 15:26 with Heb. 2:14-15.*
Often arises from the opposition
of friends or relatives. *Mic. 7:6 with*
Mat. 10:35-36.

To be carried on
Under Christ as our Captain.
Heb. 2:10.
Under the Lord's banner. *Ps. 60:4.*
With faith. *1 Tim. 1:18-19.*
With a good conscience.
1 Tim. 1:18-19.
With steadfastness in the faith.
1 Cor. 16:13; 1 Pet. 5:9 with Heb. 10:23.
With earnestness. *Jude verse 3.*
With watchfulness. *1 Cor. 16:13;*
1 Pet. 5:8.
With seriousness. *1 Thess. 5:6;*
1 Pet. 5:8.
With endurance in hardship.
2 Tim. 2:3, 10.
With self-denial. *1 Cor. 9:25-27.*
With confidence in God. *Ps. 27:1-3.*
With prayer. *Ps. 35:1-3. Eph. 6:18.*
Without earthly entanglements.
2 Tim. 2:4.
Mere professors of the faith do
not maintain. *Jer. 9:3.*

The saints

Are all engaged in. *Phil. 1:30.*

Must stand firm in. *Eph. 6:13-14.*

Are exhorted to be diligent in.
1 Tim. 6:12; Jude verse 3.

Are encouraged in. *Is. 41:11-12,
51:12; Mic. 7:8; 1 Jn. 4:4.*

Are helped by God in. *Ps. 118:13;
Is. 41:13- 14.*

Are protected by God in. *Ps. 140:7.*

Are comforted by God in.
2 Cor. 7:5-6.

Are strengthened by God in.
Ps. 20:2, 27:14; Is. 41:10.

Are strengthened by Christ in.
2 Cor. 12:9; 2 Tim. 4:17.

Are delivered by Christ in.
2 Tim. 4:18.

Thank God for victory in.
Rom. 7:25; 1 Cor. 15:57.

The armour for,

Belt of truth. *Eph. 6:14 with Is. 11:5.*

Boots of the preparation of the
gospel of faith. *Eph. 6:15 with
Is. 11:5.*

Breastplate of righteousness.
Eph. 6.14 with Is. 59:17.

Shield of faith, the. *Eph. 6:16.*

Helmet of salvation. *Eph. 6:17 and
1 Thess. 5:8 with Is. 59:17.*

Sword of the Spirit. *Eph. 6:17.*

Is called the armour of God.
Eph. 6:11.

Is called the armour of righteousness. *2 Cor. 6:7.*

Is called the armour of light.
Rom. 13:12.

Is not of this world. *2 Cor. 10:4.*

Is mighty through God.
2 Cor. 10:4-5.

The whole, is required. *Eph. 6:13.*

Must be put on. *Rom. 13:12.*
Eph. 6:11.

To be on the right hand and on
the left. *2 Cor. 6:7.*

Victory in, is

From God. *1 Cor. 15:57; 2 Cor. 2:14.*

Through Christ. *Rom. 7:25; 1 Cor.
15:27; 2 Cor. 12:9; Rev. 12:11.*

By faith. *Heb. 11:33-37; 1 Jn. 5:4-5.*

Over the devil. *Rom. 16:20; 1 Jn. 2:14.*

Over the flesh. *Rom. 7:24-25;
Gal. 5:24.*

The world. *1 Jn. 5:4-5.*

Over all that exalts itself.
2 Cor. 10:5.

Over death and the grave. *Is. 25:8,
26:19; Hos. 13:14; 1 Cor. 15:54-55.*

Triumphant. *Rom. 8:37; 2 Cor. 10:5.*

Those who overcome, will

Eat of the hidden manna.
Rev. 2:17.

Eat of the tree of life. *Rev. 2:7.*

Be clothed in white raiment.
Rev. 3:5.

Be pillars in the temple of God.
Rev. 3:12.

Sit with Christ on his throne.
Rev. 3:21.

Have a white stone, and, on it a
new name written. *Rev. 2:17.*

Have power over the nations.
Rev. 2:26.

Have the name of God written
on them by Christ. *Rev. 3:12.*

Have God as their God. *Rev. 21:7.*

Have the morning star. *Rev. 2:28.*

Inherit all things. *Rev. 21:7.*

Be content with Christ before
God the Father. *Rev. 3:5.*

Truly the the sons of God.
Rev. 21:7.

Will not be hurt by the second
death. *Rev. 2:11.*

Will not have their names
blotted out of the book of life.
Rev. 3:5.

Is illustrated. *Is. 9:6; Zech. 10:5.*

WATCHFULNESS

Christ is an example of. *Mat. 26:38,
40; Lk. 6:12.*

Is commanded. *Mk. 13:37; Rev. 3:2.*

Exhortations to. *1 Thess. 5:6; 1 Pet. 4:7.*

God specially requires, in
ministers. *Ezek. 3:17 with Is. 62:6;
Mk. 13:34.*

Ministers are exhorted to.

Acts 20:31; 2 Tim. 4:5.
Faithful ministers exercise.
Heb. 13:17.
Faithful ministers are approved
by their. Mat. 24:45-46; Lk. 12:41-44.
We should be watchful,
In prayer. Lk. 21:36; Eph. 6:18.
In thanksgiving. Col. 4:2.
In steadfastness in the faith.
1 Cor 16:13.
In taking heed. Mk. 13:33.
In seriousness. 1 Thess. 5:6; 1 Pet. 4:7.
At all times. Prov. 8:34.
In all things. 2 Tim. 4:5.
The saints pray to be kept in a
state of. Ps. 141:3.
Motives for;
An expected direction from
God. Hab. 2:1.
Uncertainty as to the time of
the coming again of Christ.
Mat. 24:42, 25:13; Mk. 13:35-36.
Incessant assaults of the devil.
1 Pet. 5:8.
Liability to be tempted. Mat. 26:41.
The blessedness of. Lk. 12:37;
Rev. 16:15.
Unfaithful ministers are devoid
of. Is. 56:10.
The wicked are averse to.
1 Thess. 5:7.
The danger of being remiss in.
Mat. 24:48-51, 25:5, 8, 12; Rev. 3:3.
Is illustrated. Lk. 12:35-36.

Three examples. **David**: Ps. 102:7.
Anna: Lk. 2:37. **Paul**: 2 Cor. 11:27.

WICKED ARE COMPARED WITH, THE

Abominable branches. Is. 14:19.
Ashes under the feet. Mal. 4:3.
Bad figs. Jer. 24:8.
Bad fish. Mat. 13:48.
Bad fruit trees. Lk. 6:43.
Beasts. Ps. 49:12. 2 Pet. 2:12.
Blighted grain. 2 Kings 19:26.
Blind, The. Zeph. 1:17. Mat. 15:14.
Bronze and iron, etc. Jer. 6:28;

Ezek. 22:18.
Briars and thorns. Is. 55:13; Ezek. 2:6.
Bulls of Bashan, The. Ps. 22:12.
Carcasses trodden under foot.
Is. 14:19.
Chaff. Job 21:18; Ps. 1:4; Mat. 3:12.
Clouds without water. Jude verse 12.
Deaf cobras. Ps. 58:4.
Dogs. Prov. 26:11; Mat. 7:6; 2 Pet. 2:22.
Dross. Ps. 119:119; Ezek. 22:18-19.
Early dew that passes away.
Hos. 13:3.
Fading oaks. Is. 1:30.
Fiery oven. Ps. 21:9; Hos. 7:4.
Fire of thorns. Ps. 118:12.
Fools building upon sand. Mat. 7:26.
Fuel of fire. Is. 9:19.
A garden without water. Is. 1:30.
Goats. Mat. 25:32.
Grass. Ps. 37:2, 92:7.
Grass on the housetop.
2 Kings 19:28.
Green bay trees. Ps. 37:35.
Green herbs. Ps. 37:2.
Horses rushing into battle. Jer. 8:6.
Idols. Ps. 115:8.
Lions greedy for prey. Ps. 17:12.
Melting wax. Ps. 68:2.
Morning-clouds. Hos. 13:3.
Moth-eaten garments. Is. 50:9, 51:8.
Passing whirlwinds. Prov. 10:25.
Potsherds. Prov. 26:23.
Raging waves of the sea. J
ude verse 13.
Rejected silver. Jer. 6:30.
Scorpions. Ezek. 2:6.
Serpents. Ps. 58:4; Mat. 23:33.
A shrub in the desert. Jer. 17:6.
Smoke. Hos. 13:3.
Stony ground. Mat. 13:5.
Stubble. Job 21:18; Mal. 4:1.
Swine. Mat. 7:6; 2 Pet. 2:22.
Tares. Mat. 18:38.
The troubled sea. Is. 57:20.
Visions of the night. Job 20:8.
Wandering stars. Jude verse 13.
Wayward children. Mat. 11:16.
Wells without water. 2 Pet. 2:17.
Wheels. Ps. 83:13.

Whitewashed tombs. *Mat. 23:27.*
Wild ass's colts. *Job 11:12.*

WIDOWS

Character of faithfulness. *Lk. 2:37;*
1 Tim. 5:5, 10.

God

Surely hears the cry of. *Ex. 22:23.*
Judges for. *Deut. 10:18. Ps. 68:5.*
Relieves. *Ps. 146:9.*
Establishes the border of.
Prov. 15:25.
Witnesses against the oppressors of. *Mal. 3:5.*
Exhorts them to trust in him.
Jer. 49:11.

Should not be

Afflicted. *Ex. 22:22.*
Oppressed. *Jer. 7:6; Zech. 7:10.*
Treated with violence. *Jer. 22:3.*
Deprived of good clothing in
pledge. *Deut. 24:17.*

Should be

Pleaded for. *Is. 1:17.*
Honoured, if widows indeed.
1 Tim. 5:3.
Relieved by their friends.
1 Tim. 5:4, 16.
Relieved by the Church. *Acts 6:1;*
1 Tim. 5:9.
Visited in their affliction. *Jas. 1:27.*
Allowed to share in our
blessings. *Deut. 14:29, 16:11, 14, 24:19-21.*
Though poor, they too may be
generous. *Mk. 12:42-43.*
When still young, they are
exposed to many temptations.
1 Tim. 5:11-14.

The saints should

Relieve. *Acts 9:39.*
Bring joy to. *Job 29:13.*
Not disappoint. *Job 31:16.*

The wicked

Do no good for. *Job 24:21.*
Send them away empty. *Job 22:9.*
Take pledges from. *Job 24:3.*
Reject the cause of. *Is. 1:23.*
Vex. *Ezek. 22:7.*
Make a prey of. *Is. 10:2; Mat. 23:14.*

Kill. *Ps. 94:6.*
Are cursed for perverting the
judgement of. *Deut. 27:19.*
Woe to those who oppress. *Is. 10:1-2.*
Blessings on those who relieve.
Deut. 14:29.
A type of Zion in her affliction.
Lam. 5:3.

WISDOM OF GOD, THE

Is one of his attributes. *1 Sam. 2:3;*
Job 9:4.

Is described as

Perfect. *Job 36:4; Job 37:10.*
Mighty. *Job 36:5.*
Universal. *Job 28:24; Dan. 2:22;*
Acts 15:18.
Infinite. *Ps. 147:5; Rom. 11:33.*
Unsearchable. *Is. 40:28; Rom. 11:33.*
Wonderful. *Ps. 139:6.*
Beyond human comprehension. *Ps. 139:6.*
Incomparable. *Is. 44:7; Jer. 10:7.*
Un-derived. *Job 21:22. Is. 40:44.*
The gospel contains treasures of.
1 Cor. 2:7.
The wisdom of the saints is
derived from. *Ezek. 7:25.*
All human wisdom is derived
from. *Dan. 2:21.*
The saints ascribe to him. *Dan. 2:20.*

Shown in

His works. *Job 37:16; Ps. 104:24, 136:5;*
Prov. 3:19; Jer. 10:12.
His counsels. *Is. 28:29; Jer. 32:19.*
His foreshowing events. *Is. 42:9;*
Is. 46:10.
Redemption. *1 Cor. 1:24; Eph. 1:8, 3:10.*
Searching the heart. *1 Chron. 28:9.*
Understanding the thoughts.
1 Chron. 28:9; Ps. 139:2.

Shown in knowing

The heart. *Ps. 44:21; Prov. 15:11;*
Lk. 16:15.
The actions. *Job 34:21; Ps. 139:2-3.*
The words. *Ps. 139:4.*
His saints. *2 Sam. 7:20; 2 Tim. 2:19.*
The way of the saints. *Job 23:10;*
Ps. 1:6.

The needs of the saints. *Deut. 2:7; Mat. 6:8.*

The afflictions of the saints. *Ex. 3:7; Ps. 142:3.*

The weaknesses of the saints. *Ps. 103:14.*

The minutest of matters. *Mat. 10:29-30.*

The most secret things. *Mat. 6:18.*

The time of judgement. *Mat. 24:36.*

The wicked. *Neh. 9:10; Job 11:11.*

The works, etc., of the wicked. *Is. 66:18.*

Nothing is concealed from. *Ps. 139:12.*

The wicked always question. *Ps. 73:11; Is. 47:10.*

Should be magnified. *Rom. 16:27; Jude verse 25.*

WITNESS OF THE HOLY SPIRIT, THE

Is absolute truth. *1 Jn. 5:6.*

Should be implicitly received. *1 Jn. 5:6, 9.*

Is borne to Christ

As Messiah. *Lk. 3:22 with Jn. 1:32-33.*

As coming to redeem and sanctify. *1 Jn. 5:6.*

As exalted to be Prince and Saviour, in giving repentance, etc. *Acts 5:31-32.*

As perfecting the saints. *Heb. 10:14-15.*

As foretold by himself. *Jn. 15:26.*

In heaven. *1 Jn. 5:7, 11.*

On earth. *1 Jn. 5:8.*

The first preaching of the gospel was confirmed by. *Acts 14:3 with Heb. 2:4.*

The faithful preaching of the apostles was accompanied by. *1 Cor. 2:4; 1 Thess. 1:5.*

Given to the saints

On believing. *Acts 15:8; 1 Jn. 5:10.*

To testify to them of Christ. *Jn. 15:26.*

As an evidence of adoption. *Rom. 8:16.*

As an evidence of Christ in them. *1 Jn. 3:24.*

As an evidence of God in them. *1 Jn. 4:13.*

Borne against all unbelievers. *Neh. 9:30; Acts 28:25-27.*

WIVES

Not to be selected from among the ungodly. *Gen. 24:3, 26:34-35, 28:1.*

Duties of, to their husbands;

To love them. *Titus 2:4.*

To respect them. *Eph. 5:33.*

To be faithful to them. *1 Cor. 7:3-5, 10.*

To be subject to them. *Gen. 3:16; Eph. 5:22, 24; 1 Pet. 3:1.*

To obey them. *1 Cor. 14:34; Titus 2:5.*

To remain with them for life. *Rom. 7:2-3.*

Should dress

Modestly. *1 Tim. 2:9-10; 1 Pet. 3:3-4.*

With propriety and seriousness. *1 Tim. 2:9.*

With a meek and quiet spirit. *1 Pet. 3:4-5.*

With good works. *1 Tim. 2:10, 5:10.*

Good wives,

Are from the Lord. *Prov. 19:14.*

Are a token of God's favour. *Prov. 18:22.*

Are a blessing to their husbands. *Prov. 12:4, 31:10, 12.*

Bring honour on their husbands. *Prov. 31:23.*

Secure the confidence of their husbands. *Prov. 31:11.*

Are praised by their husbands. *Prov. 31:28.*

Are diligent and prudent. *Prov. 31:13-27.*

Are charitable to the poor. *Prov. 31:20.*

Their duty to unbelieving husbands. *1 Cor. 7:13-14, 16; 1 Pet. 3:1-2.*

Should be silent in church. *1 Cor. 14:34.*

Should seek religious instruction from their husbands. *1 Cor. 14:35.*

Of ministers, they should be exemplary. *1 Tim. 3:11.*

Examples of good wives. **The wife of Manoah**: *Judg. 13:10.* **Orpah and Ruth**: *Ruth 1:4, 8.* **Abigail**: *1 Sam. 25:3.* **Esther**: *Esth. 2:15-17.* **Elizabeth**: *Lk. 1:6.* **Priscilla**: *Acts 18:2, 26.* **Sarah**: *1 Pet. 3:6.*

Examples of bad wives. **Samson's wife**: *Judg. 14:15-17.* **Michal**: *2 Sam. 6:16.* **Jezebel**: *1 Kings 21:25.* **Zeresh**: *Esther 5:14.* **Job's wife**: *Job 2:9.* **Herodias**: *Mk. 6:17.* **Sapphira**: *Acts 5:1-2.*

WORKS, GOOD

Christ is an example of. *Jn. 10:32; Acts 10:38.*

Are called

Good fruit. *Jas. 3:17.*

Fruit worthy of repentance. *Mat. 3:8.*

Fruits of righteousness. *Phil. 1:11.*

Works and labours of love. *Heb. 6:10.*

Are by Jesus Christ to the glory and praise of God. *Phil. 1:11.*

Those, alone, who abide in Christ, can do. *Jn. 15:4-5.*

Are worked by God in us. *Is. 26:12; Phil. 2:13.*

The Scriptures are designed to lead us to. *2 Tim. 3:16-17; Jas. 1:25.*

To be done in Christ's name. *Col. 3:17.*

Heavenly wisdom is full of. *Jas. 3:17.*

Justification is unattainable by. *Rom. 3:20; Gal. 2:16.*

Salvation is impossible by. *Eph. 2:8-9; 2 Tim. 1:9; Titus 3:5.*

The saints

Are created in Christ for. *Eph. 2:10.*

Are preordained to walk in. *Eph. 2:10.*

Are exhorted to put on. *Col. 3:12-14.*

Are full of. *Acts 9:36.*

Are zealous of. *Titus 2:14.*

Should be thoroughly equipped for all. *2 Tim. 3:17.*

Should be rich in. *1 Tim. 6:18.*

Should be careful to maintain. *Titus 3:8, 14.*

Should be established in. *2 Thess. 2:17.*

Should be fruitful in. *Col. 1:10.*

Should be perfect in. *Heb. 13:21.*

Should be prepared for all. *2 Tim. 2:21.*

Should abound in all. *2 Cor. 9:8.*

Should be ready for all. *Titus 3:1.*

Should manifest, with humility. *Jas. 3:13.*

Should provoke each other to. *Heb. 10:24.*

Should avoid all show of. *Mat. 6:1-18.*

Bring to the light their. *Jn. 3:21.*

Followed into rest by their. *Rev. 14:13.*

Holy women should manifest. *1 Tim. 2:10, 5:10.*

God remembers. *Neh. 13:14 with Heb. 6:9-10.*

Will be brought to light in the Judgement. *Eccl. 12:14 with 2 Cor. 5:10.*

In the Judgement, will be an evidence of true faith. *Mat. 25:34-40 with Jas. 2:14-20.*

Ministers should

Be a pattern for. *Titus 2:7.*

Exhort others to. *1 Tim. 6:17-18; Titus 3:1, 8, 14.*

God is glorified by. *Jn. 15:8.*

Are designed to lead others to glorify God. *Mat. 5:16; 1 Pet. 2:12.*

A blessing comes with. *Jas. 1:25.*

The wicked are disqualified from doing. *Titus 1:16.*

Illustrated. *Jn. 15:5.*

Z

ZEAL

Christ is an example of. *Ps. 69:9; Jn. 2:17*

Godly sorrow leads to. *2 Cor. 7:10-11.*

The saints produce ardent. *Ps. 119:139*

Provokes others to do good. *2 Cor. 9:2.*

Should be shown

In spirit. *Rom. 12:11.*

In well doing. *Gal. 4:18; Titus 2:14.*

In desiring the salvation of others. *Acts 26:29; Rom. 10:1.*

In contending for the faith. *Jude verse 3.*

In missionary work. *Rom. 15:19, 23.*

For the glory of God. *Num. 25:11, 13.*

For the welfare of the saints. *Col. 4:13.*

As against idolatry. *2 Kings 23:4-14*

Sometimes, is wrongly directed. *2 Sam. 21:2; Acts 22:3-4; Phil. 3:6.*

Sometimes, is not according to knowledge. *Acts 21:20; Rom. 10:2; Gal. 1:14.*

Ungodly men sometimes pretend to. *2 Kings 10:16; Mat. 23:15.*

An exhortation to. *Rom. 12:11; Rev. 3:19.*

Examples of holy zeal. **Phinehas**: *Num. 25:11, 13.* **Josiah**: *2 Kings 23:19-25.* **Apollos**: *Acts 18:25.* **The Corinthians**: *1 Cor. 14:12.* **Epaphras**: *Col. 4:12-13.*

Index of Themes

, ACCESS TO
(SEE ACCESS TO GOD)

, ANGER OF
(SEE ANGER OF GOD)

, CALL OF
(SEE CALL OF GOD)

, COMMUNION WITH
(SEE COMMUNION WITH GOD)

, COUNSELS AND PURPOSES OF
(SEE COUNSELS AND PURPOSES OF GOD)

, DELIGHTING IN
(SEE DELIGHTING IN GOD)

, DEVOTEDNESS TO
(SEE DEVOTION TO GOD)

, DISOBEDIENCE TO
(SEE DISOBEDIENCE TO GOD)

, FAITHFULNESS OF
(SEE FAITHFULNESS OF GOD)

, FAVOUR OF
(SEE FAVOUR OF GOD)

, FORGETTING
(SEE FORGETTING GOD)

, FORSAKING
(SEE FORSAKING GOD)

, GIFTS OF
(SEE GIFTS OF GOD)

, GLORY OF
(SEE GLORY OF GOD)

The Little Book of things you should know about Ministry
Reid Ferguson

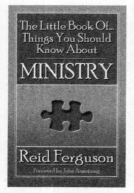

There are some astonishing gaps in the information with which church leaders are expected to guide their congregation. Some things are never said that would be of great usefulness if brought to the fore, discussed honestly and learnt from. How much pain, heartaches and mistakes would be prevented if the topics in this book were explored.

With short and thought-provoking chapters this book will enable you to think through the issues involved in leading a congregation and enable you to serve your flock with greater success.

'Reid Ferguson clearly knows ministry inside out, he knows people with all their fears and foibles but more importantly he knows God. I have no doubt that this book will help to raise the bar...'

David Meredith

'... refreshingly candid, consistently thought-provoking, and eminently practical.'

Phillip R. Johnson

'When we are dispirited; when we feel unappreciated, opposed or unsupported; the wisest responses can be considered from these pages. Read a chapter every week!'

C. Peter White

'...the compassion of the pastor's heart is evident in every thought'

Ken Jones

ISBN 1 85792 786 9

The Beginners Guide to Expository Preaching
Stephen McQuoid

Have you ever listened to a sermon and felt your heart soar as a fresh insight is given or a long-forgotten emphasis is brought back to you?

Have you ever preached a sermon and felt your heart sink as you see the lack of impact it is making on those blank faces listening to you?

It's not an easy balance to find, but Stephen McQuoid brings a refreshing dose of sensible and thoroughly Biblical advice to help us.

'Marked by practicality and realism. Both emerging and established preachers cannot fail to profit from it'.

Derek Prime

'Stephen McQuoid's readily digestible and stimulating new book will help seasoned preachers (and enable them to give themselves a good check-up). Beginners will benefit from the straightforward and sensible counsel he gives. And some, who never preach, may be helped to pray for and encourage those who do. I for one am grateful for the labour of love this little manual represents.'

Sinclair B Ferguson

'Stephen McQuoid will succeed in making preachers think hard about the passion, preparation, style and development of their preaching gift. I trust it will be a blessing and a challenge to them – it certainly was for me.'

Derek Lamont

ISBN 1 85792 769 9

Christian Focus Publications

publishes books for all ages
Our mission statement –

STAYING FAITHFUL
In dependence upon God we seek to help make His infallible Word, the Bible, relevant. Our aim is to ensure that the Lord Jesus Christ is presented as the only hope to obtain forgiveness of sin, live a useful life and look forward to heaven with Him.

REACHING OUT
Christ's last command requires us to reach out to our world with His gospel. We seek to help fulfill that by publishing books that point people towards Jesus and help them develop a Christ-like maturity. We aim to equip all levels of readers for life, work, ministry and mission.

Books in our adult range are published in three imprints.

Christian Focus contains popular works including biographies, commentaries, basic doctrine and Christian living. Our children's books are also published in this imprint.

Mentor focuses on books written at a level suitable for Bible College and seminary students, pastors, and other serious readers. The imprint includes commentaries, doctrinal studies, examination of current issues and church history.

Christian Heritage contains classic writings from the past.

Christian Focus Publications, Ltd
Geanies House, Fearn,
Ross-shire, IV20 1TW, Scotland

info@christianfocus.com